3rd Workshop on Computational Models of Reference, Anaphora and Coreference (CRAC 2020)

Held online due to COVID-19

Barcelona, Spain
12 December 2020

ISBN: 978-1-7138-2824-2

CRAC 2020

Third Workshop on Computational Models of Reference, Anaphora and Coreference

Proceedings of the Workshop

COLING 2020 Workshop
December 12, 2020
Barcelona, Spain (online)

Introduction

This is the third edition of the Workshop on Computational Models of Reference, Anaphora and Coreference (CRAC). CRAC was first held in New Orleans two years ago in conjunction with NAACL HLT 2018. CRAC and its predecessor, the Coreference Resolution Beyond OntoNotes (CORBON) workshop series that started in 2016, have arguably become the primary forum for coreference researchers to present their latest results since the demise of the Discourse Anaphora and Anaphor Resolution Colloquium series in 2011. While CORBON focuses on under-investigated coreference phenomena, CRAC has a broader scope, covering all cases of computational modeling of reference, anaphora, and coreference.

CRAC 2020 is by far the largest workshop in this workshop series in terms of the number of submissions and the number of accepted papers. Specifically, we received 23 submissions: 19 of them were from Europe, one was from the U.S. and the remaining two were from India. This geographical distribution of submissions provides suggestive evidence that coreference continues to be more actively researched in Europe than in other parts of the world. The submissions covered various aspects of reference-related topics, from resources for anaphora analysis, to different approaches to mention detection and anaphora resolution to applications. Each submission was rigorously reviewed by two to three program committee members. Based on their recommendations, we initially accepted 14 papers and conditionally accepted three papers. The three conditionally accepted papers were eventually accepted to the workshop after we made sure that the authors adequately addressed the reviewers' comments in the final camera-ready version. Overall, we were pleased with the large number of submissions as well as the quality of the accepted papers.

We started two new initiatives this year. First, with the goal of having a broad technical program, we introduced different paper categories. In addition to research papers, we welcomed survey papers, position papers, challenge papers, and demo papers. In each of these paper categories, authors were expected to report completed work. To encourage researchers to report work in progress and/or late-breaking results, we introduced another submission type, extended abstracts. Since we decided to introduce these new paper categories only in early October, many authors were not aware of these categories by the time they submitted their work. Of the 23 submissions we received, 20 were research papers, one was a position paper, one was a demo paper, and one was an extended abstract. While all of the accepted papers this year were research papers (13 long papers and 4 short papers), we are confident that these new paper categories will become increasingly popular in the future. Our second initiative involves recognizing outstanding research submitted to the workshop via a best paper award. The winner(s) will be announced at the closing session.

Due to the COVID-19 pandemic, CRAC will be organized for the first time as an online event. Authors of all accepted papers were asked to pre-record videos presenting their work, which will be made available for viewing by all attendees a week before the start of the workshop. At the workshop, each paper will be given a 5-minute oral presentation slot followed by a 5-minute discussion period.

We are grateful to the following people, without whom we could not have assembled an interesting program for the workshop. First, we are indebted to our program committee members. Owing to the unexpected increase in the number of submissions, each reviewer were assigned four papers to review. All of them did the incredible job of completing their reviews in a reviewing period that spanned less than two weeks. Second, we thank Juntao Yu for accepting our invitation to be this year's invited speaker. Juntao will give a talk on anaphora resolution beyond OntoNotes, which brings us back to the roots of our predecessor, the CORBON workshop. Third, we thank Massimo Poesio for agreeing to chair a plenary session that focuses on discussing the possibility of developing Universal Anaphora (UA), a unified, language-independent markup scheme that reflects common cross-linguistic understanding of reference-related phenomena. Motivated by Universal Dependencies, UA aims to facilitate referential analysis of the similarities and idiosyncracies among typologically different languages, support comparative evaluation of anaphora resolution systems and enable comparative linguistic studies. If successful, UA will be used to produce annotated corpora for a joint shared task by CODI (The Workshop on Computational Approaches to Discourse) and CRAC next year. Finally, we would like to thank the workshop participants for joining in.

Despite these difficult times, we look forward to an exciting online workshop. We hope you will enjoy it as much as we do!

— Maciej Ogrodniczuk, Sameer Pradhan, Yulia Grishina, and Vincent Ng

Organizing Committee and Proceedings Editors:

Maciej Ogrodniczuk, Institute of Computer Science, Polish Academy of Sciences
Sameer Pradhan, University of Pennsylvania and cemantix
Yulia Grishina, Amazon
Vincent Ng, University of Texas at Dallas

Programme Committee:

Antonio Branco, University of Lisbon
Dan Cristea, Alexandru Ioan Cuza University of Iași
Stephanie Dipper, University of Bochum
Yulia Grishina, Amazon
Veronique Hoste, Ghent University
Sandra Kübler, Indiana University
Sobha Lalitha Devi, AU-KBC Research Center, Anna University of Chennai
Emmanuel Lassalle, Machina Capital, Paris
Costanza Navaretta, University of Copenhagen
Anna Nedoluzhko, Charles University in Prague
Michal Novak, Charles University in Prague
Constantin Orasan, University of Surrey
Massimo Poesio, Queen Mary University of London
Marta Recasens, Google
Yannick Versley, Amazon
Heike Zinsmeister, University of Hamburg

Invited Speaker:

Juntao Yu, Queen Mary University of London

Table of Contents

Workshop Program: December 12, 2020

14:00–15:00 **Welcome and Invited Talk**

14:00–14:05 *Introduction*
Maciej Ogrodniczuk, Sameer Pradhan, Yulia Grishina and Vincent Ng

14:05–15:00 Invited talk: *Anaphora Resolution beyond OntoNotes*
Juntao Yu

15:00–15:10 **Short Break**

15:10–16:10 **Paper Summary Session 1: Mention Detection and Deep Learning Approaches**

15:10–15:20 *Anaphoric Zero Pronoun Identification: A Multilingual Approach*
Abdulrahman Aloraini and Massimo Poesio

15:20–15:30 *Partially-Supervised Mention Detection*
Lesly Miculicich and James Henderson

15:30–15:40 *E.T.: Entity-Transformers. Coreference Augmented Neural Language Model
for Richer Mention Representations via Entity-Transformer Blocks*
Nikolaos Stylianou and Ioannis Vlahavas

15:40–15:50 *Neural Coreference Resolution for Arabic*
Abdulrahman Aloraini, Juntao Yu and Massimo Poesio

15:50–16:00 *Sequence-to-Sequence Networks Learn the Meaning of Reflexive Anaphora*
Robert Frank and Jackson Petty

16:00–16:10 *Sequence to Sequence Coreference Resolution*
Gorka Urbizu, Ander Soraluze and Olatz Arregi

16:10–16:20 **Short Break**

16:20–17:20 **Paper Summary Session 2: Resources, Evaluation and Beyond the Identity
of Reference**

16:20–16:30 *A Benchmark of End-to-End and Deterministic Coreference Resolution
of Dutch Novels and News*
Corbèn Poot and Andreas van Cranenburgh

16:30–16:40 *A Dataset for Anaphora Analysis in French E-mails*
Hani Guenoune, Cédric Lopez, Kevin Cousot, Melissa Mekaoui
and Mathieu Lafourcade

16:40–16:50 *Integrating Knowledge Graph Embeddings to Improve Mention Representation
for Bridging Anaphora Resolution*
Onkar Pandit, Pascal Denis and Liva Ralaivola

16:50–17:00 *Reference to Discourse Topics: Introducing "Global" Shell Nouns*
Fabian Simonjetz

Workshop Program (continued): December 12, 2020

17:00–17:10   *TwiConv: A Coreference-annotated Corpus of Twitter Conversations*
Berfin Aktaş and Annalena Kohnert

17:10–17:20   *Predicting Coreference in Abstract Meaning Representations*
Tatiana Anikina, Alexander Koller and Michael Roth

17:20–17:30   Short Break

17:30–18:20   Paper Summary Session 3: Applications

17:30–17:40   *It's Absolutely Divine! Can Fine-Grained Sentiment Analysis Benefit from Coreference Resolution?*
Orphee De Clercq and Veronique Hoste

17:40–17:50   *Enhanced Labelling in Active Learning for Coreference Resolution*
Vebjørn Espeland, Beatrice Alex and Benjamin Bach

17:50–18:00   *Coreference Strategies in English-German Translation*
Ekaterina Lapshinova-Koltunski, Marie-Pauline Krielke and Christian Hardmeier

18:00–18:10   *Reference in Team Communication for Robot-Assisted Disaster Response: An Initial Analysis*
Natalia Skachkova and Ivana Kruijff-Korbayova

18:10–18:20   *Resolving Pronouns in Twitter Streams: Context can Help!*
Anietie Andy, Chris Callison-Burch and Derry Tanti Wijaya

18:20–18:30   Short Break

18:30–19:15   Plenary Session on Universal Anaphora and Best Paper Award

18:30–19:10   *Universal Anaphora Discussion Panel*
Chair: Massimo Poesio

19:10–19:15   *Best Paper Award and Closing of the Workshop*
Maciej Ogrodniczuk, Sameer Pradhan, Yulia Grishina and Vincent Ng

E.T.: Entity-Transformers
Coreference augmented Neural Language Model for richer mention representations via Entity-Transformer blocks

Nikolaos Stylianou
Aristotle University of Thessaloniki
School of Informatics
Greece
nstylia@csd.auth.gr

Ioannis Vlahavas
Aristotle University of Thessaloniki
School of Informatics
Greece
vlahavas@csd.auth.gr

Abstract

In the last decade, the field of Neural Language Modelling has witnessed enormous changes, with the development of novel models through the use of Transformer architectures. However, even these models struggle to model long sequences due to memory constraints and increasing computational complexity. Coreference annotations over the training data can provide context far beyond the modelling limitations of such language models. In this paper we present an extension over the Transformer-block architecture used in neural language models, specifically in GPT2, in order to incorporate entity annotations during training. Our model, GPT2E, extends the Transformer layers architecture of GPT2 to Entity-Transformers, an architecture designed to handle coreference information when present. To that end, we achieve richer representations for entity mentions, with insignificant training cost. We show the comparative model performance between GPT2 and GPT2E in terms of Perplexity on the CoNLL 2012 and LAMBADA datasets as well as the key differences in the entity representations and their effects in downstream tasks such as Named Entity Recognition. Furthermore, our approach can be adopted by the majority of Transformer-based language models.

1 Introduction

Language modelling is the task of transforming individual words into vector representations based on the context they appear in. Hence, distant term dependencies are an inherited issue within the task. Language models always seek for smart approaches towards incorporating context from longer distances as it allows for better representations compared to their limited context counterparts. Intuitively, imagine attempting to start reading a novel series from the second book onward, with no information about the first. The amount of information previously missed is something that cannot be acquired. However, this is the case with most language models. While an understanding of the words is present due to the contextual information at each word's occurrence, entity information that are in distant text are lost or not transferred.

Until recently, Recurrent Neural Networks (RNNs), and specifically Long Short-Term Memory (LSTM) networks, have been the core of all the state-of-the-art approaches (McCann et al., 2017; Peters et al., 2018). Thanks to the Transformers architecture (Vaswani et al., 2017), through the use of attention mechanisms, models such as XLNet (Yang et al., 2019), GPT (Radford et al., 2019) and BERT (Devlin et al., 2019) can account for even longer sequences. However, the computational limitations of the multi-head attention in the architecture make it hard to increase the contextual information in such models (Tay et al., 2020). As a result, research has been focused on introducing variations to the transformer architecture, with focus on the multi-head attention mechanism, in order to alleviate part of the computational cost and increase the contextual information available to models.

In this paper we present a novel approach, that makes use of coreference information during training a language model via our Entity-Transformer architecture, which extends the original Transformer block in Transformer-Based language models. To that end, we incorporate the important entity information

Proceedings of the 3rd Workshop on Computational Models of Reference, Anaphora and Coreference (CRAC 2020), pages 1–10,
Barcelona, Spain (online), December 12, 2020.

that would otherwise be unreachable for the model. As a result, we effectively boost the representations of the entity mentions, where entity information is present, without hindering the performance of the language model where entities are not present.

In our experiments, we extend the GPT2 architecture to formulate our model, named GPT2E and train it on the CoNLL-2012 dataset (Pradhan et al., 2012) using the annotated coreference information. We evaluate the model's performance in terms of Perplexity on the ConLL 2012 and the LAMBADA (Paperno et al., 2016) datasets and showcase the effects of such training on the word representations as well as on the downstream task of Named Entity Recognition (NER) using the CoNLL 2012 dataset. To that end, we compare GPT2E's performance to a base model (GPT2) when trained on the same data, to highlight the effects of coreference information when paird with our Entity-Transformer architecture.

2 Related Work

In the last decade, the field of Neural Language Modelling has witnessed enormous changes. With pretrained neural language models being the current go-to approach in all NLP reserach, a variety of methods models have been developed. We distinguish two major categories:

General purpose language models. Steady improvements have been achieved to this field with the use of deep RNNs and pre-training on a large number of training data (McCann et al., 2017; Peters et al., 2018). With Transformers, language models have been able to capture longer linguistic structures without the use of RNNs and surpass their RNN counterparts by a big margin (Radford et al., 2018; Devlin et al., 2019). Recent research has focused on ways of taking advantage of more context (Yang et al., 2019; Fan et al., 2020) and introducing effective methodologies to scale up the models and train them (Radford et al., 2019; Shoeybi et al., 2019; Rosset, 2019; Brown et al., 2020).

Language modelling with entity decisions. YangLM (Yang et al., 2017) was the first to incorporate entity decisions to a language model by introducing learnable entity embeddings. Alternative entity handling mechanisms are introduced in both EntityNLM (Ji et al., 2017) and SetLM (Kunz and Hardmeier, 2019) in addition to a length variable for EntityNLM. All of the aforementioned approaches are RNN-based and hence their performance is expected to be sub-par to Transformer based models. Furthermore, (Kunz and Hardmeier, 2019) concludes that language models handling entity decisions do not improve in performance with the addition of more hidden units and that the source data is of limited number and of specific genre which do not highlight the benefits of explicit entity information. Clark et al. (2019), through attention head probing, experimentally proves that BERT does model anaphoric phenomenon in the form of antecedent selection, with attention heads directly attending to the respective mention's antecedent. However, these information are not explicitly used to further enhance the model. Furthermore, ERNIE (Zhang et al., 2019), which uses knowledge graphs to infuse entity information to the model, only does so for named entities, completely ignoring pronouns and nominal mentions.

3 Our approach

In order to incorporate coreference information to a language model, we require training and testing data with entity information present and a mechanism to handle existing and non-existing entities. To that end, our proposed model, GPT2E, is based on the GPT2 language model, with changes to the Transformer block and an entity handling mechanism, which are described in the following subsections. As a result, GPT2E is a combination of multi-layer Entity-Transformer decoder blocks. The model applies multi-headed self-attention operations over the input tokens, position-wise feed-forward transformations, and entity-based attention operations. The model architecture can be described as follows:

$$h_0 = UW_e + W_p$$
$$h_l = \texttt{entity\_transformer\_block}(h_{l-1}, E) \forall_i \in [1, n] \tag{1}$$
$$P(u) = \texttt{softmax}(h_n W_e^T)$$

where $U = (u_{-k}, \ldots, u_{-1})$ is the context vector of tokens, n is the number of layers, W_e is the token embedding matrix, W_p is the position embedding matrix and E is the context vector of entity representations.

3.1 Entity-Transformer block

Entity-Transformer (ET) blocks are extensions of the transformer blocks used in GPT2, designed to handle entities in the form of vectors of shape $E_i \in \mathbb{R}^{1 \times d_{embd}}$, where d_{embd} is the embedding dimension the model outputs. Effectively, the entity representations are used directly inside the ET blocks.

The input representation first goes through a layer normalization (Ba et al., 2016) and a masked multi-head self attention layer (Vaswani et al., 2017), followed by a residual connection (He et al., 2016). The output of the residual connection is then used in a layer normalization and position-wise feed foward layer followed by another residual connection. The final residual output is used in the entity attention layer before it is forwarded outside of the Entity-Transformer block.

The entity attention layer is an adaptation of the masked multi-head self attention layer which considers Entities (E) as the Key (K) value in the Query (Q), Key (K), Value (V) attention mechanism scheme. The architecture of the Entity-Transformer blocks and the entity attention mechanism used are shown in Figure 1.

3.2 Entity handling mechanism

We maintain a persistent set of entities $\mathcal{E}$, that holds the hidden representation of the last entity's mention from our model. Each entity representation E_i is initialised as a vector of ones, which allows for minimal noise in the first occurrence of the entity. Tokens that are not part of the entity mention have a consistent entity representation $E_\emptyset$, as a vector of ones, similar to unseen entity mentions.

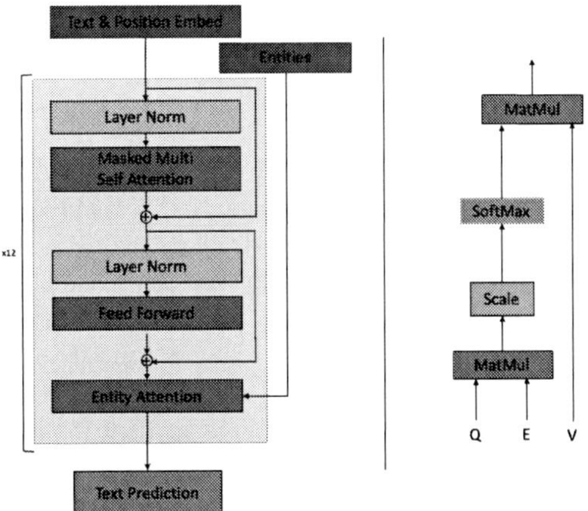

Figure 1: **(left)** Entity-Transformer Block **(right)** Entity Attention mechanism

During each training step, E_i takes the latest value of the respective entity's latest hidden representation from $\mathcal{E}$ and is updated to the new value at the end of each step. These entity representations are handled with the use of Entity-Transformer blocks. The final hidden representation of the input token, after it is affected by the previous entity representation E_i, is considered to be the new entity representations and replaces E_i in $\mathcal{E}$.

4 Experiments

Our approach is evaluated in two steps. First we evaluate our GPT2E language model, in comparison with a GPT2 model, trained on CoNLL 2012 and evaluated on both CoNLL 2012 and LAMBADA datasets. We then use the trained models to extract word representations for entity mentions based on the coreference annotations in text and measure the differences of such representations. For NER, we use the language models to extract word representatios and train the same baseline model on the CoNLL 2012 dataset.

4.1 Setup

In our experiments we use the GPT2-small configuration with 117M parameters, 12 heads and 12 layers for both GPT2 and GPT2E. Both models use a Byte-Pair Encoder to process the input, a learning rate of 2e-5 and train for 10e5 steps, with validation every 10e3 steps. We use a batch size of 1, to highlight the effect of entity updates in the system, as the entity representations are only updated at the end of each training step.

After training, we compute the differences between the representations of all entity mentions in the coreference clusters as derived from GPT2 and GPT2E. Consequently, we conduct experiments with no contextual information for each word and we also distinguish the results between using and not using entity information. We perform these experiments separately for all entities in the dataset and present the average score for different type of words based on their part-of-speech tags.

The NER models are based on the Lample et al. (2016) architecture. However, our models use only word embeddings from the pre-trained GPT2 and GPT2E models respectively, removing the character embeddings to eliminate any information input apart from the coreference-trained representations. We use a hidden size of 512 for the Bidirectional LSTMs, 0.5 dropout (Srivastava et al., 2014) between layers and a learning rate of 0.0001 with 0.9 decay per epoch with Adam (Kingma and Ba, 2014). We trained our models for 20 epoches, with early stopping and a batch size of 32.

All the experiments were run on a computer with a single Titan V 12GB graphics card, 32GB of memory and an Intel i7-8700 processor.

4.2 Datasets and Preprocessing

We chose the English CoNLL-2012 dataset for training, which is based on the OntoNotes 5.0 corpus (Weischedel et al., 2011) and contains over 1.3 million words with 35,143 entity mentions in the training set and 170 thousand words with 4,532 entity mentions in the test set making it the most suitable dataset for training a language model with coreference annotations. In the dataset common nouns, pronouns and proper nouns contribute 90% of the words in both train and test English sets. For our out of domain evaluation we chose the LAMBADA dataset. This choice was based on the premise that the dataset is primarily used for word predictions requiring broad discourse context and that the target words are mostly proper nouns and common nouns (85% fo the total target words). As a result, we expect that the importance of an entity-centric language model would be better displayed in such a scenario.

As we utilize the CoNLL-2012 dataset for both the Language Modelling task and the NER task, we formulate the data in two different ways.

Table 1: Data example from the CoNLL 2012 dataset, as formated for the task.

$X_{1:11}$	"	The	U.S.	underestimated	Noriega	all	along	"	says	Ambler	Moss
$E_{1:11}$	$\emptyset$	73	73	$\emptyset$	82	$\emptyset$	$\emptyset$	$\emptyset$	$\emptyset$	50	50
$X_{12:23}$	a	former	Ambassador	to	Panama	.	"	He	has	mastered	the	art
$E_{12:23}$	50	50	50	50	50	$\emptyset$	$\emptyset$	82	$\emptyset$	$\emptyset$	$\emptyset$	$\emptyset$

For Language Modelling, we formulate our data in a similar manner with Ji et al. (2017), as seen in Table 1. Specifically, for each token we also introduce a second variable "E" which indicates the entity in which the token is part of, using the gold coreference annotations, with a special "$\emptyset$" for tokens that are not part of an entity. For the CoNLL dataset, we populate E with the golden entities from the coreference resolution shared task. For the LAMBADA dataset we use the $\emptyset$ for all tokens. In comparison to the original data formulation described in Ji et al. (2017), we opted to not use the L variable to denote the entity length (i.e. the number of remaining tokens in the entity mention) as it's main use is enable entity mention prediction, which we do not attempt at this stage. We use Byte Pair Encoding (BPE) (Sennrich et al., 2016) for the final input representation of the word instances, similar to GPT2.

For NER, we formulate the data in a IOB format to facilitate a similar model architecture as described in Lample et al. (2016), using the gold named entities of the dataset, including nested entities.

5 Results

To evaluate the results of our Entity-Transformers architecture and the effects of corereference annotations to language modelling, we measure the change in performance of the language model using

Perplexity (PPL). Furthermore, we compute the average difference of the representations between mentions of the same entity of the GPT2E model, between each entity mention between GPT2 and GPT2E and between non-entity mentions of the same words using cosine similarity. Furthermore, we use micro-average Precision, Recall and F1 scores for the evaluation of our NER models.

For Language modelling, Table 2, shows the training and validation losses of GPT2 and GPT2E, as well as the Perplexity of the models after 10e5 training steps. The gradual changes in training and validation losses, measured every 10e3 steps, are illustrated in Figures 2 & 3 with GPT2 model in orange and GPT2E model in blue colours respectively. Similarly, Table 3 highlights the performance difference between the two trained models on the LAMBADA dataset. As both models are trained on a very limited dataset compared to other language models, we are not comparing performance in terms of accuracy.

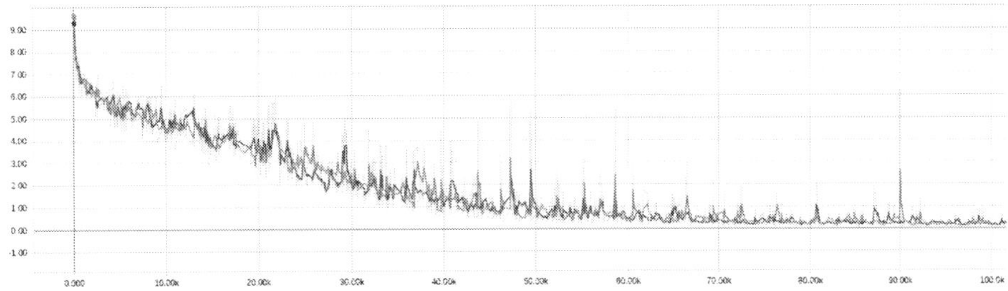

Figure 2: Training loss per step on the CoNLL 2012 dataset.

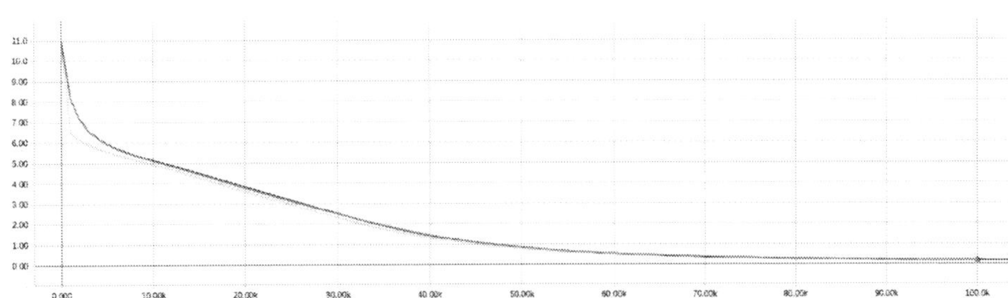

Figure 3: Validation loss per step on the CoNLL 2012 dataset.

Table 2: Perplexity and Validation loss
on the CoNLL 2012 dataset

Process	GPT2E			GPT2		
	PPL	Loss	Time per step	PPL	Loss	Time per step
Training	5.52	1.71	0.290s	4.80	1.57	0.298s
Validation	1.20	0.187	0.290s	1.19	0.184	0.298s

Table 3: Perplexity performance
on the LAMBADA dataset

Model	Perplexity
GPT2E	196.81
GPT2	219.97

In terms of Perplexity, the models show similar performances on the CoNLL 2012 dataset, while having a slight advantage at the LAMBADA dataset. The slight improvement in Perplexity of the GPT2E model over the GPT2 on the LAMBADA dataset is attributed to the target words' part-of-speech type. As described in Section 4.2, the target words of the LAMBADA dataset are mostly proper nouns and common nouns and the majority of the training mentions in the CoNLL-2012 dataset are of the same type. This behaviour is consistent with the expectations of the performance of an entity-centric language model. Both GPT2 and GPT2E models show a remarkably low Perplexity compared to EntityNLM, YangLM and SetLM of reported Perplexity 161.64, 114 and 107 respectively. However, these language models are RNN based, and gap between them is attributed to the Transformers architecture and the relatively small size of the CoNLL-2012 dataset. The added complexity of calculating the entity representations and using the Entity-Transformer blocks is contributing to 0.008 seconds per step in both training and evaluation, adding up to an additional 12 min and 6 seconds, a 2% increase in time for the complete training process.

To compare the changes in the entity mention representations when using coreference information during training we conducted a series of experiments, taking into account the existence or absence of coreference annotation. Specifically, for both models, for each entity we calculate the average similarity of its mentions with the other entity mentions, with and without the use of entity representations for GPT2E, and the average similarity between the entity representation and the entity mentions. We have limited the scope of the comparisons, using part-of-speech tags, to only nouns and proper nouns, as these will be the words that will be affected the most by our changes, given the dataset statistics presented in Section 4.2. Similarly, we calculated the average cosine similarity between the pronoun's representations of the two models as well as the differences between the two when entity representations are present.

Table 4: Cosine similarity of mention representations and their entities in different scenarios

Experiments	GPT2E without Entities	GPT2E with Entities	GPT2
Average mention similarity NN,NNS,NNP,NNPS	0.7117	0.7117	0.6971
Average entity similarity NN,NNS,NNP,NNPS	0.0489	0.0513	-0.0164
Average mention similarity PRP,PRP$	0.8250	0.8250	0.7928
Average entity similarity PRP,PRP$	0.0619	0.0566	-0.0173

Based on the results displayed in Table 4, we can infer that the mentions maintain their similarity when the coreference information are used during inference, while also have a higher average similarity than the respective mentions of the model trained without coreference annotations. However, taking into account the changing similarity scores between the entity representations and the entity mentions when we use coreference information during inference, we can conclude that there is a constant change to the representations. In the case of nouns and pronouns, that change brings the representations closer while in pronouns it has the opposite effect. Individual visual representations of the embeddings for GPT2E and GPT2 and a comparative visual representation between the two are included in the appendix section.

Table 5: NER performance using GPT2 and GPT2E representations as input.

Labels	GPT2			GPT2E		
	F1	Prec	Recall	F1	Precision	Recall
PERSON	48%	95.5%	32.5 %	51.5%	94%	35.5%
PRODUCT	8%	33%	4.5 %	23.5%	90%	13.5%
EVENT	23%	83.5%	13.5%	15%	75%	8.5%
CARDINAL	28%	81.5%	17.5%	34%	75%	23%
NORP	44.5%	72.5%	36%	48%	79%	39.5%
Overall	54%	87%	39%	57%	88%	42%

The NER model, trained using word representations from GPT2E, achieved a mean average 3% F1 increase than the one trained with GPT2 word representations. We highlight four named entities in Table 5, which showed the biggest differences between the two trained models. Specifically, we observe that the named entities of PERSON and PRODUCT, which would be directly affected by the anaphoric information in the training process, showed the greatest increase and contributed the most to the performance boost. Subsequently, EVENT entities were more commonly mislabelled while using GPT2E representations. This behaviour is credited to the use of LOCATION terms to describe events (e.g. "the Guangzhou Fair") and to generic event terms that refer to different entities based on their context (e.g. "new year" can refer to a different year) which the baseline model was unable to handle correctly when the word representations were affected by entity information.

6 Discussion and Conclusions

In this paper we demonstrated a novel architecture to use coreference information in transformer-based neural language models in order to create richer representations and its effects on downstream tasks. We introduced an extension over the Transformer blocks of GPT2, labeled Entity-Transformer, that integrates coreference information to each entity mention. To that end, we also created an entity handling mechanism to create and update entity representations. Furthermore, as our proposed architecture extends over the basic Transformer block, it can be easily adapted to other Transformer-based language models, such as BERT, and also enables further research for Transformer-based language models with explicit entity decisions which have far outperformed their RNN counterparts.

In our experiments we showcased that in terms of Language modelling, both GPT2E and GPT2, when trained on the same data, have indistinguishable performance in terms of Perplexity and GPT2E has a small computational cost that translates into a slightly longer training time. However, the difference in the similarity between entity mention representations suggests that fewer iterations and mentions of each word are required to achieve the results, assuming a large enough number of mentions. This is due to the extended contextual information present at each mention occurrence, in the form of entity representations, used when training the model. What is more, the differences in these representations directly translates to an increase in tasks such as Named Entity Recognition. As coreference is ever-present in natural language, with a better ability for a language model to understand and utilize the anaphoric phenomenon in text, we expect an increased performance in other tasks such as summarization and natural language inference.

In order for language models to use coreference information, there are two requirements that need to be met. First, the models need to replace the Transformer blocks with the Entity-Transformer blocks introduced and also adopt the entity handling mechanism to make use of entity information. Second, annotated coreference information are required throughout the training corpus. While the changes described for the language models are trivial, language models require an enormous amount of training data, making it impossible to manually annotate coreference information. However, the entity handling mechanism we introduced is not affected by the lack of entity information in the training and is only boosted by the existence of them. As a result, even sparse annotations of high confidence will allow for improvements in the representations.

In the future, we plan to extend our work, using noisy annotation provided by pretrained coreference resolvers so that we can train GPT2E to the WikiText dataset (Merity et al., 2018), creating a comparable model with the original GPT2 and other state-of-the-art language models in a wider range of tasks. Furthermore, we aim to expand the abilities of our current approach to be able to make explicit entity decisions, similar to the previously cited work. For that purpose, attention head probing techniques, which have been found to model some anaphoric phenomena (Clark et al., 2019), and transfer learning through weight initialization from a pre-trained GPT2 model will be investigated as they can contribute to significant improvements while needing less annotated training data.

Acknowledgements

This research is co-financed by Greece and the European Union (European Social Fund- ESF) through the Operational Programme "Human Resources Development, Education and Lifelong Learning" in the context of the project "Strengthening Human Resources Research Potential via Doctorate Research" (MIS-5000432), implemented by the State Scholarships Foundation (IKY).

References

Jimmy Lei Ba, Jamie Ryan Kiros, and Geoffrey E Hinton. 2016. Layer normalization. *arXiv preprint arXiv:1607.06450*.

Tom B Brown, Benjamin Mann, Nick Ryder, Melanie Subbiah, Jared Kaplan, Prafulla Dhariwal, Arvind Neelakantan, Pranav Shyam, Girish Sastry, Amanda Askell, et al. 2020. Language models are few-shot learners. *arXiv preprint arXiv:2005.14165*.

Kevin Clark, Urvashi Khandelwal, Omer Levy, and Christopher D. Manning. 2019. What does BERT look at? an analysis of BERT's attention. In *Proceedings of the 2019 ACL Workshop BlackboxNLP: Analyzing and Interpreting Neural Networks for NLP*, pages 276–286, Florence, Italy, August. Association for Computational Linguistics.

Jacob Devlin, Ming-Wei Chang, Kenton Lee, and Kristina Toutanova. 2019. BERT: Pre-training of deep bidirectional transformers for language understanding. In *Proceedings of the 2019 Conference of the North American Chapter of the Association for Computational Linguistics: Human Language Technologies, Volume 1 (Long and Short Papers)*, pages 4171–4186, Minneapolis, Minnesota, June. Association for Computational Linguistics.

Angela Fan, Thibaut Lavril, Edouard Grave, Armand Joulin, and Sainbayar Sukhbaatar. 2020. Accessing higher-level representations in sequential transformers with feedback memory. *arXiv preprint arXiv:2002.09402*.

Kaiming He, Xiangyu Zhang, Shaoqing Ren, and Jian Sun. 2016. Identity mappings in deep residual networks. In *European conference on computer vision*, pages 630–645. Springer.

Yangfeng Ji, Chenhao Tan, Sebastian Martschat, Yejin Choi, and Noah A. Smith. 2017. Dynamic entity representations in neural language models. In *Proceedings of the 2017 Conference on Empirical Methods in Natural Language Processing*, pages 1830–1839, Copenhagen, Denmark, September. Association for Computational Linguistics.

Diederik P Kingma and Jimmy Ba. 2014. Adam: A method for stochastic optimization. *arXiv preprint arXiv:1412.6980*.

Jenny Kunz and Christian Hardmeier. 2019. Entity decisions in neural language modelling: Approaches and problems. In *Proceedings of the Second Workshop on Computational Models of Reference, Anaphora and Coreference*, pages 15–19.

Guillaume Lample, Miguel Ballesteros, Sandeep Subramanian, Kazuya Kawakami, and Chris Dyer. 2016. Neural architectures for named entity recognition. In *Proceedings of the 2016 Conference of the North American Chapter of the Association for Computational Linguistics: Human Language Technologies*, pages 260–270, San Diego, California, June. Association for Computational Linguistics.

Bryan McCann, James Bradbury, Caiming Xiong, and Richard Socher. 2017. Learned in translation: Contextualized word vectors. In *Advances in Neural Information Processing Systems*, pages 6294–6305.

Stephen Merity, Nitish Shirish Keskar, and Richard Socher. 2018. An analysis of neural language modeling at multiple scales. *arXiv preprint arXiv:1803.08240*.

Denis Paperno, Germán Kruszewski, Angeliki Lazaridou, Ngoc Quan Pham, Raffaella Bernardi, Sandro Pezzelle, Marco Baroni, Gemma Boleda, and Raquel Fernández. 2016. The LAMBADA dataset: Word prediction requiring a broad discourse context. In *Proceedings of the 54th Annual Meeting of the Association for Computational Linguistics (Volume 1: Long Papers)*, pages 1525–1534, Berlin, Germany, August. Association for Computational Linguistics.

Matthew Peters, Mark Neumann, Mohit Iyyer, Matt Gardner, Christopher Clark, Kenton Lee, and Luke Zettlemoyer. 2018. Deep contextualized word representations. In *Proceedings of the 2018 Conference of the North American Chapter of the Association for Computational Linguistics: Human Language Technologies, Volume 1 (Long Papers)*, pages 2227–2237, New Orleans, Louisiana, June. Association for Computational Linguistics.

Sameer Pradhan, Alessandro Moschitti, Nianwen Xue, Olga Uryupina, and Yuchen Zhang. 2012. Conll-2012 shared task: Modeling multilingual unrestricted coreference in ontonotes. In *Joint Conference on EMNLP and CoNLL-Shared Task*, pages 1–40. Association for Computational Linguistics.

Alec Radford, Karthik Narasimhan, Tim Salimans, and Ilya Sutskever. 2018. Improving language understanding by generative pre-training. *URL https://s3-us-west-2. amazonaws. com/openai-assets/researchcovers/languageunsupervised/language understanding paper. pdf*.

Alec Radford, Jeffrey Wu, Rewon Child, David Luan, Dario Amodei, and Ilya Sutskever. 2019. Language models are unsupervised multitask learners. *OpenAI Blog*, 1(8):9.

C Rosset. 2019. Turing-nlg: A 17-billion-parameter language model by microsoft. *Microsoft Blog*.

Rico Sennrich, Barry Haddow, and Alexandra Birch. 2016. Neural machine translation of rare words with subword units. In *Proceedings of the 54th Annual Meeting of the Association for Computational Linguistics (Volume 1: Long Papers)*, pages 1715–1725, Berlin, Germany, August. Association for Computational Linguistics.

Mohammad Shoeybi, Mostofa Patwary, Raul Puri, Patrick LeGresley, Jared Casper, and Bryan Catanzaro. 2019. Megatron-lm: Training multi-billion parameter language models using gpu model parallelism. *arXiv preprint arXiv:1909.08053*.

Nitish Srivastava, Geoffrey Hinton, Alex Krizhevsky, Ilya Sutskever, and Ruslan Salakhutdinov. 2014. Dropout: a simple way to prevent neural networks from overfitting. *The Journal of Machine Learning Research*, 15(1):1929–1958.

Yi Tay, Mostafa Dehghani, Dara Bahri, and Donald Metzler. 2020. Efficient transformers: A survey. *arXiv preprint arXiv:2009.06732*.

Ashish Vaswani, Noam Shazeer, Niki Parmar, Jakob Uszkoreit, Llion Jones, Aidan N Gomez, Łukasz Kaiser, and Illia Polosukhin. 2017. Attention is all you need. In *Advances in neural information processing systems*, pages 5998–6008.

Ralph Weischedel, Eduard Hovy, Mitchell Marcus, Martha Palmer, Robert Belvin, Sameer Pradhan, Lance Ramshaw, and Nianwen Xue. 2011. Ontonotes: A large training corpus for enhanced processing. *Handbook of Natural Language Processing and Machine Translation. Springer*, page 59.

Zichao Yang, Phil Blunsom, Chris Dyer, and Wang Ling. 2017. Reference-aware language models. In *Proceedings of the 2017 Conference on Empirical Methods in Natural Language Processing*, pages 1850–1859, Copenhagen, Denmark, September. Association for Computational Linguistics.

Zhilin Yang, Zihang Dai, Yiming Yang, Jaime Carbonell, Russ R Salakhutdinov, and Quoc V Le. 2019. Xlnet: Generalized autoregressive pretraining for language understanding. In *Advances in neural information processing systems*, pages 5754–5764.

Zhengyan Zhang, Xu Han, Zhiyuan Liu, Xin Jiang, Maosong Sun, and Qun Liu. 2019. ERNIE: Enhanced language representation with informative entities. In *Proceedings of the 57th Annual Meeting of the Association for Computational Linguistics*, pages 1441–1451, Florence, Italy, July. Association for Computational Linguistics.

Appendix A. Embeddings visualizations

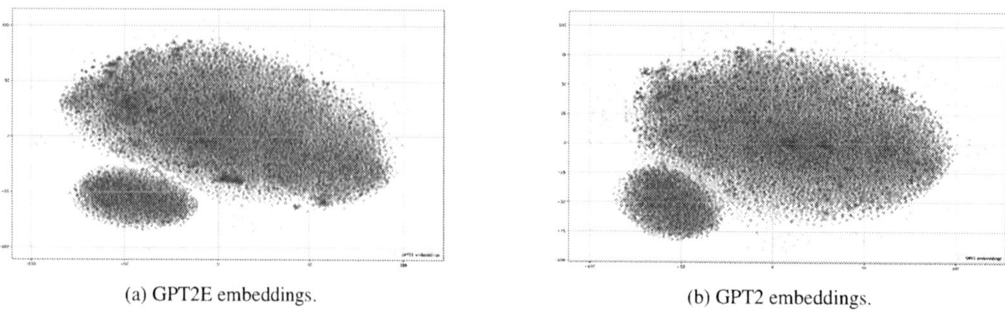

(a) GPT2E embeddings.

(b) GPT2 embeddings.

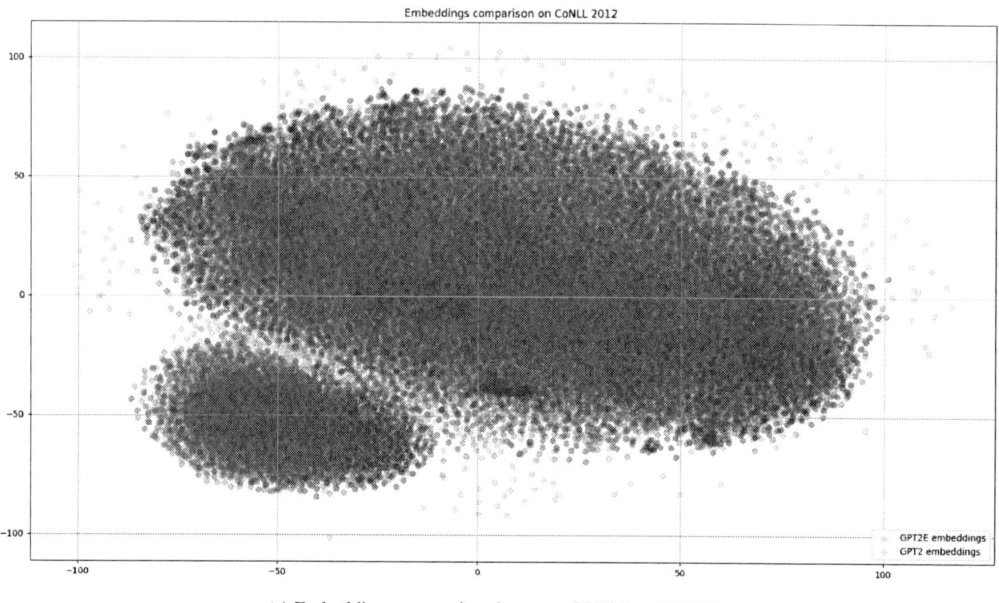

(c) Embeddings comparison between GPT2E and GPT2.

Figure 4: Visualization of the word representations of (a) GPT2E and (b) GPT2E and (c) comparison between the two, trained on the CoNLL2012 dataset, using t-SNE.

It's absolutely divine!
Can fine-grained sentiment analysis benefit from coreference resolution?

Orphée De Clercq
LT3, Ghent University
Groot-Brittannielaan 45
Ghent, Belgium
orphee.declercq@ugent.be

Véronique Hoste
LT3, Ghent University
Groot-Brittannielaan 45
Ghent, Belgium
veronique.hoste@ugent.be

Abstract

While it has been claimed that anaphora or coreference resolution plays an important role in opinion mining, it is not clear to what extent coreference resolution actually boosts performance, if at all. In this paper, we investigate the potential added value of coreference resolution for the aspect-based sentiment analysis of restaurant reviews in two languages, English and Dutch. We focus on the task of aspect category classification and investigate whether including coreference information prior to classification to resolve implicit aspect mentions is beneficial. Because coreference resolution is not a solved task in NLP, we rely on both automatically-derived and gold-standard coreference relations, allowing us to investigate the true upper bound. By training a classifier on a combination of lexical and semantic features, we show that resolving the coreferential relations prior to classification is beneficial in a joint optimization setup. However, this is only the case when relying on gold-standard relations and the result is more outspoken for English than for Dutch. When validating the optimal models, however, we found that only the Dutch pipeline is able to achieve a satisfying performance on a held-out test set and does so regardless of whether coreference information was included.

1 Introduction

In the last two decades, the field of sentiment analysis (SA) has yielded a lot of attention in both academia and commerce (see Liu (2015), Mohammad (2016) or Zhang et al. (2018) for overviews). The attention in SA research has shifted from the coarse-grained detection of the polarity of a given piece of text to the more fine-grained detection of not only polarity, but also the target of the expressed sentiment, as exemplified by the SemEval shared tasks on aspect-based sentiment analysis (Pontiki et al., (2014; 2015; 2016)). In reviews, many references to different aspects of a given product, experience, etc. are made and in a large number of cases, these references are even implicit. Regarding these implicit references, there are two options: either the referent is truly implicit meaning that the aspect can only be inferred from the implied meaning of the sentence, or the referent is an anaphor referring back to an antecedent that was or was not previously mentioned in the review.

While it has been claimed that anaphora or coreference resolution plays an important role in opinion mining to resolve the relationship between the mentioned entities in a given text and across texts (Liu, 2012), it is not clear to what extent coreference resolution actually boosts SA performance, if at all. In this paper, we investigate the potential added value of coreference resolution in the aspect-based SA of restaurant reviews for two languages: English and Dutch. By also manually annotating coreferential links in our data, we measure the incidence of referential links in our review corpus and investigate the upper bound of coreference resolution on SA performance. We reveal that although a certain number of coreferential instances are available in both languages, this does not alter the performance. On the contrary, when relying on automatic coreference resolution systems in both languages, we find that this hampers overall performance.

Proceedings of the 3rd Workshop on Computational Models of Reference, Anaphora and Coreference (CRAC 2020), pages 11–21,
Barcelona, Spain (online), December 12, 2020.

The remainder of this paper is organised as follows. In the next section, we discuss related work. In Section 3, we explain the datasets that were used for this research and how these have been annotated for both aspect-based sentiment analysis and coreference resolution. Next, in Section 4, we discuss the supervised machine learning classifier that was built and focus on how adding coreference resolution to the pipeline could alter accuracy. We present the results in Section 5, after which we conclude our work in Section 6 and offer prospects for future research.

2 Related work

The large volume of existing work on sentiment analysis from its early days until now can roughly be divided into lexicon-based and machine learning approaches. Lexicon-based methods determine the semantic orientation of a text based on scanning the words occurring in that text while relying on lexicons. Until recently, machine learning approaches were feature-based and applied supervised machine learning algorithms such as Support Vector Machines. With the advent of deep learning end-to-end approaches have also proven to perform well (Zhang et al., 2018).

Both types of approaches have been applied at various levels of a text: the document (Pang et al., 2002), paragraph (O'Hare et al., 2009), sentence (Li et al., 2010), phrase (Wilson et al., 2009) and word (Hatzivassiloglou and McKeown, 1997) level. For each of these levels, coarse-grained as well as fine-grained sentiment analysis can be performed. The latter means that the focus is not only on determining the polarity of a given utterance, but also on the identification of, for example, the source and target of the expressed sentiment (Kim and Hovy, 2006).

In the last decade, a substantial amount of research has been dedicated to target detection for aspect-based sentiment analysis (Pontiki et al., 2014). This task focuses on the detection of all sentiment expressions within a given document and the concepts and aspects (or features) to which they refer. Following the SemEval task description, aspect-based sentiment analysis can be decomposed into three subtasks: aspect term extraction, aspect term aggregation or classification and aspect term polarity estimation. The focus of the research presented here is on the second one.

The idea is to predict several predefined and domain-specific categories, i.e. a multiclass classification task. The two systems achieving the best results on this individual subtask in SemEval 2015 Task 12 both used classification to this purpose, respectively individual binary classifiers trained on each possible category which are afterwards entered in a sigmoidal feedforward network (Toh and Su, 2015) and a single Maximum Entropy classifier (Saias, 2015). When it comes to feature engineering, especially lexical features in the form of bag-of-words such as word unigrams and bigrams (Toh and Su, 2015) or word and lemma unigrams (Saias, 2015) and lexical-semantic features in the form of clusters learned from a large corpus of reference data (Saias, 2015) were used.

Since then, these benchmark SemEval datasets have been used many times to train and test neural models yielding state-of-the-art results on both this second subtask and end-to-end aspect-based sentiment analysis (Do et al., 2019) However, many methodologies start from he assumption that the target of a given polarity is explicitly lexicalized, which is certainly not always the case as people often use shorter or alternative linguistic structures, such as anaphors to refer to previously mentioned elements.

Many survey studies on sentiment analysis have claimed that the recognition of coreference is crucial for successful (aspect-based) sentiment analysis (Liu, 2012; Feldman, 2013). Stoyanov and Cardie (2006) were the first to use coreference resolution features to determine which mentions of opinion holders refer to the same entity. Early research in incorporating basic coreference resolution in sentiment analysis was conducted by Nicolov et al. (2008), who investigated how to perform sentiment analysis on parts of the document around topic terms. They demonstrated that using a proximity-based sentiment analysis algorithm can be improved by about 10%, depending on the topic, when using coreference to augment the focus area of the algorithm. The work by Kessler and Nicolov (2009), though its main focus is on finding which sentiment expressions are semantically related, provided some valuable insights in the necessity of coreference as they found that 14% of the targets expressions that had been manually labeled in their corpus were expressed in the form of pronouns. Ding and Liu (2010) introduced the problem of entity and aspect coreference resolution and aimed to determine which mentions of entities and/or aspects a certain pronoun refers to, taking a supervised machine learning approach. Their system learns a function to predict whether a pair of nouns is coreferent, building coreference chains based on feature vectors that model a variety of contextual information about the nouns. They also added two opinion-related features, which implies that they used sentiment analysis for the purpose of better coreference resolution rather than the other way around. A similar coreference resolution methodology was used by Zhao et al.(2015) to link target aspects to target objects. However, to our knowledge not much qualitative research has been performed investigating to what extent the availability of coreference information can actually help aspect-based sentiment analysis. This is the exact aim of this paper, we zoom in on the task of aspect category classification and investigate whether including coreference information prior to classification is useful.

3 Datasets and annotation

For our experiments, we rely on datasets comprising restaurant reviews in two languages, namely English and Dutch. Both datasets were released in the framework of SemEval: the English data (350 reviews) was released for the 2015 competition (Pontiki et al., 2015) and the Dutch data (400 reviews) for a rerun of this competition in 2016 (Pontiki et al., 2016).

3.1 ABSA annotation

All English and Dutch restaurant reviews were annotated following the SemEval ABSA guidelines[1]. Every review was split into sentences and a sentence was only annotated with aspect terms and categories when a polarity was expressed in the sentence. In total, 1,702 English (85%) and 1,767 Dutch (76%) sentences were found to be opinionated and further annotated with targets, aspect categories (i.e. Ambience, Drinks, Food, Location, Restaurant and Service) having different attributes (i.e. General, Prices, Quality, Style & Options and Miscellaneous) and polarity. Important for the research presented here is to note that a distinction was made between explicit and implicit targets.

Whenever there was an explicit target, the span of the terms evoking that target was included in the annotation; implicit targets were added as 'NULL' targets. As a consequence, pronouns are not annotated as separate targets, even if they refer to an explicit target. Instead, those pronouns, together with other aspects that are referred to implicitly, are added as 'NULL' targets, which are then further annotated with aspect categories and polarities. In Table 1, we give an overview of how many different aspect categories are available in both datasets, together with the number of implicit targets. We observe that 623 out of the 2,499 annotated aspect categories for English (24.9%) and 773 out of the 2,445 for Dutch (31.6%) are implicit or 'NULL' targets.

Main	Attribute	Total		Implicit	
		EN	DU	EN	DU
Ambience	General	260	240	28	56
Drinks	Prices	20	23	0	3
	Style & Options	32	38	0	4
	Quality	46	68	3	3
Food	General	1	15	0	4
	Prices	85	54	18	19
	Style & Options	133	209	19	27
	Quality	852	675	86	123
Location	General	28	34	6	7
Restaurant	General	416	437	233	296
	Prices	83	43	57	33
	Miscellaneous	100	26	51	12
Service	General	443	583	122	186
Total		2499	2445	623	773

Table 1: Total number of annotated aspect categories and implicit targets

---

[1] http://alt.qcri.org/semeval2016/task5/data/uploads/absa2016_annotationguidelines.pdf

3.2 Coreference annotation

We manually annotated each implicit or 'NULL' target by indicating whether this implicit target was clearly referential (i.e. an anaphor), whether the antecedent was also mentioned in the review or whether none of both applied. We only indicated coreferential relations constituting an identity (and thus not a part-of, etc.) relation between the anaphor and the antecedent. The following three examples exemplify this annotation procedure.

1. *I tend to judge a sushi restaurant by [its sea urchin]. [It] melted in my mouth and was perfect.*
   It = anaphor
   its sea urchin = antecedent

2. *This place is incredibly tiny. [They] refuse to seat parties of 3 or more on weekends.*
   They = anaphor
   antecedent not mentioned; 'staff' is implied

3. *Can't wait wait for my next visit.*
   No anaphor, no antecedent

The pie charts below illustrate the subdivision of these additional annotations in our datasets: for each 'NULL' target we indicated whether the implicit target was referential, and if so, whether the antecedent was mentioned (COREF) or not (EMPTY). If there was no referential relation, we labelled it as IMPLICIT.

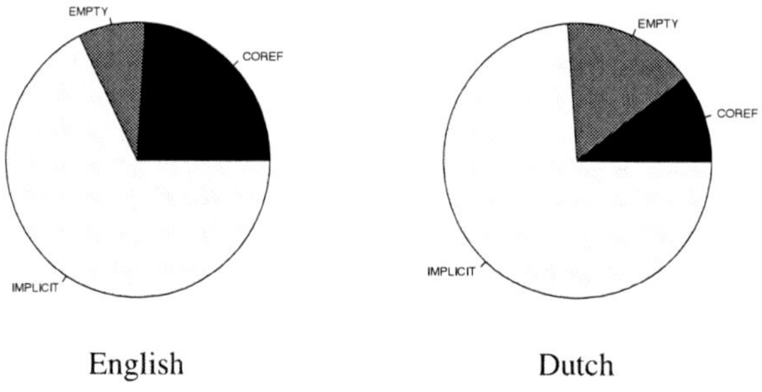

Figure 1: Pie charts visualizing the implicit target distribution in our datasets.

In both languages the vast majority is labelled as implicit. Regarding the usage of referential pronouns we observe a different tendency: in English, an anaphor is more frequently preceded by an antecedent within one review, whereas for Dutch more empty anaphors are included. Percentagewise, we see that in our English dataset 20.7% of the implicit targets are referential pronouns for which the antecedent can be discovered within the same review, whereas for Dutch this is only true for 10.34% of the implicit reviews. When performing coreference resolution prior to classification into aspect categories, we can therefore assume that this technique will be more successful for English.

4 Experimental setup

The focus of our experiments is on the task of aspect category classification. This is a fine-grained classification task requiring a system to grasp subtle differences between various main–attribute categories (e.g. *Food–General* versus *Food–Prices* versus *Food–Quality* versus *Food–Style&Options*). Moreover, as previously explained, reviewers refer to the various aspects of a restaurant in both an explicit and implicit manner. Especially those implicit targets are challenging. This is why we will investigate whether including coreference information prior to classification is useful. We envisage two experimental settings: a setting where coreferential anaphor–antecedent pairs were not derived beforehand and one where they were. In the latter setting, both gold-standard and automatically-derived coreference relations were used in order to investigate the true upper bound of incorporating this type of information.

We relied on gold-standard explicit and implicit targets for all experiments. As experimental data we employed the same train and test splits of the SemEval shared tasks on ABSA (Pontiki et al., 2016), see Table 2.

	ENGLISH		DUTCH	
	train	**test**	**train**	**test**
# targets	1654	845	1843	602
# implicits	375	248	563	210
# explicits	1279	597	1280	392

Table 2: the overall number of targets and the number of implicit and explicit targets in the datasets.

4.1 Information sources

As a baseline, we derived bag-of-words token unigram features of the sentence in which a target occurs in order to represent some of the lexical information present in each of the categories. In bag-of-words representations, each feature corresponds to a single word found in the training corpus. Besides these lexical features, features in the form of clusters derived from a large domain-specific reference corpus have also proven useful (Toh and Su, 2015; Toh and Su, 2016). Given the lack of such reference corpora for Dutch, we decided to link mentions of concepts and instances to either semantic lexicons like WordNet (Fellbaum, 1998)(English) or Cornetto (Vossen et al., 2013) (Dutch) , and to a Wikipedia-based knowledge base (Hovy et al., 2013) such as DBpedia (Lehmann et al., 2013).

This led to the creation of a set of lexico-semantic features. Six WordNet features were derived, each representing a value indicating the number of (unique) terms annotated as aspect terms from that category that (1) co-occur in the synset of the candidate term or (2) which are a hyponym/hypernymof a candidate term in the synset. Furthermore, we identified concepts in DBpedia by processing each target with DBpediaSpotlight (Mendes et al., 2011). Next, categories for each concept were created, corresponding to the categories in Wikipedia. To that end, we extracted all direct categories for each concept (`dcterms:subject`), and added the more general categories with a maximum of two levels up in the hierarchy (`skos:broader`). This process is illustrated in Figure 2. The whole process, comprising the annotation with DBpedia Spotlight and the extraction of categories, was performed using the RapidMiner LOD Extension (Paulheim and Fürnkranz, 2012).

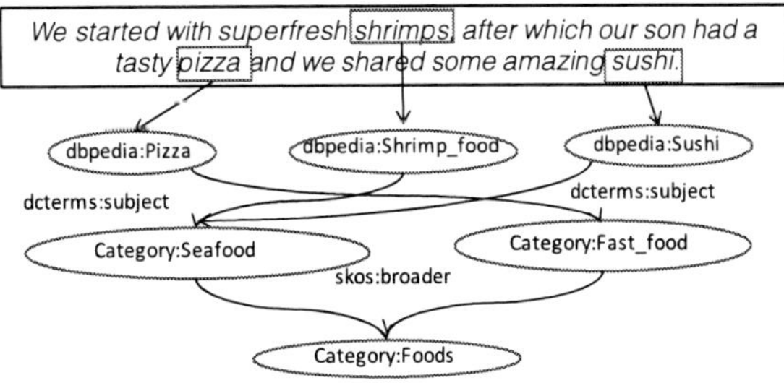

Figure 2: Example sentence in which targets are semantically enriched using DBpedia.

4.2 Coreference resolution

As all implicit aspect mentions and pronouns referring to aspects had been annotated as 'NULL' targets it was impossible to derive lexico-semantic features for these instances. However, because coreference information was added to these aspects, we hypothesized that for certain 'NULL' targets these features can actually be derived. In other words, a coreferential relation between an anaphor – pronoun – and an antecedent constituting an aspect term in itself should enable us to derive additional semantic information.

For the research presented here, we explored the added value of incorporating coreference information by including it as a separate processing step before the feature extraction. Crucial for this step is that the coreference resolution is highly accurate, since an anaphor–antecedent mismatch can also lead to a semantic information mismatch. To this purpose, we relied on existing systems in both languages: the deterministic Stanford Coreference Resolver (Lee et al., 2013) for English and the COREA system for Dutch (De Clercq et al., 2011).

The Stanford system is a rule-based system that includes a total of ten rules (or "sieves") for entity coreference, such as exact string match and pronominal resolution. The sieves are applied from highest to lowest precision, each rule adding coreference links. The COREA system is a mention-pair system (Hoste, 2016) that recasts the coreference resolution problem as a classification task: a classifier is trained to decide whether a pair of noun phrases or mentions is coreferential of not. In other words, resolving anaphor m_j can be viewed as the task of finding the mention m_i that maximizes the probability of the random variable L:

$$argmax_{m_i} P(L|m_j, m_i)$$

In the mention-pair model, each pair of NPs is represented by a feature vector containing distance, morphological, lexical, syntactic and semantic information on both NPs and the relation between them. The goal of the feature information is to enable the machine learner to distinguish between coreferential and non-coreferential relations, and for example to resolve that *it* in example 2 does not refer to *a sushi restaurant*, nor to *sushi rose*, but to *its sea urchin*. After this binary classification, a second step, a separate clustering mechanism is used to coordinate the pairwise classification decisions and to build so-called 'coreference chains'.

As we also manually annotated each 'NULL' aspect term constituting an anaphor–antecedent relation, we were able to asses the upper bound of incorporating coreference information for this task.

4.3 Optimization

Our main interest is to explore whether, and if so, how the subtask of aspect category classification, which typically relies on shallow lexical characteristics and some incorporation of semantic information, can benefit from incorporating coreference information. This is done by including coreference resolution as a preprocessing step prior to classification. To this purpose, the experiments on the training data were split in a setting where coreference relations are not derived beforehand (Setting A) and one where they are (Setting B). In the latter setting, a comparison is also made between automatically-derived and gold standard coreference information in order to assess the true upper bound.

Ten-fold cross validation experiments are conducted on the training set using LibSVM[2], version 3.17 (Chang and Lin, 2011) and we evaluate the results using accuracy as performance metric.

In both settings, we used genetic algorithms to derive the optimal feature combinations. Since each machine learning algorithm's performance is inherently dependent of the different parameters that are used, we performed a joint optimization in two different scenarios. We allow 100 generations and set the stopping criterion to a best fitness score (accuracy) that remained the same during the last five generations. Our search starts from a population of 100 individuals and all optimization experiments are performed using the Gallop toolbox (Desmet and Hoste, 2013).[3] In the first scenario (featgroups), we perform hyperparameter and feature group selection using the three feature groups we have available (i.e. bag-of-words, WordNet and DBpedia) and allow variation in LibSVM's hyperparameters. In the second scenario (indfeats), we perform hyperparameter selection and allow individual feature selection among the lexical-semantic (WordNet and DBpedia) features. The bag-of-words features are kept together as a group.

In a final experiment, the optimal settings emerging from the experiments on the training data in Setting A and B are tested on the held-out test set.

---

[3]For more information we refer to (2016) where similar experiments were performed for the task of readability prediction.

5 Results

In Setting A, coreference resolution is not performed prior to classificiation, so only the explicit aspect terms are targeted. In setting B, coreference resolution is included as an additional processing step prior to classification. Having coreference information available should allow us to derive additional semantic information for those 'NULL' targets constituting an anaphor–antecedent pair. We differentiate between a setup where we incorporate this information assuming we have a perfect coreference resolution system (GOLD), i.e. using gold-standard coreferential links, and a setup where coreference relations have been resolved automatically (AUTO). Coreference resolution as an additional processing step prior to classification. The results, expressed in accuracy, are presented in Table 3.

	ENGLISH		DUTCH	
	Joint optimization		Joint optimization	
	featgroups	indfeats	featgroups	indfeats
SETTING A	67.17	67.23	62.94	63.16
SETTING B (GOLD)	67.96	**68.20**	62.78	**63.59**
SETTING B (AUTO)	67.07	67.23	60.77	60.88

Table 3: Results of cross-validation experiments on the training data.

Overall, we observe that, when using gold information, the results increase in both languages, an accuracy of 68.20 for English and one of 63.59 for Dutch. This indicates that including coreferential links between anaphor–antecedent pairs is beneficial. If we resolve coreference automatically, however, we see that our results decrease or remain on par with the results without coreference.

From the above-mentioned results, it can also be concluded that the added value of including coreference information is not outspoken. When relying on coreference resolution systems, the performance mostly deteriorated mainly because wrong antecedents have been linked to anaphors, causing erroneous lexical-semantic features. However, our results also revealed that incorporating gold-standard anaphor-antecedent relations leads to the best overall scores in both languages after jointly optimizing LibSVM's hyperparameters and performing individual feature selection. If we compare these scores to the best individual scores achieved in setting A, we observe that the difference is more outspoken for English, which confirms our hypothesis. In the next section we will analyse whether incorporating coreference information also meant that the lexical-semantic features were considered more important.

5.1 Feature informativeness in both settings

In order to discover the added value of the lexical semantic features, we compared both optimal settings and will discuss which hyperparameters, and especially which lexical-semantic features were selected in both languages. Because, at the end of a GA optimization run, the highest fitness score may be shared by multiple individuals having different optimal feature combinations or parameter settings, we also considered runner-up individuals to that elite as valuable solutions to the search problem. This is why the features are visualized using a color range: The closer to blue, the more this feature group was turned on and the closer to red, the less important the feature group was for reaching the optimal solution. The numbers within the cells represent the same information but percentagewise.

	ENGLISH		DUTCH	
	Setting A	Setting B	Setting A	Setting B
bow	100	100	100	100
WN_AMBIENCE	100	100	100	100
WN_RESTAURANT	0	100	0	100
WN_DRINKS	100	0	100	100
WN_SERVICE	100	100	100	100
WN_LOCATION	100	100	0	100
WN_FOOD	100	100	100	100

Figure 3: Where the bag-of-words features (bow) selected and which WordNet features (WN) were selected in the optimal setting.

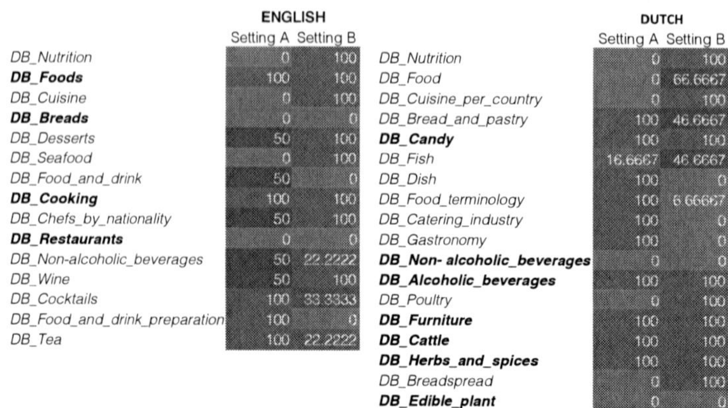

Figure 4: Which DBpedia features (DB) were selected in the optimal settings.

As can be derived from Figure 3, we observe that for both languages the bag-of-words features are crucial and always selected. Regarding the WordNet features, for English in both settings five features are selected, though not the same five. In the setting without coreference information, the feature related to the main aspect category restaurant is not selected. Whereas, in the other setting the same goes for the feature related to the aspect category drinks. For Dutch, we observe that all WordNet features are turned on when (gold-standard) coreference information has been included prior to classification.

For the DBpedia features, listed in Figure 4, there are differences between both languages. For English, we notice that only four out of the fifteen features remain unchanged in both settings, these are indicated in bold. Overall, we observe that more DBpedia features are turned on in the setting with coreference information, i.e., eight versus five features. For Dutch, seven out of the eighteen features remain unchanged and though there is a shift as to which features are selected in the optimal setting with coreference information, we see that only nine feature groups are turned on, compared to ten that were turned on in the optimal setting without coreference information.

For both languages we can conclude that including semantic information in the form of lexical-semantic features is important as a large number of these features are being selected in the optimal settings. When we look at the optimal setting with coreference information, we observe that especially for English more DBpedia features are being turned on.

5.2   Testing optimal models on held-out test sets

In a final round of experiments, the two optimal models were tested on the held-out test sets. The results are presented in Table 4.

	Train	Held-out test
Optimal EN model Setting A	67.23	57.75
Optimal EN model Setting B	**68.20**	56.92
Optimal DU model Setting A	63.16	**66.42**
Optimal DU model Setting B	63.59	**66.42**

Table 4: Comparison of the optimal results on the training data and of the held-out experiments

Though the distribution between the explicit and implicit targets does not differ between the train and test sets in both languages (Table 2), we do observe different results. For English, there is a dramatic drop in performance on the held-out test set, for setting A we achieve an accuracy of 57.75% and for setting B an even lower one of 56.92%. With these results, we are far below the best performing system at the SemEval 2016 task (Pontiki et al., 2016), but, as stated previously, we only relied on a limited amount of information sources because of comparison purposes with Dutch. Contrary to our expectations, coreference information, even when added as gold standard anaphor-antecedent pairs, does not help to reach a better performance. For Dutch, on the other hand, we achieve an accuracy of 66.42 in both settings, which is three points higher than the best accuracy scores on our training set. This result is also almost ten points higher than the best result achieved on this dataset at the SemEval 2016 task (Pontiki et al., 2016). However, these results also indicate that on our held-out test set there is no difference between the accuracy obtained with or without adding gold-standard coreference relations prior to classification.

Surprised with these outcomes regarding the added value of coreference information, especially for English where the results even deteriorated, we inspected the subdivision of the implicit aspects in both held-out test sets. We found that in the English set 240 out of the 248 implicit targets were truly implicit and that out of the eight referential anaphors, only four referred back to an antecedent within the same review. In the Dutch test set, 154 out of the 210 were truly implicit and out of the 56 referential anaphors, thirty instances constituted an anaphor-antecedent pair within the same review.

6 Conclusion

The objective of this research was to investigate to what extent coreference resolution can boost sentiment analysis performance. Our focus was on aspect-based sentiment analysis of English and Dutch restaurant reviews and more specifically the task of classifying aspect terms into predefined aspect categories. We worked with two datasets that were released and annotated in the framework of SemEval. Working with these datasets, we found that people often refer to aspect terms implicitly in both languages (24.9% in English versus 31.6% in Dutch).

This is why we investigated whether including coreference information prior to classification would be useful for pinpointing those implicit aspect terms constituting a referential relation with an antecedent. We manually annotated coreferential relations in both datasets and observed a different tendency in both languages. In English, an anaphor is frequently preceded by an antecedent within one review, whereas for Dutch the anaphors more frequently refer to extra-linguistic entities which are not explicitly mentioned in the review. When exploiting coreferential information in an aspect-based sentiment analysis pipeline, we therefore hypothesized that this would be more successful for English than for Dutch.

To investigate this, experiments were conducted in two different settings: a first setting where coreferential anaphor-antecedent pairs were not derived beforehand and a second setting where they were. In the latter setting, both gold-standard and automatically-derived coreference relations were used in order to investigate the true upper bound of incorporating this type of information. Our classifier relied on a combination of lexical (bag-of-words) and lexical-semantic information in the form of WordNet (Fellbaum, 1998) and DBpedia (Lehmann et al., 2013) features. Besides exploring the added value of coreference information, we also used a wrapper-based genetic algorithm optimization approach to optimize our classifiers and get more insights into which features are most important.

The results reveal that resolving coreferential relations prior to classification is beneficial in both settings in a setup where both the hyperparameters and individual features are jointly optimized. However, this is only the case when relying on gold-standard coreferential information and the result is more outspoken for English (from 67.23% to 68.20%) than for Dutch (from 63.16% to 63.59%). Regarding the selected features in the optimal models we could conclude that lexical bag-of-words are necessary to include and that including semantic information in the form of lexical-semantic features is also important. Comparing the optimal setting with and without performing coreference resolution prior to classification, we observe that especially for English more DBpedia features are being turned on.

In a final set of experiments we envisaged to validate these findings by testing the optimal models on a held-out test set in both languages. For English this led to poor results whereas for Dutch we were able to achieve a satisfying performance of 66.42%. In both languages, however, it was no added value to have gold-standard coreference information available before classification.

Though the results now seem to indicate that coreference information is not necessary to include in a fine-grained sentiment analysis pipeline, it will be interesting to corroborate these findings on larger datasets and on data coming from different domains. Now the focus was on resolving anaphor-antecedent pairs within one review, but in reality coreference also appears across texts which offers other interesting prospects for future research.

References

Chih-Chung Chang and Chih-Jen Lin. 2011. LIBSVM: A library for support vector machines. *ACM Transactions on Intelligent Systems and Technology*, 2(3):1–27.

Orphée De Clercq and Veronique Hoste. 2016. All mixed up? finding the optimal feature set for general readability prediction and its application to english and dutch. *COMPUTATIONAL LINGUISTICS*, 42(3):457–490.

O. De Clercq, I. Hendrickx, and V. Hoste. 2011. Cross-domain Dutch coreference resolution. In *Proceedings of the 8th International Conference on Recent Advances in Natural Language Processing (RANLP-2011)*, pages 186–193.

B. Desmet and V. Hoste. 2013. Fine-grained Dutch named entity recognition. *Language Resources and Evaluation*, pages 307–343.

X. Ding and B. Liu. 2010. Resolving Object and Attribute Coreference in Opinion Mining. In *Proceedings of the 23rd International Conference on Computational Linguistics (COLING2010)*, pages 268–276.

Hai Ha Do, PWC Prasad, Angelika Maag, and Abeer Alsadoon. 2019. Deep learning for aspect-based sentiment analysis: A comparative review. *Expert Systems with Applications*, 118:272 – 299.

Ronen Feldman. 2013. Techniques and applications for sentiment analysis. *Communications of the ACM*, 56(4):82–89.

C. Fellbaum. 1998. *WordNet: an Electronic Lexical Database*. MIT Press.

Vasileios Hatzivassiloglou and Kathleen R. McKeown. 1997. Predicting the semantic orientation of adjectives. In *Proceedings of the 35th Annual Meeting of the Association for Computational Linguistics and the 8th Conference of the European Chapter of the Association for Computational Linguistics (ACL - EACL-1997)*, pages 174–181.

Veronique Hoste. 2016. The mention-pair model. In Massimo Poesio, Roland Stuckardt, and Yannick Versley, editors, *Anaphora resolution : algorithms, resources and applications*, pages 281–295. Springer-Verlag.

Eduard Hovy, Roberto Navigli, and Simone Paolo Ponzetto. 2013. Collaboratively built semi-structured content and Artificial Intelligence: The story so far. *Artificial Intelligence*, 194:2–27.

Jason S. Kessler and Nicolas Nicolov. 2009. Targeting sentiment expressions through supervised ranking of linguistic configurations. In *The 3rd Association for the Advancement of Artificial Intelligence Conference on Weblogs and Social Media (ICWSM-2009)*, pages 90–97.

Soo-Min Kim and Eduard Hovy. 2006. Extracting opinions, opinion holders, and topics expressed in online news media text. In *Proceedings of the Workshop on Sentiment and Subjectivity in Text (SST-2006)*, pages 1–8.

H. Lee, A. Chang, Y. Peirsman, N. Chambers, M. Surdeanu, and D. Jurafsky. 2013. Deterministic coreference resolution based on entity-centric, precision-ranked rules. *Computational Linguistics*, 39(4):885–916.

Jens Lehmann, Robert Isele, Max Jakob, Anja Jentzsch, Dimitris Kontokostas, Pablo N. Mendes, Sebastian Hellmann, Mohamed Morsey, Patrick van Kleef, Sören Auer, and Christian Bizer. 2013. DBpedia – A Large-scale, Multilingual Knowledge Base Extracted from Wikipedia. *Semantic Web Journal*, 6:167–195.

Binyang Li, Lanjun Zhou, Shi Feng, and Kam-Fai Wong. 2010. A unified graph model for sentence-based opinion retrieval. In *Proceedings of the 48th Annual Meeting of the Association for Computational Linguistics (ACL-2010)*, pages 1367–1375.

Bing Liu. 2012. Sentiment analysis and opinion mining. *Synthesis Lectures on Human Language Technologies*, 5(1):1–167.

Bing Liu. 2015. *Sentiment Analysis - Mining Opinions, Sentiments, and Emotions*. Cambridge University Press.

Pablo N. Mendes, Max Jakob, Andrés García-Silva, and Christian Bizer. 2011. DBpedia Spotlight: Shedding light on the web of documents. In *Proceedings of the 7th International Conference on Semantic Systems (I-Semantics-2011)*, pages 1–8.

Saif M. Mohammad. 2016. Challenges in sentiment analysis. In D. Das, E. Cambria, and S. Bandyopadhyay, editors, *A Practical Guide to Sentiment Analysis*. Springer.

N. Nicolov, F. Salvetti, and S. Ivanova. 2008. Sentiment analysis: Does coreference matter? In *Proceedings of the Symposium on Affective Language in Human and Machine*, pages 37–40.

Neil O'Hare, Michael Davy, Adam Bermingham, Paul Ferguson, Páraic Sheridan, Cathal Gurrin, and Alan F. Smeaton. 2009. Topic-dependent sentiment analysis of financial blogs. In *Proceedings of the 1st International Conference on Information and Knowledge Management Workshop on Topic-sentiment Analysis for Mass Opinion (TSA-2009)*, pages 9–16.

Bo Pang, Lillian Lee, and Shivakumar Vaithyanathan. 2002. Thumbs up?: Sentiment classification using machine learning techniques. In *Proceedings of the 2002 Conference on Empirical Methods in Natural Language Processing (EMNLP-2002)*, pages 79–86.

Heiko Paulheim and Johannes Fürnkranz. 2012. Unsupervised Generation of Data Mining Features from Linked Open Data. In *Proceedings of the 2nd International Conference on Web Intelligence, Mining and Semantics (WIMS-2012)*, page 31.

Maria Pontiki, Dimitris Galanis, John Pavlopoulos, Harris Papageorgiou, Ion Androutsopoulos, and Suresh Manandhar. 2014. Semeval-2014 task 4: Aspect based sentiment analysis. In *Proceedings of the 8th International Workshop on Semantic Evaluation (SemEval-2014)*, pages 27–35.

Maria Pontiki, Dimitris Galanis, Haris Papageorgiou, Suresh Manandhar, and Ion Androutsopoulos. 2015. Semeval-2015 task 12: Aspect based sentiment analysis. In *Proceedings of the 9th International Workshop on Semantic Evaluation (SemEval-2015)*, pages 486–495.

Maria Pontiki, Dimitris Galanis, Haris Papageorgiou, Ion Androutsopoulos, Suresh Manandhar, Mohammad AL-Smadi, Mahmoud Al-Ayyoub, Yanyan Zhao, Bing Qin, Orphée De Clercq, Véronique Hoste, Marianna Apidianaki, Xavier Tannier, Natalia Loukachevitch, Evgeniy Kotelnikov, Núria Bel, Salud María Jiménez-Zafra, and Gülşen Eryiğit. 2016. Semeval-2016 task 5: Aspect based sentiment analysis. In *Proceedings of the 10th International Workshop on Semantic Evaluation (SemEval-2016)*, pages 19–30.

José Saias. 2015. Sentiue: Target and aspect based sentiment analysis in SemEval-2015 Task 12. In *Proceedings of the 9th International Workshop on Semantic Evaluation (SemEval-2015)*, pages 767–771, June.

Veselin Stoyanov and Claire Cardie. 2006. Partially supervised coreference resolution for opinion summarization through structured rule learning. In *Proceedings of the 2006 Conference on Empirical Methods in Natural Language Processing (EMNLP-2006)*, pages 336–344.

Zhiqiang Toh and Jian Su. 2015. NLANGP: Supervised machine learning system for aspect category classification and opinion target extraction. In *Proceedings of the 9th International Workshop on Semantic Evaluation (SemEval-2015)*, pages 496–501, June.

Zhiqiang Toh and Jian Su. 2016. NLANGP at SemEval 2016 Task 5: Improving Aspect Based Sentiment Analysis using Neural Network Features. In *Proceedings of the 10th International Workshop on Semantic Evaluation (SemEval-2016)*, pages 282–288.

P. Vossen, I. Maks, R. Segers, H. van der Vliet, M.F. Moens, K. Hofmann, E. Tjong Kim Sang, and M. de Rijke. 2013. Cornetto: a lexical semantic database for Dutch. In Peter Spyns and Jan Odijk, editors, *Essential Speech and Language Technology for Dutch, Theory and Applications of Natural Language Processing*, pages 165–184. Springer.

T. Wilson, J. Wiebe, and P. Hoffman. 2009. Recognizing contextual polarity: an exploration of features for phrase-level sentiment analysis. *Computational Linguistics*, 35(3):399–433.

Lei Zhang, Shuai Wang, and Bing Liu. 2018. Deep learning for sentiment analysis : A survey.

Y. Zhao, B. Qin, T. Liu, and W. Yang. 2015. Aspect-Object Alignment with Integer Linear Programming in Opinion Mining. *PLOS One*, 10(5).

Anaphoric Zero Pronoun Identification: A Multilingual Approach

Abdulrahman Aloraini[1,2], Massimo Poesio[1]

[1]School of Electronic Engineering and Computer Science, Queen Mary University of London
[2]Department of Information Technology, Qassim University
{a.aloraini, m.poesio}@qmul.ac.uk

Abstract

Pro-drop languages such as Arabic, Chinese, Italian or Japanese allow morphologically null but referential arguments in certain syntactic positions, called anaphoric zero-pronouns. Much NLP work on anaphoric zero-pronouns (AZP) is based on gold mentions, but models for their identification are a fundamental prerequisite for their resolution in real-life applications. Such identification requires complex language understanding and knowledge of real-world entities. Transfer learning models, such as BERT, have recently shown to learn surface, syntactic, and semantic information,which can be very useful in recognizing AZPs. We propose a BERT-based multilingual model for AZP identification from predicted zero pronoun positions, and evaluate it on the Arabic and Chinese portions of OntoNotes 5.0. As far as we know, this is the first neural network model of AZP identification for Arabic; and our approach outperforms the state-of-the-art for Chinese. Experiment results suggest that BERT implicitly encode information about AZPs through their surrounding context.

1 Introduction

Empty categories provide an important source of syntactic information about the phonetically null arguments in pro-drop languages such as Arabic (Eid, 1983), Chinese (Li and Thompson, 1979), Italian (Di Eugenio, 1990), Japanese (Kameyama, 1985), and others (Bever and Sanz, 1997; Kim, 2000). The use of empty categories started with Penn Treebanks (Marcus et al., 1993), followed by Arabic Treebank (Maamouri et al., 2004), Chinese Treebank (Xue et al., 2005) and other Penn-style series. Empty categories are used to represent traces, such as, movement operations in interrogative sentence, also to represent right node raising which is a shared argument in the rightmost constituent of a coordinate structure. Another usage of empty categories is zero-pronouns (ZP) which are omitted pronouns in places where they are expected to be, and function as overt pronouns. Anaphoric zero pronouns (AZP) are ZPs that corefer to one or more noun phrases in a preceding text. The following example of an AZP comes from the Arabic section of OntoNotes:

.. المفارقة الأخرى عن بوش هي عدم حماسته للمؤتمر الدولي، اذ انه من البداية، يريد * اجتماعا مختلفا ....

Ironically, Bush did not show any enthusiasm for the international conference, because since the beginning, (he) wanted to attend another conference ...

In the example, the ZP indicated with '*' refers to the gap position of an omitted pronoun (In OntoNotes 5.0, ZPs are denoted as * in Arabic text, and ***pro*** in Chinese). The omitted pronoun refers to a singular masculine person that has been mentioned previously, in the example "Bush/بوش". In Arabic, we deduce the reference information from the context, especially the verb that precedes the AZP, in the example the verb is "wanted/يريد". Since English is not a pro-drop language (White, 1985), the AZP gap position is translated into an overt pronoun (he). The AZP problem has inspired much research because it benefits many natural language processing tasks such as machine translation (Mitkov and Schmidt, 1998), and coreference resolution (Mitkov et al., 2000). Recently, there has been a great deal of research on AZPs for Chinese (Kong et al., 2019; Yin et al., 2018; Chang et al., 2017; Liu et al., 2017; Yin et al., 2017), Arabic (Aloraini and Poesio, 2020), Japanese (Shimazu et al., 2020), Korean (Jung and Lee, 2018), and other languages (Grigorova, 2016; Gopal and Jha, 2017). A major drawback of many existing studies is the assumption that AZP locations are given; hence, they focus primarily on resolving AZPs to their correct antecedent. However, such assumption does not reflect real-life applications. Another drawback is that current AZP identification systems rely on language-dependent features and fail to detect many AZP locations. In addition, some languages do not have an AZP identification system, one of which is Arabic.

Proceedings of the 3rd Workshop on Computational Models of Reference, Anaphora and Coreference (CRAC 2020), pages 22–32,
Barcelona, Spain (online), December 12, 2020.

To alleviate the above-mentioned limitations, we investigate the AZP identification task and study if the recently achieved state-of-the-art transfer learning methods, such as BERT (Devlin et al., 2018), can work well on identifying AZPs. Typically, AZP identification task consists of two steps. The first is the *extraction* step where potential ZP locations are extracted. The extraction procedure is based on heuristics and depend on the target language structure. The second step is *classification* step which determines which of the extracted candidate are AZP. The classification step is more challenging because of the varieties and size of the extracted candidates. In this paper, we propose a multilingual approach to AZP identification based on BERT. We make three main contributions:

- We propose a BERT-based multilingual model and evaluate on languages that differ completely in their morphological structure: Arabic and Chinese. (Arabic is morphologically rich, whereas Chinese's morphology is relatively simple (Pradhan et al., 2012))

- Ours is the first neural network-based AZP identification model for Arabic, and it substantially surpasses the current state-of-the-art on Chinese.

- Our experimental results suggest that BERT representations encode information about AZPs through their context.

The rest of the paper is organized as follows. We review Arabic and Chinese ZP-related literature, and other languages as well in Section 2. We explain our proposed model in Section 3. We discuss the evaluation settings in Section 4. We show the results and discuss them in Section 5. We conclude in Section 6.

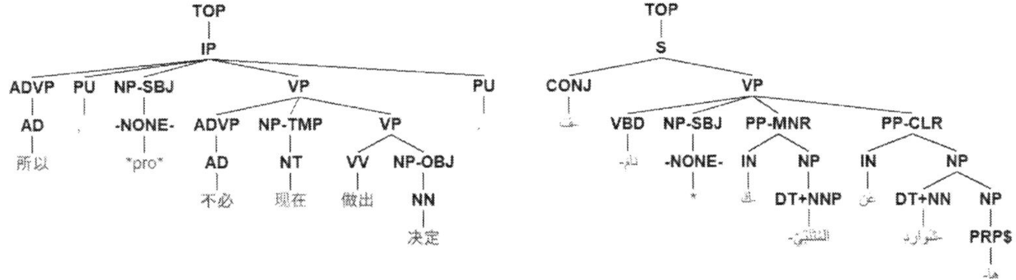

Figure 1: Chinese ZPs appear before a VP node (left), and Arabic ZPs appear after the verb of a VP head (right).In OntoNotes 5.0, Chinese AZPs are annotated as ***pro*** and Arabic AZPs as *****.

2   Related Work

AZP identification task has been considered independently, but also as a prerequisite step before AZP resolution task because the detection has a heavy impact on the resolution (Kong et al., 2019).

Arabic: There have been a few studies devoted to AZPs and empty categories in general. Green et al. (2009) proposed a conditional-random-field (CRF) sequence classifier to detect Arabic noun phrases, and captured ZPs implicitly. Bakr et al. (2009) applied a statistical approach to detect empty categories. Gabbard (2010) proposed a pipeline made of maximum entropy classifiers which jointly make a CRF to retrieve Arabic empty categories. Aloraini and Poesio (2020) proposed the first neural model for resolving Arabic AZP, but they did not consider the AZP identification step. As far as we know, no previous work has considered Arabic AZP identification.

Chinese: Converse (2006) studied AZP resolution and applied a rule-based approach that employed Hobbs algorithm (Hobbs, 1978) to resolve ZPs in the Chinese Treebank; however, did not attempt to automatically identify AZP. Yeh and Chen (2006) is another rule-based approach, for AZP resolution and also used a set of hand-engineered rules to identify AZPs. Zhao and Ng (2007), the first machine learning approach to Chinese AZPs identification and resolution, by applying decision trees incorporated with a set of syntactic and positional features. (Kong and Zhou, 2010) employed a tree kernel-based approach to AZP identification and resolution. Chen and Ng (2013) is an extension of (Zhao and Ng, 2007), they incorporated contextual features for AZP resolution and applied a combination of syntactic, lexical and other features for the identification. Chen and Ng (2014) proposed unsupervised techniques to resolve AZPs and applied a set of rules to identify AZP. Chen and Ng (2015) is another unsupervised approach on the AZP resolution. Recent approaches applying deep-learning neural networks include Chen and Ng (2016) trained a binary classifier to identify AZP and applied a feed-forward neural network to the AZP resolution; Yin et al. (2016) used (Chen and Ng, 2016)'s classifier to identify AZPs. For AZP resolution, they employed an LSTM to represent AZP and two subnetworks (general encoder and local encoder) to capture context-level and word-level information of the candidates; Yin et al. (2017) also applied (Chen and Ng, 2016)'s classifier to detect AZPs and proposed an improved deep memory network to resolve AZPs; and Liu et al. (2017), applied an attention-based neural network to resolve AZPs and enhanced the performance by training on automatically generated large-scale training data. Chang et al. (2017) focused primarily on AZP identification and applied an LSTM neural-network with text and part-of-speech information. Yin et al. (2018), also used an attention-based model, but combined their network with (Chen and Ng, 2016) features to resolve AZPs. Yin et al. (2019) applied the same heuristics in (Chen and Ng, 2015) to identify AZPs and applied a collaborative-filtering approach to resolve AZPs. Kong et al. (2019) identified AZPs using a learning-based classifier with semantic, lexical and syntactic features, and used coreferential chain information to improve AZP resolution.

Other languages: There has been also a great deal of research on identification and resolution of AZPs, particularly in Japanese (Yoshimoto, 1988; Kim and Ehara., 1995; Aone and Bennett, 1995; Seki et al., 2002; Isozaki and Hirao, 2003; Iida et al., 2006; Iida et al., 2007; Sasano et al., 2008; Sasano et al., 2009; Sasano and Kurohashi, 2011; Yoshikawa et al., 2011; Hangyo et al., 2013; Iida et al., 2015; Yoshino et al., 2013; Yamashiro et al., 2018), but also in other languages, including Korean (Han, 2004; Byron et al., 2006), Spanish (Ferrández and Peral, 2000; Rello and Ilisei, 2009), Portuguese (Rello et al., 2012), Romanian (Mihăilă et al., 2011), Bulgarian (Grigorova, 2013), and Sanskrit (Gopal and Jha, 2017). Iida and Poesio (2011) proposed the first multilingual approach for AZP resolution.

Current approaches suffer from one (or more) of the following. First, they assume AZPs are available; so they focus mainly on the resolution part. Second, they apply on a private or very small size corpus. Third, they rely on an extensive set of features or language-dependent rules to identify AZP.

3 Model

To identify AZPs, context understanding and semantic knowledge of entities are essential in Chinese (Huang, 1984) as well as in Arabic which requires, in addition, deep understanding of its complex morphology (Alnajadat, 2017). Recently, it has been shown that BERT (Devlin et al., 2018) can capture structural properties of a language, such as its surface, semantic, and syntactic aspects (Jawahar et al., 2019) which seems suitable for the AZP identification task. Therefore, we use BERT to produce representations for ZP candidates. Our model is a binary classifier that takes an automatically predicted ZP candidate as input, and classifies it as an AZP or not. In this section, we first give an overview of BERT and its adaptation modes. We then describe how we generate AZP candidates, and how we represent them. Finally, we present the training objective and hyperparameter tuning settings.

3.1 BERT

BERT is a language representation model consisting of multiple stacked Transformers (Vaswani et al., 2017). BERT was pretrained on a large amount of unlabeled text, and produces distributional vectors for words and contexts. BERT was pretrained on different settings, we use BERT-base Multilingual which was pretrained on many languages, including Chinese and Arabic, and is publicly available[1]. BERT has two modes of adaptation: feature extraction and fine-tuning. Feature extraction (also called feature-based) is when BERT representations are used as they were originally pretrained, without any further training. Fine-tuning is the process of slightly adjusting BERT's parameters for a target task. Feature extraction is computationally cheaper and might be more suitable for a specific task (Peters et al., 2019). Fine-tuning is more convenient to utilize, but restricted to several general-purpose tasks. AZP identification task was not pretrained as part of BERT tasks and not directly applicable to fine tuning mode without any modifications to BERT's architecture. We employ feature extraction mode to represent AZP candidate in our classifier.

3.2 Candidate Generation

Although ZPs are annotated in OntoNotes, our model works off automatically predicted candidates. ZP locations differ in Chinese and Arabic. In Chinese, ZPs appear before a VP node while in Arabic they appear after the head of a VP node [2]. An example of Chinese and Arabic ZP locations in Figure 1. We extract Chinese ZP locations as in (Zhao and Ng, 2007)'s work. They consider every gap before a VP node as a candidate. The number of candidates can be large. (Kong and Zhou, 2010) showed that if a VP node is in a coordinate structure or modified by an adverbial node, only its parent VP node is considered, thus decreasing the number of necessary candidates. For Arabic, we consider every gap after every head of a VP node as a candidate. A candidate is positive if it is an AZP, negative otherwise. Both approaches result in extracting many negatives examples and a small number of positive examples. The high imbalance between the two classes can make a model biased; we address the problem in Section 5.

---

[1] https://storage.googleapis.com/bert_models/2018_11_23/multi_cased_L-12_H-768_A-12.zip
[2] There are two types of word order for Arabic: Subject-Verb-Object and Verb-Subject-Object. Both are used and acceptable. In the annotation process, Arabic Treebank sets the Verb-Subject-Object as the official order.

3.3 Input Representation

We represent AZPs by their surrounding context, specifically, we represent each candidate by its VP headword and its context window of two words (left and right). Consider a sentence with a gap candidate C at position i, so its surrounding context at positions i-2, i-1, i+1, i+2.

$$sentence = (w_1, w_2, ...w_{i-2}, w_{i-1}, C_i, w_{i+1}, w_{i+2}, .., w_n) \tag{1}$$

We feed *sentence* into BERT feature extraction mode as input and it outputs *embeddings* of every word of *sentence*.

$$embeddings = BERT(sentence) \tag{2}$$

We extract the embeddings of the candidate position and its surrounding context. In our experiments, BERT Tokenizer, Wordpiece (Wu et al., 2016), segmented many Arabic words into multiple sub-tokens, each with its own embeddings. For example, the word *sleeping* might be segmented into two sub-tokens *sleep* and *##ing*. One way to represent word sub-tokens is to compute their mean; therefore, we create the function μ which computes the mean of sub-token embeddings. We join the AZP context representations together into a value called *azp*.

$$a_1 = \mu(embeddings_{(i-2)}) \tag{3}$$
$$a_2 = \mu(embeddings_{(i-1)}) \tag{4}$$
$$a_3 = \mu(embeddings_{(i)}) \tag{5}$$
$$a_4 = \mu(embeddings_{(i+1)}) \tag{6}$$
$$a_5 = \mu(embeddings_{(i+2)}) \tag{7}$$
$$azp = [a_1, a_2, a_3, a_4, a_5] \tag{8}$$

azp encodes information about the candidate context and serves as input to our classifier. It is possible to extend the AZP window to more context but we empirically find context window of size 2 to be sufficiently effective.

$$layer_1 = f(W_1 azp + b_1) \tag{9}$$
$$layer_2 = f(W_2 layer_1 + b_2) \tag{10}$$
$$output = f(W_3 layer_2 + b_3) \tag{11}$$

The binary classifier is a multi-layered perceptrons consisting of two layers and one output layer. f is the ReLU activation function (Nair and Hinton, 2010). Each layer in the classifier has learning parameters W and b. The input is then classified to be either an AZP or not.

3.4 Training Objective

The training objective of our classifier is binary cross-entropy loss:

$$J(\theta) = -\frac{1}{N} \sum_{i=1}^{N} [y_i \log \hat{y}_i + (1 - y_i) \log (1 - \hat{y}_i)] \tag{12}$$

θ represents the set of learning parameters in the model. N is the number of training data. y_i is the true label of training i and $\hat{y}_i$ its predicted label.

3.5 Hyperparameter Tuning

In the classifier, we employ two layers and initialize each one's weights using Glorot and Bengio (2010)'s method. We also add a dropout regularization between the two layers and the output layer. We tune the hyperparameters based on the development sets. Table 1 shows the hyperparameter settings.

4 Evaluation

4.1 Datasets

We evaluate our model on the Arabic and Chinese subsets of OntoNotes 5.0, which were used in the the official CoNLL-2012 shared task (Pradhan et al., 2012).

Chinese training and development sets contain AZPs, but the test set does not. Therefore, we train the model using the training set and we use the development set as the test set, a practice followed in prior research (Chen and Ng, 2013; Chen and Ng, 2014; Chen and Ng, 2016; Kong et al., 2019). We reserve 20% of the training data as a

Number of units in the first layer	800
Number of units in the second layer	600
Number of training epochs	10
Learning rate	1e-5
Dropout rate	0.5
Optimizer	Adam

Table 1: Hyperparameter settings.

Language	Category	Training	Dev	Test
Chinese	Documents	1,391	172	
	Sentences	36,487	6,083	
	Words	756,063	100,034	N/A
	AZPs	12,111	1,713	
Arabic	Documents	359	44	44
	Sentences	7,422	950	1,003
	Words	264,589	30,942	30,935
	AZPs	3,495	474	412

Table 2: Statistics on Chinese and Arabic datasets. Chinese test portion does not contain AZPs; therefore, the development portion is used for evaluation.

development set.

Arabic training, development, and test sets all have AZPs, and we use each set for its purpose. We preprocessed Arabic text by normalizing all variants of the letter "alif" and also removing all diacritics.

Detailed statistics about Chinese and Arabic dataset can be found in Table 2.

4.2 Metrics

We evaluate the results in terms of recall, precision, and F-score, as defined in (Zhao and Ng, 2007):

$$Recall = \frac{AZP\,hits}{Number\ of\ AZPs\ in\ Key}$$

$$Precision = \frac{AZP\,hits}{Number\ of\ AZPs\ in\ Response}$$

Key represents the true set of AZP entities in the dataset, and *Response* represents the system output of the identified AZPs in the model. *AZP hits* are the reported AZP positions in *Response* which occur in the same position as in *Key*.

5 Results

AZP identification results for Arabic are in Table 3, and Chinese in Table 4. The training data is highly imbalanced because of the ratio of negatives examples to the positive examples. In Arabic there are 5.6 times of negative examples compared to the positive examples, and in Chinese the negative examples are 16.2 times compared to the positive ones. To address this problem, we follow (Zhao and Ng, 2007)'s approach by changing the ratio weight r of sampling positive examples with respect to negative examples. The value r affects precision and recall scores. If r is high, precision increases but recall decreases. The effect of tuning r on precision, recall and F1 scores on Arabic and Chinese are in Figures 2 and 3 respectively. F1 scores with different variations of r are not very significant; however, we choose r that balances between the precision and recall scores.

Prior works (Chen and Ng, 2013; Chen and Ng, 2014; Chen and Ng, 2016; Chang et al., 2017; Kong et al., 2019) evaluate AZP identification under two settings: gold and system parse because annotation quality can impact the number of recovering candidates in the *extraction* step. Gold annotations are available for both languages and we also automatically parse the data with syntactic trees using the Berkeley Parser (Kitaev et al., 2018) which is a pre-trained parser using neural networks and self-attention.

5.1 Arabic

As far as we know, there has been no published proposal on Arabic AZP identification. Therefore, we implemented as a baseline (Chang et al., 2017)'s model, which employs sentence and Part-of-Speech information into a Bi-LSTM neural network to identify ZPs. We set its embedding layer to the Arabic version of Fasttext (Bojanowski et al.,

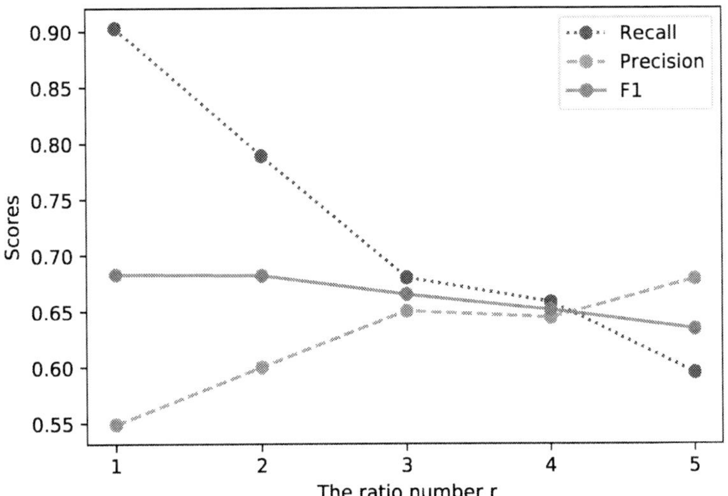

Figure 2: The effect of tuning the ratio r on recall, precision and F1 scores on the Arabic test set.

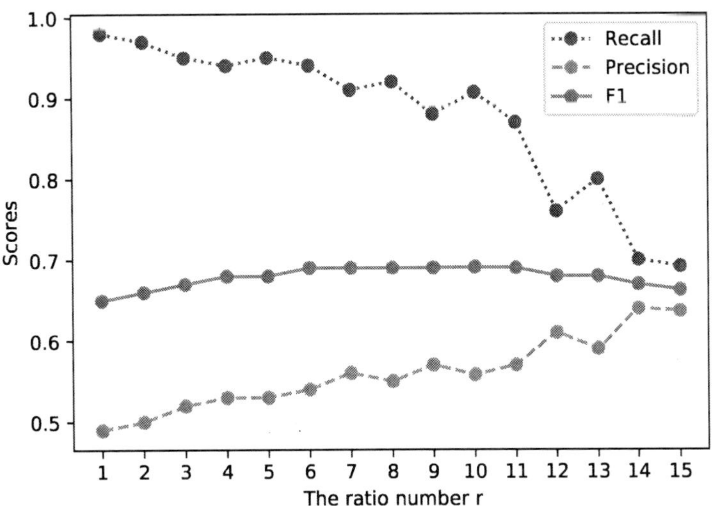

Figure 3: The effect of tuning the ratio r on recall, precision and F1 scores on the Chinese test set.

2017). We can see in Table 3 that our approach outperforms the baseline in both gold and system settings with F1 scores of 68.2% and 47.0%. There is a a big gap between gold and system parse because the automatic parser failed to recognize many VP nodes in the *extraction* step. Thus, many AZP samples were not recognized for training and evaluation which lead to a great decrease in performance. To gain additional insights into our model, we analyzed its outputs. The model correctly identifies many AZP cases, however, it struggles to recognize some patterns especially AZPs that are preceded by a verb in the first person. The errors can be attributed to the distribution of the training data. Most training AZP data are headed by verbs in the third person, and the number of verbs in the first and second persons is very small; thus, the model did not learn to classify many of these cases. A corpus that include a larger distribution of such cases can help a model to learn them.

	Settings 1: Gold Parse			Settings 2: System Parse		
	R	P	F1	R	P	F1
Baseline	**67.7**	45.2	54.2	31.7	30.6	31.1
Our model (r=2)	60.0	**78.9**	**68.2**	**38.6**	**60.1**	**47.0**

Table 3: AZP identification results for Arabic. The highest score is in **bold**.

5.2 Chinese

We compare our approach with other proposals in Table 4. As we can see, our approach achieves the highest F1 scores of 69.1% and 68.7% with gold and system parse settings, outperforming all prior proposals. The F1-score difference between our approach and the state-of-the-art approach is 4.7% with gold parse settings and 11.3% with system parse. The F1-score difference of gold and system settings of our approach is relatively small (0.4%) because the Berkeley parser annotated many VP nodes correctly. We analyzed the errors, and noticed many unidentified AZPs are located at the beginning of their samples. These cases depend on previous sentences, and their information might have not been encoded in the AZP input; thus, our model failed to identify them.

	Settings 1: Gold Parse			Settings 2: System Parse		
	R	P	F1	R	P	F1
(Chen and Ng, 2013)	50.6	55.1	52.8	30.8	34.4	32.5
(Chen and Ng, 2014)	72.4	42.3	53.4	42.3	26.8	32.8
(Chen and Ng, 2016)	75.1	50.1	60.1	43.7	30.7	36.1
(Chang et al., 2017)	63.5	**65.3**	64.4	57.2	55.7	56.4
(Kong et al., 2019)	70.1	59.4	64.3	60.2	40.2	48.2
Our model (r=10)	**90.7**	55.8	**69.1**	**81.9**	**59.2**	**68.7**

Table 4: AZP identification results for Chinese. The highest score is in **bold**.

5.3 Discussion

BERT representations work interestingly well on AZPs even though empty categories have not been considered during the BERT's pretraining. Recent works (Jawahar et al., 2019; Kovaleva et al., 2019; Goldberg, 2019; Clark et al., 2019) have shown that BERT learns various linguistic information such as, syntactic roles, coreference resolution, semantic relations and others. Our experimental results suggest that these information might be encoded in AZP contexts which make them distinctive.

Current approaches for AZP identification evaluate under two settings: gold and system annotations because the task depend highly on the annotation quality of parse trees. In our experiments, gold settings for both Arabic and Chinese achieve outstanding results. In system parse, Chinese achieves results similar to its gold setting; however, Arabic does not. The reason is that Berkeley Parser (Kitaev et al., 2018) fails to parse correctly Arabic sentences which means many correct AZP locations are not detected in the extraction step. A sophisticated Arabic parser can improve the overall performance for system-parse settings.

6 Conclusion

We proposed a BERT-based model for AZP identification. Our approach is multilingual, and we evaluate on Arabic and Chinese portions of OntoNotes. The model is the first to deal with Arabic AZP identification and the experiments demonstrated that our method surpasses the state-of-the-art on Chinese AZPs. In addition, our experimental results show that BERT learn about anaphoric zero-pronouns through their surrounding context.

References

Bashir M. Alnajadat. 2017. Pro-drop in standard arabic. In *International Journal of English Linguistics 7.1.*

Abdulrahman Aloraini and Massimo Poesio. 2020. Cross-lingual zero pronoun resolution. In *Proceedings of The 12th Language Resources and Evaluation Conference*, pages 90–98.

Chinatsu Aone and Scott William Bennett. 1995. Evaluating automated and manual acquisition of anaphora resolution strategies. In *ACL '95 Proceedings of the 33rd annual meeting on Association for Computational Linguistics*, pages 122–129.

Hitham M Abo Bakr, Khaled Shaalan, and Ibrahim Ziedan. 2009. A statistical method for detecting the arabic empty category. In *Proceedings of the Second International Conference on Arabic Language Resources and Tools, Cairo, Egypt.*

Thomas G Bever and Montserrat Sanz. 1997. Empty categories access their antecedents during comprehension: Unaccusatives in spanish. *Linguistic Inquiry*, pages 69–91.

Piotr Bojanowski, Edouard Grave, Armand Joulin, and Tomas Mikolov. 2017. Enriching word vectors with subword information. *Transactions of the Association for Computational Linguistics*, 5:135–146.

Donna K. Byron, Whitney Gegg-Harrison, and Sun-Hee Lee. 2006. Resolving zero anaphors and pronouns in korean. In *Traitement Automatique des Langues 46.1*, pages 91–114.

Tao Chang, Shaohe Lv, Xiaodong Wang, and Dong Wang. 2017. Zero pronoun identification in chinese language with deep neural networks. In *2017 2nd International Conference on Control, Automation and Artificial Intelligence (CAAI 2017)*. Atlantis Press.

Chen Chen and Vincent Ng. 2013. Chinese zero pronoun resolution: Some recent advances. In *Proceedings of the 2013 conference on empirical methods in natural language processing*, pages 1360–1365.

Chen Chen and Vincent Ng. 2014. Chinese zero pronoun resolution: An unsupervised probabilistic model rivaling supervised resolvers. In *Proceedings of the 2014 Conference on Empirical Methods in Natural Language Processing.*

Chen Chen and Vincent Ng. 2015. Chinese zero pronoun resolution: A joint unsupervised discourse-aware model rivaling state-of-the-art resolvers. In *Proceedings of the 53rd Annual Meeting of the Association for Computational Linguistics and the 7th International Joint Conference on Natural Language Processing (Volume 2: Short Papers)*, pages 320–326.

Chen Chen and Vincent Ng. 2016. Chinese zero pronoun resolution with deep neural network. In *Proceedings of the 54th Annual Meeting of the Association for Computational Linguistics (Volume 1: Long Papers)*, pages 778–788.

Kevin Clark, Urvashi Khandelwal, Omer Levy, and Christopher D Manning. 2019. What does bert look at? an analysis of bert's attention. *arXiv preprint arXiv:1906.04341.*

Susan Converse. 2006. Pronominal anaphora resolution in chinese. In *PhD Thesis, University of Pennsylvania.*

Jacob Devlin, Ming-Wei Chang, Kenton Lee, and Kristina Toutanova. 2018. Bert: Pre-training of deep bidirectional transformers for language understanding. In *arXiv preprint arXiv:1810.04805.*

B. Di Eugenio. 1990. Centering theory and the italian pronominal system. In *Proc. of the 13th COLING*, Helsinki, Finland.

Mushira Eid. 1983. On the communicative function of subject pronouns in arabic. In *Journal of Linguistics 19.2*, pages 287–303.

Antonio Ferrández and Jesús Peral. 2000. A computational approach to zero-pronouns in spanish. In *Proceedings of the 38th Annual Meeting of the Association for Computational Linguistics*, pages 166–172.

Ryan Gabbard. 2010. Null element restoration. In *Ph.D Thesis, University of Pennsylvania.*

Xavier Glorot and Yoshua Bengio. 2010. Understanding the difficulty of training deep feedforward neural networks. In *Proceedings of the thirteenth international conference on artificial intelligence and statistics.*

Yoav Goldberg. 2019. Assessing bert's syntactic abilities. In *arXiv preprint arXiv:1901.05287.*

Madhav Gopal and Girish Nath Jha. 2017. Zero pronouns and their resolution in sanskrit texts. In *The International Symposium on Intelligent Systems Technologies and Application*, pages 255–267.

Spence Green, Conal Sathi, and Christopher Manning. 2009. Np subject detection in verb-initial arabic clauses. In *Proceedings of the Third Workshop on Computational Approaches to Arabic Script-based Languages (CAASL3). Vol. 112.*

Diana Grigorova. 2013. An algorithm for zero pronoun resolution in bulgarian. In *Proceedings of the 14th International Conference on Computer Systems and Technologies.*

Diana Grigorova. 2016. Hybrid approach to zero pronoun resolution in bulgarian. In *Proceedings of the 17th International Conference on Computer Systems and Technologies 2016*, pages 331–338.

Na-Rae Han. 2004. A korean null pronouns: Classification and annotation. In *Proceedings of the 2004 ACL Workshop on Discourse Annotation. Association for Computational Linguistics, 2004.*, pages 33–40.

Masatsugu Hangyo, Daisuke Kawahara, and Sadao Kurohashi. 2013. Japanese zero reference resolution considering exophora and author/reader mentions. In *Proceedings of the 2013 Conference on Empirical Methods in Natural Language Processing*, pages 924–934.

Jerry Hobbs. 1978. Resolving pronoun references. In *Lingua*, pages 311–338.

C.-T. James Huang. 1984. On the distribution and reference of empty pronouns. In *Linguistic Inquiry, Vol. 15, No. 4*, pages 531–574.

Ryu Iida and Massimo Poesio. 2011. A cross-lingual ilp solution to zero anaphora resolution. In *Proceedings of the 49th Annual Meeting of the Association for Computational Linguistics: Human Language Technologies-Volume 1*, pages 804–813.

Ryu Iida, Kentaro Inui, and Yuji Matsumoto. 2006. Exploiting syntactic patterns as clues in zero-anaphora resolution. In *Proceedings of the 21st International Conference on Computational Linguistics and 44th Annual Meeting of the Association for Computational Linguistic*, pages 625–632.

Ryu Iida, Kentaro Inui, and Yuji Matsumoto. 2007. Zero-anaphora resolution by learning rich syntactic pattern features. In *ACM Transactions on Asian Language Information Processing, 6(4)*.

Ryu Iida, Kentaro Torisawa, Chikara Hashimoto, Jong-Hoon Oh, and Julien Kloetzer. 2015. Intra-sentential zero anaphora resolution using subject sharing recognition. In *Proceedings of the 2015 Conference on Empirical Methods in Natural Language Processing*, pages 2179–2189.

Hideki Isozaki and Tsutomu Hirao. 2003. Japanese zero pronoun resolution based on ranking rules and machine learning. In *Proceedings of the 2003 Conference on Empirical Methods in Natural Language Processing,*, pages 184–191.

Ganesh Jawahar, Benoît Sagot, and Djamé Seddah. 2019. What does bert learn about the structure of language? In *57th Annual Meeting of the Association for Computational Linguistics (ACL), Florence, Italy*.

Sangkeun Jung and Changki Lee. 2018. Deep neural architecture for recovering dropped pronouns in korean. *ETRI Journal*, 40(2):257–265.

Megumi Kameyama. 1985. *Zero Anaphora: The case of Japanese*. Ph.D. thesis, Stanford University, Stanford, CA.

Yeun-Bae Kim and Terumasa Ehara. 1995. Zero-subject resolution method based on probabilistic inference with evaluation function. In *Proceedings of the 3rd Natural Language Processing Pacific- Rim Symposium*, pages 721—727.

YOUNG-JOO Kim. 2000. Subject/object drop in the acquisition of korean: A cross-linguistic comparison. In *Journal of East Asian Linguistics 9.4*, pages 325–351.

Nikita Kitaev, Steven Cao, and Dan Klein. 2018. Multilingual constituency parsing with self-attention and pre-training. *arXiv preprint arXiv:1812.11760*.

Fang Kong and Guodong Zhou. 2010. A tree kernel-based unified framework for chinese zero anaphora resolution. In *Proceedings of the 2010 Conference on Empirical Methods in Natural Language Processing. Association for Computational Linguistics*, pages 882–891.

Fang Kong, Min Zhang, and Guodong Zhou. 2019. Chinese zero pronoun resolution: A chain-to-chain approach. *ACM Transactions on Asian and Low-Resource Language Information Processing (TALLIP)*, 19(1):1–21.

Olga Kovaleva, Alexey Romanov, Anna Rogers, and Anna Rumshisky. 2019. Revealing the dark secrets of bert. In *arXiv preprint arXiv:1908.08593*.

Charles N. Li and Sandra A. Thompson. 1979. Third person pronouns and zero anaphora in chinese discourse. In *Syntax and Semantics*, volume 12: Discourse and Syntax, pages 311–335. Academic Press.

Ting Liu, Yiming Cui, Qingyu Yin, Weinan Zhang, Shijin Wang, and Guoping Hu. 2017. Generating and exploiting large-scale pseudo training data for zero pronoun resolution. In *arXiv preprint arXiv:1606.01603*.

Mohamed Maamouri, Ann Bies, Tim Buckwalter, and Wigdan Mekki. 2004. The penn arabic treebank: Building a large-scale annotated arabic corpus. In *NEMLAR conference on Arabic language resources and tools*, volume 27, pages 466–467. Cairo.

Mitchell Marcus, Beatrice Santorini, and Mary Ann Marcinkiewicz. 1993. Building a large annotated corpus of english: The penn treebank.

Claudiu Mihăilă, Iustina Ilisei, , and Diana Inkpen. 2011. Zero pronominal anaphora resolution for the romanian language. In *Research Journal on Computer Science and Computer Engineering with Applications, POLIBITS. 42*.

Ruslan Mitkov and Paul Schmidt. 1998. On the complexity of pronominal anaphora resolution in machine translation. *STUDIES IN FUNCTIONAL AND STRUCTURAL LINGUISTICS*, pages 207–222.

Ruslan Mitkov, Richard Evans, Constantin Orasan, Catalina Barbu, Lisa Jones, and Violeta Sotirova. 2000. Coreference and anaphora: developing annotating tools, annotated resources and annotation strategies. In *Proceedings of the Discourse, Anaphora and Reference Resolution Conference (DAARC2000)*, pages 49–58. Citeseer.

Vinod Nair and Geoffrey Hinton. 2010. Rectified linear units improve restricted boltzmann machines. In *Proceedings of the 27th international conference on machine learning (ICML-10)*, pages 807–814.

Matthew Peters, Sebastian Ruder, and Noah Smith. 2019. To tune or not to tune? adapting pretrained representations to diverse tasks. In *arXiv preprint arXiv:1903.05987*.

Sameer Pradhan, Alessandro Moschitti, Nianwen Xue, Olga Uryupina, and Yuchen Zhang. 2012. Conll-2012 shared task: Modeling multilingual unrestricted coreference in ontonotes. In *Joint Conference on EMNLP and CoNLL-Shared Task. Association for Computational Linguistics, Association for Computational Linguistics.*, pages 1–40.

Luz Rello and Iustina Ilisei. 2009. A rule-based approach to the identification of spanish zero pronouns. In *Proceedings of the Student Research Workshop*, pages 60–65.

Luz Rello, Gabriela Ferraro, and Iria Gayo. 2012. A first approach to the automatic detection of zero subjects and impersonal constructions in portuguese. *Procesamiento del lenguaje natural*, 49:163–170.

Ryohei Sasano and Sadao Kurohashi. 2011. discriminative approach to japanese zero anaphora resolution with large-scale lexicalized case frames. In *Proceedings of the 5th International Joint Conference on Natural Language Processing*, pages 758–766.

Ryohei Sasano, Daisuke Kawahara, and Sadao Kurohashi. 2008. A fully-lexicalized probabilistic model for japanese zero anaphora resolution. In *Proceedings of the 22nd International Conference on Computational Linguistics*, pages 769–776.

Ryohei Sasano, Daisuke Kawahara, and Sadao Kurohashi. 2009. The effect of corpus size on case frame acquisition for discourse analysis. In *Proceedings of Human Language Technologies: The 2009 Annual Conference of the North American Chapter of the Association for Computational Linguistics*, pages 521–529.

Kazuhiro Seki, Atsushi Fujii, and Tetsuya Ishikawa. 2002. A probabilistic method for analyzing japanese anaphora integrating zero pronoun detection and resolution. In *Proceedings of the 19th International Conference on Computational Linguistics - Volume 1*, pages 1–7.

Sho Shimazu, Sho Takase, Toshiaki Nakazawa, and Naoaki Okazaki. 2020. Evaluation dataset for zero pronoun in japanese to english translation. In *Proceedings of The 12th Language Resources and Evaluation Conference*, pages 3630–3634.

Ashish Vaswani, Noam Shazeer, Niki Parmar, Jakob Uszkoreit, Llion Jones, Aidan N. Gomez, Lukasz Kaiser, and Illia Polosukhin. 2017. Attention is all you need.

Lydia White. 1985. The "pro-drop" parameter in adult second language acquisition. *Language learning*, 35(1):47–61.

Yonghui Wu, Mike Schuster, Zhifeng Chen, Quoc V. Le, Mohammad Norouzi, Wolfgang Macherey, Maxim Krikun, Yuan Cao, Qin Gao, Klaus Macherey, Jeff Klingner, Apurva Shah, Melvin Johnson, Xiaobing Liu, Łukasz Kaiser, Stephan Gouws, Yoshikiyo Kato, Taku Kudo, Hideto Kazawa, Keith Stevens, George Kurian, Nishant Patil, Wei Wang, Cliff Young, Jason Smith, Jason Riesa, Alex Rudnick, Oriol Vinyals, Greg Corrado, Macduff Hughes, and Jeffrey Dean. 2016. Google's neural machine translation system: Bridging the gap between human and machine translation. In *arXiv preprint arXiv:1609.08144*.

Naiwen Xue, Fei Xia, Fu-Dong Chiou, and Marta Palmer. 2005. The penn chinese treebank: Phrase structure annotation of a large corpus. *Natural language engineering*, 11(2):207.

Souta Yamashiro, Hitoshi Nishikawa, and Takenobu Tokunaga. 2018. Neural japanese zero anaphora resolution using smoothed large-scale case frames with word embedding. In *Proceedings of the 32nd Pacific Asia Conference on Language, Information and Computation*.

Ching-Long Yeh and Yi-Chun Chen. 2006. Zero anaphora resolution in chinese with shallow parsing. In *Journal of Chinese Language and Computing 17 (1)*, pages 41–56.

Qingyu Yin, Yu Zhang, Weinan Zhang, and Ting Liu. 2016. A deep neural network for chinese zero pronoun resolution. In *arXiv preprint arXiv:1604.05800*.

Qingyu Yin, Yu Zhang, Weinan Zhang, and Ting Liu. 2017. Chinese zero pronoun resolution with deep memory network. In *Proceedings of the 2017 Conference on Empirical Methods in Natural Language Processing*, pages 1309–1318.

Qingyu Yin, Yu Zhang, Weinan Zhang, Ting Liu, and William Yang Wang. 2018. Zero pronoun resolution with attention-based neural network. In *Proceedings of the 27th International Conference on Computational Linguistics*, pages 13–23.

Qingyu Yin, Weinan Zhang, Yu Zhang, and Ting Liu. 2019. Chinese zero pronoun resolution: A collaborative filtering-based approach. *ACM Transactions on Asian and Low-Resource Language Information Processing (TALLIP)*, 19(1):1–20.

Katsumasa Yoshikawa, Masayuki Asahara, and Yuji Matsumoto. 2011. Jointly extracting japanese predicate-argument relation with markov logic. In *Proceedings of 5th International Joint Conference on Natural Language Processing*, pages 1125–1133.

Kei Yoshimoto. 1988. Identifying zero pronouns in japanese dialogue. In *Coling Budapest 1988 Volume 2: International Conference on Computational Linguistics*.

Koichiro Yoshino, Shinsuke Mori, and Tatsuya Kawahara. 2013. Predicate argument structure analysis using partially annotated corpora. In *Proceedings of the Sixth International Joint Conference on Natural Language Processing*, pages 957–961.

Shanheng Zhao and Hwee Tou Ng. 2007. Identification and resolution of chinese zero pronouns: A machine learning approach. In *Proceedings of the 2007 Joint Conference on Empirical Methods in Natural Language Processing and Computational Natural Language Learning*, pages 541–550.

Predicting Coreference in Abstract Meaning Representations

Tatiana Anikina and **Alexander Koller**
Dept. of Language Science and Technology
Saarland Informatics Campus
Saarland University

Michael Roth
Institute for NLP
University of Stuttgart

`{tatianak|koller}@coli.uni-saarland.de`
`michael.roth@ims.uni-stuttgart.de`

Abstract

This work addresses coreference resolution in Abstract Meaning Representation (AMR) graphs, a popular formalism for semantic parsing. We evaluate several current coreference resolution techniques on a recently published AMR coreference corpus, establishing baselines for future work. We also demonstrate that coreference resolution can improve the accuracy of a state-of-the-art semantic parser on this corpus.

1 Introduction

Abstract Meaning Representations (AMRs, Banarescu et al. (2013)) are a popular type of symbolic semantic representation for semantic parsing. AMRs are labeled directed graphs whose nodes represent entities, events, properties, and states; the edges represent semantic relations between the nodes. For instance, in the example AMRs of Fig. 2, the predicate node c describes a come-back relation between the ARG1 "I" and the ARG3 "this". AMR is designed to abstract over the way in which a certain piece of meaning was expressed in language; thus "the destruction of the room by the boy" and "the boy destroyed the room" are represented by the same graph. In the example AMR, the noun phrase "university offers" is decomposed into two nodes: the predicate node *o:offer-01* and the argument node *u:university*, describing an event in which the university offers something to "I".

An AMR graphbank annotates each sentence in the corpus with an AMR graph. Recently, O'Gorman et al. (2018) introduced the Multi-Sentence AMR (MS-AMR) corpus, which adds a layer of annotation

```
-<identchain relationid="rel-3">
    <mention concept="he" id="DF-200-192400-625_7557.12" variable="h"/>
    <mention concept="person" id="DF-200-192400-625_7557.11" variable="p"/>
    <implicitrole argument="ARG0" id="DF-200-192400-625_7557.12"
                  parentconcept="want-01" parentvariable="w2"/>
</identchain>
```

Figure 1: Coreference chain from MS-AMR.

on top of the AMR-2017 graphbank that represents coreference and implicit arguments beyond the sentence level. An example is shown in Fig. 1. Each *<identchain>* element collects mentions of the same entity; these mentions are not pieces of text as in other coreference annotation schemes, but nodes in the AMR graphs. The annotation also specifies what implicit roles of predicate nodes the entity fills.

In this paper, we make two contributions. First, we evaluate the performance of different coreference resolution tools on the MS-AMR annotations. We evaluate these on the token level (by projecting the coreference annotations from the nodes to the sentences) and on the node level (by projecting the tools' coreference predictions to the nodes of the graphs) and find that AllenNLP with SpanBERT embeddings (Joshi et al., 2020) generally performs best.

Second, we show for the first time how the output of a coreference system can be integrated into the predictions of a state-of-the-art AMR parser. We use the neural semantic parser of Lindemann et al.

33

Proceedings of the 3rd Workshop on Computational Models of Reference, Anaphora and Coreference (CRAC 2020), pages 33–38,
Barcelona, Spain (online), December 12, 2020.

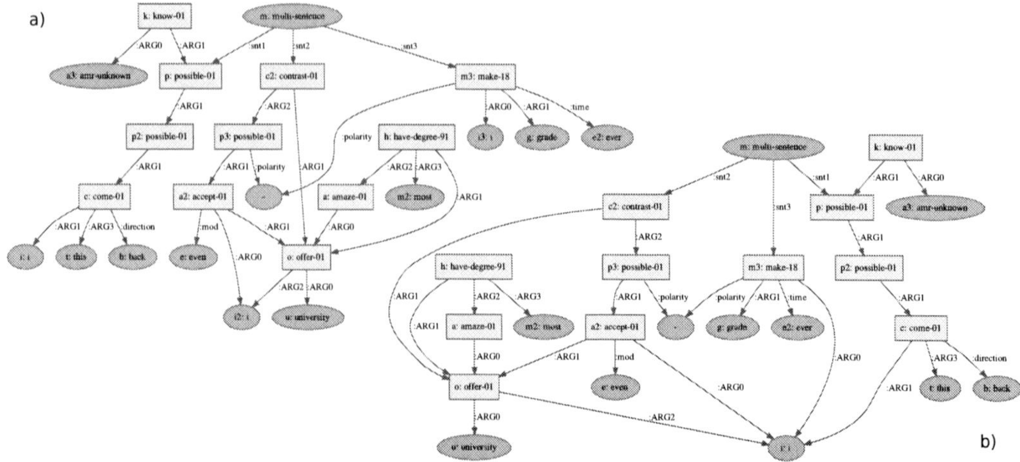

Figure 2: AMRs, (a) before and (b) after merge for *"Maybe **I** can come back from this, who knows. **I**'ve got the most amazing university offers, but **I** can't even accept them - **I**'ll never make the grades."*

(2019), which compositionally predicts a graph for the input sentence. We exploit this compositional structure to map coreferent input tokens to nodes in the predicted graph, and obtain an improvement of three points Smatch f-score over a coreference-unaware baseline.

2   Coreference in MS-AMR

Coreference resolution tools typically predict coreference between *tokens* in a text, but MS-AMR annotates coreference between *nodes* in the AMR graphs. To perform coreference resolution on MS-AMR, we therefore have to map between the token level and the node level. The MS-AMR corpus contains annotations which map between tokens and nodes, but this mapping is not always one-to-one. In the example shown in Fig. 2 (a), the two tokens "who knows" are aligned to the single node p. The nodes *a3:amr-unknown* and *h:have-degree-91* are left unaligned.

Furthermore, AMR graphs sometimes contain nodes that participate in the coreference chains but are not realized at the token level. For instance, in the sentence "speak to a doctor" the predicate *speak-01* has an ARG0 *you* which is a separate node in the graph even though it does not have any token alignment.

We evaluate coreference tools on MS-AMR in two different modes: *token-level*, where we project MS-AMR coreference annotations from nodes to tokens and compare them against the predicted token-level coreference annotations; and *node-level*, where we project token-level coreference predictions to MS-AMR nodes and compare them against the MS-AMR annotations. Because of the node–token mismatch explained above, we can project to the token level only coreference annotations between nodes that are aligned to tokens. We retained only coreference chains with at least two members. This reduces the 87 coreference chains between 425 mentions in the original MS-AMR test set to 69 coreference chains between 385 mentions. 35% of these chains consist only of two mentions although there are also some very long chains with more than 30 elements, mostly pronouns.

For the node-level evaluation and the Smatch-based evaluation (see below), we used the unmodified coreference annotations on the nodes.

3   Comparative Evaluation of Coreference Resolution Tools

We compared the output of the deterministic CoreNLP (Lee et al., 2013) and neural CoreNLP (Clark and Manning, 2016) coreference resolvers and tested two versions of the AllenNLP (Lee et al., 2017) coreference tool based on the GloVe (Pennington et al., 2014) and SpanBERT (Joshi et al., 2020) embeddings respectively. These tools were chosen due to their availability and their strong accuracy on English.

	MUC			B^3			$CEAF\ \phi_3$			$CEAF\ \phi_4$		
	P	R	F	P	R	F	P	R	F	P	R	F
AllenNLP (GloVe)	0.61	0.51	0.55	0.42	0.40	0.39	0.46	0.44	0.45	0.20	0.26	0.22
AllenNLP (SpanBERT)	0.60	0.56	0.58	0.44	0.44	**0.43**	0.50	0.49	**0.49**	0.24	0.28	**0.25**
CoreNLP (determin.)	0.45	0.50	0.47	0.35	0.35	0.32	0.35	0.39	0.37	0.14	0.27	0.18
CoreNLP (neural)	0.63	0.56	**0.59**	0.40	0.38	0.37	0.48	0.42	0.45	0.22	0.23	0.22

Table 1: Coreference evaluation at the token level for AllenNLP and CoreNLP.

	MUC			B^3			$CEAF\ \phi_3$			$CEAF\ \phi_4$		
	P	R	F	P	R	F	P	R	F	P	R	F
AllenNLP (GloVe)	0.62	0.37	0.45	0.31	0.29	0.28	0.51	0.34	0.39	0.32	0.23	0.26
AllenNLP (SpanBERT)	0.69	0.42	**0.50**	0.32	0.30	**0.30**	0.58	0.35	**0.43**	0.42	0.24	**0.30**
CoreNLP (determin.)	0.51	0.33	0.39	0.26	0.22	0.22	0.46	0.29	0.34	0.26	0.21	0.22
CoreNLP (neural)	0.64	0.37	0.46	0.31	0.28	0.27	0.51	0.33	0.39	0.30	0.22	0.24

Table 2: Coreference evaluation at the node level for AllenNLP and CoreNLP.

To evaluate the performance at the **token level**, the gold alignments were extracted and each coreference chain from the MS-AMR dataset was mapped to the corresponding span in the text. These annotations represent the gold standard to which we compared the system annotations. In order to annotate coreference chains, a separate text file was created for each document with the sentences representing the document AMRs. Then each document text was processed with different coreference resolution systems to generate the predictions. For the token-level evaluation we compared the system output directly to the coreferent tokens in the MS-AMR test set and for the node-level evaluation we first projected token annotations to the graph nodes using the gold alignments and then compared the node coreference chains.

Table 1 reports the token-level results on the MS-AMR test data using several metrics: MUC, B^3, mention-based $CEAF\ \phi_3$ and entity-based $CEAF\ \phi_4$. The evaluation shows that the neural version of CoreNLP achieves the best MUC f-score (0.59), followed by the SpanBERT version of AllenNLP (0.58). Neural CoreNLP and AllenNLP with GloVe show similar results in terms of B^3, $CEAF\ \phi_3$ and $CEAF\ \phi_4$. Overall, SpanBERT AllenNLP achieves the best performance and deterministic CoreNLP performs the worst in all metrics. The difference in scores is due to the way how metrics define the coreference: in terms of links (for MUC) or in terms of clusters (B^3 and $CEAF$).

Neural CoreNLP and AllenNLP are reasonable baselines for AMR coreference resolution, although the results seem to be worse than state-of-the-art performance reported on news and narrative texts. One problem might be that the MS-AMR corpus contains text snippets from blog data, including misspellings, jargon and incorrect grammar. Also the conversational style used in blogs poses challenges for the coreference tools since they do not distinguish between posts made by different authors.

The results of the **node-level** evaluation can be found in Table 2. They are based on mapping the predicted annotations to the nodes defined in the gold AMR graphs. The reason to perform both token and node-level evaluation is that coreference chains differ depending on whether their members are tokens or nodes. For example, there are four instances of token "I" in the text corresponding to the AMR in Fig. 2 (a) but the graph contains only three i nodes (i, $i2$ and $i3$) because the predicates $a2{:}accept\text{-}01$ and $o{:}offer\text{-}01$ share the argument node $i2{:}i$. So, the number of mentions in each chain varies depending on whether the evaluation is done at the token or node level. Moreover, the node-level evaluation includes the full set of annotated nodes in the gold standard, not only those that can be aligned to tokens. At the node level, the SpanBERT version of AllenNLP achieves the best results in all metrics.

4 AMR parsing with coreference

Coreference is not an isolated task in MS-AMR parsing; in order to predict the gold annotations, coreference information needs to be incorporated into AMR graphs predicted by a semantic parser. We thus

	AMR parser			AMR parser + AllenNLP			AMR parser + oracle		
	P	R	F	P	R	F	P	R	F
macro-average:	0.57	0.52	0.54	0.61	0.54	0.57	0.63	0.56	0.59
micro-average:	0.57	0.50	0.53	0.60	0.53	0.56	0.63	0.55	0.58

Table 3: Smatch evaluation of document-level coreference annotations.

extended the AMR parser of Lindemann et al. (2019) with coreference information.

First, we prepared gold annotations at the document level. For this, we combined the individual AMRs from each document into a single graph to represent document-level annotations. The coreference chains were extracted from the gold annotations of the MS-AMR corpus, and coreferent nodes in the document graph were merged following the procedure described in (O'Gorman et al., 2018).

Second, we ran Lindemann's parser on each sentence separately and combined the predicted AMR graphs into a document-level graph. Then we ran SpanBERT AllenNLP (henceforth just AllenNLP) on each document text, and mapped each token-level prediction to the nodes the Lindemann parser predicted for those tokens. We collapsed the coreferent nodes by replacing all edges into a node for a coreferent token by edges into the first node of the coreference chain; see O'Gorman et al. (2018) for details. For example, in Fig. 2 (a) there are three coreferent nodes $i{:}i$, $i2{:}i$ and $i3{:}i$. Since all three nodes represent the same entity the corresponding edges can be rearranged to point to the same node $i{:}i$ as shown in Fig. 2 (b).

We evaluated the performance of Lindemann's parser, with and without the added coreference information, on the complete MS-AMR test data. To this end, we computed the Smatch score (Cai and Knight, 2013) for the predicted vs. gold document-level graphs. Table 3 shows the micro- and macro-average Smatch precision, recall and f-score for the documents from the test set. The left column indicates the scores obtained by comparing the gold AMRs with coreference to the ones generated by the parser without coreference. The middle column shows the scores for the gold MS-AMR graphs versus the parser output augmented with coreference predictions. The overall improvement in f-score is around three points Smatch f-score. The right column shows the scores obtained by augmenting Lindemann's parser output with the gold coreference chains extracted from the MS-AMR corpus (i.e. oracle predictions).

It is worth noting that the overall Smatch score is much lower than on other AMR graphbanks; for instance, Lindemann et al. (2019) report a Smatch f-score of 0.75 for their parser on the AMR-2017 test set. Even on the MS-AMR test corpus without coreference links (i.e. pure sentence-by-sentence parsing), the parser only gets a score of 0.61, indicating that this is a harder corpus than AMR-17. This then drops to 0.53 once nodes in the gold graphs are merged based on the coreference annotations.

5   Discussion

The coreference chains annotated in the MS-AMR corpus are quite heterogeneous. At the token level, mentions of the same chain can be expressed as verbs, nouns or pronouns and Fig. 3 illustrates one example where the chain includes different concepts at the node level: *it*, *thing*, *harm-01*, *cut-01*. Such chains are hard to predict for the AllenNLP coreference model because they are realized as

```
-<identchain relationid="rel-1">
    <mention concept="it" id="DF-200-192400-625_7557.9" variable="i2"/>
    <mention concept="thing" id="DF-200-192400-625_7557.24" variable="t3"/>
    <mention concept="it" id="DF-200-192400-625_7557.27" variable="i2"/>
    <mention concept="harm-01" id="DF-200-192400-625_7557.35" variable="h"/>
    <mention concept="cut-01" id="DF-200-192400-625_7557.3" variable="c4"/>
    <mention concept="do-02" id="DF-200-192400-625_7557.17" variable="d2"/>
    <mention concept="cut-01" id="DF-200-192400-625_7557.8" variable="c"/>
    <mention concept="this" id="DF-200-192400-625_7557.29" variable="t"/>
    <mention concept="harm-01" id="DF-200-192400-625_7557.1" variable="h"/>
    <mention concept="cut-01" id="DF-200-192400-625_7557.6" variable="c"/>
    <mention concept="it" id="DF-200-192400-625_7557.36" variable="i"/>
    <mention concept="thing" id="DF-200-192400-625_7557.28" variable="t2"/>
</identchain>
```

Figure 3: Heterogeneous coreference chain from MS-AMR.

different parts of speech and are semantically nontrivial (harm/cut). 35% of all coreference chains in the test set are heterogeneous, i.e. they include entities that are expressed with multiple different parts of speech.

On the one hand, AMR parsing already resolves some cases of coreference within the AMR graphs.

For instance, in Fig. 2 (a) a single node *o:offer-01* aligns to coreferent tokens "offers" and "them". On the other hand, some AMR nodes can build coreference chains but do not have any token alignments. For example, a sentence like "speak to a doctor" has a separate node "you" as ARG0 of "speak-01" in the AMR graph. However, this node does not correspond to any token in the text. 9% of all coreferent mentions in the MS-AMR test set do not have any alignments and the token-based coreference resolvers are not able to handle them.

Incorrect (or incomplete) node-token alignments can hurt the performance. 10% of all coreferent nodes in the test set refer to generic concepts like *t:thing* or *p:person*. This becomes a problem when AllenNLP finds the coreference with more specific nodes such as *d:dad* in Fig. 4. Token "dad" is aligned to the node *d:dad* in the AMR graph whereas the more generic node *p:person* does not have an alignment. However, the gold coreference chain includes only *p:person* as a member which results in the wrong classification of *d:dad* as false positive although both nodes actually correspond to the same entity. This example illustrates the problem when the gold annotation includes generic concepts that are represented in the AMR graphs but not realized at the token level.

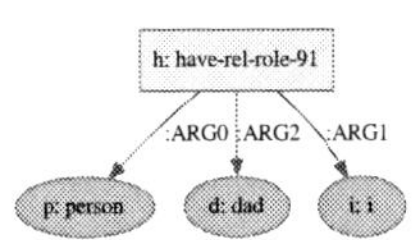

Figure 4: AMR for *"my dad"*.

We also found cases of incorrectly resolved personal pronouns because some texts were extracted from forums and the speaker could switch in the middle of the conversation, so that *I* and *you* would get a different meaning. For example, one document in the MS-AMR test set contains the following text: "Or should $[I]_1$ ... just keep an eye on the anxiety until it becomes a problem? Well $[I]_2$ wouldn't try to keep an eye on anxiety for a start because that will make $[u]_1$ tense." The first sentence has the pronoun $[I]_1$ that refers to the same entity as $[u]_1$ in the second sentence and the $[I]_2$ pronoun in the second sentence corresponds to a different speaker. Since the input text for the coreference tool does not include any meta information about the speakers the tool resolves both occurrences of "I" as referring to the same entity. This issue affects 9% of the coreference chains from the MS-AMR test set.

6 Conclusion

In this paper, we evaluated two popular coreference resolution tools on the MS-AMR dataset, and found that the SpanBERT version of AllenNLP performs best in both a token-level and a node-level evaluation. We further extended a state-of-the-art AMR parser with predicted coreference information, and obtained a three-point improvement in Smatch score.

The coreference models we have used here were quite conservative, in that they relied only on textual information. In the future, it would be interesting to extend them with features based on the AMR graphs, which abstract over some surface details. It would also be interesting to predict bridging coreference relations and include those in the parser output too.

Acknowledgments. We thank Jonas Groschwitz and Matthias Lindemann for fruitful discussions and for their help with the Lindemann et al. parser. We also thank Tim O'Gorman for providing the MS-AMR corpus.

References

Laura Banarescu, Claire Bonial, Shu Cai, Madalina Georgescu, Kira Griffitt, Ulf Hermjakob, Kevin Knight, Philipp Koehn, Martha Palmer, and Nathan Schneider. 2013. Abstract meaning representation for sembanking. In *Proceedings of the 7th Linguistic Annotation Workshop and Interoperability with Discourse, LAW-ID@ACL 2013, August 8-9, 2013, Sofia, Bulgaria*, pages 178–186.

Shu Cai and Kevin Knight. 2013. Smatch: an evaluation metric for semantic feature structures. In *Proceedings of the 51st Annual Meeting of the Association for Computational Linguistics, ACL 2013, 4-9 August 2013, Sofia, Bulgaria, Volume 2: Short Papers*, pages 748–752.

Kevin Clark and Christopher D. Manning. 2016. Improving coreference resolution by learning entity-level distributed representations. In *Proceedings of the 54th Annual Meeting of the Association for Computational Linguistics, ACL 2016, August 7-12, 2016, Berlin, Germany, Volume 1: Long Papers*.

Mandar Joshi, Danqi Chen, Yinhan Liu, Daniel S. Weld, Luke Zettlemoyer, and Omer Levy. 2020. Spanbert: Improving pre-training by representing and predicting spans. *Trans. Assoc. Comput. Linguistics*, 8:64–77.

Heeyoung Lee, Angel X. Chang, Yves Peirsman, Nathanael Chambers, Mihai Surdeanu, and Dan Jurafsky. 2013. Deterministic coreference resolution based on entity-centric, precision-ranked rules. *Computational Linguistics*, 39(4):885–916.

Kenton Lee, Luheng He, Mike Lewis, and Luke Zettlemoyer. 2017. End-to-end neural coreference resolution. In *Proceedings of the 2017 Conference on Empirical Methods in Natural Language Processing, EMNLP 2017, Copenhagen, Denmark, September 9-11, 2017*, pages 188–197.

Matthias Lindemann, Jonas Groschwitz, and Alexander Koller. 2019. Compositional semantic parsing across graphbanks. In *Proceedings of the 57th Conference of the Association for Computational Linguistics, ACL 2019, Florence, Italy, July 28- August 2, 2019, Volume 1: Long Papers*, pages 4576–4585.

Tim O'Gorman, Michael Regan, Kira Griffitt, Ulf Hermjakob, Kevin Knight, and Martha Palmer. 2018. AMR beyond the sentence: the multi-sentence AMR corpus. In *Proceedings of the 27th International Conference on Computational Linguistics, COLING 2018, Santa Fe, New Mexico, USA, August 20-26, 2018*, pages 3693–3702.

Jeffrey Pennington, Richard Socher, and Christopher D. Manning. 2014. Glove: Global vectors for word representation. In *Proceedings of the 2014 Conference on Empirical Methods in Natural Language Processing, EMNLP 2014, October 25-29, 2014, Doha, Qatar, A meeting of SIGDAT, a Special Interest Group of the ACL*, pages 1532–1543.

Sequence to Sequence Coreference Resolution

Gorka Urbizu
Elhuyar Fundation
gurbizu@elhuyar.eus

Ander Soraluze and **Olatz Arregi**
HiTZ Center, Ixa NLP group,
University of the Basque Country
{ander.soraluze, olatz.arregi}@ehu.eus

Abstract

Until recently, coreference resolution has been a critical task on the pipeline of any NLP task involving deep language understanding, such as machine translation, chatbots, summarization or sentiment analysis. However, nowadays, those end tasks are learned end-to-end by deep neural networks without adding any explicit knowledge about coreference. Thus, coreference resolution is used less in the training of other NLP tasks or trending pretrained language models. In this paper we present a new approach to face coreference resolution as a sequence to sequence task based on the Transformer architecture. This approach is simple and universal, compatible with any language or dataset (regardless of singletons) and easier to integrate with current language models architectures. We test it on the ARRAU corpus, where we get 65.6 F1 CoNLL. We see this approach not as a final goal, but a means to pretrain sequence to sequence language models (T5) on coreference resolution.

1 Introduction

Coreference resolution is a Natural Language Processing (NLP) task which consists on identifying and clustering all the expressions referring to the same real-world entity in a text. NLP tasks that include language understanding such as text summarisation (Steinberger et al., 2016; Kopeć, 2019), chatbots (Agrawal et al., 2017; Zhu et al., 2018), sentiment analysis (Krishna et al., 2017) or machine translation (Werlen and Popescu-Belis, 2017; Ohtani et al., 2019) can benefit from coreference resolution. And until recently, coreference resolution has been a critical task on the pipelines of those systems.

However, with the recent rising trend of building end-to-end deep neural networks, for any NLP task where the data available in that language or domain is huge, current models are able to learn the end task without any explicit training on coreference resolution. This is even more evident in the case of the huge unsupervisedly pretrained language models (LM) that are already able to resolve coreference (Clark et al., 2019; Tenney et al., 2019), as BERT (Devlin et al., 2019), RoBERTa (Liu et al., 2019), T5 (Raffel et al., 2019), or GPT3 (Brown et al., 2020) which are used to boost results on any downstream task.

Those pretrained language models have also improved notably the results obtained at coreference resolution. Combining the SotA neural coreference resolution system (Lee et al., 2017) at the time with pretrained language models (ELMo, BERT, SpanBERT) improves results by a large margin.

Despite coreference resolution was already useful in NLP end tasks before the irruption of deep learning in NLP, and getting very significant improvements on the results with it, nowadays most of the tasks that require deep language understanding, are approached without having coreference resolution in mind.

Src:	Even	the	smallest	person	can	change	the	course	of	history	.
Trg:	(0	_	_	0)	_	_	(1	_	_	(2)|1)	_

Table 1: Example of sequence to sequence approach for coreference resolution.

Proceedings of the 3rd Workshop on Computational Models of Reference, Anaphora and Coreference (CRAC 2020), pages 39–46,
Barcelona, Spain (online), December 12, 2020.

In this paper, we introduce a new approach to solve coreference resolution as a sequence to sequence task (as shown in Table 1) using a Transformer (Vaswani et al., 2017), that opens a path towards unifiying the approaches used in coreference resolution with the trending pretrained LMs and other NLP tasks, while simplifying the neural architecture used for coreference resolution.

We test our approach on the English ARRAU corpus (Uryupina et al., 2020), which includes singletons. We train our model on coreference resolution as a sequence to sequence task, where the neural network learns to produce the coreference relations as output from the raw text in the source.

In the following Section 2 we review the state of the art of the field. In Section 3 we describe how we approached coreference resolution as a sequence to sequence task, we present the neural architecture and corpora we used. In Section 4 we report our results, and lastly, we present our conlusions and future work in Section 5.

2 State of the Art

The SotA for English coreference resolution, improved a lot since the revolution of deep learning in NLP. The first end-to-end neural model (Lee et al., 2017) obtained big improvements over previous models. Since then, pretrained LMs improved a lot those results; adding ELMo (Peters et al., 2018), BERT (Devlin et al., 2019) and SpanBert (Joshi et al., 2020) to the model, improved by a large margins the SotA at the moment (Lee et al., 2018; Kantor and Globerson, 2019; Joshi et al., 2019; Joshi et al., 2020).

Furthermore, we would like to underline different approaches as reinforcement learning (Fei et al., 2019) and neural MCDM and fuzzy weighting techniques (Hourali et al., 2020), which improved results.

There have been only two works which already have tried to combine language models and coreference resolution at training. In the first one, T5 (Raffel et al., 2019), they use coreference resolution among other tasks to train a neural language model on text to text, but the coreference task is approached as a simple binary mention-pair task, which does not reflect all the advances done at resolving coreference. In the second one, CorefQA (Wu et al., 2020), they adress coreference resolution as query-based span prediction for which they convert coreference resolution into a QA task, where the model has to find the coreferential mentions in the text. Although they get the best results obtained to this day, their approach still uses a windowing technique of length 512, and needs to create questions automatically from the text.

Models	F1
(Lee et al., 2017)	68.8
(Lee et al., 2018)	73.0
(Fei et al., 2019)	73.8
(Kantor and Globerson, 2019)	76.6
(Joshi et al., 2019)	77.1
(Joshi et al., 2020)	79.6
(Hourali et al., 2020)	80.0
(Wu et al., 2020)	83.1

Table 2: The state of the art for English coreference resolution: F1 scores at CoNLL metric, for Ontonotes/CoNLL-2012 dataset.

We should keep in mind that, apart of the well studied English language, there are lots of other less researched languages. Yet we already have neural models for some of those languages: Polish (Nitoń et al., 2018), Japanese (Shibata and Kurohashi, 2018), French (Grobol, 2019), Basque (Urbizu et al., 2019), Telegu (Annam et al., 2019), Russian (Sboev et al., 2020) Persian (Sahlani et al., 2020) and cross-linguals (Cruz et al., 2018; Kundu et al., 2018) with varied results depending on corpus sizes and architectures.

3 Sequence to Sequence Coreference Resolution

Coreference resolution has been historically divided in two subtasks. The first one is mention detection, where possible candidates for a mention are located in the text. The second one would be to find those which have coreferential relations, among the mentions. This second task has been approached as a clustering problem, where mention-pair models evolved into entity-mention models, and their respectives ranking models. Some of this approaches have issues with making the correct global decisions, and those who handle this more appropriately, have higher computational cost. In the following subsection, we present our approach, which solves these two subtasks at once in a simpler way.

3.1 Our Approach

There are many ways to annotate or indicate coreference relations on a text, such as using 2 columns, which was used on the Ontonotes corpus (Pradhan et al., 2007) for the CONLL task (Pradhan et al., 2011; Pradhan et al., 2012). On the left we have the raw text word by word, and on the right, the coreference relations expressed in a parenthetical structure, were parenthesis are used to delimitate mentions, and numbers to refer the coreference clusters that the mentions belong.

Text:	Coreference:
you	(0)
love	–
me	(1)

Table 3: Two column annotation.

Source:	You	love	me
Target:	(0)	–	(1)

Table 4: Sequence to sequence task.

This annotation system shows that the task is similar to sequence-labeling tasks, where the labels of the second row are not discrete. To handle this problem, we propose a sequence to sequence approach. In source we would have the raw text, and in the target, the coreference annotation corresponding to the source text in the parenthetical structure.

To make the task easier to learn, as there are many equivalent ways to represent the same coreference relations, we rewrite all the numbers referring to coreference clusters in the training dataset, with ascendent numbers starting from 0, from left to right, keeping the coreference relations.

3.2 Transformer Model

We choose the architecture of Transformer, as it gives good results for many sequence to sequence tasks. Although keeping source and target sequences of the same length helps the model to create the outputs of the correct length, this creates the problem of huge vocabularies in source and target, which makes training the model harder, and more memory consuming.

To solve this issue, we use fixed vocabularies on source and target sequences. On source, we use BPE (Bojanowski et al., 2017) to segment words in subword units, with which we get a small closed vocabulary of 16K tokens. On target, we divide the labels of coreference resolution which contains more than one coreference relation within it, so that we avoid conplex labels, as (8)|122)|68)|128), which are hard to learn correctly: (8) | 122) | 68) | 128). Doing this, we decrease the size of the target vocabulary significantly (1.7K).

Src:	Even	the	small@@	est	person	can	change	the	course	of	history	.
Trg:	(0	–	–	0)	–	–	(1	–	–	(2)	|	1) –

Table 5: Example of source and target sequences.

As we can see in the example above, the aligment that we got previously is gone, so the model will have to learn to align source and target tokens, which a Transformer should do easily, as seen in tasks such as machine translation with this architecture. Furthermore, with those changes the source and target vocabularies sizes decrease a lot, making easier to understand the text and produce correct target tokens.

We do not use any pretrained word embeddings or LMs, or any other linguistic, distance or speaker features. We have chosen fairseq implementation of the Transformer (Ott et al., 2019) with standard hyperparameters. We set the max length of the source and target sequences at 1024. As coreference resolution is a document level task, it might happen that the document that we want to process has more than 1024 tokens in source or target after applying BPE and labels division. To handle that, a model with longer sequences should be trained (increasing significantly memory requirements), or a windowing strategy could be used. But we do not try any of this here, to keep computational costs low[1].

3.3 Datasets

We tested our approach on the ARRAU corpus (Uryupina et al., 2020), an English dataset which includes singletons. They had been ignored due to the division on mention detection and clustering tasks, and the specific corpora made for the second one. We train our Transformer model just to carry out both tasks at once. We used all coreference relations of the dataset. The corpus has 350K words, and its already divided on train, dev and test subsets.

As we do not add any pretrained word embeddings or any LMs to the model, the ARRAU corpus is not big enough to learn the task of language understanding in the encoder part and it has a limited vocabulary in the training. Thus, we used an auxiliary corpus for the training. We chose PreCo corpus, which is an English coreference corpus of over 10M words, which also includes singletons (Chen et al., 2018). Both datasets were converted to the mentioned two column format from their respective enriched annotations.

3.4 Data Augmentation

We used data augmentation to increase the amount of training instances. For this purpose, we took all the combinations of consecutive sentences for the training. Given the document $S_A - S_Z$, where S is a sentence: S_A , S_A-S_B, ..., S_A-S_B-S_C-...-S_Z; S_B, S_B-S_C, ... S_B-S_C-S_D-...-S_Z; ...; S_Y, S_Y-S_Z; S_Z.

With this technique, we do not improve much the dataset for source sequences, as it would be the same sentences repeated in different lengths. However, the repeated parts of the sequences in the source, would have their coreference relations represented by different numbers in the target sequences:

	You	love	cats	.	I	love	cats	.	My	dog	hates	cats	.
S_A-S_B-S_C Src:	You	love	cats	.	I	love	cats	.	My	dog	hates	cats	.
S_A-S_B-S_C Trg:	(0)	–	(1)	–	(2)	–	(1)	–	(3 | (2)	3)	–	(1)	–
S_B-S_C Src:					I	love	cats	.	My	dog	hates	cats	.
S_B-S_C Trg:					(0)	–	(1)	–	(2 | (0)	2)	–	(1)	–
S_C Src:									My	dog	hates	cats	.
S_C Trg:									(0 | (1)	0)	–	(2)	–

Table 6: Training sequences after data augmentation, and its effect on the target cluster numbers.

Furthermore, having sequences of a single sentence in the training, makes the beginning of the learning process easier. Later, the model will be able to learn to resolve coreference for whole documents at once.

3.5 Post-processing

Once we get the output prediction sequences, we need to post-process a bit the output with the 3 following processes. First, we correct the unclosed (or unopened) patenthesis or mentions, deleting them. Then, we group the different coreference relations referring to the same token again (just removing the space between each of the | in the output). Finally, we correct the length of the output sequence, removing tokens, or adding extra "_" tokens at the end until it matches the length of the source text. We can see the changes made to the predicted sequence at post-procesing in the following example:

	Even	the	small@@	est	person	can	change	the	course	of	history	.
Src:	Even	the	small@@	est	person	can	change	the	course	of	history	.
Trg:	(0	–	–		0)	–	–	(1	–	–	(2)	| 1) –
Pred:	(0	–	–		0)	–	–	(1	(2	–	(3)	| 1)
Post:	(0	–	–		0)	–	–	(1	–	–	(3)|1)	–

Table 7: Example of the post-procesing applied to the predicted sequences.

---

[1] We trained the model on a single Nvidia Rtx 2080Ti GPU (11GB) for 24h.

4   Results

For the evaluation of our new sequence to sequence approach and the transformer model we built, we use the coreference official scorer (Pradhan et al., 2014) to get the results of the most used metrics on the task on the ARRAU testing split. We obtain 77.2 F1 at mention detection (MD), 64.9 F1 at MUC, 66.5 F1 at B^3, 65.3 F1 at CEAF$_e$ and 65.6 F1 on the CoNLL metric. They are quite good results for a simple approach which does not use any external information as pretrained word embeddings or LMs, or any linguistic, distance or speaker features other than the auxiliary dataset we used, which just added the amount of raw text and its coreferential relations we had. Our model is able to detect most of the mentions, including singletons, and it does cluster correctly correferential mentions to a certain extent, including those that are at a very long distance[2].

	MD	MUC	B^3	CEAF$_m$	CEAF$_e$	BLANC	LEA	CoNLL
This work	77.2	64.9	66.5	66.7	65.3	59.9	58.0	65.6
(Yu et al., 2020)	—	78.2	78.8	—	76.8	—	—	77.9

Table 8: Our F1 results in comparison with previous best results on the ARRAU dataset.

The best results on the ARRAU dataset are those presented at Yu et al. (2020). Results obtained in this work are not completely comparable with our work, as we do not process documents longer than 1024 tokens (~800 words, keeping 72% of the documents), while they only test their system with the RST subset of the test set. However, we include the comparison in table 8, to put our results into context, and as we can see, we are not able to match their results.

5   Conclusions and Future Work

All in all, in this work we present a novel approach, as far as we know, the first time where coreference resolution has been learned as a simple sequence to sequence task, using just a Transformer, an architecture that rules the NLP field. We got 65.6 F1 CoNLL on the ARRAU corpus, and despite not getting the best results on the dataset, we proved that a Transformer is enough to learn the task, from raw text, without any features or pre-trained word-embeddings or LMs. The results obtained are quite good, as this approach have room for improvements at architecture level, hyperparameter tuning, and the integration of pretrained LMs. This approach may help at unifing the coreference resolution with other NLP models, where this task could be used at pretraining sequence to sequence LMs (T5). Our code and model are available at: `https://github.com/gorka96/text2cor`.

There are many aspects of this approach worth to continue researching. To begin with, we limited the maximum length of the sequences to 1024 tokens for simplicity, nevertheless, to be able to process longer documents, we will need to train Transformer models with longer maximum positions. To handle the increment in memory and computational costs, architectures that do not use full attention as reformer (Kitaev et al., 2020) or longformer (Beltagy et al., 2020) could be considered. Moreover, we would like to verify that this method is as universal as we said here, trying datasets without singletons, low-resourced languages, and multilingual or cross-lingual settings. Finally, using this approach to train a sequence to sequence language model like T5, would be interesting.

Acknowledgements

This research was partially supported by the Department of Industry of the Basque Government (Deep-Text project, KK-2020/00088) and by the European Commission (LINGUATEC project, EFA227/16). We thank the three anonymous reviewers whose comments and suggestions contributed to improve this work.

---

[2]Sample of the output: `https://github.com/gorka96/text2cor/blob/main/pred_example.txt`

References

Samarth Agrawal, Aditya Joshi, Joe Cheri Ross, Pushpak Bhattacharyya, and Harshawardhan M Wabgaonkar. 2017. Are word embedding and dialogue act class-based features useful for coreference resolution in dialogue. In *Proceedings of PACLING*.

Vinay Annam, Nikhil Koditala, and Radhika Mamidi. 2019. Anaphora resolution in dialogue systems for south asian languages. *arXiv preprint arXiv:1911.09994*.

Iz Beltagy, Matthew E. Peters, and Arman Cohan. 2020. Longformer: The long-document transformer. *arXiv:2004.05150*.

Piotr Bojanowski, Edouard Grave, Armand Joulin, and Tomas Mikolov. 2017. Enriching word vectors with subword information. *Transactions of the Association for Computational Linguistics*, 5:135–146.

Tom B Brown, Benjamin Mann, Nick Ryder, Melanie Subbiah, Jared Kaplan, Prafulla Dhariwal, Arvind Neelakantan, Pranav Shyam, Girish Sastry, Amanda Askell, et al. 2020. Language models are few-shot learners. *arXiv preprint arXiv:2005.14165*.

Hong Chen, Zhenhua Fan, Hao Lu, Alan Yuille, and Shu Rong. 2018. Preco: A large-scale dataset in preschool vocabulary for coreference resolution. In *Proceedings of the 2018 Conference on Empirical Methods in Natural Language Processing*, pages 172–181.

Kevin Clark, Urvashi Khandelwal, Omer Levy, and Christopher D Manning. 2019. What does bert look at? an analysis of bert's attention. In *Proceedings of the 2019 ACL Workshop BlackboxNLP: Analyzing and Interpreting Neural Networks for NLP*, pages 276–286.

André Ferreira Cruz, Gil Rocha, and Henrique Lopes Cardoso. 2018. Exploring Spanish corpora for Portuguese coreference resolution. In *2018 Fifth International Conference on Social Networks Analysis, Management and Security (SNAMS)*, pages 290–295. IEEE.

Jacob Devlin, Ming-Wei Chang, Kenton Lee, and Kristina Toutanova. 2019. Bert: Pre-training of deep bidirectional transformers for language understanding. In *Proceedings of the 2019 Conference of the North American Chapter of the Association for Computational Linguistics: Human Language Technologies, Volume 1 (Long and Short Papers)*, pages 4171–4186.

Hongliang Fei, Xu Li, Dingcheng Li, and Ping Li. 2019. End-to-end deep reinforcement learning based coreference resolution. In *Proceedings of the 57th Annual Meeting of the Association for Computational Linguistics*, pages 660–665.

Loïc Grobol. 2019. Neural coreference resolution with limited lexical context and explicit mention detection for oral french. In *Second Workshop on Computational Models of Reference, Anaphora and Coreference*, page 8.

Samira Hourali, Morteza Zahedi, and Mansour Fateh. 2020. Coreference resolution using neural mcdm and fuzzy weighting technique. *International Journal of Computational Intelligence Systems*.

Mandar Joshi, Omer Levy, Luke Zettlemoyer, and Daniel S Weld. 2019. Bert for coreference resolution: Baselines and analysis. In *Proceedings of the 2019 Conference on Empirical Methods in Natural Language Processing and the 9th International Joint Conference on Natural Language Processing (EMNLP-IJCNLP)*, pages 5807–5812.

Mandar Joshi, Danqi Chen, Yinhan Liu, Daniel S Weld, Luke Zettlemoyer, and Omer Levy. 2020. Spanbert: Improving pre-training by representing and predicting spans. *Transactions of the Association for Computational Linguistics*, 8:64–77.

Ben Kantor and Amir Globerson. 2019. Coreference resolution with entity equalization. In *Proceedings of the 57th Annual Meeting of the Association for Computational Linguistics*, pages 673–677.

Nikita Kitaev, Łukasz Kaiser, and Anselm Levskaya. 2020. Reformer: The efficient transformer. *arXiv preprint arXiv:2001.04451*.

Mateusz Kopeć. 2019. Three-step coreference-based summarizer for polish news texts. *Poznan Studies in Contemporary Linguistics*, 55(2):397–443.

M Hari Krishna, K Rahamathulla, and Ali Akbar. 2017. A feature based approach for sentiment analysis using svm and coreference resolution. In *2017 International Conference on Inventive Communication and Computational Technologies (ICICCT)*, pages 397–399. IEEE.

Gourab Kundu, Avi Sil, Radu Florian, and Wael Hamza. 2018. Neural cross-lingual coreference resolution and its application to entity linking. In *Proceedings of the 56th Annual Meeting of the Association for Computational Linguistics (Volume 2: Short Papers)*, volume 2, pages 395–400.

Kenton Lee, Luheng He, Mike Lewis, and Luke Zettlemoyer. 2017. End-to-end Neural Coreference Resolution. In *Proceedings of the 2017 Conference on Empirical Methods in Natural Language Processing*, pages 188–197.

Kenton Lee, Luheng He, and Luke Zettlemoyer. 2018. Higher-order coreference resolution with coarse-to-fine inference. In *Proceedings of the 2018 Conference of the North American Chapter of the Association for Computational Linguistics: Human Language Technologies, Volume 2 (Short Papers)*, pages 687–692.

Yinhan Liu, Myle Ott, Naman Goyal, Jingfei Du, Mandar Joshi, Danqi Chen, Omer Levy, Mike Lewis, Luke Zettlemoyer, and Veselin Stoyanov. 2019. Roberta: A robustly optimized bert pretraining approach. *arXiv preprint arXiv:1907.11692*.

Bartłomiej Niton, Paweł Morawiecki, and Maciej Ogrodniczuk. 2018. Deep neural networks for coreference resolution for Polish. In *Proceedings of the Eleventh International Conference on Language Resources and Evaluation (LREC-2018)*, pages 395–400.

Takumi Ohtani, Hidetaka Kamigaito, Masaaki Nagata, and Manabu Okumura. 2019. Context-aware neural machine translation with coreference information. In *Proceedings of the Fourth Workshop on Discourse in Machine Translation (DiscoMT 2019)*, pages 45–50.

Myle Ott, Sergey Edunov, Alexei Baevski, Angela Fan, Sam Gross, Nathan Ng, David Grangier, and Michael Auli. 2019. fairseq: A fast, extensible toolkit for sequence modeling. In *Proceedings of NAACL-HLT 2019: Demonstrations*.

Matthew E. Peters, Mark Neumann, Mohit Iyyer, Matt Gardner, Christopher Clark, Kenton Lee, and Luke Zettlemoyer. 2018. Deep contextualized word representations. In *Proc. of NAACL*.

Sameer Pradhan, Eduard Hovy, Mitch Marcus, Martha Palmer, Lance Ramshaw, and Ralph Weischedel. 2007. OntoNotes: A Unified Relational Semantic Representation. In *Proceedings of the International Conference on Semantic Computing*, (ICSC '07), pages 517–526, Washington, DC, USA. IEEE Computer Society.

Sameer Pradhan, Lance Ramshaw, Mitchell Marcus, Martha Palmer, Ralph Weischedel, and Nianwen Xue. 2011. CoNLL-2011 Shared Task: Modeling Unrestricted Coreference in OntoNotes. In *Proceedings of the Fifteenth Conference on Computational Natural Language Learning: Shared Task*, CONLL Shared Task '11, pages 1–27, Portland, Oregon.

Sameer Pradhan, Alessandro Moschitti, Nianwen Xue, Olga Uryupina, and Yuchen Zhang. 2012. CoNLL-2012 Shared Task: Modeling Multilingual Unrestricted Coreference in OntoNotes. In *Joint Conference on EMNLP and CoNLL - Shared Task*, pages 1–40, Jeju Island, Korea, July. Association for Computational Linguistics.

Sameer Pradhan, Xiaoqiang Luo, Marta Recasens, Eduard Hovy, Vincent Ng, and Michael Strube. 2014. Scoring Coreference Partitions of Predicted Mentions: A Reference Implementation. In *Proceedings of the 52nd Annual Meeting of the Association for Computational Linguistics (Volume 2: Short Papers)*, pages 30–35, Baltimore, Maryland, June. Association for Computational Linguistics.

Colin Raffel, Noam Shazeer, Adam Roberts, Katherine Lee, Sharan Narang, Michael Matena, Yanqi Zhou, Wei Li, and Peter J Liu. 2019. Exploring the limits of transfer learning with a unified text-to-text transformer. *arXiv preprint arXiv:1910.10683*.

Hossein Sahlani, Maryam Hourali, and Behrouz Minaei-Bidgoli. 2020. Coreference resolution using semantic features and fully connected neural network in the persian language. *International Journal of Computational Intelligence Systems*, 13(1):1002–1013.

A Sboev, R Rybka, and A Gryaznov. 2020. Deep neural networks ensemble with word vector representation models to resolve coreference resolution in russian. In *Advanced Technologies in Robotics and Intelligent Systems*, pages 35–44. Springer.

Tomohide Shibata and Sadao Kurohashi. 2018. Entity-centric joint modeling of japanese coreference resolution and predicate argument structure analysis. In *Proceedings of the 56th Annual Meeting of the Association for Computational Linguistics (Volume 1: Long Papers)*, pages 579–589.

Josef Steinberger, Mijail Kabadjov, and Massimo Poesio. 2016. Coreference applications to summarization. In *Anaphora Resolution*, pages 433–456. Springer.

Ian Tenney, Dipanjan Das, and Ellie Pavlick. 2019. Bert rediscovers the classical nlp pipeline. In *Proceedings of the 57th Annual Meeting of the Association for Computational Linguistics*, pages 4593–4601.

Gorka Urbizu, Ander Soraluze, and Olatz Arregi. 2019. Deep cross-lingual coreference resolution for less-resourced languages: The case of basque. In *Proceedings of the 2nd Workshop on Computational Models of Reference, Anaphora and Coreference (CRAC 2019), co-located with NAACL 2019*.

Olga Uryupina, Ron Artstein, Antonella Bristot, Federica Cavicchio, Francesca Delogu, Kepa J Rodriguez, and Massimo Poesio. 2020. Annotating a broad range of anaphoric phenomena, in a variety of genres: the arrau corpus. *Natural Language Engineering*, 26(1):95–128.

Ashish Vaswani, Noam Shazeer, Niki Parmar, Jakob Uszkoreit, Llion Jones, Aidan N Gomez, Łukasz Kaiser, and Illia Polosukhin. 2017. Attention is all you need. In *Advances in neural information processing systems*, pages 5998–6008.

Lesly Miculicich Werlen and Andrei Popescu-Belis. 2017. Using coreference links to improve spanish-to-english machine translation. In *Proceedings of the 2nd Workshop on Coreference Resolution Beyond OntoNotes (COR-BON 2017)*, pages 30–40.

Wei Wu, Fei Wang, Arianna Yuan, Fei Wu, and Jiwei Li. 2020. Corefqa: Coreference resolution as query-based span prediction. In *Proceedings of the 58th Annual Meeting of the Association for Computational Linguistics*, pages 6953–6963.

Juntao Yu, Alexandra Uma, and Massimo Poesio. 2020. A cluster ranking model for full anaphora resolution. In *Proceedings of The 12th Language Resources and Evaluation Conference*, pages 11–20.

Pengfei Zhu, Zhuosheng Zhang, Jiangtong Li, Yafang Huang, and Hai Zhao. 2018. Lingke: a fine-grained multi-turn chatbot for customer service. In *Proceedings of the 27th International Conference on Computational Linguistics: System Demonstrations*, pages 108–112.

TwiConv: A Coreference-annotated Corpus of Twitter Conversations

Berfin Aktaş
SFB1287
Research Focus Cognitive Sciences
University of Potsdam, Germany
`berfinaktas@uni-potsdam.de`

Annalena Kohnert
Department of Language Science
and Technology
Saarland University, Germany
`akohnert@coli.uni-saarland.de`

Abstract

This article introduces TwiConv, an English coreference-annotated corpus of microblog conversations from Twitter. We describe the corpus compilation process and the annotation scheme, and release the corpus publicly, along with this paper. We manually annotated nominal coreference in 1756 tweets arranged in 185 conversation threads. The annotation achieves satisfactory annotation agreement results. We also present a new method for mapping the tweet contents with distributed stand-off annotations, which can easily be adapted to different annotation tasks.

1 Introduction and Related Work

Microblog texts from Twitter present a discourse genre that carries non-standard language characteristics (e.g., noisy or informal language with abbreviations, purposeful typos, use of non-alphanumerical symbols such as #- and @-characters, misspellings, etc.) and is therefore challenging for NLP applications (Ritter et al., 2011; Sikdar and Gambäck, 2016). There exist a number of Twitter datasets annotated at different linguistic layers for investigating a variety of NLP tasks on this genre, including sentiment analysis (Cieliebak et al., 2017), named entity recognition (Derczynski et al., 2016), and event coreference resolution (Chao et al., 2019). Aktaş et al. (2018) tested an out-of-the-box nominal coreference resolution system trained on OntoNotes (Hovy et al., 2006; Weischedel et al., 2011) on Twitter data and showed that the system performs with much lower scores than the original reported values on that data. Hence, tweets are a complicated genre also for the task of nominal coreference resolution.

We introduce TwiConv, a nominal coreference-annotated corpus of English-language Twitter posts with the intent to explore the coreference features in conversational Twitter texts. Our annotation scheme is based on (Grishina and Stede, 2016), yet with some domain-driven adaptations. Twitter's Developer Policy[1] does not allow publishing the tweet contents. Therefore, most of the tweet datasets distribute the unique tweet IDs and annotations without the tweet text. However, if the tokenization of the corpus in concern is realized through a relatively complicated procedure or contains manual corrections, stand off annotation layers may not match with the text content in the compiled corpus. We thus present a distribution method for mapping the original tweet texts with our annotations. To our knowledge, TwiConv is the first tweet corpus for nominal coreference.

The remainder of paper is organized as follows. We describe the corpus compilation process in Section 2. In Section 3, we present the annotation principles along with a description of quality assurance methods. The main statistics of our corpus are presented in Section 4. Format of the distributed corpus and data sharing methodology are described in Section 5. Section 6 summarizes the presented work.

---

[1] `developer.twitter.com/en/developer-terms/policy`

Proceedings of the 3rd Workshop on Computational Models of Reference, Anaphora and Coreference (CRAC 2020), pages 47–54,
Barcelona, Spain (online), December 12, 2020.

2 Corpus Compilation

2.1 Data collection

We used *twarc*[2] to collect English-language tweets from the Twitter stream on several (non-adjacent) days in December, 2017. We did not filter for topics in any way, since that is not a concern for this corpus. Instead, our aim was to collect threads (conversations) by recursively retrieving parent tweets, whose IDs are taken from the `in_reply_to_id` field of the tweet object returned by the Twitter API. We then used a script from (Scheffler, 2017), which constructs the full conversational tree structure for any tweet that generated replies. A single *thread* (in our terminology) is a path from the root to a leaf node of that tree. For the purposes of this study, we are not interested in alternative replies and other aspects of the tree structure; so we kept only one of the longest threads (paths) from each tree and discarded everything else. Therefore, the data set does not contain any overlaps in tweet sequences. A sample thread structure with one example coreference chain annotation is illustrated in Appendix A.

2.2 Tokenization

It is well known that tokenization is a crucial preparatory step for doing any kind of NLP on texts. We experimented with two different tokenizers: the Stanford *PTBTokenizer* (Manning et al., 2014) and *Twokenizer* (Gimpel et al., 2011). It turned out that these systems have different strengths in handling challenging cases. For instance, only PTBTokenizer can handle the apostrophes (e.g., contracted verb forms and possessive markers). On the other hand, Twokenizer is stronger in recognizing the punctuation symbols even if they are not surrounded by whitespace. These cases are illustrated in Appendix B.

We thus decided to implement a tokenization pipeline where the output of the Twokenizer is given as input to the PTBTokenizer. The outcome of this pipeline process is compatible with Penn Treebank conventions[3] and, therefore, with the other corpora following the same conventions, such as OntoNotes (Weischedel et al., 2013) and Switchboard (Calhoun et al., 2010). We found that the number of tokens increased in the second step of the pipeline by 4%, and only 5% of newly generated tokens are erroneous over-generated tokens. Therefore, we don't consider over-tokenization as a potential problem for token-based compatibility with other corpora.

2.3 Sentence Segmentation

We followed a semi-automated segmentation procedure to split the tokenized tweets into sentences. We first segmented the text using the SoMaJo sentence splitter for English (Proisl and Uhrig, 2016). SoMaJo deals well with common Twitter tokens such as links, hashtags and abbreviations but fails when sentences in the same tweet start with lowercase letters or hashtags, and when the user does not use any punctuation. Therefore, we manually corrected the boundaries detected by SoMaJo.

3 Annotation

3.1 Annotation Principles

In our scheme, *markables* are phrases with nominal or pronominal heads. All nominal expressions, such as names, definite/indefinite noun phrases, pronouns, and temporal expressions are annotated for coreference. Non-referential pronouns, predicative copula constructions, and appositions are also annotated and distinguished by the attribute values assigned to them. Elements of the web language such as usernames and hashtags are considered as markables as well. Links and emojis are treated according to their grammatical roles. We illustrate these cases in Appendix C. We annotated all chains including singletons. Chains can contain several markables from the same tweet (intra-tweet) or from different replies (inter-tweet), which can lead to 1st, 2nd and 3rd pronouns referring to the same entity within one thread as in Example 1. We do not allow dicontinuous markables, therefore split antecedents and their co-referring mentions are annotated as separate markables (Example 3) unless they occur as compound phrases (Example 2)[4].

---

(1) ⌐ Thanks to [you]$_i$, [I]$_j$ can now understand the whole conversation.
     ⌐ [You]$_j$ are welcome.

(2) [The baby and I]$_i$ are listening to [our]$_i$ favourite music.

(3) [I]$_i$ met [him]$_j$ at [our]$_k$ favourite café.

We used the MMAX2 tool (Müller and Strube, 2006) for annotations and customized its default settings according to our scheme. We defined comprehensive attributes for chains and mentions. All chains should be assigned a representative mention (i.e., the most descriptive mention in the chain), a semantic class (i.e., the semantic category of the entity) and genericity value (i.e., whether the referred entity is specific or generic). Mentions are assigned a nominal form (np_form) and grammatical role.

3.2 Annotation Quality

We applied the following procedures to assess and evaluate the quality of manual annotations.

1. **Automated Checks** We validated the consistency of the annotations by applying a number of automated procedures checking whether the constraints specified in the guideline are applied uniformly.

2. **Review of Annotations** We reviewed the annotations of the first 27 threads (15% of all threads in the corpus). In total, 33 problematic annotation cases were detected during this review, which affected approximately 50 mentions. Most of the problematic cases were due to incorrect selection of mention span or assignment of wrong attributes for different features specified in the guideline. The proportion of detected problems affects only 2% of all mentions in this sub-corpus. Therefore we did not see the necessity to extend the review process to the entire corpus.

3. **Inter-Annotator Agreement** We assessed the inter-annotator agreement (IAA) to evaluate the reliability of our annotation process. In the first version of the TwiConv corpus, we annotated only the coreference chains containing 3rd person pronouns. We conducted the inter-annotator agreement evaluation on this first version of the corpus. The most common annotator errors were different selection of mentions (missing or spurious markables), missing chains if they only contained very few mentions or the splitting of one chain into two, as well as occasional differences in markable span boundaries.

   We then extended the guideline (GL) and annotated all the coreference chains in the second version of the dataset. The changes in the extended GL only concern attributes, which are not addressed in the IAA study. Therefore, we are confident that this agreement study can assess our final scheme in terms of mention detection and chain linking.

   Artstein and Poesio (2008) propose the use of Krippendorff's α (Krippendorff, 1980) for set-based agreement tasks such as coreference annotations. Following their proposal, we used Krippendorff's α to measure the IAA for 12 randomly selected threads. Two linguistics students annotated this sub-corpus. We computed the IAA for mention detection and chain linking. We calculated the Krippendorff's α by following the methodology described in (Passonneau, 2006) and found its value as 0.872 ($\alpha \geq .800$) which indicates reliability of our data annotations for research purposes.

4 Corpus Overview

The resulting TwiConv corpus consists of 1756 tweets in 185 threads, with the average length of a tweet being 153 characters. We present additional descriptive statistics for TwiConv corpus in Table 1 and for annotations in Table 2.

5 Corpus Distribution

5.1 Corpus format

The annotations are stored in a CoNLL format (i.e., tab-separated) with 17 columns in total, one file per Twitter thread. The content of each column is described in Table 3 and an example is presented

# of threads	185
# of tweets	1756
# of tokens	48172
# of sentences	3503
# of clauses	6719
average thread length (token)	260.4
average sentence length (token)	13.6

Table 1: General statistics on the corpus

# of mentions:	12374
# of chains:	7035
# of non-singleton (ns) chains:	1734
# of intra-tweet coref chains (ns):	674
# of inter-tweet coref chains (ns):	1060
# of username mentions:	124
# of mentions including hashtag:	94
Average mention length (in tokens):	1.94

Table 2: Descriptive statistics of the coreference annotations

in Appendix E. The Part-of-Speech tags and parses in column 4 and 5 are automatically created with Stanford Parser (Manning et al., 2014) with no manual correction. Empty lines indicate sentence breaks.

Column	Content	Column	Content
0	Thread ID	9	NP form/reference type
1	Thread No	10	Coreference ID
2	Token No in sentence	11	Clause boundary
3	Token	12	Shortest NP boundary
4	POS tag	13	Longest NP boundary
5	Parse info	14	Grammatical role
6	Speaker/User handle	15	Genericity
7	Representative mentions	16	[Tweet No in thread]_[Sentence
8	Semantic class		No in tweet]_[Token No in sentence]

Table 3: Column content in CoNLL format corpus

It is possible that different mentions start at the same token, e.g. "My Twitter username" marks both the beginning of the pronoun mention "My" as well the full definite noun mention "My Twitter username". In this case, we used pipe symbols ("|") to separate the annotations for different mentions. The order of the annotations separated by the pipe symbol remained the same for the entire line, meaning that the order of annotations in pipe-separated columns is always the same.

Further, some annotations such as NP form and grammatical role have sub-categories, which we express by slashes ("/"): e.g. *ppers/anaphora* marks a personal pronoun that functions as an anaphoric expression. Similarly, the grammatical role *other* can be either appositive, vocative or other (e.g., *other/vocative*), but those sub-categories were only assigned to the *other* type, not to subjects, prepositional phrases etc.

We used the automatically created parses to detect the clause and NP boundaries (both for shortest and longest NP spans) in tweets. We manually corrected the detected boundaries and added boundary information to the data files (i.e., boundary start and end tokens are specified in columns 11-13 in Table 3). The last column in the data files represent the relative order of tokens in the texts.

5.2 Sharing Method

Due to Twitter's Developer Policy, we have to refer to tweets via their ID, through which the message text as well as other tweet-related information can be downloaded.

In order to share the data, we use a method similar to the distribution of the CoNLL-2012 Shared Task Data (Pradhan et al., 2012) and provide skeleton files which include all annotations, but no tokens from the Twitter message and no usernames (instead, they are replaced by underscore characters). For each token, the ID of the tweet from which the token originates is indicated at the end of the corresponding line. As we have tokenized the data, we also provide reference files to recreate our tokenization steps. To create those *diff* files, we compared files with the whitespace tokenized tweets (with one token per line) to ones with the tweets with our final tokenization (one token per line as well) with the Linux program *diff*. We share only those tokens in the *diff* files that were affected by the tokenization method or other forms of modification such as encoding differences for emoticons. For a sample representation, see Appendix D.

After downloading all still available tweets, they have to be transformed into above described format (whitespace tokenized, one token per line, one file per tweet). We provide an assembly script that will use these tweet files, the skeleton files and *diff* files to create the complete CoNLL files with all annotations and tokens[5]. The script itself contains no information about the content of the annotations and can be re-used for any other tweets, given that the *diff* and skeleton files (following the CoNLL-style format described in Table 3) have been generated correctly. For unavailable tweets, the tokens will remain anonymized (meaning the underscore character remains).

6 Conclusion

We have developed a comprehensive annotation scheme for annotating nominal coreference in English Twitter conversations and fully annotated 1756 tweets arranged in 185 threads. Assessment of annotations and correction of erroneous cases were made via inter-annotator agreement evaluation, partial review, and automated checks. We distribute the corpus without tweet contents and introduce tools for researchers to map the tweet texts, captured using the tweet IDs, with the shared annotations. We hope that the release of the TwiConv corpus will increase the interest in coreference studies on this genre.

Acknowledgements

We thank the anonymous reviewers and Manfred Stede for their helpful observations and suggestions. This work is funded by the Deutsche Forschungsgemeinschaft (DFG, German Research Foundation) - Projektnummer 317633480 - SFB 1287, Project A03.

References

Berfin Aktaş, Tatjana Scheffler, and Manfred Stede. 2018. Anaphora resolution for twitter conversations: An exploratory study. In *Proceedings of the First Workshop on Computational Models of Reference, Anaphora and Coreference (CRAC@NAACL 2018)*, pages 1–10, New Orleans, Louisiana, June. Association for Computational Linguistics.

Ron Artstein and Massimo Poesio. 2008. Survey article: Inter-coder agreement for computational linguistics. *Computational Linguistics*, 34(4):555–596.

Sasha Calhoun, Jean Carletta, Jason M. Brenier, Neil Mayo, Dan Jurafsky, Mark Steedman, and David Beaver. 2010. The nxt-format switchboard corpus: A rich resource for investigating the syntax, semantics, pragmatics and prosody of dialogue. *Language Resources and Evaluation*, 44(4):387–419, 12.

W. Chao, P. Wei, Z. Luo, X. Liu, and G. Sui. 2019. Selective expression for event coreference resolution on twitter. In *2019 International Joint Conference on Neural Networks (IJCNN)*.

Mark Cieliebak, Jan Milan Deriu, Dominic Egger, and Fatih Uzdilli. 2017. A twitter corpus and benchmark resources for german sentiment analysis. In *Proceedings of the Fifth International Workshop on Natural Language Processing for Social Media*, pages 45–51.

Leon Derczynski, Kalina Bontcheva, and Ian Roberts. 2016. Broad Twitter corpus: A diverse named entity recognition resource. In *Proceedings of COLING 2016, the 26th International Conference on Computational Linguistics: Technical Papers*, pages 1169–1179, Osaka, Japan, December. The COLING 2016 Organizing Committee.

Kevin Gimpel, Nathan Schneider, Brendan O'Connor, Dipanjan Das, Daniel Mills, Jacob Eisenstein, Michael Heilman, Dani Yogatama, Jeffrey Flanigan, and Noah A. Smith. 2011. Part-of-speech tagging for twitter: Annotation, features, and experiments. In *Proceedings of the 49th Annual Meeting of the Association for Computational Linguistics: Human Language Technologies: Short Papers - Volume 2*, HLT '11, pages 42–47, Stroudsburg, PA, USA. Association for Computational Linguistics.

---

[5]Scripts and data to reproduce the corpus can be found at `https://github.com/berfingit/TwiConv`

Yulia Grishina and Manfred Stede, 2016. *Parallel coreference annotation guidelines.*, November.

Eduard Hovy, Mitchell Marcus, Martha Palmer, Lance Ramshaw, and Ralph Weischedel. 2006. OntoNotes: The 90% solution. In *Proceedings of the Human Language Technology Conference of the NAACL, Companion Volume: Short Papers*, pages 57–60, New York City, USA, June. Association for Computational Linguistics.

K. Krippendorff. 1980. *Content Analysis: An Introduction To Its Methodology.* Sage commtext series. Sage Publications.

Christopher D. Manning, Mihai Surdeanu, John Bauer, Jenny Finkel, Steven J. Bethard, and David McClosky. 2014. The Stanford CoreNLP natural language processing toolkit. In *Association for Computational Linguistics (ACL) System Demonstrations*, pages 55–60.

Christoph Müller and Michael Strube. 2006. Multi-level annotation of linguistic data with mmax2. In Joybrato Mukherjee Sabine Braun, Kurt Kohn, editor, *Corpus Technology and Language Pedagogy: New Resources, New Tools, New Methods.*

Rebecca Passonneau. 2006. Measuring agreement on set-valued items (MASI) for semantic and pragmatic annotation. In *Proceedings of the Fifth International Conference on Language Resources and Evaluation (LREC'06)*, Genoa, Italy, May. European Language Resources Association (ELRA).

Sameer Pradhan, Alessandro Moschitti, Nianwen Xue, Olga Uryupina, and Yuchen Zhang. 2012. CoNLL-2012 Shared Task: Modeling Multilingual Unrestricted Coreference in OntoNotes. In *Joint Conference on EMNLP and CoNLL-Shared Task*, pages 1–40.

Thomas Proisl and Peter Uhrig. 2016. SoMaJo: State-of-the-art tokenization for German web and social media texts. In *Proceedings of the 10th Web as Corpus Workshop (WAC-X) and the EmpiriST Shared Task*, pages 57–62, Berlin. Association for Computational Linguistics (ACL).

Alan Ritter, Sam Clark, Mausam, and Oren Etzioni. 2011. Named entity recognition in tweets: An experimental study. In *Proceedings of the Conference on Empirical Methods in Natural Language Processing*, EMNLP '11, page 1524–1534, USA. Association for Computational Linguistics.

Tatjana Scheffler. 2017. Conversations on twitter. In Darja Fišer and Michael Beißwenger, editors, *Researching computer-mediated communication: Corpus-based approaches to language in the digital world*, pages 124–144. University Press, Ljubljana.

Utpal Kumar Sikdar and Björn Gambäck. 2016. Feature-rich twitter named entity recognition and classification. In *Proceedings of the 2nd Workshop on Noisy User-generated Text (WNUT)*, pages 164–170, Osaka, Japan, December. The COLING 2016 Organizing Committee.

Ralph Weischedel, Eduard Hovy, Mitchell Marcus, Martha Palmer, Robert Belvin, Sameer Pradan, Lance Ramshaw, and Nianwen Xue. 2011. Ontonotes : A large training corpus for enhanced processing. In Joseph Olive, Caitlin Christianson, and John McCary, editors, *Handbook of Natural Language Processing and Machine Translation.*

Ralph Weischedel, Martha Palmer, Mitchell Marcus, Eduard Hovy, Sameer Pradhan, Lance Ramshaw, Nianwen Xue, Ann Taylor, Jeff Kaufman, Michelle Franchini, Mohammed El-Bachouti, Robert Belvin, and Ann Houston. 2013. Ontonotes release 5.0 ldc2013t19. *Web Download. Linguistic Data Consortium, Philadelphia, PA.*

Appendices

Appendix A: Thread sample

> The only Russia collusion occurred when [@HillaryClinton]ᵢ conspired to sell US Uranium to a Russian oligarch while [she]ᵢ was in charge.
>
>> Why is the mainstream media so quiet? Probably because [#theSecretaryofState]ᵢ is still powerfull.
>>
>>> Haven't you heard , dear???? [HRC]ᵢ is NOT president!!!
>>>
>>>> .[She]ᵢ doesn't have to be a President to face crimes [she]ᵢ committed, dear .

Appendix B: Tokenization examples

	String	Twokenizer	PTBTokenizer	TwiConv Pipeline
1	aren't	aren't (1)[6]	are, n't (2)	are, n't (2)
2	you've	you've (1)	you, 've (2)	you, 've (2)
3	London's	London's (1)	London, 's (2)	London, 's (2)
4	here:)Because	here, :), Because (3)	here:)Because (1)	here, :), Because (3)
5	..	.. (1)	., . (2)	., . (2*)

Table 4: Tokenization output

Appendix C: Twitter mention examples

(4) .. [@SomeUser] just said twice that.. *("username" as a mention)*

(5) this doesn't pass [the #smelltest] *("hashtag" as part of a mention)*

(6) [] are fools ... *("emoji" as a mention)*

(7) If crashing, please refer to this: **[https://exampleurl.com]** *("link" as a mention)*

Appendix D: Tokenization differences

```
This
is
just
a
test.
Hi
Twitter!
```

Figure 1: Example Tweet, whitespaced tokenized

```
5,6c5
< test
< .
---
> test
8,9c7
< Twitter
< !
---
> Twitter!
```

Figure 2: *diff* file example

Appendix E: CoNLL-formatted sample annotation

```
#begin document (001_987654321000000000.branch1.); part 0
001_987654321000000000.branch1.   0   0   This  DT   (ROOT(S(NP*)  SomeUsername   -   -   pds/cataphora   (0)   CL0   NP_S(   NP_L(   -   -   0_0_0
001_987654321000000000.branch1.   0   1   is  VBZ   (VP*   SomeUsername   -   -   -   -   -   )NP_S   -   -   -   0_0_1
001_987654321000000000.branch1.   0   2   just  RB   (ADVP*   SomeUsername   -   -   -   -   -   -   -   -   0_0_2
001_987654321000000000.branch1.   0   3   a  DT   (NP*   SomeUsername   representative_men   -   indefnp/none   (1   -   NP_S()   )NP_L   -   -   0_0_3
001_987654321000000000.branch1.   0   4   test  NN   *)))   SomeUsername   -   -   -   1)   -   -   -   -   0_0_4
001_987654321000000000.branch1.   0   5   .  .   *))   SomeUsername   -   -   -   -   CL0   -   -   -   -   0_0_5

001_987654321000000000.branch1.   0   0   Hi  UH   (ROOT(INTJ*   SomeUsername   -   -   -   -   CL1   -   -   -   -   0_1_0
001_987654321000000000.branch1.   0   1   Twitter  NNP   (NP*)   SomeUsername   representative_men   -   ne/none   (2)   -   -   -   -   -   0_1_1
001_987654321000000000.branch1.   0   2   !  .   *))   SomeUsername   -   -   -   -   CL1   -   -   -   -   0_1_2

#end document
```

Figure 3: Example CoNLL file

Integrating knowledge graph embeddings to improve mention representation for bridging anaphora resolution

Onkar Pandit[1], Pascal Denis[1] and Liva Ralaivola[2]

1- MAGNET, Inria Lille - Nord Europe, Villeneuve d'Ascq, France
onkar.pandit@inria.fr, pascal.denis@inria.fr
2- Criteo AI Lab, Paris, France. l.ralaivola@criteo.com

Abstract

Lexical semantics and world knowledge are crucial for interpreting bridging anaphora. Yet, existing computational methods for acquiring and injecting this type of information into bridging resolution systems suffer important limitations. Based on explicit querying of external knowledge bases, earlier approaches are computationally expensive (hence, hardly scalable) and they map the data to be processed into high-dimensional spaces (careful handling of the curse of dimensionality and overfitting has to be in order). In this work, we take a different and principled approach which naturally addresses these issues. Specifically, we convert the external knowledge source (in this case, WordNet) into a graph, and learn embeddings of the graph nodes of low dimension to capture the crucial features of the graph topology and, at the same time, rich semantic information. Once properly identified from the mention text spans, these low dimensional graph node embeddings are combined with distributional text-based embeddings to provide enhanced mention representations. We illustrate the effectiveness of our approach by evaluating it on commonly used datasets, namely ISNotes (Markert et al., 2012) and BASHI (Rösiger, 2018). Our enhanced mention representations yield significant accuracy improvements on both datasets when compared to different standalone text-based mention representations.

1 Introduction

An *anaphor* is an expression whose interpretation depends upon a previous expression in the discourse, an *antecedent*. A *Bridging anaphor* is a special type of anaphor where there is non-identical or associative relation with its antecedent (Clark, 1975), as in the following example:

"*Starbucks* has a new take on the unicorn frappuccino. **One employee** accidentally leaked a picture of the secret new drink."

In this case, the anaphor **One employee** depends on the antecedent *Starbucks* for the complete interpretation and holds non-identical relationship with the antecedent, hence, a bridging anaphor.

We here address the problem of learning from a set of anaphor-antecedent pairs a predictor capable of accurately identify such pairs in unseen texts. More precisely, if bridging resolution comprises two main tasks, *bridging anaphora recognition* and *bridging anaphora resolution*, we solely focus on the task of *bridging anaphora resolution* and assume that bridging anaphor recognition has already been performed.

Semantic information on anaphor-antecedent pairs plays a crucial role in resolving bridging anaphora. Consider again the previous example: if the resolution system has the knowledge that Starbucks is a company and companies have employees, then it is easy to establish the link between them. Standard text-based features either hand-crafted or automatically extracted from word embeddings (Mikolov et al., 2013a, Pennington et al., 2014), are not sufficient for bridging resolution (Hou, 2018b). Earlier systems (Poesio et al., 2004, Lassalle and Denis, 2011) have proposed to extract this information from knowledge bases, the web, or raw text through queries of the form "X *of* Y". The estimated number of occurrences in these sources gives the probability of relations between X and Y. These types of queries were generalized by (Hou et al., 2013) where all queries of the type "X *preposition* Y", i.e. beyond

Proceedings of the 3rd Workshop on Computational Models of Reference, Anaphora and Coreference (CRAC 2020), pages 55–67,
Barcelona, Spain (online), December 12, 2020.

the mere "of" preposition, were considered. However, these approaches extract only shallow features, capturing relations between pair of nodes instead of taking advantage of broader information that is present in knowledge graphs. Therefore, attempting to extend these strategies to take into account a larger amount of information on mentions may translate into learning problems where the input space is of high dimension, which might be a hurdle when dealing with moderate size datasets – for instance, the datasets that we consider here, i.e ISNotes (Markert et al., 2012) and ARRAU (Uryupina et al., 2019) respectively contain 663 training pairs and 5512 training pairs.

Recently proposed approaches tried to remedy these shortcomings (Hou, 2018b, Hou, 2018a). Hou learned embeddings on the pairs of nouns present in the text which are connected by prepositional or possessive structure (e.g. "X *of* Y"). She creates "pseudo knowledge" by generating these noun-pairs and learn embeddings on these pairs. Her approach is better at capturing fine-grained semantics than *vanilla* word embeddings such as Word2Vec (Mikolov et al., 2013a), Glove (Pennington et al., 2014), etc. however, it still depends on the presence of the required noun-pairs in the corpus. The use of knowledge graphs, either manually or automatically constructed, can alleviate this problem as they contain general semantic and world-knowledge. We empirically demonstrate that embeddings constructed on these graphs indeed provide additional information and complement these text-based embeddings.

In the present work, we propose to use *low-dimensional* graph node embeddings on knowledge graphs to capture semantic information. We use WordNet [1] (Fellbaum, 1998) as a knowledge graph in the experiments, though our approach can be extended to any knowledge graph. We hypothesize that the low-dimensional vectors learned on the nodes of WordNet graph capture lexical semantics such as hypernymy, hyponymy, meronymy, etc. as well as general relatedness between nodes. This way we eliminate the cumbersome task of manually designing features as well as the burden of querying. Moreover, as we shall see, the low dimensionality of the embedding space does not go against its use with small datasets. But obtaining node embeddings for a mention is non-trivial a task, as it requires mapping a potentially ambiguous multi-token expression onto a specific node in the graph (synset in case of WordNet). This entails several key steps, such as: (i) *mention normalization* where the mention is mapped to a standardized form which might be present in the graph, (ii) handling the *absent knowledge* case where the referred entity is unavailable in the knowledge graph and possibly (iii) *sense disambiguation* in the presence of multiple senses for the mention. We propose simple yet effective heuristics to address these issues, as detailed in the coming sections. These knowledge graph embeddings are combined with distributional text-based embeddings to produce improved mention representations.

We address the problem of bridging resolution as a ranking problem, where the trained model assigns a score to anaphor-candidate antecedent pairs, preferring this ranking approach over a classification perspective for it to be less sensitive to class-imbalance, and making it focused on learning relative scores. Specifically, we train a ranking SVM model to predict scores for anaphor-candidate antecedent pairs, an approach that has been successfully applied to the related task of coreference resolution (Rahman and Ng, 2009). We observe that integrating node embeddings with text-based embeddings produces increased accuracy, substantiating the ability of graph node embeddings in capturing the semantic information.

2 Related Work

Bridging anaphora resolution. Earlier approaches (Poesio et al., 1997, Poesio and Vieira, 1998, Poesio et al., 2004, Lassalle and Denis, 2011) put restrictions on the resolution task either by constraining the types of noun-phrases (NP) to be considered as bridging anaphor or by restricting relations between bridging anaphors and antecedent where most of the approaches tackle specific type of anaphor like definite noun-phrases. A pairwise model combining lexical semantic features as well as salience features to perform bridging resolution limited to mereological relations only is studied by (Poesio et al., 2004) on the GNOME corpus. Lexical distance is used as one feature in their approach. WordNet (Fellbaum, 1998) is used to acquire the distance. For a noun head X of an anaphor x and Y of potential antecedent y, the query of the form "X *of* Y" is provided to WordNet. But recall in WordNet is low, so as an alternative,

---

[1] WordNet is a lexical database and not a knowledge graph in the stricter sense. But, the graph is constructed over it, to be subsequently used as the knowledge graph.

Google API is used to get the distance between anaphor-antecedent. The API yields number of hits, from which lexical distance is calculated. Based on this method (Lassalle and Denis, 2011) developed a system that resolves mereological bridging anaphors in French.

Improving on the previous approach, (Hou et al., 2013) proposed a generic query with all possible prepositions. Their query is formulated as "*X preposition Y*" instead of limiting to *of* preposition. They propose a *global* model as opposed to previous approaches that relied only on *local* features. In this model, they infer links globally instead of choosing from candidate set of the specific anaphor as they argue that the probability of noun phrase (NP) being antecedent increases if it is already antecedent to another anaphor. Their assumption is opposite to the local salience hypothesis of (Sidner, 1979) as the local models indirectly assume that the most salient candidate among the nearest context is the best suitable for antecedent. Rule-based *full bridging resolution* system is proposed in (Hou et al., 2014) where they devised rules for linking anaphors to antecedents. Some of the rules as well as the corresponding features are acquired by querying the knowledge sources, albeit different queries such as a query to get a list of nouns which denote a part of building — *wall, window,* or list of personal relations — *husband, sister,* etc. They also propose a learning-based system by converting the rules into features but observe slight gain.

The work (Hou, 2018b) created word embeddings for bridging (embeddings_PP) by exploring the syntactic structure of noun phrases (NPs) to derive contexts for nouns in the GloVe model. She generalizes previous approaches of querying as her PP context model uses all prepositions for all nouns in big corpora. The deterministic approach proposed in (Hou, 2018a) is the extension to the work done in (Hou, 2018b) which creates new embeddings (embedding_bridging) by combining embeddings_PP and GloVe. Her approach is efficient and solves the scalability and curse of dimensionality issues. But her approach depends on the presence of the NP having a specific syntactic structure so that the algorithm can identify it as "*X preposition Y*". This algorithm misses those anaphor-antecedent pairs which do not possess this structure. The work (Roesiger et al., 2018) uses neural networks trained on the relation classification tasks to get the semantic information between anaphor and antecedent. This information is integrated into the state-of-the-art systems for coreference and bridging resolution. The system fails at capturing broader semantic relations as only six semantic relations are predicted with neural networks, due to this they observe marginal improvement in the bridging resolution.

All the previous works assume that the mentions are detected, i.e., noun phrases are presented and the task is to choose the correct NP as an antecedent. This is discarded in the latest system, BARQA (Hou, 2020). She casts bridging anaphora resolution as a question answering problem where answer produces antecedent for an anaphor. She also pointed out that most of the previous approaches relied only on the features of the antecedent-anaphor ignoring the context around them. However, she ignores any semantic information and relies on BERT (Devlin et al., 2018) architecture to capture both contextual information as well as required common sense knowledge.

Knowledge Graph Embeddings Graph embeddings represent graph (whole or sub-graph) or nodes with the lower dimensional vector. The work (Hamilton et al., 2017) details a generic framework of the commonly used graph embedding algorithms. In recent times, embedding algorithms specifically for knowledge graphs have been proposed — RESCAL (Nickel et al., 2011), DistMult (Yang et al., 2014), ComplEx (Trouillon et al., 2016), HolE (Nickel et al., 2016) learn embeddings for knowledge graph completion, (Bansal et al., 2019) propose A2N neighborhood attention-based technique, (Xu and Li, 2019) embed relations with dihedral groups whereas (Nathani et al., 2019) employ graph attention network to acquire embeddings. In this work, we used WordNet as a knowledge graph so we are interested in the graph node embeddings learned particularly on WordNet (Goikoetxea et al., 2015, Saedi et al., 2018, Kutuzov et al., 2019). Though, (Goikoetxea et al., 2015, Saedi et al., 2018) do not produce embeddings for senses present in WordNet as they encode corresponding words. However, `path2vec` (Kutuzov et al., 2019) produces embeddings for each sense present in WordNet by optimizing graph-based similarity metric. The use of knowledge graph embeddings to infuse common sense knowledge into NLP systems is becoming popular, and our work falls into this category. Language model (Peters et al., 2019), domain-specific natural language inference (NLI) (Sharma et al., 2019), entity disambiguation (Sevgili et al., 2019) have been some of the tasks where graph embeddings have been used. To the best of our knowledge, this is the first work where graph embeddings are used for bridging anaphora resolution.

3   Knowledge-aware mention representation

In this paper, we propose a new, knowledge-aware mention representations for bridging resolution. These representations combine two components: (i) distributional embeddings learned from raw text data, and (ii) graph node embeddings learned from relational data obtained from a knowledge graph. Specifically, the final representation v_m for a mention m is obtained by concatenating the text-based contextual embeddings g_m and the knowledge graph node embeddings h_m: $v_m = [g_m, h_m]$.

For the distributional embeddings g_m, we use off-the-shelf word embeddings such as word2vec (Mikolov et al., 2013a), glove (Pennington et al., 2014), BERT (Devlin et al., 2018), or embeddings_pp (Hou, 2018b). Except for BERT, we average over embeddings of the mention's head word and common nouns appearing in the mention before the head, as mentioned in (Hou, 2018a). With BERT, mention embeddings are obtained by averaging over embeddings of all the words of the mention.

However, obtaining knowledge graph-based embeddings h_m for the mention is a much more challenging task, comprising different steps. Before detailing those steps, we first briefly describe the knowledge graph – WordNet and how we compute node embeddings in the following paragraphs.

Knowledge Graph is a graph with nodes being entities or abstract concepts and edges denoting the relation between them. A node in the knowledge graph can be a real-world entity such as a person, a place, etc. or can be an abstract concept such as a word, a sense, etc. A knowledge graph can be domain-specific (WordNet (Fellbaum, 1998) captures the semantic relation between words and meanings) or open domain (DBpedia (Lehmann et al., 2015) for general-purpose knowledge). The central purpose of knowledge graphs is to store common sense knowledge in a structured format so that machines can easily access it. In this work, we have used WordNet as a knowledge repository but our approach is generic and can be applied with any other knowledge graph.

WordNet (Fellbaum, 1998) primarily consists of *synsets*, i.e., a set of synonyms of words. The *synsets* which refer to the same concept are grouped together giving it a thesaurus-like structure. Each *synset* consists of its definition and small example showing its use in a sentence. The *synsets* are connected with different relations such as synonymy, antonymy, hypernymy, hyponymy, meronymy, etc. In addition to the semantic knowledge, it also includes a bit of common sense knowledge such as real world entities like cities, countries and famous people. However, WordNet stores this knowledge as a database in its basic form, so a graph is constructed based on WordNet for further use. Subsequently, the node embeddings learned on this graph will automatically capture the semantic information associated with the senses.

We briefly discuss different WordNet node embedding algorithms used in our study. We use random walk and neural language model based embeddings (Goikoetxea et al., 2015), matrix factorization based WordNet embeddings (Saedi et al., 2018) and graph-similarity based path2vec (Kutuzov et al., 2019) embeddings. The important distinction between these methods is that the first two algorithms (Goikoetxea et al., 2015, Saedi et al., 2018) produce word embeddings and path2vec produces embeddings corresponding to each sense present in WordNet. The path2vec algorithm naturally encodes WordNet nodes as it actually produces embeddings for senses as opposed to (Goikoetxea et al., 2015, Saedi et al., 2018) algorithms as they conflate all the senses to produce word embeddings instead of generating embeddings for each sense while losing some finer semantic information in the process.

The approach proposed by (Goikoetxea et al., 2015) is based on the well-known neural language model Continuous Bag of Words and Skip-gram (Mikolov et al., 2013b). The main idea is to produce artificial sentences from WordNet and to apply the language models on these sentences to produce word embeddings. For this, they perform random walk starting at any arbitrary vertex in WordNet, then map each WordNet sense to the corresponding word to produce an artificial sentence. Each random walk produces a sentence, repeating this process several times gives a collection of sentences. Finally, this collection of sentences is considered as the corpus for learning word embeddings.

A different approach based on matrix factorization is taken in (Saedi et al., 2018) to produce embeddings. The procedure starts by creating the adjacency matrix M from WordNet graph. The element

M_{ij} in the matrix M is set to 1 if there exists any relation between words w_i and w_j. [2] Furthermore, words which are not connected directly but via other nodes should also have an entry in the matrix, albeit with lower weights than 1. Accordingly, matrix M_G is constructed to get the overall affinity strength between words. In the analytical formulation, M_G can be constructed from the adjacency matrix M as $M_G = (I - \alpha M)^{-1}$ where I is the identity matrix and $0 < \alpha < 1$ decay factor to control the effect of longer paths over shorter ones. Following that, matrix M_G is normalized to reduce the bias towards words which have more number of senses and finally a Principal Component Analysis is applied to get vectors.

The `path2vec` (Kutuzov et al., 2019) learns embeddings based on a pairwise similarity between nodes. The fundamental concept is that pairwise similarity between nodes of the graph should remain the same after their projection in the vector space. The model is flexible enough to consider any user-defined similarity measure while encoding. The objective function is designed to produce such embeddings for nodes which reduce the difference between actual graph-based pairwise similarity and vector similarity. It also preserves the similarity between adjacent nodes. Formally, for the graph $G = (V, E)$ where V, E denote a set of vertices and edges, respectively, the objective is —

$$\sum_{(a,b)\in\mathcal{V}} \min_{\mathbf{v}_a, \mathbf{v}_b} \left((\mathbf{v}_a^T \mathbf{v}_b - s(a,b))^2 - \alpha(\mathbf{v}_a^T \mathbf{v}_n + \mathbf{v}_b^T \mathbf{v}_m) \right)$$

where n, m are adjacent nodes of nodes a, b respectively, $s(a, b)$ is the user-defined similarity measure between a, b and $\mathbf{v}_a, \mathbf{v}_b, \mathbf{v}_n, \mathbf{v}_m$ denote the embeddings of a, b, n, m, respectively. To show the ability of their model in adapting to different pairwise similarity measures.

Mention normalization. The first step for being able to align a mention with a particular node in the knowledge base and ultimately its graph embedding, is to convert the mention into a normalized form that can be easily matched. Consider mentions like *the wall, one employee, beautiful lady* or *the famous scientist Einstein*; none of these can be directly matched to a knowledge graph node (in this case WordNet synset [3]). We propose to normalize them into a single word, respectively to *wall, employee, lady* and *Einstein*. We design simple rules to normalize mentions. For this, as a first step, we remove articles and commonly used quantifiers like *the, a, an, one, all* etc. from the mention. If we find an entry in the knowledge graph with this modified word then we get the corresponding embedding, otherwise, we go a step further and extract the *head* of the mention and try to obtain embeddings for it. Specifically, we use the parsed tree of the mention and Collins' head finder algorithm (Collins, 2003) to get the head.

Absence of Knowledge. Even after mention normalization, it might still be possible that a mention cannot be aligned with a node in the knowledge graph, simply because some entities are not present therein. This leads to the unavailability of the corresponding node embeddings. We use zero vector of the same dimensions to resolve these cases where node embeddings are absent.

Sense disambiguation The knowledge graph may contain multiple concepts or senses for a given entity. This is the case in all the knowledge graphs. The reason is that the same word has many senses or refer to different real world entities. For example, the word *bank* can refer to *a financial institution* or *the land alongside the river*, the entity *Michael Jordan* can refer to *the scientist* or *the basketball player*. Due to this ambiguity, there are multiple node embeddings for the same mention as they capture entirely different concepts [4]. However, recognizing the correct sense is crucial to get accurate embedding. We explore two simple heuristics to tackle the issue of multiple senses of an entity — 1. *Lesk* (Lesk, 1986) algorithm to get the correct sense of the mention depending on the context. 2. Unweighted average over embeddings of all the senses of the mention.

4 Ranking Model

Let $\mathcal{D}$ be the given document containing $\mathcal{M} = \{m_1, m_2, \cdots, m_{n_m}\}$, n_m number of mentions. Let $\mathcal{A} = \{a_1, a_2, \cdots, a_{n_a}\}$ denote the set of all anaphors and $\mathcal{A} \subset \mathcal{M}$. Let a be any anaphor in the set $\mathcal{A}$

---

[2] They also experimented by weighting relations differently (e.g. 1 for hypernymy, hyponymy, antonymy and synonymy, 0.8 for meronymy and holonymy and 0.5 for others) but obtained the best results without weighting.

[3] In case of WordNet embeddings from (Goikoetxea et al., 2015, Saedi et al., 2018), normalized mention is mapped to words.

[4] This difficulty does not arise in the cases where embeddings are learned for words instead of senses (Goikoetxea et al., 2015, Saedi et al., 2018). But, the problem is prevalent for node embeddings learned for actual nodes of the graph.

and j be its position in the set $\mathcal{M}$, then E_a be the set of candidate antecedents for a which is defined as $E_a = \{m_i : m_i \in \mathcal{M}, i < j\}$. Let T_a and F_a be the set of true antecedents and false candidate antecedents of a such that $T_a \cup F_a = E_a, T_a \cap F_a = \emptyset$. Let each anaphor a is represented with the feature vector v_a and candidate antecedent e represented with v_e where $e \in E_a$. Then the goal is to predict score $s(v_a, v_e)$ between anaphor a and candidate antecedent e. The score denotes the possibility of anaphor a having bridging relation with the candidate antecedent e, so a higher score denotes a higher chance of e being true antecedent.

The model is trained to reduce the ranking loss calculated based on the scores obtained between anaphor-candidate antecedents. The ranking strategy is fairly obvious $-$ for an anaphor a high scoring candidate antecedent from E_a is ranked higher than the low scoring one. Let this prediction ranking strategy be r' and true ranking is given by r^*. For a candidate antecedent, if predicted rank is not the same as true rank then it is called discordant candidate, otherwise concordant. The difference between true and predicted ranking strategy can be measured with Kendall's rank correlation coefficient $- \tau$. Formally, concordant C, discordant D candidates and τ are calculated as $-$

$$C = \sum_{(t,f) \in (T_a \times F_a)} \mathbb{I}_{s(v_a,v_t) > s(v_a,v_f)} \ , \quad D = |T_a \times F_a| - C \quad and \quad \tau(r^*, r') = \frac{C - D}{C + D}$$

where $\mathbb{I}$ is an indicator function which takes value 1 if $s(v_a, v_t) > s(v_a, v_f)$ else 0 and $|\cdot|$ denotes cardinality of the set. The empirical ranking loss (Joachims, 2002) captures the number of wrongly predicted ranks which is given as $-$

$$\mathcal{L} = \frac{1}{n_a} \sum_{i=1}^{n_a} -\tau(r_i^*, r_i')$$

Inference We consider all the anaphors in the test document separately. For each anaphor, we consider all previously occurring mentions as candidate antecedents [5] and find out the compatibility score for each anaphor-candidate antecedent pair with the above ranking model. We apply best first strategy to choose the most appropriate antecedent from the list of candidate antecedents. In this strategy, the highest scoring pair is selected as anaphor-antecedent pair. Formally, let a be any anaphor and E_a denote a set of candidate antecedents for a. Let $s(a, e)$ be the score between a and e where $e \in E_a$. Let $\hat{e}_a$ be the predicted antecedent of a which is given by - $\hat{e}_a = argmax_{e \in E_a} s(a, e)$

5 Experimental Setup

Data We used ISNotes (Markert et al., 2012) and BASHI (Rösiger, 2018) datasets for experiments. ISNotes and BASHI consist of 50 different OntoNotes documents, containing 663 and 459 anaphors, respectively. BASHI dataset annotates *comparative* anaphors as bridging anaphors which are 115 in numbers, remaining are *referential* anaphors. Following the setup from (Hou, 2020), we only consider 344 referential bridging anaphors in this work as well from the BASHI dataset. In the experiments, we implemented nested cross-validation to select the best hyperparameter combination. The setup is $-$ first we make 10 sets of train and test documents containing 45 and 5 documents respectively with 10-fold division. Then at each fold, 45 training documents are further divided into 5 sets of 36-9 actual training and development documents. Each hyperparameter combination is trained on these 5-sets and evaluated. The highest averaged accuracy over the 5-sets of development documents gives the best hyperparameter combination. Once the best hyperparameter setting is obtained the SVM model is re-trained over 45 documents (36+9). For each fold number of accurately linked anaphors is calculated. The accurately predicted number of anaphors over each fold is added to get the total number of accurately linked anaphors from the complete dataset. Thus, the system is evaluated by the accuracy of predicted pairs (Hou, 2020).

For the training data, we have positive samples where we know true anaphor-antecedent pairs but no negative samples. We generate these pairs by considering all the noun phrases (NPs) which occur

---

[5]In ISNotes dataset 71% of anaphors have antecedent either in the previous two sentences or the first sentence of the document. So, mentions only from the previous two sentences and the first sentence are considered as candidate antecedents. We apply the same strategy for BASHI dataset as well.

Data	Our Experiments						SOTA	
	WV	GV	BE	EP	BEP	−	SYS	ACC
ISNotes								
−	25.94	27.60	<u>32.87</u>	31.08	37.10	-	PMIII	36.35
+ PL	26.40	28.61	34.39	31.81	43.87*	20.06	MMII	41.32
+ PA	24.74	30.92	33.18	33.24	39.82*	19.53	EB	39.52
+ RW	27.75	27.6	34.12	33.24	**46.30***	22.06	MMEB	46.46
+ WNV	21.71	25.13	31.69	26.80	33.28	17.64	BARQA	50.08
BASHI								
−	22.92	17.48	<u>31.23</u>	28.51	33.52	-	PMIII	-
+ PL	30.95	21.49	35.53	29.26	36.68*	16.44	MMII	-
+ PA	24.07	19.2	35.24	29.48	**38.94***	17.62	EB	29.94
+ RW	26.64	18.91	34.38	28.91	38.83*	15.75	MMEB	-
+ WNV	20.92	18.05	26.36	21.20	27.80	12.97	BARQA	38.66

Table 1: Results of our experiments and state-of-the-art models over two datasets – ISNotes and BASHI. In our experiments section, we present results for different text-based embeddings – word2vec (WV), glove (GV), BERT (BE), embeddings_pp (EP), BERT + embeddings_pp (BEP) and the last column – shows the absence of text-based embeddings. Also, in each row, WordNet node embeddings based on different algorithms, except the first row, are added – path2vec with Lesk (PL), path2vec with averaged senses (PA), random walk based (RW) and WordNet embeddings (WNV). The other section of the table – SOTA, shows results with previously proposed systems – Pairwise Model III (PMIII), MLN model II (MMII) (Hou et al., 2013), embeddings_bridging (EB) (Hou, 2018a), the combination of embeddings_bridging and MLN model (MMEB) and the latest system, BARQA (Hou, 2020). The results with ∗ are statistically signficant in comparison to the results based only on text embeddings with p-value $< 10^{-4}$ with McNemar's test and Wilcoxon signed-rank test.

before the anaphor in the window of some fixed number of sentences. All the mention pairs which do not hold bridging relations are considered as negative samples for training. Similarly at the test time, for an anaphor, all the previous mentions in the fixed window size are considered as candidate antecedents.

Implementation We obtained pre-trained word2vec (Mikolov et al., 2013a), Glove (Pennington et al., 2014), BERT (Devlin et al., 2018) and embeddings_pp (Hou, 2018b) embeddings. We used spanBERT (Joshi et al., 2020) embeddings in our experiments as it gave better results in (Hou, 2020). Also, we used pre-trained WordNet embeddings provided by respective authors of (Goikoetxea et al., 2015, Saedi et al., 2018, Kutuzov et al., 2019). In the case of path2vec (Kutuzov et al., 2019), embeddings learned with different similarity measures such as – Leacock-Chodorow similarities (Leacock and Chodorow, 1998); Jiang-Conrath similarities (Jiang and Conrath, 1997); Wu-Palmer similarities (Wu and Palmer, 1994); and Shortest path similarities (Lebichot et al., 2018), are provided. We experimented with all the four similarity measures and found out that the shortest path based similarity measure produced better results most of the time, so we have used those embeddings in our experiments. We used python implementation of *Lesk* algorithm from *nltk*[6] library to select the best sense from multiple senses of the mention. Two sentences previous to mention and two sentences after the mention, including the sentence in which the mention occurs, are given to this algorithm as a context for a mention.

Both anaphor and candidate antecedent's embeddings are obtained as mentioned above, afterwards, element-wise product of these vectors is provided to the ranking SVM. We also did preliminary experiments with the concatenation of the vectors but element-wise product gave better results. We used SVM^{rank} (Joachims, 2006) implementation for our experiments. In the experiments with SVM, we did grid search over C = 0.001,0.01,0.1,1, 10,100 with the use of *linear* kernel. We also use *random fourier features (rff)* trick proposed by (Rahimi and Recht, 2008) to approximate non-linear kernels. We found, use of non-linear kernels slightly improved results in comparison to linear kernels so reported only those

---

[6] https://www.nltk.org/_modules/nltk/wsd.html

results. We also varied different widow sizes of sentences — 2,3,4 and all previous sentences, in addition to NPs from the first sentence (salience), to get candidate antecedents for an anaphor. Out of these settings, the window size of 2 and salience have yielded the best results which are reported here.

6 Results

Comparison between distributional and graph embeddings is shown in Table 1 in our experiments section. The first row corresponding to ISNotes and BASHI dataset shows results with only text-based embeddings. We observe that on both the datasets the best performance is obtained with the use of BERT embeddings showing the efficacy of these embeddings when only one type of text-based embeddings is used. It shows that the context of the mention plays important role in resolving bridging anaphora. The second best scores are obtained with embeddings_pp which are specially designed embeddings for the task. We also observe further improvement in the results when two best performing text-based embeddings — BERT and embeddings_pp are combined (noted as BEP in the Table)[7].

The following rows (2-4) of Table 1 show the results obtained with the addition of WordNet information with different embeddings algorithms — path2vec (Kutuzov et al., 2019)(PL and PA), random walk based embeddings (Goikoetxea et al., 2015) (RW) and WordNet embeddings (Saedi et al., 2018)(WNV). The results from these rows in comparison with the result from the first row prove the effectiveness of the external information and substantiates our claims [8]. Interestingly, it also shows that BERT though trained on a huge unlabelled corpus is not inherently efficient at capturing common sense knowledge required for bridging anaphora resolution. Though, it has been competitive at capturing relational knowledge required for other nlp tasks like question answering (Petroni et al., 2019). Moreover, external information seems to be complementing embeddings_pp embeddings which are custom tailored for bridging tasks, further consolidating our claims. We compare results from path2vec Lesk (PL) with path2vec average (PA) to see which strategy of disambiguation is effective. But the observations are not conclusive, as in some cases performance with the use of averaging strategy is better than choosing the best sense with Lesk. The reason is that Lesk is a naive algorithm which considers overlapping words in the context to get the best sense. Further, in each row of the second last column of the table, results obtained by combining external information with BERT embeddings and embeddings_pp show that even the best performing text-based embeddings can still benefit from the external information.

Comparison between different WordNet embeddings We first examine the effectiveness of external knowledge without any text-based embeddings. These scores are noted in the last column of our experiments section against each WordNet graph node embeddings. The lower scores in this column in comparison with text-based embeddings reveal that the features learned with WordNet embeddings are not sufficient and should be complemented with the contextual features. This observation further substantiates our observation of higher scores with BERT embeddings showing the importance of context (Table 1, the first row). Further, we consider results from averaged embedding over senses (PA) for comparing path2vec with the other two embeddings as it is the closest analogous setting to correlate. This comparison shows, there is no best algorithm amongst these WordNet embeddings as sometimes we get better results with path2vec and sometimes with random walk based embeddings. This result is surprising as even after losing some semantic information, RW produces competent results compared to path2vec. This might be happening because of errors in sense disambiguation with path2vec.

Comparison with previous studies The results of different state-of-the-art systems on both the datasets are presented in SOTA section of Table 1. These results are obtained from Hou's latest work (Hou, 2020). In BARQA (Hou, 2020), mentions are also detected in her model, so we considered results where gold mentions are considered for the equal comparison. We observe that, on ISNotes dataset, our model's performance is better than rule-based approaches from Pairwise Model III and MLN model II (Hou et al., 2013), embeddings_bridging based deterministic approach from (Hou, 2018a) and competitive

---

[7]We combine BERT and embeddings_pp embeddings by concatenating both the vectors

[8]Except with the addition of WordNet embeddings (WNV) as results with WNV are mostly inferior in comparison with only text-based embeddings. Lower coverage for WNV, around 65% as opposed to 90% for the other two embeddings as only 60,000 words were present in pre-trained WNV embeddings, might be the possible reason. Also, the vector dimension is significantly higher — 850 in comparison to 300 for the other two.

Mention Mapping Error		Mention Sense Selection	
Mention	Normalized Mention	Mention	Selected Sense
Los Angeles, Cali.	Angeles	[...] future generations of memory **chips**	electronic equipment
Hong Kong	Kong	The move by the coalition of political **parties** [...]	organization
U.S.S.R	U.S.S.R	[...] when the rising Orange River threatened to swamp the **course** [...]	route
IBM	IBM	[...] U.S. industry to head off **the Japanese**, who now dominate [...]	language
politburo member Joachim Herrman	Herrman	[...] potential investors at race **tracks** [...]	magnetic paths
U.S. district judge Jack B. Weinstein	Weinstein	The Thoroughbred Owners and Breeders **Association** [...]	a group of organisms

Table 2: **Mention Mapping Error** lists examples of mentions for which no entry is found in WordNet after normalization. The first three mentions are not found because of normalization error but the next three entities are not present in WordNet. **Mention Sense Selection** notes a few mentions and their senses selected by Lesk algorithm. For the first three mentions, Lesk disambiguates correctly but fails in the next three. The correct senses of the last three are *Japanese people*, *racecourse* and *organization*, respectively.

in comparison with the combination of MLN model and embeddings_bridging but lags to BARQA model. The reason might be that MLN model combines hand-crafted rules in addition to carefully crafted embeddings. On the other hand, BARQA system is trained on additional data obtained by forming quasi-bridging pairs. However, with BASHI dataset we observe best results, as the model achieves significant gains in comparison with embeddings_bridging and moderate gains against BARQA.

7 Error Analysis

7.1 Mention normalization and sense disambiguation

ISNotes dataset contains 663 anaphors and combining those with candidate antecedents of each anaphor we get more than 9500 mentions out of which 10% of mentions can not be mapped to WordNet entries. The situation is similar in the case of BASHI dataset as around 8% of the 5933 mentions can not be mapped to WordNet entries.

We analyze cases where normalized mention is failed to map to any sense in WordNet. There are broadly two reasons for not getting WordNet entry for the mention — 1. Normalization error 2. Inherent limitations of WordNet. We note down some of the examples from each category in the Table 2. The first three mentions are wrongly normalized as Los Angeles to Angeles and Hong Kong to Kong, otherwise, both the cities are present in WordNet. The cases like U.S.S.R shows limitations of our simple normalization approach, the normalization should map U.S.S.R to Soviet Russia which is present in WordNet. The other three examples show the inherent limitations of WordNet as those entities are absent from WordNet.

WordNet contains multiple senses for a given word because of which we get on an average 7 senses for the given mention. We used a simple *Lesk* algorithm for disambiguation which takes into account the context of the normalized mention to determine the correct sense. We present some examples of disambiguation with Lesk in Table 2. It correctly disambiguates in the first three examples but fails for the following three. This is because of the count of overlapping words between sense's context and definition in WordNet. For example, the last example contains words like blood, breeder in the context because of which it selects sense as *a group of organisms* and not an *organization*.

7.2 Anaphor-antecedent predictions

We analyze a few anaphor-antecedent pairs which were identified incorrectly with BERT-based mention representation but with the addition of WordNet information, we were able to correct it. The underlined and bold lettered phrases denote antecedent and anaphor, respectively.

(1). Staar Surgical Co.'s board said that it has removed Thomas R. Waggoner [...]. [..] that John R. Ford resigned as **a director**, and that Mr. Wolf was named a member of the board.

(2). So far this year, rising demand for OPEC oil and production restraint by some members have kept **prices** firm despite rampant cheating by others.

(3). One building was upgraded to red status while people were taking things out, and a resident who was not allowed to go back inside called up **the stairs** to his girlfriend, telling her to keep [...].

WordNet contains relations where *company* and *director* are related where director works at company. The *OPEC oil* is stored as a corporation which in turn is related to *prices* and *stairs* are part of *building*. This information is present in WordNet which has been used for resolving these pairs as opposed to relying only on the textual information in case of mention representation only with BERT.

Conversely, we also observed a few pairs where the addition of extra information has been detrimental. The italic faced phrase is the selected antecedent with WordNet based system but without WordNet correct antecedent (shown with underline) was selected for boldfaced anaphor.

(4).Within the same nine months, *News Corp.* [...]. Meanwhile, American Health Partners, publisher of American Health magazine, is deep in debt, and Owen Lipstein, **founder**[...].

(5)[...]   *the magnificent dunes where the Namib Desert meets the Atlantic Ocean* [...]Since this treasure chest [...] up a diamond from **the sand**.

(6).The space shuttle Atlantis landed [...] that dispatched *the Jupiter - bound Galileo space probe.* **The five astronauts** returned [...].

Example 4, *News Corporation* is closer to **founder** than Partners as head word is Partners for the long phrase. Thus, the system assigns higher scores to wrong candidate antecedent. Similarly, in example 5, the *dunes* are closer to **sand** than treasure chest. In the example 6, WordNet contains Atalantis as legendary island and not as a space shuttle thus **astronauts** is closer to space probe than island, thus receiving a higher score than the correct antecedent. These mistakes can be attributed to the process of normalizing mentions as well as limitations of WordNet. Interestingly, these examples show the inadequacy of BERT in capturing the *partOf* relation but efficacy of capturing some form of relatedness of the terms.

8   Conclusion

We presented a simple approach of incorporating external semantic knowledge for bridging anaphora resolution. We combined contextual embeddings learned only on the text with the knowledge graph node embeddings. We establish the potency of knowledge graph embeddings with the experiments with the use of different WordNet graph embeddings on the ISNotes and BASHI datasets. Though we apply a simplistic approach to solve mention normalization, absent knowledge resolution and sense disambiguation to obtain node embeddings, we achieve competitive results on both the datasets. Moreover, this study opens up further investigation into the design of sophisticated methods to incorporate knowledge graph embeddings for bridging anaphora resolution such as improved mention normalization and sense disambiguation, incorporating knowledge from multiple knowledge sources.

Acknowledgements

We thank the three anonymous reviewers for their comments and feedback. This work was supported by the French National Research Agency via grant no ANR-16-CE33-0011-01 as well as by CPER Nord-Pas de Calais/FEDER DATA Advanced data science and technologies 2015-2020.

References

Trapit Bansal, Da-Cheng Juan, Sujith Ravi, and Andrew McCallum. 2019. A2N: Attending to neighbors for knowledge graph inference. In *Proceedings of the 57th Annual Meeting of the Association for Computational Linguistics*, pages 4387–4392, Florence, Italy, July. Association for Computational Linguistics.

Herbert H. Clark. 1975. Bridging. In *Theoretical Issues in Natural Language Processing*.

Michael Collins. 2003. Head-driven statistical models for natural language parsing. *Computational Linguistics*, 29(4):589–637.

Jacob Devlin, Ming-Wei Chang, Kenton Lee, and Kristina Toutanova. 2018. Bert: Pre-training of deep bidirectional transformers for language understanding. *arXiv preprint arXiv:1810.04805*.

Christiane Fellbaum. 1998. *WordNet: An Electronic Lexical Database*. Bradford Books.

Josu Goikoetxea, Aitor Soroa, and Eneko Agirre. 2015. Random walks and neural network language models on knowledge bases. In *Proceedings of the 2015 Conference of the North American Chapter of the Association for Computational Linguistics: Human Language Technologies*, pages 1434–1439, Denver, Colorado, May–June. Association for Computational Linguistics.

William L. Hamilton, Rex Ying, and Jure Leskovec. 2017. Representation learning on graphs: Methods and applications. cite arxiv:1709.05584Comment: Published in the IEEE Data Engineering Bulletin, September 2017; version with minor corrections.

Yufang Hou, Katja Markert, and Michael Strube. 2013. Global inference for bridging anaphora resolution. In *Proceedings of the 2013 Conference of the North American Chapter of the Association for Computational Linguistics: Human Language Technologies*, pages 907–917, Atlanta, Georgia, June. Association for Computational Linguistics.

Yufang Hou, Katja Markert, and Michael Strube. 2014. A rule-based system for unrestricted bridging resolution: Recognizing bridging anaphora and finding links to antecedents. In *Proceedings of the 2014 Conference on Empirical Methods in Natural Language Processing (EMNLP)*, pages 2082–2093, Doha, Qatar, October. Association for Computational Linguistics.

Yufang Hou. 2018a. A deterministic algorithm for bridging anaphora resolution. In *Proceedings of the 2018 Conference on Empirical Methods in Natural Language Processing*, pages 1938–1948, Brussels, Belgium, October-November. Association for Computational Linguistics.

Yufang Hou. 2018b. Enhanced word representations for bridging anaphora resolution. In *Proceedings of the 2018 Conference of the North American Chapter of the Association for Computational Linguistics: Human Language Technologies, Volume 2 (Short Papers)*, pages 1–7, New Orleans, Louisiana, June. Association for Computational Linguistics.

Yufang Hou. 2020. Bridging anaphora resolution as question answering. In *Proceedings of the 58th Annual Meeting of the Association for Computational Linguistics*, pages 1428–1438, Online, July. Association for Computational Linguistics.

Jay J. Jiang and David W. Conrath. 1997. Semantic similarity based on corpus statistics and lexical taxonomy. In *Proceedings of the 10th Research on Computational Linguistics International Conference*, pages 19–33, Taipei, Taiwan, August. The Association for Computational Linguistics and Chinese Language Processing (ACLCLP).

Thorsten Joachims. 2002. Optimizing search engines using clickthrough data. In *Proceedings of the Eighth ACM SIGKDD International Conference on Knowledge Discovery and Data Mining*, KDD 02, page 133142, New York, NY, USA. Association for Computing Machinery.

Thorsten Joachims. 2006. Training linear svms in linear time. In *Proceedings of the 12th ACM SIGKDD International Conference on Knowledge Discovery and Data Mining*, KDD 06, page 217226, New York, NY, USA. Association for Computing Machinery.

Mandar Joshi, Danqi Chen, Yinhan Liu, Daniel S. Weld, Luke Zettlemoyer, and Omer Levy. 2020. Spanbert: Improving pre-training by representing and predicting spans. *Transactions of the Association for Computational Linguistics*, 8:64–77.

Andrey Kutuzov, Mohammad Dorgham, Oleksiy Oliynyk, Chris Biemann, and Alexander Panchenko. 2019. Learning graph embeddings from WordNet-based similarity measures. In *Proceedings of the Eighth Joint Conference on Lexical and Computational Semantics (*SEM 2019)*, pages 125–135, Minneapolis, Minnesota, June. Association for Computational Linguistics.

Emmanuel Lassalle and Pascal Denis. 2011. Leveraging different meronym discovery methods for bridging resolution in french. In Iris Hendrickx, Sobha Lalitha Devi, António Horta Branco, and Ruslan Mitkov, editors, *Anaphora Processing and Applications - 8th Discourse Anaphora and Anaphor Resolution Colloquium, DAARC 2011, Faro, Portugal, October 6-7, 2011. Revised Selected Papers*, volume 7099 of *Lecture Notes in Computer Science*, pages 35–46. Springer.

Claudia Leacock and Martin Chodorow, 1998. *Combining Local Context and WordNet Similarity for Word Sense Identification*, volume 49, pages 265–. 01.

Bertrand Lebichot, Guillaume Guex, Ilkka Kivimäki, and Marco Saerens. 2018. A constrained randomized shortest-paths framework for optimal exploration. *CoRR*, abs/1807.04551.

Jens Lehmann, Robert Isele, Max Jakob, A. Jentzsch, D. Kontokostas, Pablo N. Mendes, S. Hellmann, M. Morsey, Patrick van Kleef, S. Auer, and C. Bizer. 2015. Dbpedia - a large-scale, multilingual knowledge base extracted from wikipedia. *Semantic Web*, 6:167–195.

Michael Lesk. 1986. Automatic sense disambiguation using machine readable dictionaries: How to tell a pine cone from an ice cream cone. In *Proceedings of the 5th Annual International Conference on Systems Documentation*, SIGDOC 86, page 2426, New York, NY, USA. Association for Computing Machinery.

Katja Markert, Yufang Hou, and Michael Strube. 2012. Collective classification for fine-grained information status. In *Proceedings of the 50th Annual Meeting of the Association for Computational Linguistics (Volume 1: Long Papers)*, pages 795–804, Jeju Island, Korea, July. Association for Computational Linguistics.

Tomas Mikolov, Kai Chen, Greg S. Corrado, and Jeffrey Dean. 2013a. Efficient estimation of word representations in vector space.

Tomas Mikolov, Wen-tau Yih, and Geoffrey Zweig. 2013b. Linguistic regularities in continuous space word representations. In *Proceedings of the 2013 Conference of the North American Chapter of the Association for Computational Linguistics: Human Language Technologies*, pages 746–751, Atlanta, Georgia, June. Association for Computational Linguistics.

Deepak Nathani, Jatin Chauhan, Charu Sharma, and Manohar Kaul. 2019. Learning attention-based embeddings for relation prediction in knowledge graphs. In *Proceedings of the 57th Annual Meeting of the Association for Computational Linguistics*, pages 4710–4723, Florence, Italy, July. Association for Computational Linguistics.

Maximilian Nickel, Volker Tresp, and Hans-Peter Kriegel. 2011. A three-way model for collective learning on multi-relational data. In *Proceedings of the 28th International Conference on International Conference on Machine Learning*, ICML11, page 809816, Madison, WI, USA. Omnipress.

Maximilian Nickel, Lorenzo Rosasco, and Tomaso Poggio. 2016. Holographic embeddings of knowledge graphs. In *Proceedings of the Thirtieth AAAI Conference on Artificial Intelligence*, AAAI16, page 19551961. AAAI Press.

Jeffrey Pennington, Richard Socher, and Christopher Manning. 2014. Glove: Global vectors for word representation. In *Proceedings of the 2014 Conference on Empirical Methods in Natural Language Processing (EMNLP)*, pages 1532–1543, Doha, Qatar, October. Association for Computational Linguistics.

Matthew E. Peters, Mark Neumann, Robert L. Logan IV, Roy Schwartz, Vidur Joshi, Sameer Singh, and Noah A. Smith. 2019. Knowledge enhanced contextual word representations.

Fabio Petroni, Tim Rocktäschel, Sebastian Riedel, Patrick Lewis, Anton Bakhtin, Yuxiang Wu, and Alexander Miller. 2019. Language models as knowledge bases? In *Proceedings of the 2019 Conference on Empirical Methods in Natural Language Processing and the 9th International Joint Conference on Natural Language Processing (EMNLP-IJCNLP)*, pages 2463–2473, Hong Kong, China, November. Association for Computational Linguistics.

Massimo Poesio and Renata Vieira. 1998. A corpus-based investigation of definite description use. *Computational Linguistics*, 24(2):183–216.

Massimo Poesio, Renata Vieira, and Simone Teufel. 1997. Resolving bridging references in unrestricted text. In *Operational Factors in Practical, Robust Anaphora Resolution for Unrestricted Texts*.

Massimo Poesio, Rahul Mehta, Axel Maroudas, and Janet Hitzeman. 2004. Learning to resolve bridging references. In *Proceedings of the 42nd Annual Meeting of the Association for Computational Linguistics (ACL-04)*, pages 143–150, Barcelona, Spain, July.

Ali Rahimi and Benjamin Recht. 2008. Random features for large-scale kernel machines. In J. C. Platt, D. Koller, Y. Singer, and S. T. Roweis, editors, *Advances in Neural Information Processing Systems 20*, pages 1177–1184. Curran Associates, Inc.

Altaf Rahman and Vincent Ng. 2009. Supervised models for coreference resolution. In *Proceedings of the 2009 Conference on Empirical Methods in Natural Language Processing*, pages 968–977, Singapore, August. Association for Computational Linguistics.

Ina Roesiger, Maximilian Köper, Kim Anh Nguyen, and Sabine Schulte im Walde. 2018. Integrating predictions from neural-network relation classifiers into coreference and bridging resolution. In *Proceedings of the First Workshop on Computational Models of Reference, Anaphora and Coreference*, pages 44–49, New Orleans, Louisiana, June. Association for Computational Linguistics.

Ina Rösiger. 2018. BASHI: A corpus of wall street journal articles annotated with bridging links. In *Proceedings of the Eleventh International Conference on Language Resources and Evaluation (LREC 2018)*, Miyazaki, Japan, May. European Language Resources Association (ELRA).

Chakaveh Saedi, António Branco, João António Rodrigues, and João Silva. 2018. WordNet embeddings. In *Proceedings of The Third Workshop on Representation Learning for NLP*, pages 122–131, Melbourne, Australia, July. Association for Computational Linguistics.

Özge Sevgili, Alexander Panchenko, and Chris Biemann. 2019. Improving neural entity disambiguation with graph embeddings. In *Proceedings of the 57th Annual Meeting of the Association for Computational Linguistics: Student Research Workshop*, pages 315–322, Florence, Italy, July. Association for Computational Linguistics.

Soumya Sharma, Bishal Santra, Abhik Jana, Santosh Tokala, Niloy Ganguly, and Pawan Goyal. 2019. Incorporating domain knowledge into medical NLI using knowledge graphs. In *Proceedings of the 2019 Conference on Empirical Methods in Natural Language Processing and the 9th International Joint Conference on Natural Language Processing (EMNLP-IJCNLP)*, pages 6092–6097, Hong Kong, China, November. Association for Computational Linguistics.

Candace L. Sidner. 1979. *Towards a computational theory of definite anaphora comprehension in English discourse*. Ph.D. thesis, Massachusetts Institute of Technology, Cambridge, MA, USA.

Tho Trouillon, Johannes Welbl, Sebastian Riedel, ric Gaussier, and Guillaume Bouchard. 2016. Complex embeddings for simple link prediction.

Olga Uryupina, Ron Artstein, Antonella Bristot, Federica Cavicchio, Francesca Delogu, Kepa J. Rodriguez, and Massimo Poesio. 2019. Annotating a broad range of anaphoric phenomena, in a variety of genres: The arrau corpus. *Natural Language Engineering*, pages 1–34, 05.

Zhibiao Wu and Martha Palmer. 1994. Verbs semantics and lexical selection. In *Proceedings of the 32nd Annual Meeting on Association for Computational Linguistics*, ACL 94, page 133138, USA. Association for Computational Linguistics.

Canran Xu and Ruijiang Li. 2019. Relation embedding with dihedral group in knowledge graph. In *Proceedings of the 57th Annual Meeting of the Association for Computational Linguistics*, pages 263–272, Florence, Italy, July. Association for Computational Linguistics.

Bishan Yang, Wen tau Yih, Xiaodong He, Jianfeng Gao, and Li Deng. 2014. Embedding entities and relations for learning and inference in knowledge bases.

Reference to Discourse Topics: Introducing "Global" Shell Nouns

Fabian Simonjetz
Linguistics Department
Ruhr-Universität Bochum
Bochum, Germany
`fabian.simonjetz@rub.de`

Abstract

Shell nouns (SNs) are abstract nouns like *fact*, *issue*, and *decision*, which are capable of referring to non-nominal antecedents, much like anaphoric pronouns. As an extension of classical anaphora resolution, the automatic detection of SNs alongside their respective antecedents has received a growing research interest in recent years but proved to be a challenging task. This paper critically examines the assumption prevalent in previous research that SNs are typically accompanied by a specific antecedent, arguing that SNs like *issue* and *decision* are frequently used to refer, not to specific antecedents, but to global discourse topics, in which case they are out of reach of previously proposed resolution strategies that are tailored to SNs with explicit antecedents. The contribution of this work is three-fold. First, the notion of global SNs is defined; second, their qualitative and quantitative impact on previous SN research is investigated; and third, implications for previous and future approaches to SN resolution are discussed.

1 Introduction

Traditionally, the primary concern of anaphora resolution (AR) has been the systematic identification of coreference between pronouns and NPs whereas less prototypical forms of anaphoric relations such as bridging anaphora and reference to abstract objects still remain comparatively unexplored (Poesio et al., 2016). One notable exception to this are *shell nouns* (SNs; Schmid, 2000), abstract nouns such as *fact*, *decision*, or *issue*, whose idiosyncratic referring properties have received growing research attention in the last couple of years.

The defining characteristic of SNs lies in their capability to refer to abstract, proposition-like entities usually expressed by non-nominal syntactic constituents such as full sentences (example 1), *that*-clauses (example 2), or infinitive clauses (example 3).[1]

(1)   If the subject prefers to look at one stimulus rather than another we can assume that he has detected a difference between them. **This idea** had a great influence upon the thinking of Schopenhauer who followed up its implications more thoroughly than did Kant.

(2)   It must have seemed clear to him at once that Tolkien was a man of literary genius, and **this fact** only brought home to him his own sense of failure as a writer.

(3)   The Lake District Planning Board has sought to limit new houses to local people, but **this attempt** was overturned by the Secretary of State for the Environment.

The way SNs are interpreted in unison with syntactic clauses from their context bears a striking resemblance to anaphora, and it is this observation that sparked efforts to approach SNs from a computational perspective with the ultimate goal of automatically detecting SNs alongside their respective antecedents. This task – termed *SN resolution* (Kolhatkar, 2015) – is usually approached in the same way as traditional

---

[1]SNs are printed in boldface, and antecedents are underlined. The examples (1–3) are drawn from the British National Corpus (`http://www.natcorp.ox.ac.uk`).

Proceedings of the 3rd Workshop on Computational Models of Reference, Anaphora and Coreference (CRAC 2020), pages 68–78,
Barcelona, Spain (online), December 12, 2020.

AR, i.e., the context of a SN instance is scanned for (non-nominal) antecedent candidates which are then passed to an ML-based ranking algorithm that determines the best match. However, the wide range of syntactic shapes SN antecedents can take on adds significantly to the complexity of the problem which, along with other factors, makes major simplifications necessary so as to make the task more feasible.

Part of the difficulty of quantitative approaches to SNs has been attributed to the existence of so-called "long-distance antecedents" (Kolhatkar, 2015, p. 38). On the grounds of examples like (4–5), Kolhatkar argues that SNs can occur far away from the antecedents they refer to, and accordingly, allows her system to obtain antecedent candidates from up to four sentences preceding the SN instance plus the sentence hosting the SN.

(4)   The sense of a public struggling with a morally difficult issue was dramatically conveyed when the survey asked: "Would you approve or disapprove of someone you know having an abortion?" Thirty-nine percent said they would approve and 32 percent said they would disapprove. But 25 percent more volunteered a response not included in the question: they said their view would depend on the circumstances involved. An additional 5 percent did not know. The lack of a clear majority for either of the unequivocal responses to **this question** may be the best indicator of where public opinion really stands on abortion.

(5)   New York is one of only three states that do not allow some form of audio-visual coverage of court proceedings. Some lawmakers worry that cameras might compromise the rights of the litigants. But a 10-year experiment with courtroom cameras showed that televised access enhanced public understanding of the judicial system without harming the legal process. New York's backwardness on **this issue** hurts public confidence in the judiciary...

Long-distance antecedents do not only make the task of SN resolution significantly more complex while offering only a rather small potential benefit, they are also problematic from a theoretical perspective because they stand in contrast to research on pronominal anaphora that found non-nominal antecedents to be of low salience, and hence, to be accessible for subsequent anaphoric reference for only a limited amount of time. Kolhatkar (2015, p. 38) attributes the seemingly increased anaphoric range of SNs to their richer semantics when compared to pronouns, arguing that the additional information conveyed by the nouns makes it possible for less recent antecedents to be identified. However, this does not seem to fully explain the remarkably long distances reported for some SN instances. For example, Kolhatkar (2015, p. 61) mentions a case where the antecedent occurs six sentences prior to the SN, and the longest distance I am aware of is an instance of the SN *issue* with an (albeit nominal) antecedent eleven sentences back in the data by Simonjetz and Roussel (2016)[2], which raises the question of whether such examples are adequately analyzed as anaphora.

A hint at a possible answer to this question can be found in work by Ariel (1988) who found NPs that refer to *discourse topics* (DTs), i.e., the central entities the discourse is about, to be viable antecedents for subsequent pronominal reference for longer distances than would normally be expected, indicating that DTs are highly accessible even if they have not been mentioned recently. Aside from NPs, DTs can also be expressed by questions or propositions (Watson Todd, 2016), and if it is possible for expressions as semantically unspecific as pronouns to refer to non-local antecedents as long as they correspond to DTs, it seems likely that SNs, which often carry a "topic-like" meaning (e.g., *theory, idea, issue, question*, and – obviously – *topic*), are suitable devices to refer to (propositional) DTs. Thus, the SNs *question* and *issue* in examples (4) and (5) can be taken to refer to the topics their respective discourses are about.

Much unlike the obligatory antecedents of SNs like in examples (1–3), DTs are accessible for anaphoric reference regardless of whether or not they are explicitly realized in the discourse. Even if an adequate description of the DT is present as is the case in examples (4–5), it appears that the marked spans of text lack the direct anaphoric relation present in examples (1–3). Accordingly, we can draw a distinction between

1. *Proper* antecedents that are locally available for immediate reference via a SN or pronoun, and

---

[2]The data is available at https://github.com/ajroussel/shell-nouns-data and the example can be found in turn t_02-06-11_37.

2. *Apparent* antecedents that are merely descriptions of what the SN in question refers to – often, the DT – without standing in a direct anaphoric relation.

As realizations of two distinct underlying processes, topic-referring SNs (henceforth *global SNs*) on the one hand, and SNs with antecedents in their close vicinity (*local SNs*) on the other, have different properties, which renders SN resolution strategies as previously proposed much less, if at all, adequate for the resolution of the former.

The remainder of this paper will specify the details of the implications of this observation, starting with an overview of related work in SN annotation and resolution (Section 2), followed by an examination of the (qualitative and quantitative) impact of global SNs on the tasks of SN annotation and resolution (Section 3). Next, implications for previous and future research are discussed (Section 4) and complemented by some concluding remarks (Section 5).

2 Background

2.1 Schmid's Definition of Shell Nouns

Schmid (1997; 2000; 2018) defines SNs as a class of abstract nouns that feature an "inherent semantic gap" (Schmid, 2018, p. 111) which has to be filled with context-specific information generally represented by non-nominal syntactic units such as *that-* and *to*-clauses, or sentences and longer stretches of the discourse. The central observations underlying the notion of SNs are not new; anaphoric or deictic links between (pro-)nouns and abstract entities have been an area of interest within the linguistic and philosophical literature for more than half a century. Among the plethora of similar notions are *container nouns* (Vendler, 1967), *general nouns* (Halliday and Hasan, 1976), *situation reference* (Fraurud, 1992), *reference to abstract objects* (Asher, 1993), *discourse deixis* (Webber, 1988; Webber, 1991), *carrier nouns* (Ivanič, 1991), *labels* (Francis, 1994), *signalling nouns* (Flowerdew, 2003; Flowerdew and Forest, 2015), *abstract anaphora* (Dipper and Zinsmeister, 2012), *non-nominal antecedent anaphora* (Roussel et al., 2018; Kolhatkar et al., 2018), and others. What is innovative about SNs (and what makes them appealing for computational linguists) is their syntactically driven definition: while related notions largely rely on theoretical and philosophical considerations that are hard to operationalize, SNs are defined by Schmid (2000, p. 3) in terms of a set of syntactic patterns (examples 6–7) which serve as a fairly objective (though not perfect) linguistic test to identify SNs and as templates for corpus queries to automatically gather SNs.

(6) Determiner + (Premodifier) + SN + postnominal *that*-clause, *wh*-clause or *to*-infinitive
The (deplorable) fact that I have no money.

(7) Determiner + (Premodifier) + SN + *be* + complementing *that*-clause, *wh*-clause or *to*-infinitive
The (big) problem was that I had no money.

Schmid (2000) based his considerations about the theoretical and cognitive aspects of SNs on data retrieved from the Cobuild corpus by means of the patterns (6–7). The automatic resolution of SNs, however, has not been attempted until more than a decade later when SNs were recognized as a stepping stone to approach anaphora with non-nominal antecedents.

2.2 Shell Noun Annotation

Prior to implementing automatic SN resolution systems, it is necessary to manually generate gold standard data for the purposes of investigating the properties of SNs as well as establishing a data base for training and testing systems later on. Kolhatkar and Hirst (2012; 2014) and Kolhatkar (2015) explore both crowd-sourcing and expert annotations of the SN *issue* and other nouns in Medline abstracts and New York Times articles. Another expert annotation was published by Simonjetz and Roussel (2016) who present a study of parallel English and German SNs in Europarl data. Occasionally, SNs are annotated as a subset of other forms of anaphora (Poesio and Modjeska, 2002; Poesio and Artstein, 2008; Flowerdew and Forest, 2015), and there is an extensive amount of relevant literature on the annotation and resolution of pronouns with non-nominal antecedents, overviews of which can be found, e.g., in Dipper and Zinsmeister (2010), Roussel et al. (2018), and Kolhatkar et al. (2018).

The manual annotation (and the automatic resolution, for that matter) of SNs broadly consists of three steps:

1. Identification of relevant SN instances

2. Identification of the source sentence hosting the antecedent

3. Identification of the exact antecedent within the source sentence

The first step is relatively straightforward as SNs are a semi-open class, i.e., while an exhaustive list of all SNs would be difficult to compile, there are a few hundred lexemes that are widely used as SNs (Schmid, 2000). Thus, finding relevant SNs in a corpus is for the most part a matter of matching tokens or lemmas with a list of SNs, as carried out by Kolhatkar and colleagues, who look at a number of SN lexemes that occur with an accompanying demonstrative *this* and manually exclude irrelevant instances in postprocessing (Kolhatkar and Hirst, 2012; Kolhatkar et al., 2013; Kolhatkar and Hirst, 2014; Kolhatkar, 2015). A similar approach has been pursued by Simonjetz and Roussel (2016) and Roussel (2018), i.e., an exhaustive annotation of SNs without preselecting specific nouns has not been attempted so far.

After the target nouns have been determined, annotators are instructed to identify the sentence hosting the antecedent of the SN. This step does not pose great practical difficulty either, as preprocessing essentially consists of sentence-splitting the data. Kolhatkar and Hirst (2012) and Simonjetz and Roussel (2016) do not treat the selection of an antecedent source sentence as a separate step, but Kolhatkar et al. (2013), Kolhatkar and Hirst (2014), and Kolhatkar (2015), found higher agreement for this simpler subtask than for the annotation of exact antecedent spans, indicating that annotators will often agree with respect to the approximate location of the antecedent.

The most challenging part of SN resolution is the identification of exact antecedent spans which, accordingly, received the most research attention. While antecedents in traditional anaphora and coreference resolution are for the most part restricted to NPs, SN antecedents can come in a variety of syntactic shapes, are not necessarily continuous, and may even span multiple sentences. As elaborated by Kolhatkar (2015), treating all syntactic constituents as markables is impractical as it would result in a high number of candidates most of which are either very unlikely or overlap significantly with each other, which could cause confusion among annotators. Thus, most previous work opted for allowing free spans of text to be annotated as SN antecedents, resulting in a more straightforward, yet harder to evaluate task.

Due to the lack of a shared set of items to choose from, freely annotated data cannot be evaluated on a binary hit-or-miss basis – reliability metrics need to account for and quantify the degree of overlap between annotators. In wide use are variants of Krippendorff's (unitizing) α (Krippendorff, 2013), chance-corrected reliability coefficients specifically designed for the annotation of free spans of text that have been employed to determine the reliability of SN antecedent annotation, e.g., by Kolhatkar and Hirst (2012), Kolhatkar et al. (2013), Kolhatkar (2015), and Simonjetz and Roussel (2016). Still, the agreement estimates returned by Krippendorff's α and other metrics of inter-annotator agreement are difficult to interpret and an imperfect solution, as they fail to incorporate semantic knowledge which would be desirable for the task of SN resolution. To illustrate, consider example (5), where two annotators could arrive at the same understanding of the SN, yet annotate distinct spans of text, e.g., "audio-visual coverage of court proceedings" versus "courtroom cameras". This would result in a low agreement even though the selected spans of text virtually mean the same thing. Likewise, the very same amount of overlap between two non-identical annotations could either reflect a different interpretation of the SN (if the antecedents describe fundamentally different concepts) or an insignificant difference if, e.g., annotators agree with respect to the core concept but decided to include or dismiss a (possibly lengthy) adjunct.

2.3 Shell Noun Resolution

The first approach to automatically resolve the SN *issue* has been offered by Kolhatkar and Hirst (2012). Their contribution consists of an annotation of instances of *this issue* in Medline abstracts followed by an automatic resolution approach that consists of a candidate extraction and ranking procedure. With the annotation showing reliable results, the candidate ranking model was trained and evaluated based on a range of syntactic and semantic factors as well as the distance between the SN and the candidate. This work was later expanded by Kolhatkar et al. (2013), Kolhatkar and Hirst (2014), and Kolhatkar (2015) in particular, by successively expanding the range of included SN lexemes, increasing the amount of data, and improving the ML-based resolution. On the basis of the findings and data from these studies, at least two more approaches to SN resolution have been published, namely Marasovic et al. (2017), a neural network approach which covers a wider range of SNs, and an approach to resolve German SNs by Roussel (2018).

Even though some progress has been made in the resolution of SNs, the approaches presented to date are still far from a full-fledged, general purpose SN resolution system. Domains are mostly restricted to Medline abstracts and NYT articles, and a number of additional simplifications have been adopted, e.g., by limiting the task to a few SN lexemes. In addition, different studies deal with different subtasks of the resolution. Marasovic et al. (2017), e.g., focus on the identification of the exact antecedent span within the source sentence (step 3 above) and treat the antecedent's source sentence itself as given.

Due to the problems posed by annotating SNs, the open questions regarding best practices to deal with the inherent vagueness of SN usage, the absence of a large-scale, general purpose data set for SNs, and the lack of an agreed upon evaluation metric, a comparison of previous work on SN resolution is difficult (Kolhatkar et al., 2018). The notion of global SNs as shown below may help to partly disentangle this complex picture.

2.4 Discourse Topics

In contrast to the well researched notion of sentence topics, *discourse topics* are a concept without a generally accepted formal definition (Ariel, 1988; Asher, 2004; Watson Todd, 2016). As for many other applications, a "pretheoretical" (Watson Todd, 2016, p. 9) notion of DTs as 'descriptions of what a discourse or discourse section is about' will suffice for our considerations, though.

According to Watson Todd (2016, p. 50), there are three common ways to express DTs, i.e., propositions, questions, and NPs. As SNs generally refer to "proposition-like pieces of information" (Schmid, 2000, p. 4), it appears reasonable to adopt a definition that views DTs as propositions in line with, e.g., the seminal work by Asher (1993) and Asher and Lascarides (2003) in the framework of SDRT. Occasionally, it will be necessary to expand this view to questions, concepts, events, and the like, but the details of the semantic types of SN antecedents are of no concern here and have been subject to detailed examinations elsewhere (Fraurud, 1992; Asher, 1993; Schmid, 2000; Kolhatkar, 2015, and others). For instance, the topics of the discourses in examples (4) and (5) can be informally characterized as a question and as the concept of allowing trials to be filmed, respectively.

Specifying the topic(s) of a given discourse is a challenging task that defies a simple formalization (Watson Todd, 2016). The topics of the examples above are rather straightforward to identify, but this is usually not the case for more complex discourses. That being said, deciding whether or not a given SN is global or local does not require the intended topic to be specified, hence the question of how to approach DTs formally is not of primary concern for this work.

What is important for the argument put forward here is the fact that DTs, though an integral part of discourse structure, are systematically left implicit (Asher and Lascarides, 2003; Asher, 2000; Asher, 2004). This is dramatically illustrated by the Question under Discussion (QUD) view of discourse structure (Roberts, 2012) which models all utterances of a discourse as answers to underlying questions the speaker seeks to address, and while these questions may be explicitly expressed as in example (4), they usually are not. Global SNs then are SNs that refer to DTs for which the presence of an antecedent cannot be presupposed, which renders them principally out of reach of a resolution via a candidate extraction and ranking strategy. Even if an appropriate topic description is available, coincidentally matching descriptions must not be mistaken for proper antecedents as in examples (1–3) (cf. Section 4).

3 Global Shell Nouns

3.1 Global Vs. Local Shell Nouns

In Schmid's (2000) patterns, the constituent subcategorized by the SN functions as syntactically determined antecedent by conveying a proposition that occupies the argument slot inherent in the semantic structure of the SN. As illustrated by the examples (1–3), the SN can alternatively derive its argument from its nearby context, sometimes even across a sentence boundary. What is common to all these cases is that a proposition (or other abstract object) is temporarily salient enough to be available for anaphoric reference and gets immediately picked up by a SN to construct a unified meaning in a classical compositional semantic fashion. In that respect, such *local* SNs follow the same principles as pronouns that refer to non-nominal antecedents, and it is likely that they can be solved by means of similar strategies by identifying the antecedents that are accessible when the anaphor is expressed and, subsequently, selecting the best match(es).

The apparent antecedents of *global* SNs, on the other hand, can occur several sentences away from the SN, contradicting the well accepted finding that non-nominal antecedents are only available for pronominal reference right after being uttered (Passonneau, 1991; Webber, 1991; Fraurud, 1992; Asher, 1993; Poesio and Modjeska, 2002; Gundel et al., 2003, and others). The richer semantics of SNs when compared to pronouns could in part be responsible for this (Kolhatkar, 2015), but this leaves open the question of how possible antecedents are handled in the discourse model in the first place.

If non-nominal antecedent candidates are kept in a stack-like structure like NPs in Centering (Grosz et al., 1995; Poesio and Modjeska, 2002), we need to assume that the interlocutors permanently keep track of one or two highly accessible non-nominal antecedents that are available for pronouns, and additionally, a considerable number of less recent (and thus less salient) antecedents, which can be referred to by SNs only. However, if that is the case, it seems odd that such antecedents are generally referred to by SNs accompanied by the demonstrative determiner *this* (cf. examples 4–5) which indicates a *high* accessibility of the antecedent (Gundel et al., 2003; Poesio and Modjeska, 2002). Thus, global SNs refer to pieces of information that have not necessarily been uttered recently, yet are highly accessible, both of which are attributes of DTs.

Instead of analyzing the underlined portions of the discourses in examples (4–5) as instances of long-distance antecedents, we can view them as stretches of text that function as *topic descriptions*. Even though the subsequent SNs then refer to the very topics described by the apparent antecedents, they do so only as a result of a meta-linguistic interpretation of the discourse without reflecting an underlying, direct anaphoric process. That is, annotators arrive at these antecedents by first, understanding the SN as referring to a DT; second, identifying the intended topic; and third, scanning the text for a suitable paraphrase of it.

The process of interpreting global SNs thus gives the impression of being a combination of semantic-pragmatic tasks like word sense disambiguation, topic detection, question answering, key phrase extraction, etc. Bearing little resemblance to the much more compositional interpretation of local SNs, it appears that entirely different criteria need to be applied to global SNs, as factors previously assumed to play a role for the resolution of SNs as a whole, like the syntactic shape of the antecedent, distance to the SN, and local discourse structure, seem to be primarily relevant for the subset of local SNs.

3.2 Evidence for Global Shell Nouns

So far, global and local SNs have not been investigated separately, which makes it difficult to assess the impact of global SNs on the resolution of the class as a whole. However, by analyzing the previously published data by Kolhatkar et al. (2013) and Kolhatkar (2015) it can be shown that global SNs tend to be harder to annotate and to resolve, which is in line with the idea that the processes underlying global SN resolution are more complex than for local SNs.

As SNs need to be semantically compatible with their antecedents (Schmid, 2000), we can expect nouns with a "topic-like" semantics to be more likely to refer to DTs than others. Furthermore, given that newspaper articles tend to be about everyday and social *issues* and *questions* as well as political and court *decisions*, it is possible to divide the selection of SNs in Kolhatkar et al. (2013) into a local (*fact*,

	Fact	*Reason*	*Issue*	*Decision*	*Question*	*Possibility*	*All*
$c < .5$	8%	8%	36%	21%	13%	7%	16%
$.5 \leq c < .6$	6%	6%	13%	8%	7%	5%	8%
$.6 \leq c < .8$	24%	25%	31%	31%	22%	27%	27%
$.8 \leq c < 1.$	22%	23%	11%	14%	19%	25%	18%
$c = 1.$	40%	38%	9%	26%	39%	36%	31%
Average c	.83	.82	.61	.72	.80	.83	.76

Table 1: Results of the crowd-sourcing annotation by (Kolhatkar et al., 2013, p. 116)

reason, possibility) and a global subset (*issue, question, decision*), with the latter being much more likely to refer to topics.

Among the annotation experiments conducted by Kolhatkar et al. (2013), the most important for our purposes is the task where crowd-workers were asked to select the host sentence of the antecedent without specifying an exact constituent. If topics are represented by spans of text that can occur anywhere in the text, are more difficult to pinpoint, more likely to be discontinuous, and potentially left implicit, the source sentences of topic descriptions can be expected to be more difficult to locate than the antecedents of local SNs, i.e., a better performance can be expected for the nouns *fact, reason*, and *possibility*, than for *issue, question*, and *decision*.

Kolhatkar et al. (2013) report confidence levels as returned by the CrowdFlower[3] platform they used for the task (see Table 1). A low confidence means less agreement, so it is obvious that annotators agreed the least for the three nouns with a topic-like meaning. In light of these results, Kolhatkar et al. (2013, p. 116) recognize a special status of *issue* and *decision*, noting they "had a large number of low-confidence ($c < 0.5$) instances, bringing in the question of reliability of antecedent annotation of these nouns". Further explanation is not provided, and the data is not publicly available, but it seems likely that the lower annotation confidence for topic-like SNs has to do with global references.

Additional evidence for a difference in behavior between global and local SNs can be drawn from the distance to their respective antecedents, which can be expected to be longer for the former. Varada Kolhatkar kindly provided a data set from her study (Kolhatkar, 2015) consisting of a collection of antecedent sentences and SN strings alongside a link to their respective source articles in the NYT corpus. By means of these data, average distances from the SNs to their antecedents (ignoring cataphoric instances) can be calculated as 1.3 for *issue* (n=265); 1.2 for both *decision* (n=343) and *question* (n=376); 1 for *possibility* (n=268); and 0.8 for both *fact* (n=436) and *reason* (n=412). As the data did not include the exact positions of the SNs and the antecedents in the source articles, their locations had to be determined heuristically, hence the results may not be entirely accurate, but there is a clear tendency that global nouns exhibit higher average distances.

This is further supported by the baseline algorithm presented by Kolhatkar (2015, p. 121) that selects as antecedent the sentence preceding the host sentence of the SN which gives us an idea of the distribution of antecedent distances. Table 2 shows the ratio of antecedents with a distance of 1 according to this data. As expected, the three global nouns have the lowest percentage of adjacent antecedents. While this could also indicate a higher number of sentence-internal antecedents, it is likely that long-distance antecedents are responsible for the lower number of nearby antecedents.

Kolhatkar (2015, p. 119) notes that the nouns *issue* and *decision* are also idiosyncratic with respect to the distribution of the syntactic types of their antecedents, exhibiting less sentences and clauses, and more NPs and VPs. According to her, this is a result of the nouns being more flexible than others regarding the types of abstract objects they can refer to, but it could also be an indicator of the meta-linguistic nature of global SN interpretation outlined above, following the intuition that annotators who look for topic descriptions based on semantic considerations – as opposed to the more syntactically driven task of finding proper antecedents – will tend to select a higher number of syntactically atypical antecedents.

---

[3] http://crowdflower.com/

	reason	*fact*	*possibility*	*question*	*decision*	*issue*
Antecedent in PS	44%	40%	34%	25%	21%	19%

Table 2: Percentage of antecedents found in the sentence preceding the SN (Kolhatkar, 2015, p. 121)

Finally, the results of the resolution systems reported by Kolhatkar et al. (2013) and Kolhatkar (2015) consistently show a lower performance for the nouns *issue* and *decision*, which is hardly surprising as difficulties in the annotation can be expected to propagate to the final resolution.

3.3 Annotation Experiment

In order to gain a more direct (if preliminary) assessment of how frequent global SNs are, a small annotation experiment has been conducted. To this end, four German SNs have been selected: *Entscheidung* ('decision') and *Angelegenheit* ('issue') as examples of topic-like SNs, and *Tatsache* ('fact') and *Problem* ('problem') as local SNs. For each noun, 20 articles have been collected from the German online newspaper *Die Zeit*, each containing one instance of the noun accompanied by the demonstrative determiner *diese(r)* ('this').

After receiving an introduction about SNs and the idea of global reference, two German native speakers majoring in linguistics were instructed to carefully read the articles and decide whether they think the SNs in question were GLOBAL or LOCAL. In addition, they were allowed to mark the nouns as COREF-ERENTIAL if they thought it was part of an anaphoric chain and did not directly refer to a non-nominal antecedent, or UNCLEAR if they could not decide for sure. One of the articles (containing an instance of the German pendant of *fact*) had to be dismissed, resulting in a total number of 79 items.

The two analysts agreed in 52 cases (65.8%), 43 (54.4%) of which they evaluated as LOCAL, and 7 (8.9%) as GLOBAL. The global items consisted of one instance of *decision*, two instances of *problem*, and 4 instances of *issue*, i.e., the latter has been agreed by the analysts to be global 20% of the time.

While only looking at a small sample, this study suggests that references to DTs are a considerable factor at least for some SNs, particularly the noun *issue*. The experiment also revealed that a simple global/local distinction is too coarse as SNs can be used to refer to local DTs, i.e., DTs of discourse *sections*, which caused uncertainty among the annotators who reported after the study that they were sometimes unsure whether references to topics of the host paragraph of the SN had to be annotated as GLOBAL or LOCAL. Furthermore, the annotators often found the nouns *fact*, *decision*, and *problem* easy to identify as local instances with syntactically prominent antecedents in their close vicinity, while *issue* was generally hard to annotate due to its vague semantics.

4 Discussion

The fact that the global/local distinction has not been acknowledged in previous work appears to be a major cause of misunderstanding of SNs which led to flaws in annotation and resolution approaches. The majority of the criteria previously employed to resolve SNs are only applicable to local SNs, whereas the resolution of global SNs is a novel, separate task that needs additional steps to be introduced into the resolution pipeline. This is particularly apparent in the factor of distance between the SN and its antecedent.

Although distance is very important for evaluating the accessibility of local antecedents, it is in principle irrelevant for the resolution of global SNs, as spans of text describing the DT can occur virtually anywhere in the text or even be left implicit, which puts both resolution systems and human annotators in an awkward position: they are expected to look for an antecedent where there is none, resulting in a high uncertainty and variance across annotations. Furthermore, it appears that the anaphoric range of SNs has been overestimated as a result of topic references being analyzed as long-distance antecedents. The data from previous studies suggest that local SNs will only rarely refer to an antecedent further away than one sentence, and any antecedent that occurs further away than that is either still accessible because of properties of the local discourse structure (Webber, 1991; Asher, 2008) or it is not an antecedent in the sense of a reflection of an underlying anaphoric process.

Regarding annotation, it needs to be asked whether a classic annotation setting is appropriate for global SNs. Annotators will be biased to annotate *something* in the vicinity of the target noun even if the available context does not provide a stretch of text that perfectly matches their understanding of the noun. In order to avoid such bias, it might be preferable to approach SNs by means of a more open question answering task, asking annotators to paraphrase what they think the target noun means in context, and subsequently comparing their answers with each other and with the source text. Ideally, such a strategy would provide a more accurate picture of how SNs are understood. The evaluation of free text answers is very difficult and not well researched, though, but it bears resemblance, e.g., to the evaluation of answers to reading comprehension tasks (Hahn and Meurers, 2012), which could be adapted to SN research.

Due to their semantics, some SNs lend themselves more readily to a global reading than others. Such tendencies are both domain- and text-specific, but it is fair to assume that the nouns *issue*, and, to a lesser extent, *decision*, are likely to refer to the overall topic in the domain of newspaper articles. The focus of previous work on instances of such nouns seems to have caused an over-representation of topic references in the data. This is further amplified by limiting the considerations to instances of nouns with the demonstrative determiner *this*, which is associated with a high accessibility of the antecedent (Kolhatkar, 2015). As shown by the data by Simonjetz and Roussel (2016), SNs with an accompanying *that* tend to refer to closer antecedents (average distance=0.84 sentences; n=18) than SNs with *this* (d=1.13; n=23), indicating that the former might be correlated with local, and the latter with global SNs. As nouns with a less topic-like meaning like *fact* proved to be much easier to annotate and resolve, SN resolution might be better off focusing on such nouns first, expanding the data to determiners other than *this* to prevent a bias towards topic references.

Assuming that topic referents compete with locally available, explicit antecedents, the factors that are helpful for the resolution of local SNs are probably also helpful for identifying global SNs, following the intuition that if there is no suitable antecedent nearby, the SN derives its information elsewhere. Thus, what both human annotators and resolution systems are missing is the option to disregard the available local antecedents in favor of a discourse topic. As a tentative strategy to account for such an option, the set of antecedent candidates could be extended by one or more pseudo-antecedents representing the discourse topic(s). The candidate set would then consist of antecedents extracted from the close proximity of the SN and a number of topic descriptions, making for a considerably reduced search space and leaving human annotators and automatic resolvers free to choose among explicit antecedents and topics as equally viable options. Future work will need to explore the details of such an approach, addressing questions such as how to extract topic information, how to generate antecedent candidates from topic(s), how to treat features such as distance and phrase type for such antecedents, etc.

5   Conclusion

Quantitative approaches to SNs have proved difficult both in terms of annotation and automatic resolution, and part of this difficulty seems to be due to misconceptions about the interplay between SNs and their context. The prevalent assumption that the occurrence of a SN "*typically* [emphasis added] involves a full-fledged clausal antecedent" (Marasovic et al., 2017, p. 222) seems to have caused more harm than good by raising wrong expectations about SN antecedents, which apparently caused references to DTs to be mistaken for long-distance antecedents. The evidence from theoretical work on anaphoric reference to non-nominal antecedents, practical approaches to SNs, and the annotation experiment outlined above, suggest that some SNs, notably *issue* and *decision* – which much of previous work on SN resolution is based on – are frequently used to refer to DTs that may or may not be explicitly present in the discourse. Crucially, the detection of spans of text that match a topic description is an entirely different task than the resolution of local SNs. Future research will need to find ways to deal with global SNs, topic antecedents, and other implicit sources of abstract referents, in order to make manual annotation and automatic resolution systems more reliable.

References

Mira Ariel. 1988. Referring and Accessibility. *Journal of linguistics*, 24(1):65–87.

Nicholas Asher and Alex Lascarides. 2003. *Logics of conversation*. Cambridge University Press, Cambridge.

Nicholas Asher. 1993. *Reference to Abstract Objects in Discourse*. Kluwer, Dordrecht.

Nicholas Asher. 2000. Events, facts, propositions, and evolutive anaphora. In James Higginbotham, Fabio Pianesi, and Achille C. Varzi, editors, *Speaking of events*, pages 123–150. Oxford University Press, New York.

Nicholas Asher. 2004. Discourse topic. *Theoretical Linguistics*, 30(2–3):163–201.

Nicholas Asher. 2008. Troubles on the right frontier. In Anton Benz and Peter Kühnlein, editors, *Constraints in Discourse*, pages 29–52. John Benjamins Publishing Company, Amsterdam.

Stefanie Dipper and Heike Zinsmeister. 2010. Towards a standard for annotating abstract anaphora. *Proceedings of the LREC 2010 workshop on Language Resources and Language Technology Standards*, pages 54–59.

Stefanie Dipper and Heike Zinsmeister. 2012. Annotating abstract anaphora. *Language Resources and Evaluation*, 46(1):37–52.

John Flowerdew and Richard W. Forest. 2015. *Signalling nouns in English*. Cambridge University Press, Cambridge.

John Flowerdew. 2003. Signalling nouns in discourse. *English for Specific Purposes*, 22(4):329–346.

Gill Francis. 1994. Labelling discourse: An aspect of nominal-group lexical cohesion. In M. Coulthart, editor, *Advances in written text analysis*, pages 83–101, London. Routledge.

Kari Fraurud. 1992. Situation reference: What does "it" refer to? In *Processing noun phrases in natural discourse*, Department of Linguistics, Stockholm University. PhD thesis.

Barbara J. Grosz, Scott Weinstein, and Aravind K. Joshi. 1995. Centering: A framework for modeling the local coherence of discourse. *Computational Linguistics*, 21(2):203–225.

Jeanette K Gundel, Michael Hegarty, and Kaja Borthen. 2003. Cognitive status, information structure, and pronominal reference to clausally introduced entities. *Journal of Logic, Language and Information*, 12(3):281–299.

Michael Hahn and Detmar Meurers. 2012. Evaluating the meaning of answers to reading comprehension questions: A semantics-based approach. In *Proceedings of the Seventh Workshop on Building Educational Applications Using NLP*, pages 326–336.

Michael A. K. Halliday and Ruqaiya Hasan. 1976. *Cohesion in english*. Longman, London.

Roz Ivanič. 1991. Nouns in search of a context: A study of nouns with both open- and closed-system characteristics. *IRAL – International Review of Applied Linguistics in Language Teaching*, 29(2):93–114.

Varada Kolhatkar and Graeme Hirst. 2012. Resolving "this-issue" anaphora. In *Proceedings of the 2012 Conference on Empirical Methods in Natural Language Processing*, pages 1255–1265, Jeju Island, Korea.

Varada Kolhatkar and Graeme Hirst. 2014. Resolving shell nouns. In *Proceedings of the 2014 Conference on Empirical Methods in Natural Language Processing (EMNLP)*, pages 499–510, Doha, Qatar.

Varada Kolhatkar, Heike Zinsmeister, and Graeme Hirst. 2013. Annotating anaphoric shell nouns with their antecedents. In *Proceedings of the 7th Linguistic Annotation Workshop & Interoperability with Discourse*, pages 112–121, Sofia, Bulgaria.

Varada Kolhatkar, Adam Roussel, Stefanie Dipper, and Heike Zinsmeister. 2018. Anaphora with non-nominal antecedents in computational linguistics: A survey. *Computational Linguistics*, 44(3):547–612.

Varada Kolhatkar. 2015. *Resolving Shell Nouns*. Ph.D. thesis, University of Toronto.

Klaus Krippendorff. 2013. *Content analysis: An introduction to its methodology*. Sage, Thousand Oaks, CA, USA, 3rd edition.

Ana Marasovic, Leo Born, Juri Opitz, and Anette Frank. 2017. A mention-ranking model for abstract anaphora resolution. In *Proceedings of the 2017 Conference on Empirical Methods in Natural Language Processing*, pages 221–232.

Rebecca J. Passonneau. 1991. Some facts about centers, indexicals, and demonstratives. In *29th Annual Meeting of the Association for Computational Linguistics*, pages 63–70, Berkeley, California, USA. Association for Computational Linguistics.

Massimo Poesio and Ron Artstein. 2008. Anaphoric annotation in the ARRAU corpus. *Proceedings of the Sixth International Conference on Language Resources and Evaluation (LREC'08)*.

Massimo Poesio and Natalia N. Modjeska. 2002. The THIS-NPs hypothesis: A corpus-based investigation. *Proceedings of the 4th Discourse Anaphora and Anaphor Resolution Colloquium (DAARC 2002)*, pages 157–162.

Massimo Poesio, Roland Stuckardt, and Yannick Versley. 2016. *Anaphora resolution: Algorithms, resources, and applications*. Springer, Heidelberg, Berlin.

Craige Roberts. 2012. Information structure in discourse: Towards an integrated formal theory of pragmatics. *Semantics and Pragmatics*, 5.

Adam Roussel, Stefanie Dipper, Sarah Jablotschkin, and Heike Zinsmeister. 2018. Towards the automatic resolution of anaphora with non-nominal antecedents: Insights from annotation. In *Proceedings of the 14th Conference on Natural Language Processing (KONVENS 2018)*, pages 178–191, Vienna, Austria.

Adam Roussel. 2018. Detecting and resolving shell nouns in German. In *Proceedings of the Workshop on Computational Models of Reference, Anaphora and Coreference*, pages 61–67, New Orleans, Louisiana.

Hans-Jörg Schmid. 1997. Constant and ephemeral hypostatization. In Bernard Caron, editor, *Proceedings of the 16th International Congress of Linguists*, Paris. Elsevier.

Hans Jörg Schmid. 2000. *English abstract nouns as conceptual shells: From corpus to cognition*. De Gruyter, Berlin, New York.

Hans-Jörg Schmid. 2018. Shell nouns in English: A personal roundup. *Caplletra*, 64:109–128.

Fabian Simonjetz and Adam Roussel. 2016. Crosslinguistic annotation of German and English Shell Noun complexes. In *Proceedings of the 13th Conference on Natural Language Processing (KONVENS 2016)*, pages 265–278.

Zeno Vendler. 1967. *Linguistics in philosophy*. Cornell University Press, Ithaca, NY, USA.

Richard Watson Todd. 2016. *Discourse topics*, volume 269 of *Pragmatics & Beyond New Series*. John Benjamins Publishing Company, Amsterdam.

Bonnie Lynn Webber. 1988. Discourse deixis: Reference to discourse segments. In *Proceedings of the 26th Annual Meeting on Association for Computational Linguistics*, ACL '88, pages 113–122, Stroudsburg, PA, USA. Association for Computational Linguistics.

Bonnie Lynn Webber. 1991. Structure and ostension in the interpretation of discourse deixis. *Language and Cognitive Processes*, 6(2):107–135.

A Benchmark of Rule-Based and Neural
Coreference Resolution in Dutch Novels and News

Corbèn Poot
CLCG, University of Groningen
c.poot@student.rug.nl

Andreas van Cranenburgh
CLCG, University of Groningen
a.w.van.cranenburgh@rug.nl

Abstract

We evaluate a rule-based (Lee et al., 2013) and neural (Lee et al., 2018) coreference system on Dutch datasets of two domains: literary novels and news/Wikipedia text. The results provide insight into the relative strengths of data-driven and knowledge-driven systems, as well as the influence of domain, document length, and annotation schemes. The neural system performs best on news/Wikipedia text, while the rule-based system performs best on literature. The neural system shows weaknesses with limited training data and long documents, while the rule-based system is affected by annotation differences. The code and models used in this paper are available at https://github.com/andreasvc/crac2020

1 Introduction

In recent years, the best results for coreference resolution of English have been obtained with end-to-end neural models (Lee et al., 2017b, 2018; Joshi et al., 2019, 2020; Wu et al., 2020). However for Dutch, the existing systems are still using either a rule-based (van der Goot et al., 2015; van Cranenburgh, 2019) or a machine learning approach (Hendrickx et al., 2008a; De Clercq et al., 2011). The rule-based system dutchcoref (van Cranenburgh, 2019) outperformed previous systems on two existing datasets and also presented a corpus and evaluation of literary novels (RiddleCoref).

In this paper we compare this rule-based system to an end-to-end neural coreference resolution system: e2e-Dutch. This system is a variant of Lee et al. (2018) with BERT token representations. We evaluate and compare the performance of e2e-Dutch to dutchcoref on two different datasets: (1) the SoNaR-1 corpus (Schuurman et al., 2010), a genre-balanced corpus of 1 million words, and (2) the RiddleCoref corpus of contemporary novels (van Cranenburgh, 2019). This provides insights into (1) the relative strengths of a neural system versus a rule-based system for Dutch coreference, and (2) the effect of domain differences (news/Wikipedia versus literature).

The two datasets we consider vary greatly in terms of overall size and length of the individual documents; the training subset of RiddleCoref contains only 23 documents (novel fragments) compared to 581 documents for SoNaR-1. However, the average number of sentences per document is higher for RiddleCoref than for SoNaR-1 (295.78 vs. 64.28 respectively). We also conduct an error analysis for both of the systems to examine the types of errors that the systems make.

2 Related work

The main differences between traditional and neural approaches can be summarized as follows:

- Rule-based systems are knowledge-intensive; machine learning systems are data-driven but require feature engineering; end-to-end neural systems only require sufficient training data and hyperparameter tuning to perform well.
- Rule-based and machine learning coreference systems rely on features from syntactic parses and named-entities provided by an NLP pipeline whereas neural systems rely on distributed representations; end-to-end systems do not require any other features.

Proceedings of the 3rd Workshop on Computational Models of Reference, Anaphora and Coreference (CRAC 2020), pages 79–90,
Barcelona, Spain (online), December 12, 2020.

System	CoNLL	System	CoNLL
Rule-based (Lee et al., 2011)	58.3	End-to-end (Lee et al., 2017b)	68.8
Perceptron (Fernandes et al., 2012)	58.7	Higher-order + CTF + ELMo (Lee et al., 2018)	73.0
Hybrid: rules + ML (Lee et al., 2017a)	63.2	Finetuning BERT base (Joshi et al., 2019)	73.9
Embeddings (Wiseman et al., 2015)	63.4	Finetuning BERT large (Joshi et al., 2019)	76.9
+ RL (Clark and Manning, 2016a)	65.3	Pretraining SpanBERT (Joshi et al., 2019)	79.6
+ Entity embeddings (Clark and Manning, 2016b)	65.7	SpanBERT + QA (Wu et al., 2020)	83.1

Table 1: English coreference scores on the OntoNotes CoNLL 2012 shared task dataset. ML: Machine Learning, RL: Reinforcement Learning, CTF: Coarse-to-Fine, QA: Question Answering.

- The rule-based system by Lee et al. (2013) is entity-based and exploits global features, while end-to-end systems such as Lee et al. (2017b) rank mentions and make greedy decisions based on local features. Although Lee et al. (2018) does approximate higher-order inference, their model does not build representations of entities.

The rest of this section discusses the current best systems for Dutch and English.

2.1 Dutch coreference resolution

The largest dataset available for Dutch coreference resolution is the SoNaR-1 dataset (Schuurman et al., 2010) which consists of 1 million words annotated for coreference. This corpus was a continuation of the Corea project (Bouma et al., 2007; Hendrickx et al., 2008a,b). De Clercq et al. (2011) present a cross-domain coreference resolution study conducted on this corpus. They use a mention-pair system, which was originally developed with the KNACK-2002 corpus and then further improved in the Corea project, and observe that the influence of domain and training size is large, thus underlining the importance of this large and genre-balanced SoNaR-1 dataset.

The current best coreference resolution system for Dutch is called "dutchcoref" (van Cranenburgh, 2019) and is based on the rule-based Stanford system (Lee et al., 2011, 2013). This system improved on the systems in the SemEval-2010 shared task (Recasens et al., 2010) and a previous implementation of the Stanford system for Dutch (GroRef; van der Goot et al., 2015). The main focus of van Cranenburgh (2019) was evaluating coreference on literary texts, for which a corpus and evaluation is presented. Most coreference resolution systems are evaluated using newswire texts, but a domain such as literary text presents its own challenges (Bamman, 2017); for example, novels are longer than news articles, and novels can therefore contain longer coreference chains.

2.2 English Coreference resolution

The main benchmark for English is the CoNLL 2012 shared task (Pradhan et al., 2012). Table 1 reports a timeline of results for this task, which shows the dramatic improvements brought by neural networks, especially the end-to-end systems on the right. Neural coreference systems improved on previous work but were still relying on mention detection rules, syntactic parsers, and heavy feature engineering (Table 1, left). They were outperformed by the first end-to-end coreference resolution system by Lee et al. (2017b). This system looks at all the spans (expressions) in a text, up to a maximum length, and then uses a span-ranking model that decides for each span which previous spans are good antecedents, if any. The spans themselves are represented by word embeddings.

Although the models by Clark and Manning (2016a) and Lee et al. (2017b) are computationally efficient and scalable to long documents, they are heavily relying on first order models where they are only scoring pairs of mentions. Because they make independent decisions regarding coreference links, they might make predictions which are locally consistent but globally inconsistent (Lee et al., 2018). Lee et al. (2018) introduce an approximation of higher-order inference, which uses the span-ranking architecture from Lee et al. (2017b) described above in an iterative fashion, and also propose a coarse-to-fine approach to lower the computational cost of this iterative higher-order approximation. Further improvements over Lee et al. (2017b) were obtained through the use of deep contextualized ELMo (Peters et al., 2018) word

	RiddleCoref			SoNaR-1		
	Train	Dev	Test	Train	Dev	Test
documents	23	5	5	581	135	145
sentences	6803	1525	1536	37,346	10,585	11,671
tokens	105,517	28,042	28,054	635,191	171,293	197,392
sents per doc	295.78	305	307.2	64.28	78.41	80.49
avg sent len	15.51	18.39	18.26	17	16.18	16.91
mentions	25,194	6584	6869	182,311	50,472	57,172
entities	9041	2643	3008	128,142	37,057	39,904
mentions/tokens	0.24	0.23	0.24	0.29	0.29	0.29
mentions/entities	2.79	2.49	2.28	1.42	1.36	1.43
entities/tokens	0.09	0.09	0.11	0.20	0.22	0.20
% pronouns	40.4	35.7	38.1	11.6	11.3	11.0
% nominal	47.0	49.4	52.8	70.8	70.4	71.9
% names	12.6	14.9	9.1	17.6	18.3	17.1

Table 2: Dataset statistics

embeddings. The current state-of-the-art scores are even higher by using BERT finetuning (Joshi et al., 2019, 2020; Wu et al., 2020) However, this paper focuses on the model by Lee et al. (2018).

Bamman et al. (2020) present coreference results on English literature with an end-to-end model comparable to the one used in this paper, except for using a separate mention detection step. However, their dataset consist of a larger number of shorter novel fragments (2000 words). They report a CoNLL score of 68.1 on the novel fragments.

3 Coreference corpora

In this paper we consider entity coreference and focus on the relations of identity and predication. The rest of this section describes the two Dutch corpora we use.

3.1 SoNaR-1: news and Wikipedia text

The SoNaR-1 corpus (Schuurman et al., 2010) contains about 1 million words of Dutch text from various genres, predominantly news and Wikipedia text. Coreference was annotated from scratch (i.e., annotation did not proceed by correcting the output of a system), based on automatically extracted markables. The markables include singleton mentions but also non-referring expressions such as pleonastic pronouns. The annotation was not corrected by a second annotator. Hendrickx et al. (2008b) estimated the inter-annotator agreement of a different corpus with the same annotation scheme and obtained a MUC score of 76 % for identity relations (which form the majority).

We have created a genre-balanced train/dev/test split for SoNaR-1 of 70/15/15. The documents are from a range of different genres and we therefore ensure that the subsets are a stratified sample in terms of genres, to avoid distribution shifts between the train and test set.[1]

We convert the SoNaR-1 coreference annotations from MMAX2 format into the CoNLL-2012 format. Since dutchcoref requires parse trees as input, we use the manually corrected Lassy Small treebank (van Noord et al., 2006; Van Noord, 2009), which is a superset of the SoNaR-1 corpus.[2] We align the Lassy Small trees at the sentence and token level to the SoNaR-1 coreference annotations, since there are some differences in tokenization and sentence order.[3] We also add gold standard NER annotations from SoNaR-1. The manually corrected trees lack some additional features produced by the Alpino parser (van Noord, 2006) which are needed by dutchcoref; we merge these predicted features into the gold standard trees.

---

[1] Cf. `https://gist.github.com/CorbenPoot/ee1c97209cb9c5fc50f9528c7fdcdc93`

[2] We could also evaluate with predicted parses from the Alpino parser, but components of the Alpino parser have been trained on subsets of Lassy Small, so predicted parses of Lassy Small are not representative of Alpino's heldout performance.

[3] The conversion script is part of `https://github.com/andreasvc/dutchcoref/`

3.2 RiddleCoref: contemporary novels

The RiddleCoref corpus consists of contemporary Dutch novels (both translated and originally Dutch), and was presented in van Cranenburgh (2019). The corpus is a subset of the Riddle of Literary Quality corpus of 401 bestselling novels (Koolen et al., 2020). This dataset was annotated by correcting the output of dutchcoref. Most novels in the dataset were corrected by two annotators, with the second performing another round of correction after the first. In this dataset, mentions include singletons and are manually corrected; i.e., only expressions that refer to a person or object are annotated as mentions. Besides this difference, relative clauses and discontinuous constituents have different boundaries (minimal spans).

The system by van Cranenburgh (2019) is a rule-based system that does not require a training data, and therefore the dev/test split used in this paper is not suitable for a supervised system. To avoid this issue, we create a new train/dev/test split which reserves 70% for training data. We also evaluate dutchcoref on this new split. The new dev and test sets have no overlap with the original development set on which the rules of dutchcoref were tuned.

No gold standard parse trees are available for the novels. Instead, we use automatically predicted parses from the Alpino parser (van Noord, 2006).

3.3 Dataset statistics

Table 2 shows statistics of the two datasets and their respective splits. The documents in RiddleCoref are almost four times as long as those in SoNaR-1, and this is reflected in a higher number of mentions per entity, while SoNaR-1 has a higher density of entities to tokens. We also see a difference due to the more selective, manual annotation of mentions: almost 30% of SoNaR-1 tokens are part of a mention, compared to less than 25% for RiddleCoref. Finally, we see large differences in the proportion of pronouns, nominals and names, due to the genre difference.

4 Coreference systems

We now describe the two coreference systems, dutchcoref and e2e-Dutch, which we evaluate on the coreference corpora described in the previous section.

4.1 Rule-based: dutchcoref

The dutchcoref system[4] (van Cranenburgh, 2019) is an implementation of the rule-based coreference system by Lee et al. (2011, 2013). The input to the system consists of Alpino parse trees (van Noord, 2006), which include named entities. The system infers information about speakers and addressees of direct speech using heuristic rules. This information is used for coreference decisions. Note that this information is not given as part of the input.

We have made some improvements to the rules of this system in order to make it more compatible with the SoNaR-1 annotations; this was however based only on the output of a single document in the development set, as well as on the original, RiddleCoref development set on which dutchcoref was developed. When evaluating on SoNaR-1, we apply rules to filter links and mentions from the output to adapt to the annotation scheme of this dataset.

4.2 End-to-end, neural: e2e-Dutch

The e2e-Dutch system[5] is fully end-to-end in the sense that it is trained only on the token and coreference column of the CoNLL files of the dataset, without using any metadata. Our data does not contain speaker information which is used by models trained on the OntoNotes dataset (Hovy et al., 2006). In addition, models trained on OntoNotes use genre information; while our data does have genre metadata, we have not experimented with using this feature. For English, such information provides additional improvement in scores (Lee et al., 2017b).

---

[4] https://github.com/andreasvc/dutchcoref

[5] The e2e-Dutch system is being developed as part of the Filter Bubble project at the VU and eScience center. The specific commit we used is https://github.com/Filter-Bubble/e2e-Dutch/tree/056dcf7d3d711a3c7b8cda241a16cdd76158a823

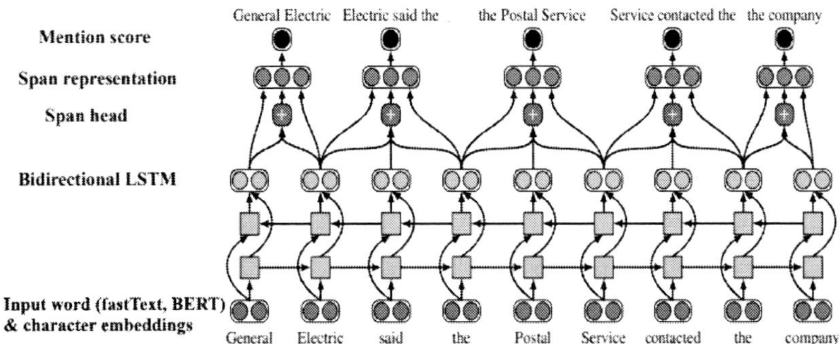

Figure 1: Overview of the first step of the end-to-end model in which the embedding representations and mention scores are computed. The model considers all possible spans up to a maximum width but only a small subset is shown here. Figure adapted from Lee et al. (2017b).

The model that e2e-Dutch is based on (Lee et al., 2018) uses a combination of character n-gram embeddings, non-contextual word embeddings (GloVe; Pennington et al., 2014) and contextualized word embeddings (ELMo; Peters et al., 2018). These embeddings are concatenated and fed into a bidirectional LSTM. Span heads are approximated using an attention mechanism; while this step is intended to approximate syntactic heads, it does not rely on parse tree information. Figure 1 shows an overview of the model. e2e-Dutch adapts this architecture by adding support for singletons; i.e., during mention detection, each span is classified as not a mention, a singleton, or a coreferent mention.

Character n-gram embeddings are extracted by iterating over the data and feeding the character n-grams to a Convolutional Neural Network (CNN) which then represents these n-grams as learned 8-dimensional embeddings. The GloVe embeddings were replaced with fastText[6] embeddings (Grave et al., 2018). We also trained fastText embeddings on our own datasets but saw a performance decrease; we therefore stick with pre-trained embeddings. Lastly, the ELMo embeddings were replaced by BERT (Devlin et al., 2019) token embeddings, since BERT tends to outperform ELMo (Devlin et al., 2019) and because there is a pretrained, monolingual Dutch BERT model available whose pretraining data includes novels (BERTje; Vries et al., 2019). However, there is no overlap between the 7000+ novels that BERTje is trained on and the RiddleCoref corpus. Whenever there is a mismatch between the subtokens of BERT and the tokens in the coreference data, the model takes the average of the BERT subtoken embeddings as token representation. The last BERT layer is used for the token representation; however, recent research has showed that layer 9 actually performs best for Dutch coreference (de Vries et al., 2020). Note also that we do not finetune BERT for this task, contrary to Joshi et al. (2019); this is left for future work.

We use some different hyperparameters compared to Lee et al. (2018). Our model only considers up to 30 antecedents per span instead of 50; this only leads to marginally worse performance, a 0.03 decrease in the LEA F1-score, while reducing the computational cost substantially. During training, each document is randomly truncated at 30 sentences, but different random parts are selected at each epoch. We have experimented with higher values for this parameter with RiddleCoref, but only obtained marginal improvements (0.01 difference), and did not pursue this further. The top span ratio controls the number of mentions that are considered and determines the precision/recall tradeoff for mentions. We experimented with tuning this parameter, but settled on the default of 0.4. Mentions up to 50 tokens long are considered.

During training, the model is evaluated every 1500 epochs (2500 for SoNaR-1). If the CoNLL score on the development set does not increase after three rounds, training is stopped.

5   Evaluation

Before presenting our main benchmark results, we discuss the issue of coreference evaluation metrics.

---

[6]We use Fasttext common crawl embeddings, https://fasttext.cc/docs/en/crawl-vectors.html

System	dataset	Mentions			LEA			CoNLL
		R	P	F1	R	P	F1	
dutchcoref	RiddleCoref, dev	86.85	85.84	86.34	49.18	58.03	**53.24**	**65.91**
e2e-Dutch	RiddleCoref, dev	83.12	87.65	85.33	48.37	50.99	49.65	64.81
dutchcoref	RiddleCoref, test	87.65	90.80	89.20	50.83	64.78	**56.97**	**69.86**
e2e-Dutch	RiddleCoref, test	81.95	89.00	85.33	44.82	50.48	47.48	63.55
dutchcoref	SoNaR-1, dev	64.88	86.78	74.25	37.98	52.23	43.98	55.45
e2e-Dutch	SoNaR-1, dev	90.24	88.09	89.16	65.02	65.55	**65.29**	**71.53**
dutchcoref	SoNaR-1, test	65.32	85.94	74.22	37.87	52.55	44.02	55.91
e2e-Dutch	SoNaR-1, test	88.96	86.81	87.87	60.67	62.48	**61.56**	**68.45**

Table 3: Coreference results (predicted mentions, including singletons).

5.1 Metrics

The challenge with evaluating coreference resolution lies in the fact that it involves several levels: mentions, links and entities. Results can be correct on one level and incorrect on another, and the levels interact. One of the most important factors in coreference performance is the performance of mention detection, since an incorrect or missed mention can lead to a large number of missed coreference links (especially for a long coreference chain). We therefore report mention scores. It turns out that mention performance also has a large influence on coreference evaluation metrics (Moosavi and Strube, 2016). We will use two coreference metrics. The CoNLL score (Pradhan et al., 2011) is the standard benchmark, but it does not have a precision and recall score, and the MUC, B^3, and CEAFe metrics on which it is based have their own flaws. Therefore we will also look at the LEA metric (Moosavi and Strube, 2016). LEA gives more weight to larger entities, so that mistakes on more important chains have more effect on the score than mistakes on smaller entities.

Unless otherwise noted, all our results include singletons. Evaluating with and without singletons will affect all of the scores, and the two datasets differ in the way they annotated singletons. Singletons inflate coreference scores due to the mention identification effect. Since most mentions are easy to identify based on form, singletons reduce the informativeness of the coreference score. SoNaR-1 includes automatically extracted markables instead of manually annotated mentions, as in RiddleCoref. The automatically extracted markables are more numerous and easier to identify (they were extracted based on syntax) than manually annotated mentions that are restricted to potentially referring expressions (a semantic distinction). One possibility to rule out the mention identification effect completely is to present the systems with gold mentions. However, this still leaves the singleton-effect. If singletons are included, the system will not know which of the gold mentions are singletons, and this can lead to incorrect coreference links. A dataset with more singletons (such as SoNaR-1) will thus have more potential for incorrect coreference links (precision errors). If singleton mentions are excluded from the set of gold mentions, it is given that all mentions are coreferent. The system should then use this information and force every mention to have at least one link. However, this requires re-training or re-designing the coreference system, and does not allow us to do a realistic end-to-end coreference evaluation. We are therefore stuck with the complications that come with combining mention identification and coreference resolution.

5.2 Results

The main results are presented in Table 3. For RiddleCoref, dutchcoref outperforms e2e-Dutch by a 6 point margin. For SoNar-1, e2e-Dutch comes out first, and the gap is even larger. Despite the advantage dutchcoref has due to its use of gold standard parse trees, its performance is lower than e2e-Dutch. We can see from the mention recall score that dutchcoref misses a large number of potential mentions; this may be due to the fact that SoNaR-1 markables include singletons and non-referential mentions. However, dutchcoref also has a lower LEA recall, so the gap with e2e-Dutch on SoNar-1 is not only due to mention

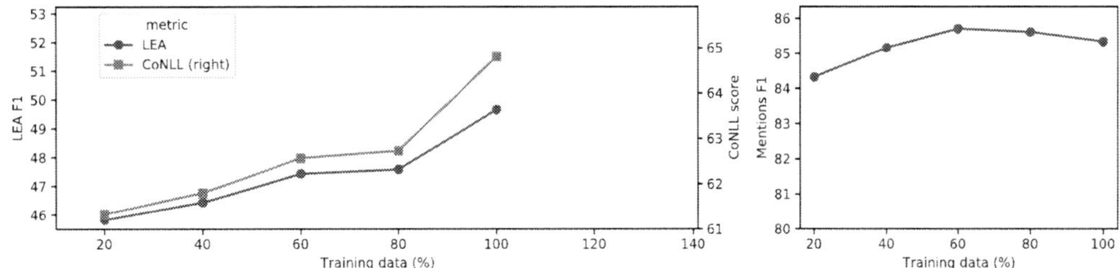

Figure 2: Learning curve of e2e-Dutch on RiddleCoref dev set, showing performance as a function of amount of training data (initial segments of novels).

Novel	System	Mentions			LEA			CoNLL
		R	P	F1	R	P	F1	
Forsyth_Cobra	dutchcoref	90.67	93.14	**91.89**	62.82	74.83	**68.30**	**77.42**
Forsyth_Cobra	e2e-Dutch	78.31	85.23	81.62	39.82	44.27	41.93	55.71
Japin_Vaslav	dutchcoref	86.19	92.78	**89.36**	44.57	61.39	**51.65**	65.79
Japin_Vaslav	e2e-Dutch	83.13	91.75	87.22	49.23	50.89	50.05	**66.09**
Proper_GooischeVrouwen	dutchcoref	88.20	91.12	89.63	58.65	66.95	**62.53**	**72.29**
Proper_GooischeVrouwen	e2e-Dutch	87.60	92.21	**89.85**	50.10	44.74	47.27	64.77
Royen_Mannentester	dutchcoref	87.15	86.01	86.57	44.66	58.21	50.54	65.01
Royen_Mannentester	e2e-Dutch	87.90	89.94	**88.91**	54.48	56.19	**55.32**	**69.93**
Verhulst_LaatsteLiefde	dutchcoref	86.24	87.70	**86.96**	45.38	59.66	**51.55**	**66.09**
Verhulst_LaatsteLiefde	e2e-Dutch	82.66	87.98	85.23	41.58	48.77	44.89	61.38

Table 4: Performance difference between e2e-Dutch and dutchcoref for each individual novel

performance. While results for different datasets and languages are not comparable, the performance difference for SoNaR-1 has the same order of magnitude as the difference for OntoNotes between the comparable rule-based and neural systems of Lee et al. (2011) and Lee et al. (2018) in Table 1.

RiddleCoref is much smaller than the SoNaR-1 dataset. Is there enough training data for the neural model? Figure 2 shows a learning curve for e2e-Dutch. This curve suggests that for the coreference scores the answer is no, because the performance does not reach a plateau—instead the curve is steep until the end. The performance of dutchcoref is the top of the plot; if we extrapolate the curve linearly, we might expect e2e-Dutch to outperform dutchcoref with 1.1–1.3 times the current training data. However, as an anonymous reviewer pointed out, training curves are usually logarithmic, so more training data may be required. Mention performance does reach a plateau, which suggests this task is easier.

6 Analysis

The previous section showed some surprising results. We now take a closer look at the differences between the two coreference systems, datasets, and the annotations.

6.1 Rule-based versus neural coreference

See Table 4 for a novel by novel comparison of dutchcoref and e2e-Dutch. On 3 out of 5 novels, dutchcoref is better on both LEA F1 and CoNLL. Interestingly, on 1 novel, LEA F1 and CoNLL disagree on the ranking of the systems. Mention performance is high across all novels, except for a large discrepancy on Forsyth in which e2e-Dutch scores 10 points lower.

To get more insight in the particular errors made by the systems, we perform an error analysis using the tool by Kummerfeld and Klein (2013).[7] This tool attributes errors to mention spans, missing or extra

---

[7]We adapted this tool for Dutch: `https://github.com/andreasvc/berkeley-coreference-analyser`

System	Dataset	Span Error	Conflated Entities	Extra Mention	Extra Entity	Divided Entity	Missing Mention	Missing Entity
dutchcoref	RiddleCoref	73	476	130	96	587	379	154
e2e-Dutch	RiddleCoref	47	321	101	36	420	511	369
dutchcoref	SoNaR-1	352	2432	2327	1772	2640	2469	1519
e2e-Dutch	SoNaR-1	203	1187	895	695	1994	3428	2330

Table 5: Error types and their respective counts for both systems and datasets

Dataset	System	error	name	nom.	pron.	Incorrect part			Rest of entity			Divided		Conflated	
						Na	No	Pr	Na	No	Pr	d.c.	e2e	d.c.	e2e
RiddleCoref	d.c.	extra	5	83	42	-	-	1+	-	1+	1+	104	66	118	74
RiddleCoref	e2e	extra	6	55	40	-	-	1+	1+	1+	1+	202	49	11	72
RiddleCoref	d.c.	missing	11	163	205	-	-	1+	-	1+	-	62	66	156	31
RiddleCoref	e2e	missing	115	274	122	-	1+	-	-	1+	-	22	30	33	20
SoNaR-1	d.c.	extra	544	1473	310	-	1+	1+	-	1+	1+	33	31	16	13
SoNaR-1	e2e	extra	175	550	170	-	1+	-	-	1+	1+	34	18	33	6
SoNaR-1	d.c.	missing	283	1842	344	-	1+	1+	1+	1+	1+	36	29	2	12
SoNaR-1	e2e	missing	825	2124	479	-	-	1+	-	-	1+	15	11	25	14
						Other						79	120	82	79

Table 6: Left: Counts of missing and extra mention errors by mention type. Right: A breakdown of conflated/divided entity errors on RiddleCoref grouped by Name/Nominal/Pronoun composition; 1+ means that the entity contains one or more mentions of the given type.

mentions/entities, and entities which are divided (incorrectly split) or conflated (incorrectly merged). We use the default configuration of ignoring singletons mentions, but add an option to support the Dutch parse tree labels. Table 5 shows an overview of these error types by the systems on the RiddleCoref and SoNaR-1 test sets. We can see that e2e-Dutch makes less errors of all types, except for missing mentions and entities, which is due to its lower mention recall. Even though e2e-Dutch showed a high score for mention recall on SoNaR-1 in Table 3, we actually find that dutchcoref and e2e-Dutch both show a similarly low mention recall when singletons are excluded (65.8 and 64.3, respectively). Finally, note that a lower mention recall means that there is less opportunity to make errors of other types, so this comparison is not conclusive.

To understand what is going on with mention identification, we can look at a breakdown by mention type, see Table 6. We see that e2e-Dutch produces substantially less extra nominal (NP) mentions, but is otherwise similar. In terms of missing mentions, e2e-Dutch makes substantially more errors on names and nominals, but on RiddleCoref it has less missing pronouns, while it has more missing pronouns with SoNaR-1. Although pronouns form a closed class, the issue of pleonastic pronouns still makes pronoun mention detection non-trivial for RiddleCoref, where pleonastic pronouns are not annotated as mentions. Since dutchcoref has no rules to detect non-pleonastic uses of potentially pleonastic pronouns, it defaults to treating them as non-mentions. For SoNaR-1, the performance difference on missing mentions may be due to information from the gold parse trees which is used by dutchcoref; for example the possessive *zijn* (his) has the same form as the infinitive of the verb to be, but POS tags disambiguate this, and this information is not available to e2e-Dutch.

Finally, we can try to understand the coreference link errors. Table 6 shows the counts of link errors on RiddleCoref by the two systems, with the entities categorized by their configuration. We see that for both dutchcoref and e2e-Dutch, the most common divided and conflated entity errors have a pronoun present in the incorrect part, although dutchcoref makes more of these errors. We can thus reconfirm the finding by Kummerfeld and Klein (2013) and van Cranenburgh (2019) who report that the most common link error involves pronouns. Coreference resolution for Dutch provides an extra challenge in the fact that the third person singular pronouns can refer to either biological or linguistic gender (Hoste, 2005).

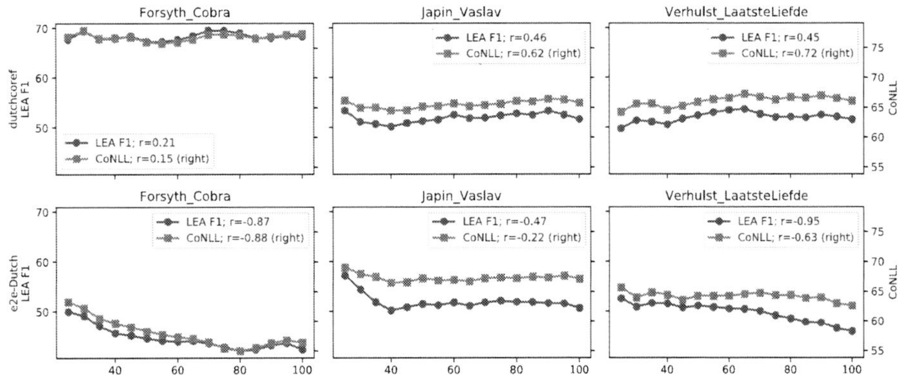

Figure 3: Coreference scores as a function of document length. Gold and system output are truncated at different lengths (based on % of words, rounded to the nearest sentence boundary); r is the Pearson correlation coefficient.

System	Dataset	Mentions	Singletons	Mentions F1	LEA F1	CoNLL
dutchcoref	RiddleCoref	predicted	excluded	80.56	48.15	56.21
e2e-Dutch	RiddleCoref	predicted	excluded	79.94	45.31	54.90
dutchcoref	RiddleCoref	predicted	included	86.34	53.24	65.91
e2e-Dutch	RiddleCoref	predicted	included	85.33	49.65	64.81
dutchcoref	RiddleCoref	gold	included	100	61.89	75.84
e2e-Dutch	RiddleCoref	gold	included	100	55.17	72.01
dutchcoref	SoNaR-1	predicted	excluded	63.57	39.71	46.96
e2e-Dutch	SoNaR-1	predicted	excluded	67.08	46.18	52.76
dutchcoref	SoNaR-1	predicted	included	74.25	43.98	55.45
e2e-Dutch	SoNaR-1	predicted	included	89.16	65.29	71.53
dutchcoref	SoNaR-1	gold	included	100	59.34	70.90
e2e-Dutch	SoNaR-1	gold	included	100	74.88	80.61

Table 7: Development set results under different conditions.

6.2 RiddleCoref (novels) versus SoNaR-1 (news/Wikipedia)

Are the scores on the two datasets comparable? There are several issues which hinder the comparison: document length, domain differences, and mention annotation.

We first look at document length. It could be that the evaluation metrics are influenced by document length, since longer documents offer more opportunities for errors. We will investigate this effect by truncating the documents before evaluation, while keeping other factors such as the model or training data constant. We truncate after running the coreference system because we want to focus on the effect of document length on the evaluation, and we have no reason to expect the coreference systems to behave differently on truncated texts. We truncate the novels at different lengths based on the number of words, rounded to the nearest sentence. Note that truncating does not cause additional errors, because gold and system output are both truncated. Figure 3 shows coreference scores as a function of document length for the novels. We conclude that e2e-Dutch seems to perform worse on longer documents, based on the negative correlation of scores and document length. While LEA weighs larger entities more, we also see this effect with the CoNLL score, so it is not an artifact of the LEA metric. Moreover, we do not see the effect for dutchcoref, so the effect is not inherent to the coreference metrics. The documents in SoNaR-1 are much shorter (number of sentences and words), and this may be an advantage for e2e-Dutch. Joshi et al. (2019) report a similar document length effect for English with their end-to-end model.

Table 2 shows there is large difference in distribution of pronouns, names, and noun phrases, which are not equally difficult. Novels tend to have a larger proportion of pronouns. However, it is hard to say a priori whether this would make novels easier or more difficult in terms of coreference.

In order to see the influence of the mention identification effect, as well as the influence of evaluating with and without singletons, Table 7 shows a comparison on the development set. Note that in our experiments with e2e-Dutch, singletons are always included during training; excluding singletons only refers to excluding them from the system output and gold data during evaluation. We see that ignoring singletons has a counter-intuitively large effect on coreference scores, while it has a relatively small effect on mention identification for RiddleCoref, but a large effect with SoNaR-1. However, whether singletons are included or not does not change the ranking of the systems. Finally, when gold mentions are given during evaluation we see the large effect that mention identification has downstream, although again the ranking is preserved.

6.3 SoNaR-1 annotation issues

Since the gap between the performance of e2e-Dutch and dutchcoref on SoNaR-1 is so large, we take a quick look at the SoNaR-1 annotations of a single development set document (WR-P-E-C-0000000021), in order to understand the errors made by dutchcoref. However, it is apparent that part of these errors are actually errors in the annotation. The first thing that stands out are mentions with exact string matches which are not linked; for example: Amsterdam (5x), Hilversum (6x), *de zeventiende eeuw* (the seventeenth century, 4x), etc. Other errors are due to missing mentions; for example, 2 out of 10 mentions of the artist Japix are missing, probably because the name occurs twice as part of a possessive. A corpus based on semi-automatic annotation would not contain such errors, while it is understandable that such links are easy to overlook in a longer document when manually annotating from scratch.

An example of a questionable mention boundary (with corrected boundary underlined):

(1)   [Hij] was [<u>burgemeester van Franeker</u> en later <u>gedeputeerde van Friesland in de Staten-Generaal</u>].
[He] was [<u>mayor of Franeker</u> and later <u>deputy of Frisia in the Senate</u>].

This is actually an example of a downside of semi-automatic annotation, at least if there is no correction, since the markable boundaries of SoNaR-1 were automatically extracted and could not be changed by annotators. For the RiddleCoref corpus, such boundaries were corrected.

An example of a missing anaphoric link (second *hij* was not linked):

(2)   Een vers aan [Caspar Barlaeus]$_1$ ondertekent [hij]$_2$ met 'Dando petere solitus' dat wil zeggen: [hij]$_2$ schrijft poëzie in de hoop betere verzen terug te krijgen .
A verse to [Caspar Barlaeus]$_1$ he$_2$ signes with 'Dando petere solitus' which is to say: he$_2$ writes poetry in the hope to get better verses back.

This only scratches the surface of the SoNaR-1 annotations. A more systematic study should be done.

7 Conclusion

We found large gaps in performance for the two systems across the two domains, but this result is not conclusive due to several reasons, which are as follows. The neural system shows a weakness with the long documents in the novel corpus, but also needs more training data to reach its full potential. The rule-based system should be better adapted to the SoNaR-1 annotation scheme, but the neural system's capacity to adapt to arbitrary annotation conventions does not necessarily imply better linguistic performance. To maximize the comparability and usefulness of the corpora, their annotations should be harmonized, which involves manual mention annotation. In future work we want to improve the neural system by using genre metadata and finetuning BERT, and the rule-based system should be extended to a hybrid system by adding supervised classifiers.

Acknowledgements

We are grateful to Gertjan van Noord and Peter Kleiweg for help with preprocessing the Lassy Small treebank, to Wietse de Vries and Malvina Nissim for comments on the evaluation, and to three anonymous reviewers for their suggestions.

References

David Bamman. 2017. Natural language processing for the long tail. In *Proceedings of Digital Humanities*.

David Bamman, Olivia Lewke, and Anya Mansoor. 2020. An annotated dataset of coreference in English literature. In *Proceedings of The 12th Language Resources and Evaluation Conference*, pages 44–54.

Gosse Bouma, Walter Daelemans, Iris Hendrickx, Véronique Hoste, and Anne-Marie Mineur. 2007. The COREA-project: manual for the annotation of coreference in Dutch texts. Technical report, University of Groningen.

Kevin Clark and Christopher D. Manning. 2016a. Deep reinforcement learning for mention-ranking coreference models. In *Proceedings of EMNLP*, pages 2256–2262.

Kevin Clark and Christopher D. Manning. 2016b. Improving coreference resolution by learning entity-level distributed representations. In *Proceedings of ACL*, pages 643–653.

Andreas van Cranenburgh. 2019. A Dutch coreference resolution system with an evaluation on literary fiction. *Computational Linguistics in the Netherlands Journal*, 9:27–54.

Orphée De Clercq, Véronique Hoste, and Iris Hendrickx. 2011. Cross-domain Dutch coreference resolution. In *Proceedings of RANLP*, pages 186–193.

Jacob Devlin, Ming-Wei Chang, Kenton Lee, and Kristina Toutanova. 2019. BERT: Pre-training of deep bidirectional transformers for language understanding. In *Proceedings of NAACL*, pages 4171–4186.

Eraldo Fernandes, Cícero dos Santos, and Ruy Milidiú. 2012. Latent structure perceptron with feature induction for unrestricted coreference resolution. In *Joint Conference on EMNLP and CoNLL - Shared Task*, pages 41–48.

Rob van der Goot, Hessel Haagsma, and Dieke Oele. 2015. GroRef: Rule-based coreference resolution for Dutch. In *CLIN26 shared task*.

Edouard Grave, Piotr Bojanowski, Prakhar Gupta, Armand Joulin, and Tomas Mikolov. 2018. Learning word vectors for 157 languages. In *Proceedings of LREC*.

Iris Hendrickx, Gosse Bouma, Frederik Coppens, Walter Daelemans, Veronique Hoste, Geert Kloosterman, Anne-Marie Mineur, Joeri van der Vloet, and Jean-Luc Verschelde. 2008a. A coreference corpus and resolution system for Dutch. In *Proceedings of LREC*.

Iris Hendrickx, Veronique Hoste, and Walter Daelemans. 2008b. Semantic and syntactic features for Dutch coreference resolution. In *Computational Linguistics and Intelligent Text Processing*, pages 351–361, Berlin, Heidelberg. Springer Berlin Heidelberg.

Véronique Hoste. 2005. *Optimization issues in machine learning of coreference resolution*. Ph.D. thesis, Universiteit Antwerpen. Faculteit Letteren en Wijsbegeerte.

Eduard Hovy, Mitchell Marcus, Martha Palmer, Lance Ramshaw, and Ralph Weischedel. 2006. OntoNotes: The 90% solution. In *Proceedings of NAACL*, pages 57–60.

Mandar Joshi, Danqi Chen, Yinhan Liu, Daniel S. Weld, Luke Zettlemoyer, and Omer Levy. 2020. SpanBERT: Improving pre-training by representing and predicting spans. *Transactions of the Association for Computational Linguistics*, 8:64–77.

Mandar Joshi, Omer Levy, Luke Zettlemoyer, and Daniel Weld. 2019. BERT for coreference resolution: Baselines and analysis. In *Proceedings of EMNLP-IJCNLP*, pages 5807–5812.

Corina Koolen, Karina van Dalen-Oskam, Andreas van Cranenburgh, and Erica Nagelhout. 2020. Literary quality in the eye of the Dutch reader: The national reader survey. *Poetics*.

Jonathan K. Kummerfeld and Dan Klein. 2013. Error-driven analysis of challenges in coreference resolution. In *Proceedings of EMNLP*, pages 265 277.

Heeyoung Lee, Angel Chang, Yves Peirsman, Nathanael Chambers, Mihai Surdeanu, and Dan Jurafsky. 2013. Deterministic coreference resolution based on entity-centric, precision-ranked rules. *Computational Linguistics*, 39(4):885–916.

Heeyoung Lee, Yves Peirsman, Angel Chang, Nathanael Chambers, Mihai Surdeanu, and Dan Jurafsky. 2011. Stanford's multi-pass sieve coreference resolution system at the CoNLL-2011 shared task. In *Proceedings of CoNLL*, pages 28–34.

Heeyoung Lee, Mihai Surdeanu, and Dan Jurafsky. 2017a. A scaffolding approach to coreference resolution integrating statistical and rule-based models. *Natural Language Engineering*, 23(5):733–762.

Kenton Lee, Luheng He, Mike Lewis, and Luke Zettlemoyer. 2017b. End-to-end neural coreference resolution. In *Proceedings of EMNLP*, pages 188–197.

Kenton Lee, Luheng He, and Luke Zettlemoyer. 2018. Higher-order coreference resolution with coarse-to-fine inference. In *Proceedings of NAACL*, pages 687–692.

Nafise Sadat Moosavi and Michael Strube. 2016. Which coreference evaluation metric do you trust? A proposal for a link-based entity aware metric. In *Proceedings of ACL*, pages 632–642.

Gertjan van Noord. 2006. At last parsing is now operational. In *TALN06. Verbum Ex Machina. Actes de la 13e conference sur le traitement automatique des langues naturelles*, pages 20–42.

Gertjan van Noord, Ineke Schuurman, and Vincent Vandeghinste. 2006. Syntactic annotation of large corpora in STEVIN. In *Proceedings of LREC*.

Jeffrey Pennington, Richard Socher, and Christopher Manning. 2014. GloVe: Global vectors for word representation. In *Proceedings of EMNLP*, pages 1532–1543.

Matthew Peters, Mark Neumann, Mohit Iyyer, Matt Gardner, Christopher Clark, Kenton Lee, and Luke Zettlemoyer. 2018. Deep contextualized word representations. In *Proceedings of NAACL*, pages 2227–2237.

Sameer Pradhan, Alessandro Moschitti, Nianwen Xue, Olga Uryupina, and Yuchen Zhang. 2012. CoNLL-2012 shared task: Modeling multilingual unrestricted coreference in OntoNotes. In *Joint Conference on EMNLP and CoNLL - Shared Task*, pages 1–40.

Sameer Pradhan, Lance Ramshaw, Mitchell Marcus, Martha Palmer, Ralph Weischedel, and Nianwen Xue. 2011. CoNLL-2011 shared task: Modeling unrestricted coreference in OntoNotes. In *Proceedings of CoNLL*, pages 1–27.

Marta Recasens, Lluís Màrquez, Emili Sapena, M. Antònia Martí, Mariona Taulé, Véronique Hoste, Massimo Poesio, and Yannick Versley. 2010. SemEval-2010 task 1: Coreference resolution in multiple languages. In *Proceedings of SemEval*, pages 1–8.

Ineke Schuurman, Véronique Hoste, and Paola Monachesi. 2010. Interacting semantic layers of annotation in SoNaR, a reference corpus of contemporary written Dutch. In *Proc. of LREC*, pages 2471–2477.

Gertjan Van Noord. 2009. Huge parsed corpora in Lassy. In *Proceedings of TLT7*, Groningen, The Netherlands. LOT.

Wietse de Vries, Andreas van Cranenburgh, and Malvina Nissim. 2020. What's so special about BERT's layers? A closer look at the NLP pipeline in monolingual and multilingual models. In *Findings of EMNLP*.

Wietse de Vries, Andreas van Cranenburgh, Arianna Bisazza, Tommaso Caselli, Gertjan van Noord, and Malvina Nissim. 2019. BERTje: A Dutch BERT model. arXiv:1912.09582.

Sam Wiseman, Alexander M. Rush, Stuart Shieber, and Jason Weston. 2015. Learning anaphoricity and antecedent ranking features for coreference resolution. In *Proceedings of ACL*, pages 1416–1426.

Wei Wu, Fei Wang, Arianna Yuan, Fei Wu, and Jiwei Li. 2020. CorefQA: Coreference resolution as query-based span prediction. In *Proceedings of ACL*, pages 6953–6963.

Partially-supervised Mention Detection

Lesly Miculicich[†‡] **James Henderson**[†]
[†] Idiap Research Institute, Switzerland
[‡]École Polytechnique Fédérale de Lausanne (EPFL), Switzerland
{lmiculicich, jhenderson}@idiap.ch

Abstract

Learning to detect entity mentions without using syntactic information can be useful for integration and joint optimization with other tasks. However, it is common to have partially annotated data for this problem. Here, we investigate two approaches to deal with partial annotation of mentions: weighted loss and soft-target classification. We also propose two neural mention detection approaches: a sequence tagging, and an exhaustive search. We evaluate our methods with coreference resolution as a downstream task, using multitask learning. The results show that the recall and F1 score improve for all methods.

1 Introduction

Mention detection is the task of identifying text spans referring to an entity: named, nominal or pronominal (Florian et al., 2004). It is a fundamental component for several downstream tasks, such as coreference resolution (Soon et al., 2001), and relation extraction (Mintz et al., 2009); and it can help to maintain coherence in large text generation (Clark et al., 2018), and contextualized machine translation (Miculicich et al., 2018). Previous studies tackled mention detection jointly with named entity recognition (Xu et al., 2017; Katiyar and Cardie, 2018; Ju et al., 2018; Wang et al., 2018). There, only certain types of entities are considered (e.g., person, location), and the goal is to recognize mention spans and their types. In this study, we are interested in discovering entity mentions, which can potentially be referred to in the text, without the use of syntactic parsing information. Our long term objective is to have a model that keeps track of entities in a document for word disambiguating language modeling and machine translation.

Data from coreference resolution is suitable for our task, but the annotation is partial in that it contains only mentions that belong to a coreference chain, not singletons. Nevertheless, the missing mentions have approximately the same distribution as the annotated ones, so we can still learn this distribution from the data. Figure 1 shows an example from Ontonotes V.5 dataset (Pradhan et al., 2012) where "the taxi driver" is annotated in sample 1 but not in 2. Thus, we approach mention detection as a partially supervised problem and investigate two simple techniques to compensate for the fact that some negative examples are true mentions: weighted loss functions and soft-target classification. By doing this, the model is encouraged to predict more false-positive samples, so it can detect potential mentions which were not annotated. We implement two neural mention detection methods: a sequence tagging approach, and an exhaustive search approach. The first method is novel, whereas the other is similar to previous work (Lee et al., 2017). We evaluate both techniques for coreference resolution by implementing a multitask learning system. We show that the proposed techniques help the model increase recall significantly with a minimal decrease in precision. In consequence, the F1 score of the mention detection and coreference resolution improves for both methods, and the exhaustive search approach yields a significant improvement over the baseline coreference resolver.

Our contributions are:

i We investigate two techniques to deal with partially annotated data.

Proceedings of the 3rd Workshop on Computational Models of Reference, Anaphora and Coreference (CRAC 2020), pages 91–98,
Barcelona, Spain (online), December 12, 2020.

> 1. [They] informed the [taxi driver] and asked
>   [him] to take the vehicle outside ...
>
> 2. On [our] way back , the taxi driver gave
>   [us] an explanation ...

Figure 1: Samples from CoNLL 2012. Annotated mentions are within brackets, non-annotated ones are underlined.

  ii We propose a sequence tagging method for mention detection that can model nested mentions.

  iii We improve an exhaustive search method for mention detection.

  iv We approach mention detection and coreference resolution as multitask learning and improve both tasks' recall.

The rest of the paper is organized as follows. Sections 2 and 3 describe the two mention detection approaches we use in our experiments. Section 4 presents the proposed methods to deal with partially annotated mentions. We use coreference resolution as a proxy task for testing our methods which is described in Section 5. Section 6 contains the experimental setting and the analysis of results. Section 7 contains related work to this study. Finally, the final conclusion is drawn Section 8.

2 Sequence tagging model

Several studies have tackled mention detection and named entity recognition as a tagging problem. Some of them use one-to-one sequence tagging techniques (Lample et al., 2016; Xu et al., 2017), while others use more elaborate techniques to include nested mentions (Katiyar and Cardie, 2018; Wang et al., 2018). Here, we propose a simpler yet effective tagging approach that can manage nested mentions.

We use a sequence-to-sequence model, which allows us to tag each word with multiple labels. The words are first encoded and contextualized using a recurrent neural network, and then a sequential decoder predicts the output tag sequence. During decoding, the model keeps a pointer into the encoder, indicating the word's position, which is being tagged at each time step. The tagging is done using the following set of symbols: $\{[,],+,-\}$. The brackets "[" and "]" indicate that the tagged word is the starting or ending of a mention respectively, the symbol "+" indicates that one or more mention brackets are open, and "-" indicates that none mention bracket is open. The pointer into the encoder moves to the next word only after predicting "+" or "-"; otherwise, it remains in the same position. Figure 2 shows a tagging example indicating the alignments of words with tags.

Given a corpus of sentences $X = (x_1, ..., x_M)$, the goal is to find the parameters Θ which maximize the log likelihood of the corresponding tag sequences $Y = (y_1, ..., y_T)$:

$$P_\Theta(Y|X) = \prod_{t=1}^{T} P_\Theta(y_t|X, y_1, ..., y_{t-1}) \tag{1}$$

The next tag probability is estimated with a softmax over the output vector of a neural network:

$$P_\Theta(y_t|X, y_1, ..., y_{t-1}) = softmax(o_t) \tag{2}$$

$$o_t = relu(W_o \cdot [d_t, h_i] + b_o) \tag{3}$$

where W_o, b_o are parameters of the network, d_t is the vector representation of the tagged sequence at time-step t, modeled with a long-short term memory (LSTM) (Hochreiter and Schmidhuber, 1997), and h_i is the vector representation of the pointer's word at time t contextualized with a bidirectional LSTM (Graves and Schmidhuber, 2005).

$$(h_1, ..., h_M) = BiLSTM(X) \tag{4}$$

$$d_t = LSTM(y_1, ..., y_{t-1}) \tag{5}$$

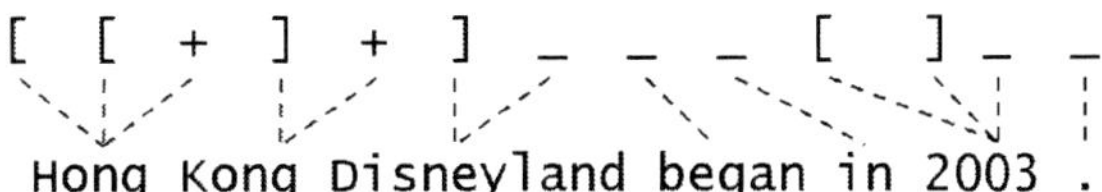

Figure 2: Tagged sentence example

where the decoder is initialized with the last states of the bidirectional encoder, $d_0 = h_M$. The i-th word pointed to at time t is given by:

$$i \leftarrow \begin{cases} 0, & \text{if } t = 0 \\ i + 1, & \text{if } t > 0 \text{ and } y_{t-1} \in \{+, -\} \\ i, & \text{otherwise} \end{cases} \tag{6}$$

At decoding time, we use a beam search approach to obtain the sequence. The complexity of the model is linear with respect to the number of words. It can be parallelized at training time, given that it uses ground-truth data for the conditioned variables. However, it cannot be parallelized during decoding because of its autoregressive nature.

3 Span scoring model

Our span scoring model of mention detection is similar to the work of Lee et al. (2017) for solving coreference resolution, and to Ju et al. (2018) for nested named mention detection, as both are exhaustive search methods. The objective is to score all possible spans m_{ij} in a document, where i and j are the starting and ending word positions of the span in the document. For this purpose, we minimize the binary cross-entropy with the labels y:

$$H(y, P_\Theta(m)) = -\frac{1}{M^2} \sum_{i=1}^{M} \sum_{j=1}^{M} (y_{m_{ij}} * log(P_\Theta(m_{ij})) + (1 - y_{m_{ij}}) * log(1 - P_\Theta(m_{ij}))) \tag{7}$$

where Θ are the parameters of the model, $y_{m_{ij}} \in [0, 1]$ is one when there is a mention from position i to j. If $y_{m_{ij}}$ is zero when there is no mention annotated, this is the same as maximizing the log-likelihood. Nevertheless, we will consider models where this is not the case.

The probability of detection is estimated as:

$$P_\Theta(m_{ij}) = \sigma(V \cdot relu(W_m \cdot m_{ij} + b_m)) \tag{8}$$

$$m_{ij} = relu(W_h \cdot [h_i, h_j, \tilde{x}_{ij}] + b_h) \tag{9}$$

where V, W_m, W_h are weight parameters of the model, b_m, b_h are biases, and m_{ij} is a representation of the span from position i to j. It is calculated with the contextualized representations of the starting and ending words h_i, h_j, and the average of the word embeddings $\tilde{x}_{ij}$:

$$(h_1, ..., h_M) = BiLSTM(X) \tag{10}$$

$$\tilde{x}_{ij} = \frac{1}{j - i} \sum_{k=i}^{j} x_k \tag{11}$$

The complexity of this model is quadratic with respect to the number of words. However, it can be parallelized at training and decoding time. Lee et al. (2017) uses an attention function over the embeddings instead of an average. That approach is less memory efficient and requires the maximum length of spans as a hyperparameter. Also, they include embeddings of the span lengths which are learned during training. As shown in the experimental part, these components do not improve the performance of our model.

4   Partially annotated data

The partial annotation of coreference data for mention detection means that not labeled spans may be true mentions of entities. Thus, the approach of treating spans without mention annotations as true negative examples would be incorrect. On the other hand, the ideal solution of sampling all possible mention annotations, which are consistent with the given partial annotation, would be intractable. We want to modify the model's loss function in such a way that, if the system predicts a false-positive, the loss is reduced. This encourages the model to favor recall over precision by predicting more mention-like spans, even when they are not labeled. We assume that it is possible to learn the true mention distribution using the annotated mention samples by extrapolating the non-annotated mentions, and we propose two ways to encourage the model to do so.

Weighted loss function: We use a weighted loss function with weight $w \in \{0, 1\}$ for negative examples only. The *sequence tagging* model makes word-wise decisions; thus, we consider words tagged as "out of mention", $y_t =$ "-", as negative examples, while the rest are positives. Although this simplification has the potential to increase inconsistencies, e.g., having non-ending or overlapping mentions, we observe that the LSMT-based model can capture the simple grammar of the tag labels with very few mistakes. For *span scoring*, the distinction between negative and positive examples is clear, given that the decisions are made for each span.

Soft-target classification: Soft-targets allow us to have a distribution over all classes instead of having a single class annotation. Thus, we applied soft-targets to negative examples to reflect the probability that they could actually be positive ones. For *sequence tagging*, we set the target of negative examples, $y_t =$ "-", to $(\rho, \rho, \rho, 1 - 3\rho)$ corresponding to the classes ([,], +, -). For *span scoring*, we change the target of negative examples to $y_{neg} = \rho$. In both cases, ρ is the probability of the example being positive.

5   Coreference Resolution

We use multitask learning to train the mention detection together with coreference resolution. The weights to sum the loss functions of each task are estimated during training, as in Cipolla et al. (2018). The sentence encoder is shared, and the output of mention detection serves as input to coreference resolution. We use the coreference resolver proposed by Lee et al. (2017). It uses a pair-wise scoring function s between a mention m_k and each of its candidate antecedents m_a, defined as:

$$s(m_k, m_a) = s_c(m_k, m_a) + s_m(m_k) + s_m(m_a) \tag{12}$$

where s_c is a function that assesses whether two mentions refer to the same entity. We modified the mention detection score s_m.

For the *sequence tagging* approach, the function s_m serves as a bias value and it is calculated as:

$$s_m = v.P(y_{t_i} = \text{"["}).P(y_{t_j} = \text{"]"}) \tag{13}$$

where y_{t_i} and y_{t_j} are the labels of the first and last words of the span, and v is a scalar parameter learned during training. At test time, only mentions in the one-best output of the mention detection model are candidate mentions for the coreference resolver. During training, the set of candidate mentions includes both the spans detected by the mention detection model and the ground truth mentions. The mention decoder is run for one pass with ground-truth labels in the conditional part of the probability function (Eq. 2), to get the mention detection loss, and run for a second pass with predicted labels to provide input for the coreferece task and compute the coreference loss.

For the *span scoring* approach, s_m is a function of the probability defined in Eq. 8, scaled by a parameter v learned during training.

$$s_m = v.P(m_{i,j}) \tag{14}$$

Model	Rec.	Prec.	F1
Sequence tagging	73.7	77.5	75.6
Span scoring	72.7	79.2	75.8
+ span size emb.	71.6	80.1	75.6
- avg. emb. + att. emb.	72.1	78.9	75.4

Table 1: Mention detection evaluation

Instead of the end-to-end objective of Lee et al. (2017), we use a multitask objective, which adds the loss function of mention detection. We do not prune mentions with a maximum length, nor impose any maximum number of mentions per document. We use the probability of the mention detector with a threshold of τ for pruning.

6 Experiments and Results

We evaluate our model on the English OntoNotes set from the CoNLL 2012 shared-task (Pradhan et al., 2012), which has 2802 documents for training, 343 for development, and 348 for testing. The setup is the same as Lee et al. (2017) for comparison purposes, with the hyper-parameters ρ, w, τ optimized on the development set. We use the average F1 score as defined in the shared-task (Pradhan et al., 2012) for evaluation of mention detection and coreference resolution.

6.1 Mention detection

First, we evaluate our stand-alone mention detectors. For this evaluation, all unannotated mentions are treated as negative examples. Table 1 show the results on the test set with models selected using the best F1 score with $\tau{=}0.5$, on the development set. We can see that *sequence tagging* performs almost as well as *span scoring* in F1 score, even though the latter is an exhaustive search method. We also evaluate the *span scoring* model with different components from Lee et al. (2017). By adding the span size vector, the precision increases but the recall decreases. Replacing the average embedding $\bar{x}$ with attention over the embeddings requires a limited span size for memory efficiency, resulting in decreased performance.

6.2 Coreference Resolution

Table 2 shows the results obtained for our multitask systems for coreference resolution and mention detection with and without the loss modification. The *sequence tagging* method obtains lower performance compared to *span scoring*. This result can be attributed to its one-best method to select mentions, in contrast to *span scoring*, where uncertainty is fully integrated with the coreference system. The *span scoring* method performs similarly to the coreference resolution baseline, showing that the naive introduction of a loss for mention detection does not improve performance (although we find it does decrease convergence time). However, adding the modified mention loss does improve coreference performance. For *sequence tagging*, the weighted loss results in higher performance, while for the *span scoring*, soft-targets work best. In both cases, the recall increases with a small decrease in precision, which improves the F1 score of mention detection and improves coreference resolution.

6.3 Recall performance

Figure 3 shows a comparison of the mention detection methods in terms of recall. The unmodified *sequence tagging* model achieves 73.7% recall, and by introducing a weighted loss at $w{=}0.01$, it reaches 90.5%. The lines show the variation of recall for the *span scoring* method with respect to the detection threshold of τ. The dotted line represents the unmodified model, while the continuous line represents the model with soft-targets at $\rho{=}0.1$, which shows higher recall for every τ.

7 Related Work

Lee et al. (2017) proposed the first end-to-end coreference resolution that does not require heavy feature engineering for word representations. Their mention detection is done by considering all spans in a

Model	Mention			Coref.
	Rec.	Prec.	F1	Avg. F1
Lee et al. (2017)	–	–	–	67.2
Sequence tagging	73.1	84.9	78.6	59.9
+ wt. loss w=0.01	77.3	83.2	80.1	64.1
+ soft-target ρ=0.1	74.3	84.0	78.8	61.2
Span scoring	75.3	88.3	81.3	67.0
+ wt. loss w=0.3	76.3	88.1	81.8	67.1
+ soft-target ρ=0.1	78.4	87.9	82.9	67.6

Table 2: Coreference resolution evaluation (CoNLL 2012)

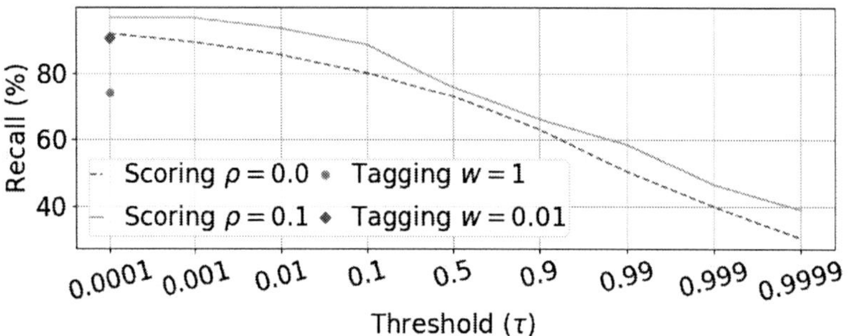

Figure 3: Recall of the *mention scoring* function with respect to the detection threshold τ. Values for the *sequence tagging* are referential

document as the candidate mentions, and the learning signal is coming indirectly from the coreference annotation. Zhang et al. (2018) used a similar approach but introducing a direct learning signal for the mention detection, which is done by adding a loss for mention detection with a scaling factor as hyperparameter. This allows a faster convergence at training time. Lee et al. (2018) proposed a high-order coreference resolution where the mention representation are inferred over several iterations of the model. However, the mention detection part is same as in (Lee et al., 2017). The following studies proposed improvements over this work (Fei et al., 2019; Joshi et al., 2019; Joshi et al., 2020) but maintaining the same method for mention detection.

Name entity recognition has been largely studied in the community. However, many of these models ignored the nested entity names. Katiyar and Cardie (2018) presents a nested named entity recognition model using a recurrent neural network that includes extra connections to handle nested mention detection. Ju et al. (2018) uses stack layers to model the nested mentions, and (Wang et al., 2018) use an stack recurrent network. Lin et al. (2019) proposed a sequence-to-nuggets architecture for nested mention detection. Li et al. (2019) uses pointer networks and adversarial learning. Shibuya and Hovy (2020) uses CRF with a iterative decoder that detect nested mentions from the outer to the inner tags. Yu et al. (2020) use a bi-affine model with a similar method as in (Lee et al., 2017).

8 Conclusion

We investigate two simple techniques to deal with partially annotated data for mention detection and propose two methods to approach it: a Weighted loss function and a soft-target classification. We evaluate them on coreference resolution and mention detection with a multitask learning approach. We show that the techniques effectively increase the recall of mentions and coreference links with a small decrease in precision, thus, improving the F1 score. In the future, we plan to use these methods to maintain coherence over long distances when reading, translating, and generating large text, by keeping track of abstract representations of entities.

Acknowledgements

We are grateful for the support of the Swiss National Science Foundation under the project LAOS, grant number "FNS-30216"

References

Roberto Cipolla, Yarin Gal, and Alex Kendall. 2018. Multi-task learning using uncertainty to weigh losses for scene geometry and semantics. In *2018 IEEE/CVF Conference on Computer Vision and Pattern Recognition*, pages 7482–7491. IEEE.

Elizabeth Clark, Yangfeng Ji, and Noah A. Smith. 2018. Neural text generation in stories using entity representations as context. In *Proceedings of the 2018 Conference of the North American Chapter of the Association for Computational Linguistics: Human Language Technologies, Volume 1 (Long Papers)*, pages 2250–2260, New Orleans, Louisiana, June. Association for Computational Linguistics.

Hongliang Fei, Xu Li, Dingcheng Li, and Ping Li. 2019. End-to-end deep reinforcement learning based coreference resolution. In *Proceedings of the 57th Annual Meeting of the Association for Computational Linguistics*, Florence, Italy, July. Association for Computational Linguistics.

R Florian, H Hassan, A Ittycheriah, H Jing, N Kambhatla, X Luo, N Nicolov, and S Roukos. 2004. A statistical model for multilingual entity detection and tracking. In *HLT-NAACL 2004: Main Proceedings*, pages 1–8, Boston, Massachusetts, USA, May 2 - May 7. Association for Computational Linguistics.

Alex Graves and Jürgen Schmidhuber. 2005. Framewise phoneme classification with bidirectional lstm and other neural network architectures. *Neural Networks*, 18(5-6):602–610.

Sepp Hochreiter and Jürgen Schmidhuber. 1997. Long-short term memory. *Neural Computation*, 9(8):1735–1780.

Mandar Joshi, Omer Levy, Luke Zettlemoyer, and Daniel Weld. 2019. BERT for coreference resolution: Baselines and analysis. In *Proceedings of the 2019 Conference on Empirical Methods in Natural Language Processing and the 9th International Joint Conference on Natural Language Processing (EMNLP-IJCNLP)*, pages 5803–5808, Hong Kong, China, November. Association for Computational Linguistics.

Mandar Joshi, Danqi Chen, Yinhan Liu, Daniel S. Weld, Luke Zettlemoyer, and Omer Levy. 2020. SpanBERT: Improving pre-training by representing and predicting spans. *Transactions of the Association for Computational Linguistics*, 8:64–77.

Meizhi Ju, Makoto Miwa, and Sophia Ananiadou. 2018. A neural layered model for nested named entity recognition. In *Proceedings of the 2018 Conference of the North American Chapter of the Association for Computational Linguistics: Human Language Technologies, Volume 1 (Long Papers)*, pages 1446–1459, New Orleans, Louisiana, June. Association for Computational Linguistics.

Arzoo Katiyar and Claire Cardie. 2018. Nested named entity recognition revisited. In *Proceedings of the 2018 Conference of the North American Chapter of the Association for Computational Linguistics: Human Language Technologies, Volume 1 (Long Papers)*, pages 861–871, New Orleans, Louisiana, June. Association for Computational Linguistics.

Guillaume Lample, Miguel Ballesteros, Sandeep Subramanian, Kazuya Kawakami, and Chris Dyer. 2016. Neural architectures for named entity recognition. In *Proceedings of the 2016 Conference of the North American Chapter of the Association for Computational Linguistics: Human Language Technologies*, pages 260–270, San Diego, California, June. Association for Computational Linguistics.

Kenton Lee, Luheng He, Mike Lewis, and Luke Zettlemoyer. 2017. End-to-end neural coreference resolution. In *Proceedings of the 2017 Conference on Empirical Methods in Natural Language Processing*, pages 188–197, Copenhagen, Denmark, September. Association for Computational Linguistics.

Kenton Lee, Luheng He, and Luke Zettlemoyer. 2018. Higher-order coreference resolution with coarse-to-fine inference. In *Proceedings of the 2018 Conference of the North American Chapter of the Association for Computational Linguistics: Human Language Technologies, Volume 2 (Short Papers)*, pages 687–692, New Orleans, Louisiana, June. Association for Computational Linguistics.

Jing Li, Deheng Ye, and Shuo Shang. 2019. Adversarial transfer for named entity boundary detection with pointer networks. In *IJCAI*, pages 5053–5059.

Hongyu Lin, Yaojie Lu, Xianpei Han, and Le Sun. 2019. Sequence-to-nuggets: Nested entity mention detection via anchor-region networks. In *Proceedings of the 57th Annual Meeting of the Association for Computational Linguistics*, pages 5182–5192.

Lesly Miculicich, Dhananjay Ram, Nikolaos Pappas, and James Henderson. 2018. Document-level neural machine translation with hierarchical attention networks. In *Proceedings of the 2018 Conference on Empirical Methods in Natural Language Processing*, pages 2947–2954, Brussels, Belgium, October-November. Association for Computational Linguistics.

Mike Mintz, Steven Bills, Rion Snow, and Daniel Jurafsky. 2009. Distant supervision for relation extraction without labeled data. In *Proceedings of the Joint Conference of the 47th Annual Meeting of the ACL and the 4th International Joint Conference on Natural Language Processing of the AFNLP*, pages 1003–1011, Suntec, Singapore, August. Association for Computational Linguistics.

Sameer Pradhan, Alessandro Moschitti, Nianwen Xue, Olga Uryupina, and Yuchen Zhang. 2012. Conll-2012 shared task: Modeling multilingual unrestricted coreference in ontonotes. In *Joint Conference on EMNLP and CoNLL - Shared Task*, pages 1–40, Jeju Island, Korea, July. Association for Computational Linguistics.

Takashi Shibuya and Eduard Hovy. 2020. Nested named entity recognition via second-best sequence learning and decoding. *Transactions of the Association for Computational Linguistics*, 8:605–620.

Wee Meng Soon, Hwee Tou Ng, and Daniel Chung Yong Lim. 2001. A machine learning approach to coreference resolution of noun phrases. *Computational Linguistics*, 27(4):521–544.

Bailin Wang, Wei Lu, Yu Wang, and Hongxia Jin. 2018. A neural transition-based model for nested mention recognition. In *Proceedings of the 2018 Conference on Empirical Methods in Natural Language Processing*, pages 1011–1017, Brussels, Belgium, October-November. Association for Computational Linguistics.

Mingbin Xu, Hui Jiang, and Sedtawut Watcharawittayakul. 2017. A local detection approach for named entity recognition and mention detection. In *Proceedings of the 55th Annual Meeting of the Association for Computational Linguistics (Volume 1: Long Papers)*, pages 1237–1247, Vancouver, Canada, July. Association for Computational Linguistics.

Juntao Yu, Bernd Bohnet, and Massimo Poesio. 2020. Named entity recognition as dependency parsing. *arXiv preprint arXiv:2005.07150*.

Rui Zhang, Cicero Nogueira dos Santos, Michihiro Yasunaga, Bing Xiang, and Dragomir Radev. 2018. Neural coreference resolution with deep biaffine attention by joint mention detection and mention clustering. In *Proceedings of the 56th Annual Meeting of the Association for Computational Linguistics (Volume 2: Short Papers)*, pages 102–107, Melbourne, Australia, July. Association for Computational Linguistics.

Neural Coreference Resolution for Arabic

Abdulrahman Aloraini[1,2]*   **Juntao Yu**[1]*   **Massimo Poesio**[1]

[1]Queen Mary University of London, United Kingdom
[2]Qassim University, Saudi Arabia
`{a.aloraini, juntao.yu, m.poesio}@qmul.ac.uk`

Abstract

No neural coreference resolver for Arabic exists, in fact we are not aware of any learning-based coreference resolver for Arabic since (Björkelund and Kuhn, 2014). In this paper, we introduce a coreference resolution system for Arabic based on Lee et al's end-to-end architecture combined with the Arabic version of BERT and an external mention detector. As far as we know, this is the first neural coreference resolution system aimed specifically to Arabic, and it substantially outperforms the existing state-of-the-art on OntoNotes 5.0 with a gain of 15.2 points CONLL F1. We also discuss the current limitations of the task for Arabic and possible approaches that can tackle these challenges.

1 Introduction

Coreference resolution is the task of grouping mentions in a text that refer to the same real-world entity into clusters (Poesio et al., 2016) . Coreference resolution is a difficult task that requires reasoning, context understanding, and background knowledge of real-world entities, and has driven research in both natural language processing and machine learning, particularly since the release of the ONTONOTES multilingual corpus providing annotated coreference data for Arabic, Chinese and English and used for the 2011 and 2012 CONLL shared tasks (Pradhan et al., 2012). Since then, there has been substantial research on English coreference, most recently using neural coreference approaches (Lee et al., 2017; Lee et al., 2018; Kantor and Globerson, 2019a; Joshi et al., 2019b; Joshi et al., 2019a; Yu et al., 2020b; Wu et al., 2020), leading to a significant increase in the performance of coreference resolvers for English. By contrast, there has been almost no research on Arabic coreference; the performance for Arabic coreference resolution has not improved much since the CONLL 2012 shared task, and in particular no neural architectures have been proposed–the current state-of-the-art system remains the model proposed in (Björkelund and Kuhn, 2014). In this paper we close this very obvious gap by proposing what to our knowledge is the first neural coreference resolver for Arabic.[1]

One explanation for this lack of research might simply be the lack of training data large enough for the task. Another explanation might be that Arabic is more problematic than English because of its rich morphology, its many dialects, and/or its high degree of ambiguity. We explore the first of these possibilities. Coreference resolution can be further divided into two subtasks–mention detection and mention clustering–as illustrated in Figure 1. In early work, coreference's two subtasks were usually carried out in a pipeline fashion (Soon et al., 2001; Fernandes et al., 2014; Björkelund and Kuhn, 2014; Wiseman et al., 2015; Wiseman et al., 2016; Clark and Manning, 2016a; Clark and Manning, 2016b), with candidate mentions selected prior the mention clustering step. Since Lee et al. (2017) introduced an end-to-end neural coreference architecture that achieved state of the art by carrying out the two tasks jointly, as first proposed by Daume and Marcu (2005), most state-of-the-art systems have followed this approach. However, no end-to-end solution was attempted for Arabic. We intend to explore whether an end-to-end solution would be practicable with a corpus of more limited size.

---

* Equal contribution. Listed by alphabetical order.

[1]The code is available at `https://github.com/juntaoy/aracoref`

Proceedings of the 3rd Workshop on Computational Models of Reference, Anaphora and Coreference (CRAC 2020), pages 99–110,
Barcelona, Spain (online), December 12, 2020.

1. Mention Detection	<u>Obama</u> nominated <u>Clinton</u> as <u>his</u> secretary of state on Monday. <u>He</u> chose <u>her</u> because <u>she</u> had foreign affairs experience.
2. Mention Clustering	<u>Obama</u> nominated <u>Clinton</u> as <u>his</u> secretary of state on Monday. <u>He</u> chose <u>her</u> because <u>she</u> had foreign affairs experience.

Figure 1: The first step in coreference resolution is mention detection. The detected mentions are underlined. The second step is mention clustering. We have two clusters {Obama, his, he} and {Clinton, her, she}. The mention detector might identify other words as mentions, but for simplicity we present only the mentions of the two clusters.

The approach we followed to adapt the state-of-the-art English coreference resolution architecture to Arabic is as follows. We started with a strong baseline system (Lee et al., 2018; Kantor and Globerson, 2019a), enhanced with contextual BERT embeddings (Devlin et al., 2019). We then explored three methods for improving the model's performance for Arabic. The first method is to pre-process Arabic words with heuristic rules. We follow Althobaiti et al. (2014) to normalize the letters with different forms, and removing all the diacritics. This results in a substantial improvement of 7 percentage points over our baseline. The second route is to replace multilingual BERT with a BERT model trained only on the Arabic texts (ARABERT) (Antoun et al., 2020). Multilingual BERT is trained with 100+ languages; as a result, it is not optimized for any of them. As shown by Antoun et al. (2020), monolingual BERT trained only on the Arabic texts has better performance on various NLP tasks. We found the same holds for coreference: using embeddings from monolingual BERT, the model further improved the CONLL F1 by 4.8 percentage points. Our third step is to leverage the end-to-end system with a separately trained mention detector (Yu et al., 2020a). We show that a better mention detection performance can be achieved by using a separately trained mention detector. And by using a hybrid training strategy between the end-to-end and pipeline approaches (end-to-end annealing) our system gains an additional 0.8 percentage points. Our final system achieved a CONLL F1 score of 63.9%, which is is 15% more than the previous state-of-the-art system (Björkelund and Kuhn, 2014) on Arabic coreference with the CONLL dataset. Overall, we show that the state-of-the-art English coreference model can be adapted to Arabic coreference leading to a substantial improvement in performance when compared to previous feature-based systems.

2 Related Work

2.1 English Coreference Resolution

Like with other natural language processing tasks, most state-of-the-art coreference resolution systems are evaluated on English data. Coreference resolution for English is an active area of research. Until the appearance of neural systems, state-of-the-art systems for English coreference resolution were either rule-based (Lee et al., 2011) or feature-based (Soon et al., 2001; Björkelund and Nugues, 2011; Fernandes et al., 2014; Björkelund and Kuhn, 2014; Clark and Manning, 2015). Wiseman et al. (2015) introduced a neural network-based approach to solving the task in a non-linear way. In their system, the heuristic features commonly used in linear models are transformed by a tanh function to be used as the mention representations. Clark and Manning (2016b) integrated reinforcement learning to let the model optimize directly on the B^3 scores. Lee et al. (2017) first presented a neural joint approach for mention detection and coreference resolution. Their model does not rely on parse trees; instead, the system learns to detect mentions by exploring the outputs of a bi-directional LSTM. Lee et al. (2018) is an extended version of Lee et al. (2017) mainly enhanced by using ELMo embeddings (Peters et al., 2018), in addition, the use of second-order inference enabled the system to explore partial entity level features and further improved the system by 0.4 percentage points. Later the model was further improved by Kantor and Globerson

(2019a) who use BERT embeddings (Devlin et al., 2019) instead of ELMo embeddings. In these systems, both BERT and ELMo embeddings are used in a pre-trained fashion. More recently, Joshi et al. (2019b) fine-tuned the BERT model for coreference, resulting in a small further improvement. Later, Joshi et al. (2019a) introduces SPANBERT which is trained for tasks that involve spans. Using SPANBERT, they achieved a substantial gain of 2.7% when compared with the Joshi et al. (2019b) model. Wu et al. (2020) reformulate the coreference resolution task as question answering task and achieved the state-of-the-art results by pretrain the system first on the large question answering corpora.

2.2 Arabic Coreference Resolution

There have been several studies of Arabic coreference resolution; in particular, several of the systems involved in the CONLL 2012 shared task attempted Arabic as well. li (2012) used syntactic parse trees to detect mentions, and compared pairs of mention based on their semantic and syntactic features. Zhekova and Kübler (2010) proposed a language independent module that requires only syntactic information and clusters mentions using the memory-based learner TiMBL (Daelemans et al., 2004). Chen and Ng (2012) detected mentions by employing named entity and language-dependent heuristics. They employed multiple sieves (Lee et al., 2011) for English and Chinese, but only used an exact match sieve for Arabic because other sieves did not provide better results. Björkelund and Nugues (2011) considered all noun phrases and possessive pronouns as mentions, and trained two types of classifier: logistic regression and decision trees. Stamborg et al. (2012) extracted all noun phrases, pronouns, and possessive pronouns as mentions. Then they applied (Björkelund and Nugues, 2011)'s solver which consists of various lexical and graph dependency features. Uryupina et al. (2012) adapted for Arabic the BART (Versley et al., 2008) coreference resolution system, which consists of five components: pre-processing pipeline, mention factory, feature extraction module, decoder and encoder. Fernandes et al. (2014) defined a set of rules based on parse tree information to detect mentions, and utilized a latent tree representation to learn coreference chains. Similarly Björkelund and Kuhn (2014) adopted a tree representation approach to cluster mentions, but improved the learning strategy and introduced non-local features to capture more information about coreference relations. There have been other research studies related to anaphora resolution (Trabelsi et al., 2016; Bouzid et al., 2017; Beseiso and Al-Alwani, 2016; Abolohom and Omar, 2015), but they only considered pronominal anaphora. Aloraini and Poesio (2020) also considered a specific type of pronominal anaphora, zero-pronoun anaphora. All current approaches suffer from a number of limitations, one of which is that most of them rely on an extensive set of hand-chosen features.

3 System architecture

3.1 The Baseline System

We use the Lee et al. (2018) system as our baseline and replace their ELMo embeddings with the BERT recipe of Kantor and Globerson (2019a). The input of the system is the concatenated embeddings $((emb_t)_{t=1}^T)$ of both word and character levels. The word-level fastText (Bojanowski et al., 2016) and BERT (Devlin et al., 2019) embeddings are used together with the character embeddings learned from a convolution neural network (CNN) during training. The input is then put through a multi-layer bi-directional LSTM to create the token representations $((x_t)_{t=1}^T)$. The $(x_t)_{t=1}^T$ are used together with head representations (h_i) to form the mention representations (M_i). The h_i of a mention is calculated as the weighted average of its token representations $(\{x_{b_i}, ..., x_{e_i}\})$, where b_i and e_i are the indices of the start and the end of the mention respectively. The mention score $(s_m(i))$ is then computed by a feedforward neural network to determine the likeness of a candidate to be mention. Formally, the system computes h_i, M_i and $s_m(i)$ as follows:

$$\alpha_t = \text{FFNN}_\alpha(x_t)$$

$$a_{i,t} = \frac{exp(\alpha_t)}{\sum_{k=b_i}^{e_i} exp(\alpha_k)}$$

101

$$h_i = \sum_{t=b_i}^{e_i} a_{i,t} \cdot x_t$$

$$M_i = [x_{b_i}, x_{e_i}, h_i, \phi(i)]$$

$$s_m(i) = \text{FFNN}_m(M_i)$$

where $\phi(i)$ is the mention width feature embeddings. To make the task computationally tractable, the system only considers mentions up to a maximum width of 30 tokens (i.e. $e_i - b_i < 30$). Further pruning on candidate mentions is applied before approaching the antecedent selection step. The model keeps a small portion (0.4 mention/token) of the top-ranked spans according to their mention scores ($s_m(i)$).

Next, the system uses a bilinear function to compute a light-weight mention pair scores ($s_c(i, j)$) between all the valid mention pairs[2]. The scores are then used to select top candidate antecedents for all candidate mentions (coarse antecedent selection). More precisely, the $s_c(i, j)$ are computed as follows:

$$s_c(i, j) = M_i^\top W_c M_j$$

After that, the system further computes a more accurate mention pair scores between the mentions and their top candidate antecedents $s_a(i, j)$:

$$P_{(i,j)} = [M_i, M_j, M_i \circ M_j, \phi(i, j)]$$

$$s_a(i, j) = \text{FFNN}_a(P_{(i,j)})$$

where $P_{(i,j)}$ is the mention pair representation, M_i, M_j is the representation of the antecedent and anaphor respectively, $\circ$ denotes element-wise product, and $\phi(i, j)$ is the distance feature between a mention pair.

The next step is to compute the final pairwise score ($s(i, j)$). The system adds an artificial antecedent ϵ to deal with cases of non-mentions, discourse-new mentions or cases when the antecedent does not appear in the candidate list. The $s(i, j)$ is calculated as follows:

$$s(i, j) = \begin{cases} 0 & i = \epsilon \\ s_m(i) + s_m(j) + s_c(i, j) + s_a(i, j) & i \neq \epsilon \end{cases}$$

For each mention the predicted antecedent is the one that has the highest $s(i, j)$. An anaphora-antecedent link will be created only if the predicted antecedent is not ϵ.

Additionally, the model has an option to use higher-order inference to allow the system to access entity level information. We refer the reader to the original Lee et al. (2018) paper for more details. We use the default setting of Lee et al. (2018) to do second-order inference. The final clusters are created using the anaphora-antecedent pairs predicted by the system. Figure 2 shows the proposed system architecture of our system.

3.2 Data Pre-processing

Arabic is a morphologically rich language. Thus, training on Arabic texts that are not pre-processed properly can suffer from sparsity (various forms for the same word) and ambiguity (same form corresponding to multiple words). There are two reasons for these problems. First, certain letters can have different forms which are usually misspelled, such as the various forms of the letter "alif". Second, the placement of diacritics on words which are assumed to be undiacritized (Habash and Sadat, 2006). Therefore, we follow the steps proposed in (Althobaiti et al., 2014) to pre-process the data. These steps include:

- Normalizing the various forms of the letter "alif" (إ,أ,آ) to the letter "ا".

- Removing all diacritic marks.

We show an example of an original and pre-processed sentence from OntoNotes 5.0 in Table 1. Pre-processing the data increases the overall performance of coreference system with 7 percentage points more as we will see in Section 5.

---

[2]Candidate mentions are paired with all the mentions appeared before them (candidate antecedents) in the document.

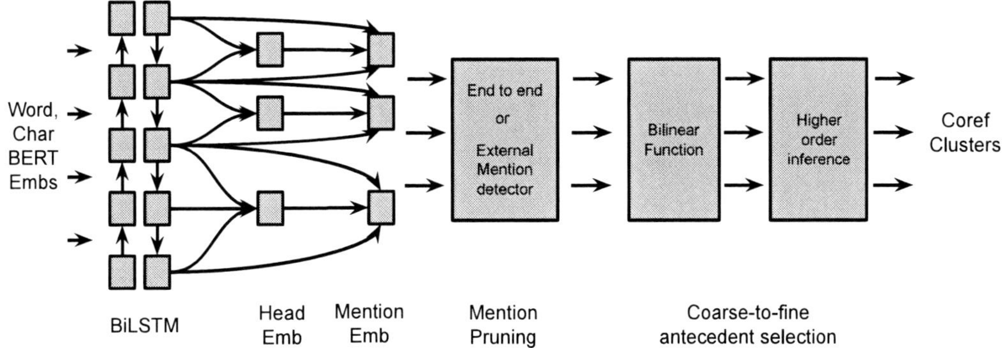

Figure 2: The proposed system architecture.

| Original text | إلى ذلكَ كَتَبَت مِئاتِ المَقالاتِ النَّقْدِيةِ الأَدَبِيةِ |
| pre-processed text | الى ذلك كتبت مئات المقالات النقدية الادبية |

Table 1: An example on how we pre-process Arabic text. The letter "alif" is normalized and all diacritic marks are removed.

3.3 Multilingual vs. monolingual BERT

BERT (Devlin et al., 2019) is a language representation model consisting of multiple stacked Transformers (Vaswani et al., 2017). BERT was pretrained on a large amount of unlabeled text, and produces distributional vectors for words and contexts. Recently, it has been shown that BERT can capture structural properties of a language, such as its surface, semantic, and syntactic aspects (Jawahar et al., 2019) which seems related to what we need for the coreference resolution. Therefore, we set BERT to produce embeddings for the mentions. BERT is available for English, Chinese, and there is a version for multiple languages, called multilingual BERT [3]. Multilingual BERT is publicly available and covers a wide range of languages including Arabic. Even though the multilingual version provides great results for many languages, it has been shown their monolingual counterparts to achieve better. Therefore, recent research adopts the monolingual approach to pretrain BERT, developing, e.g., CamemBERT for French (Martin et al., 2019), ALBERTo for Italian (Polignano et al., 2019), and others (Lee et al., 2020; Souza et al., 2019; Kuratov and Arkhipov, 2019). AraBERT (Antoun et al., 2020) is a monolingual BERT model for Arabic which was pre-trained on a collection of Wikipedia and newspaper articles. There are two versions, AraBERT 0.1 and AraBERT 1.0, the difference being that the latter pretrained on the word morphemes obtained using Farasa (Darwish and Mubarak, 2016). The two versions yield relatively similar scores in various NLP tasks. In our experiments, we used AraBERT 0.1 because empirically it proved more compatible with the coreference resolution system.

3.4 Mention Detection

Mention detection is a crucial part of the coreference resolution system, better candidate mentions usually lead to better overall performance. As suggested by Yu et al. (2020a), a separately trained mention detector can achieve a better mention detection performance when compared to its end-to-end counterpart. In this work, we adapt the state-of-the-art mention detector of Yu et al. (2020a) to aid our system. In their paper, Yu et al. (2020a) evaluated three different architectures for English mention detection task, we use their best settings (BIAFFINE MD) and replace their ELMo embeddings with BERT embeddings in the same way

---

[3]https://github.com/google-research/bert

Algorithm 1: End-to-end annealing algorithm.

Input: Training step: N; Candidate mentions from external mention detector: $\text{CANDIDATE}_{\text{EXTERNAL}}$

Output: Trainable variables: W

1   $n = 0$;

2   **while** $n \leq N$ **do**

3      $\text{PIPELINE}_{\text{RATIO}} \leftarrow n/N$;

4      $rand = random.random()$;

5   **if** $rand \leq \text{PIPELINE}_{\text{RATIO}}$ **then**

6         $\text{CANDIDATEMENTION} \leftarrow \text{CANDIDATE}_{\text{EXTERNAL}}$;

7   **else**

8   Generate mention candidates $\text{CANDIDATE}_{\text{END-TO-END}}$;

9         $\text{CANDIDATEMENTION} \leftarrow \text{CANDIDATE}_{\text{END-TO-END}}$;

10   **end**

11   Predict antecedent for candidate mentions;

12   Compute training loss;

13   Update W;

14      $n \leftarrow n + 1$

15 **end**

Models	Joint			Separate		
	R	P	F1	R	P	F1
BASELINE (MULTIBERT)	85.6	24.4	38.0	**88.1**	25.2	39.2
MULTIBERT+PRE	91.2	26.0	40.5	**93.3**	26.6	41.5
ARABERT+PRE	92.5	26.4	41.1	**95.5**	27.2	42.4

Table 2: The mention detection performance comparison between the separately and jointly trained mention detectors in a high recall setting.

we did for our coreference system[4]. The BIAFFINE MD uses contextual word embeddings and a multi-layer bi-directional LSTM to encode the tokens. It then uses a biaffine classifier (Dozat and Manning, 2017) to assign every possible span in the sentence a score. Finally, the candidate mentions are chosen according to their scores. In addition to the standard high-F1 setting, the system has a further option (high-recall) to output top mentions in the proportion of the number of tokens, this is similar to our mention detection part of the system. Here we use the high-recall settings of the mention detector we modify the baseline system to allow the system using the mentions supplied by the external mention detector.

To confirm our hypothesis that a separately trained mention detector can achieve a better mention detection performance, we compare the mention detection performance of our system with the separately trained mention detector. For our system, we train the models end-to-end and assess the quality of candidate mentions before feeding them into the mention clustering part of the system. Table 2 shows the comparison of both systems in three different settings (MULTIBERT (baseline), MULTIBERT+PRE (multilingual BERT and data pre-processing), ARABERT+PRE (ARABERT and data pre-processing)). As we can see from the table, the separately trained mention detector constantly have a better recall of up to 3% when compared with the jointly trained mention detector[5].

The preliminary experiments show that by simply using the mentions generated by the external mention detector in a pipeline setting result in a lower coreference resolution performance. We believe this is mainly because in an end-to-end setting, the model is exposed to different negative mention examples;

---

[4]We tried to add the fastText and character-based embeddings to the system but found they do not improve the mention detection results

[5]Here we only care about the recall as the number of candidate mentions is fixed

Category	Training	Dev	Test
Documents	359	44	44
Sentences	7,422	950	1,003
Words	264,589	30,942	30,935

Table 3: Statistics on Arabic portion of CONLL-2012.

Parameter	Value
bi-directional LSTM layers/size/dropout	3/200/0.4
FFNN layers/size/dropout	2/150/0.2
CNN filter widths/size	[3,4,5]/50
Char/fastText/Feature embedding size	8/300/20
BERT embedding size/layer	768/Last 4
Embedding dropout	0.5
Max span width	30
Max num of antecedents	50
Mention/token ratio	0.4
Optimiser	Adam (1e-3)
Training step	400K

Table 4: Hyperparameters for our models.

hence, has a better ability to handle false positive candidates. To leverage the benefits between better candidate mentions and more negative mention examples, we introduce a new hybrid training strategy (end-to-end annealing) that initially training the system in an end-to-end fashion and linearly decreasing the usage of end-to-end approach. At the end of the training, the system is trained purely in a pipeline fashion. The resulted system is then tested in a pipeline fashion. Algorithm 1 shows the details of our end-to-end annealing training strategy.

4 Experimental Setup

Since the BERT models are large, the fine-tuning approaches are more computationally expensive: GPU/TPUs with large memory (32GB+) are required. In this work, we use BERT embeddings in a pre-trained fashion to make our experiment feasible on a GTX-1080Ti GPU with 11GB memory.

4.1 Dataset

We run our model on the Arabic portion of OntoNotes 5.0, which were used in the the official CONLL-2012 shared task (Pradhan et al., 2012). The data is divided into three splits: train, development, and test. We used each split for its purpose, the train for training the model, the development for optimizing the settings, and the test for evaluating the overall performance. Detailed information about the number of documents, sentences, and words can be found in Table 3.

4.2 Evaluation Metrics

For our evaluation on the coreference system, we use the official CONLL 2012 scoring script v8.01 to score our predictions. Following standard practice, we report recall, precision, and F1 scores for MUC, B^3 and $CEAF_{\phi_4}$ and the average F1 score of those three metrics. For our experiments on the mention detection we report recall, precision and F1 scores for mentions.

4.3 Hyperparameters

We use the default settings of Lee et al. (2018), and replace their GloVe/ELMo embeddings with the fastText/BERT embeddings. Table 4 shows the hyperparameters used in our system.

Models	MUC			B^3			CEAF$_{\phi_4}$			Avg.
	R	P	F1	R	P	F1	R	P	F1	F1
Björkelund and Nugues (2011)	43.9	52.5	47.8	35.7	49.8	41.6	40.5	41.9	41.2	43.5
Fernandes et al. (2012)	43.6	49.7	46.5	38.4	47.7	42.5	48.2	45.0	46.5	45.2
Björkelund and Kuhn (2014)	47.5	53.3	50.3	44.1	49.3	46.6	49.2	49.5	49.3	48.7
BASELINE (MULTIBERT)	45.7	66.9	54.3	38.8	64.3	48.4	45.7	57.9	51.1	51.3
MULTIBERT+PRE	56.1	67.1	61.1	50.0	63.4	56.0	54.8	61.1	57.8	58.3
ARABERT+PRE	62.3	70.8	66.3	56.3	65.8	60.7	58.8	**66.1**	62.2	63.1
ARABERT+PRE+MD	**63.2**	**70.9**	**66.8**	**57.1**	**66.3**	**61.3**	**61.6**	65.5	**63.5**	**63.9**

Table 5: Coreference resolution results on Arabic test set.

Models	R	P	F1
BASELINE (MULTIBERT)	56.5	79.1	65.9
MULTIBERT+PRE	67.4	78.8	72.6
ARABERT+PRE	70.6	79.9	75.0
ARABERT+PRE+MD	**72.9**	**80.4**	**76.4**

Table 6: Mention detection results on Arabic test set.

5 Evaluation

5.1 Results

Baseline We first evaluate our baseline system using the un-pre-processed data and the multilingual BERT model. As we can see from Table 5, the baseline system already outperforms the previous state-of-the-art system which is based on handcrafted features by a large margin of 2.6 percentage points. The better F1 scores are mainly as a result of a much better precision in all three metrics evaluated, the recall is lower than the previous state-of-the-art system (Björkelund and Kuhn, 2014).

Data pre-processing We then apply heuristic rules to pre-process the data. The goal of pre-processing is to reduce the sparsity of the data by normalizing the letters that have different forms and removing the diacritics. By doing so, we created a 'clean' version of the data. As we can see from Table 5, the simple pre-processing on the data achieved a large gain of 7 percentage points when compared with the baseline model trained on the original data. Since the pre-processing largely reduced the data sparsity, the recall of all three matrices has been largely improved. We further compare the mention scores of two models (see Table 6). As illustrated in the table, the system trained on the pre-processed data achieved a much better recall and a similar precision when compared with the baseline. This suggests that data pre-processing is an efficient and effective way to improve the performance of the Arabic coreference resolution task.

Language Specific BERT Embeddings Next, we evaluate the effect of the language-specific BERT embeddings. The monolingual BERT model (ARABERT) trained specifically on Arabic Wikipedia and several news corpora has been shown that it can outperform the multilingual BERT model on several NLP tasks for Arabic. Here we replace the multilingual BERT model with the ARABERT model to generate the pre-trained word embeddings. We test our system with ARABERT on the pre-processed text, the results are shown in Table 5 and Table 6. As we can see from the Tables, the model enhanced by the ARABERT achieved large gains of 4.7 and 2.4 percentage points when compared to the model using multilingual BERT on coreference resolution and mention detection respectively. Both recall and precision are improved for all the metrics evaluated which confirmed the finding in Antoun et al. (2020) that ARABERT model is better suited for Arabic NLP tasks.

External Mention Detector Finally, we use a separately trained mention detector to guide our models with a better candidate mentions. We train a mention detector using the same CONLL 2012 Arabic datasets and store the top-ranked mentions in the file. We use the top-ranked mentions from the external mention

Corpora	Language	Tokens	Documents
ACE	English	~960,000	-
	Chinese	~615,000	-
	Arabic	~500,000	-
OntoNotes	English	~1,600,000	2384
	Chinese	~950,000	1729
	Arabic	~300,000	447

Table 7: General domain coreference resolution corpora that include Arabic.

detector in a pipeline fashion, the mentions are fixed during the training of the coreference resolution task. We use the output of the mention detector model trained on the pre-processed data and using the ARABERT embeddings as this model performs best over three settings we tested (see Table 2). We use the end-to-end annealing training strategy proposed in Section 3.4 to train our model with both end-to-end and pipeline approaches. The model is then tested in a pipeline fashion. Table 5 shows our results on coreference resolution, the model enhanced by the external mention detector achieved a gain of 0.8% when compared to the pure end-to-end model. We further compared the mention detection performance between two models in Table 6, as expected the new model has a much better mention recall (2.3%) when compared to the pure end-to-end model (ARABERT+PRE), this suggests our training strategy successfully transferred the higher recall achieved by the external mention detector to our coreference system.

Overall, our best model enhanced by the data pre-processing, monolingual Arabic BERT and the external mention detector achieved a CONLL F1 score of 63.9% and this is 15.2 percentage points better than the previous state-of-the-art system (Björkelund and Kuhn, 2014) on Arabic coreference resolution.

5.2 Discussion

Coreference resolution is a difficult task, and even more so for languages such as Arabic with more limited resourced. The main challenge is the lack of large scale coreference resolution corpora. At present there are two multilingual coreference corpora that cover Arabic. The first is the Automatic Content Extraction (ACE) (Doddington et al., 2004) which has ~500,000 tokens, but mentions are restricted to seven semantic types[6] and some can be singletons (mentions that do not corefer). The second is OntoNotes (Pradhan et al., 2012), which covers all entities and does not consider singletons, but the size is smaller than ACE, with ~300,000 tokens. A summary of the two corpora in Table 7. OntoNotes has been the standard for coreference resolution evaluation since the CONLL-2012 shared task. However, its Arabic portion is small and this scarcity poses a considerable barrier to improving coreference resolution.

Another challenge of the task is the absence of large pre-trained language models. There are two versions of BERT: BERT-base and BERT-large. BERT-large integrates more parameters to encode better representations for mentions which usually leads to a better performance in many NLP tasks. ARABERT and multilingual BERT are pre-trained using the BERT-base approach because BERT-large is computationally expensive. We are not aware of any publicly available BERT-large for Arabic that we could have used in our experiments. We surmise that a BERT-large version of Arabic can improve the overall performance as shown in prior works (Joshi et al., 2019b; Kantor and Globerson, 2019b).

6   Conclusion

In this paper, we modernize the Arabic coreference resolution task by adapting state-of-the-art English coreference system to the Arabic language. We start with a strong baseline system and introduce three methods (data pre-processing, language-specific BERT, external mention detector) to effectively enhance the performance of the Arabic coreference resolution. Our final system enhanced by all three methods achieved a CONLL F1 score of 63.9% and improved the state-of-the-art result on Arabic coreference resolution task by more than 15 percentage points.

---

[6]The semantic types are person, organization, geo-political entity, location, facility, vehicle, and weapon.

Acknowledgements

This research was supported in part by the DALI project, ERC Grant 695662, in part by the Human Rights in the Era of Big Data and Technology (HRBDT) project, ESRC grant ES/M010236/1.

References

Abdullatif Abolohom and Nazlia Omar. 2015. A hybrid approach to pronominal anaphora resolution in arabic. *Journal of Computer Science*, 11(5):764.

Abdulrahman Aloraini and Massimo Poesio. 2020. Cross-lingual zero pronoun resolution. In *Proceedings of The 12th Language Resources and Evaluation Conference*, pages 90–98.

Maha Althobaiti, Udo Kruschwitz, and Massimo Poesio. 2014. Aranlp: A java-based library for the processing of arabic text.

Wissam Antoun, Fady Baly, and Hazem Hajj. 2020. Arabert: Transformer-based model for arabic language understanding. *arXiv preprint arXiv:2003.00104*.

Majdi Beseiso and Abdulkareem Al-Alwani. 2016. A coreference resolution approach using morphological features in arabic. *International Journal of Advanced Computer Science and Applications*, 7(10):107–113.

Anders Björkelund and Pierre Nugues. 2011. Exploring lexicalized features for coreference resolution. In *Proceedings of the Fifteenth Conference on Computational Natural Language Learning: Shared Task*, pages 45–50.

Anders Björkelund and Jonas Kuhn. 2014. Learning structured perceptrons for coreference resolution with latent antecedents and non-local features. In *Proceedings of the 52nd Annual Meeting of the Association for Computational Linguistics (Volume 1: Long Papers)*, pages 47–57.

Piotr Bojanowski, Edouard Grave, Armand Joulin, and Tomas Mikolov. 2016. Enriching word vectors with subword information. *arXiv preprint arXiv:1607.04606*.

Saoussen Mathlouthi Bouzid, Fériel Ben Fraj Trabelsi, and Chiraz Ben Othmane Zribi. 2017. How to combine salience factors for arabic pronoun anaphora resolution. In *2017 IEEE/ACS 14th International Conference on Computer Systems and Applications (AICCSA)*, pages 929–936. IEEE.

Chen Chen and Vincent Ng. 2012. Combining the best of two worlds: A hybrid approach to multilingual coreference resolution. In *Joint Conference on EMNLP and CoNLL-Shared Task*, pages 56–63.

Kevin Clark and Christopher D. Manning. 2015. Entity-centric coreference resolution with model stacking. In *Association for Computational Linguistics (ACL)*.

Kevin Clark and Christopher D. Manning. 2016a. Deep reinforcement learning for mention-ranking coreference models. In *Empirical Methods on Natural Language Processing (EMNLP)*.

Kevin Clark and Christopher D. Manning. 2016b. Improving coreference resolution by learning entity-level distributed representations. In *Association for Computational Linguistics (ACL)*.

Walter Daelemans, Jakub Zavrel, Kurt Van Der Sloot, and Antal Van den Bosch. 2004. Timbl: Tilburg memory-based learner. *Tilburg University*.

Kareem Darwish and Hamdy Mubarak. 2016. Farasa: A new fast and accurate arabic word segmenter. In *Proceedings of the Tenth International Conference on Language Resources and Evaluation (LREC'16)*, pages 1070–1074.

H. Daume and D. Marcu. 2005. A large-scale exploration of effective global features for a joint entity detection and tracking model. In *Proc. HLT/EMNLP*, Vancouver.

Jacob Devlin, Ming-Wei Chang, Kenton Lee, and Kristina Toutanova. 2019. Bert: Pre-training of deep bidirectional transformers for language understanding. In *Proceedings of the 2019 Annual Conference of the North American Chapter of the Association for Computational Linguistics (NAACL)*.

George R Doddington, Alexis Mitchell, Mark A Przybocki, Lance A Ramshaw, Stephanie M Strassel, and Ralph M Weischedel. 2004. The automatic content extraction (ace) program-tasks, data, and evaluation. In *Lrec*, volume 2, pages 837–840. Lisbon.

Timothy Dozat and Christopher Manning. 2017. Deep biaffine attention for neural dependency parsing. In *Proceedings of 5th International Conference on Learning Representations (ICLR)*.

Eraldo Fernandes, Cícero dos Santos, and Ruy Milidiú. 2012. Latent structure perceptron with feature induction for unrestricted coreference resolution. In *Joint Conference on EMNLP and CoNLL - Shared Task*, pages 41–48, Jeju Island, Korea, July. Association for Computational Linguistics.

Eraldo Rezende Fernandes, Cícero Nogueira dos Santos, and Ruy Milidiú. 2014. Latent trees for coreference resolution. In *Computational Linguistics, 40(4)*, pages 801–835.

Nizar Habash and Fatiha Sadat. 2006. Arabic preprocessing schemes for statistical machine translation. In *Proceedings of the Human Language Technology Conference of the NAACL, Companion Volume: Short Papers*, pages 49–52.

Ganesh Jawahar, Benoît Sagot, and Djamé Seddah. 2019. What does bert learn about the structure of language? In *57th Annual Meeting of the Association for Computational Linguistics (ACL), Florence, Italy*.

Mandar Joshi, Danqi Chen, Yinhan Liu, Daniel S Weld, Luke Zettlemoyer, and Omer Levy. 2019a. Spanbert: Improving pre-training by representing and predicting spans. *arXiv preprint arXiv:1907.10529*.

Mandar Joshi, Omer Levy, Luke Zettlemoyer, and Daniel Weld. 2019b. BERT for coreference resolution: Baselines and analysis. In *Proceedings of the 2019 Conference on Empirical Methods in Natural Language Processing and the 9th International Joint Conference on Natural Language Processing (EMNLP-IJCNLP)*, pages 5803–5808, Hong Kong, China, November. Association for Computational Linguistics.

Ben Kantor and Amir Globerson. 2019a. Coreference resolution with entity equalization. In *Proceedings of the 57th Annual Meeting of the Association for Computational Linguistics*, pages 673–677, Florence, Italy, July. Association for Computational Linguistics.

Ben Kantor and Amir Globerson. 2019b. Coreference resolution with entity equalization. In *Proceedings of the 57th Annual Meeting of the Association for Computational Linguistics*, pages 673–677.

Yuri Kuratov and Mikhail Arkhipov. 2019. Adaptation of deep bidirectional multilingual transformers for russian language. *arXiv preprint arXiv:1905.07213*.

Heeyoung Lee, Yves Peirsman, Angel Chang, Nathanael Chambers, Mihai Surdeanu, and Dan Jurafsky. 2011. Stanford's multi-pass sieve coreference resolution system at the conll-2011 shared task. In *CONLL Shared Task '11 Proceedings of the Fifteenth Conference on Computational Natural Language Learning: Shared Task*, pages 28–34.

Kenton Lee, Luheng He, Mike Lewis, and Luke Zettlemoyer. 2017. End-to-end neural coreference resolution. *Proceedings of the 2017 Conference on Empirical Methods in Natural Language Processing*.

Kenton Lee, Luheng He, and Luke Zettlemoyer. 2018. Higher-order coreference resolution with coarse-to-fine inference. *Proceedings of the 2018 Annual Conference of the North American Chapter of the Association for Computational Linguistics*.

Sangah Lee, Hansol Jang, Yunmee Baik, Suzi Park, and Hyopil Shin. 2020. Kr-bert: A small-scale korean-specific language model. *arXiv preprint arXiv:2008.03979*.

Baoli li. 2012. Learning to model multilingual unrestricted coreference in ontonotes. In *Joint Conference on EMNLP and CoNLL2012-Shared Task*.

Louis Martin, Benjamin Muller, Pedro Javier Ortiz Suárez, Yoann Dupont, Laurent Romary, Éric Villemonte de la Clergerie, Djamé Seddah, and Benoît Sagot. 2019. Camembert: a tasty french language model. *arXiv preprint arXiv:1911.03894*.

Matthew E. Peters, Mark Neumann, Mohit Iyyer, Matt Gardner, Christopher Clark, Kenton Lee, and Luke S. Zettlemoyer. 2018. Deep contextualized word representations. In *Proceedings of the 2018 Annual Conference of the North American Chapter of the Association for Computational Linguistics*.

M. Poesio, R. Stuckardt, and Y. Versley. 2016. *Anaphora Resolution: Algorithms, Resources and Applications*. Springer, Berlin.

Marco Polignano, Pierpaolo Basile, Marco de Gemmis, Giovanni Semeraro, and Valerio Basile. 2019. Alberto: Italian bert language understanding model for nlp challenging tasks based on tweets. In *CLiC-it*.

Sameer Pradhan, Alessandro Moschitti, Nianwen Xue, Olga Uryupina, and Yuchen Zhang. 2012. Conll-2012 shared task: Modeling multilingual unrestricted coreference in ontonotes. In *Joint Conference on EMNLP and CoNLL-Shared Task. Association for Computational Linguistics, Association for Computational Linguistics.*, pages 1–40.

Wee M. Soon, Daniel C. Y. Lim, and Hwee T. Ng. 2001. A machine learning approach to coreference resolution of noun phrases. *Computational Linguistics*, 27(4), December.

Fabio Souza, Rodrigo Nogueira, and Roberto Lotufo. 2019. Portuguese named entity recognition using bert-crf. *arXiv preprint arXiv:1909.10649.*

Marcus Stamborg, Dennis Medved, Peter Exner, and Pierre Nugues. 2012. Using syntactic dependencies to solve coreferences. In *Joint Conference on EMNLP and CoNLL2012-Shared Task.*

Fériel Ben Fraj Trabelsi, Chiraz Ben Othmane Zribi, and Saoussen Mathlouthi. 2016. Arabic anaphora resolution using markov decision process. In *International Conference on Intelligent Text Processing and Computational Linguistics*, pages 520–532. Springer.

Olga Uryupina, Alessandro Moschitti, and Massimo Poesio. 2012. Bart goes multilingual: the unitn/essex submission to the conll-2012 shared task. In *Joint Conference on EMNLP and CoNLL-Shared Task*, pages 122–128.

Ashish Vaswani, Noam Shazeer, Niki Parmar, Jakob Uszkoreit, Llion Jones, Aidan N. Gomez, Lukasz Kaiser, and Illia Polosukhin. 2017. Attention is all you need.

Yannick Versley, Simone Paolo Ponzetto, Massimo Poesio, Vladimir Eidelman, Alan Jern, Jason Smith, Xiaofeng Yang, and Alessandro Moschitti. 2008. Bart: A modular toolkit for coreference resolution. In *Proceedings of the ACL-08: HLT Demo Session*, pages 9–12.

Sam Wiseman, Alexander M Rush, Stuart Shieber, and Jason Weston. 2015. Learning anaphoricity and antecedent ranking features for coreference resolution. In *Proceedings of the 53rd Annual Meeting of the Association for Computational Linguistics and the 7th International Joint Conference on Natural Language Processing (Volume 1: Long Papers)*, volume 1, pages 1416–1426.

Sam Wiseman, Alexander M Rush, and Stuart M Shieber. 2016. Learning global features for coreference resolution. In *Proceedings of the 2016 Conference of the North American Chapter of the Association for Computational Linguistics: Human Language Technologies*, pages 994–1004.

Wei Wu, Fei Wang, Arianna Yuan, Fei Wu, and Jiwei Li. 2020. CorefQA: Coreference resolution as query-based span prediction. In *Proceedings of the 58th Annual Meeting of the Association for Computational Linguistics*, pages 6953–6963, Online, July. Association for Computational Linguistics.

Juntao Yu, Bernd Bohnet, and Massimo Poesio. 2020a. Neural mention detection. In *Proceedings of The 12th Language Resources and Evaluation Conference*, pages 1–10, Marseille, France, May. European Language Resources Association.

Juntao Yu, Alexandra Uma, and Massimo Poesio. 2020b. A cluster ranking model for full anaphora resolution. In *Proceedings of The 12th Language Resources and Evaluation Conference*, pages 11–20, Marseille, France, May. European Language Resources Association.

Desislava Zhekova and Sandra Kübler. 2010. Ubiu: A language-independent system for coreference resolution. In *Proceedings of the 5th International Workshop on Semantic Evaluation*, page 96–99.

Enhanced Labelling in Active Learning for Coreference Resolution

Vebjørn Espeland
School of Informatics
University of Edinburgh &
Opus 2 International
s1471720@ed.ac.uk

Benjamin Bach
School of Informatics
University of Edinburgh
bbach@inf.ed.ac.uk

Beatrice Alex
School of Literature, Languages
and Cultures
Edinburgh Futures Institute
University of Edinburgh
balex@ed.ac.uk

Abstract

In this paper we describe our attempt to increase the amount of information that can be retrieved through active learning sessions compared to previous approaches. We optimise the annotator's labelling process using active learning in the context of coreference resolution. Using simulated active learning experiments, we suggest three adjustments to ensure the labelling time is spent as efficiently as possible. All three adjustments provide more information to the machine learner than the baseline, though a large impact on the F1 score over time is not observed. Compared to previous models, we report a marginal F1 improvement on the final coreference models trained using for two out of the three approaches tested when applied to the English OntoNotes 2012 Coreference Resolution data. Our best-performing model achieves 58.01 F1, an increase of 0.93 F1 over the baseline model.

1 Introduction

Coreference resolution (CR) is the task of resolving which noun phrases (NP) in a text are referring to the same entity. It is related to entity linking, but does not involve an external knowledge base. It is an important task in information extraction, as a step in structuring the unstructured information in natural language. CR has traditionally been a difficult problem, as it is hard to accurately predict coreference links without extensive real-world knowledge.

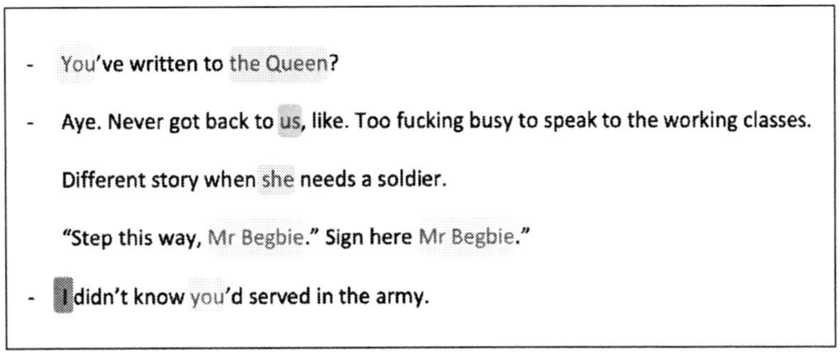

Figure 1: Different types of coreference resolution. An anaphoric pair of noun phrases is marked in green, and a cataphoric pair is marked in yellow. From "T2: Trainspotting" (Boyle, 2017)

An example of different levels of CR is shown in Figure 1. The mentions "us" and "I" are both singletons, and are not coreferring with anything in this text. The noun phrase "she" is anaphoric (where the pronoun points *backwards* to its antecedent) with "the Queen". The pronoun "You" in "You've" is coreferring with "Mr Begbie", but the pronoun is pointing *forward* to its coreferent, this type of coreference is cataphoric coreference.

Proceedings of the 3rd Workshop on Computational Models of Reference, Anaphora and Coreference (CRAC 2020), pages 111–121,
Barcelona, Spain (online), December 12, 2020.

Many of the most successful coreference resolution approaches have used hand-crafted corpora, such as ACE (NIST, 2004), GAP (Webster et al., 2018) and OntoNotes (Pradhan et al., 2012). Models trained using these datasets, though comparatively successful, do not necessarily generalise to domain specific data, or noisy data. Making these big datasets is also a very expensive task, which is very difficult for low resource languages.

Active learning is a human-in-the-loop approach to machine learning, where a sample selection algorithm chooses the most informative samples for a human to annotate. This approach will reduce the total amount of samples which need to be labelled to achieve high accuracy, and in some cases it accelerates the otherwise expensive process of hand-crafting fully labelled datasets. Iteratively training and labelling this way would lead to higher accuracy models faster than training with random sampling.

The most expensive part of dataset creation is the labelling effort of the annotators. Therefore using the annotator's time as efficiently as possible should be a key focus in developing active learning techniques. As previous research (Section 2.2) has focused on which samples to label, this article will focus on improving the use of the annotator's time. The objective of this research is to improve the amount of information that can be retrieved through the active learning sessions.

Aiming to use the annotator's time as efficiently as possible, this article suggests three improvements to recent developments in active learning for coreference resolution. We investigate whether it is effective to label all the instances of an entity once the user has been asked to provide the first label of the entity. We also suggest an improvement based on allowing the user to edit an incorrectly identified mention and then provide coreference information, rather than disregarding that candidate coreferent pair. Finally, for mentions which are the first instances of their entity, such as the example of "Mr Begbie" above, we allow the user to provide cataphoric labels. We use the English OntoNotes 2012 Coreference Resolution dataset provided by the CoNLL 2012 shared task (Pradhan et al., 2012) to simulate dataset creation using active learning techniques.

In this paper we firstly review the related work on coreference resolution and active learning in Section 2. Then in Section 3 and 4 we explain the experimental methodology and review the results. Finally in Section 5 and 6 we analyse the results before our conclusions and directions for future work.

2 Related work

2.1 Coreference resolution

A detailed review of the early research in coreference resolution was made by Ng (2010). I will summarise this in short in this section, and move on to reviewing the later research, especially the approaches using deep learning.

Past coreference resolution research can be divided into two approaches: mention-pair and mention-ranking. The mention-pair models attempt to reduce the coreference resolution challenge to a binary problem, whether two NPs are coreferring or not. Aone and Bennett (1995) and McCarthy and Lehnert (1995) were early proponents of this method. The mention-ranking models aim to rank the candidate antecedent mentions according to likelihood of coreferring. Connolly et al. (1997) were the first to apply this approach. Other mention ranking approaches include Iida et al. (2003), Yang et al. (2003), and Yang et al. (2008).

Durrett and Klein (2013) tried to reduce the amount of expensive hand-crafted features. This idea was picked up by Wiseman et al. (2015). The benefit of using neural networks is that the fine-tuning of these features is left in the hidden layers of the network. With the arrival of word-embedding techniques after the very influential paper by Mikolov et al. (2013), much of the research in natural language processing (NLP), including coreference resolution, took a step in the direction of using neural networks.

Clark and Manning (2016a) used a deep neural network to capture a larger set of learned, continuous features indicating that more entity-level information is beneficial to the coreference task. Based on this finding, they trained a neural mention-ranking model using reinforcement learning (Clark and Manning, 2016b). They claimed that, despite being less expressive than the entity-centric models of Haghighi and Klein (2010; Clark and Manning (2015), their model is faster, more scalable and simpler to train.

Lee et al. (2017) presented a neural end-to-end coreference resolution system, without using a syntactic parser or a mention detector to extract the candidate mentions. They combined context-dependent boundary representations with an attention mechanism for NP head finding, inspired by Durrett and Klein (2013) to treat aggregated spans of words as a unit. The likelihood of two spans being coreferent is determined by merging the likelihood of either span being a mention with the likelihood of them coreferring.

Finally, with the arrival of transformers and BERT (Devlin et al., 2018), the field of NLP took another leap forward. Coreference resolution approaches using BERT include Joshi et al. (2019) and Joshi et al. (2020).

2.2 Active learning

When building a dataset for NLP tasks, a human annotator would normally have to label every single sample in the dataset which is a very expensive process. The use of active learning is an appealing solution to creating and labelling datasets, as the human annotator would only have to annotate the most informative samples. There are two main considerations in the active learning process outside of user interface design: how to choose which samples to label, and how to label them. The first consideration has been the most researched, the second is the focus of this article.

There is an array of techniques to choose which samples to label next. Using an informativeness measure such as entropy enables an algorithm to choose the samples with the highest uncertainty. Lewis and Gale (1994), Gasperin (2009) and Schein and Ungar (2007) use this technique with varying degrees of success. Other methods include ensemble models like query-by-committee (QBC) and cluster-outlier methods. Sachan et al. (2015) reviewed these and found that all these methods performed better than random sampling, and that the ensemble model is the best performing one. Settles (2009) reviewed general active learning literature, and Olsson (2009) reviewed the AL literature within the scope of NLP. Recently, Shen et al. (2017) used active learning for named entity recognition, achieving close to state-of-the-art results with only 25% of the training data.

For deciding what to do with the selected samples, the dominant approach has been binary pairwise selection for potential manual coreference annotation (Gasperin, 2009; Laws et al., 2012; Zhao and Ng, 2014; Sachan et al., 2015). This approach pairs up candidate mentions with candidate antecedents, and the annotator can discard or accept a mention-pair dependent on whether they are coreferring or not. Sachan et al. (2015) introduced *must-link* (ML) and *cannot-link* (CL) constraints as a method of storing user annotations. The mention-pairs which where deemed coreferent received the ML constraint, and the ones deemed not coreferent received the CL constraint, where the coreference likelihood of those pairs was set to 1 and 0 respectively. Applying transitivity (if A is coreferent with B, and B with C, then A and C must also be coreferent) to these constraints means more labels can be distributed without extra labelling.

Li et al. (2020) improved on the mention-pair constraints by using span embeddings instead of mentions, as successfully applied to coreference resolution in Lee et al. (2017). They also augmented the pair-wise annotation with a second step of marking the first occurrence of the entity if the span pair is not coreferent, introducing the notion of discrete annotations.

The marking of the first occurrence of the entity allows the annotator to cluster the entities. Together with the notion of transitivity, this makes annotation more efficient, as it makes use of some false negatives. However, this approach, though better than pairwise decision, still does not make use of the false positives. It also ignores readily available information about other occurrences of the entity in question.

It takes time for an annotator to find the *first* sample of the highlighted entity, particularly if the document they are labelling is more than a few sentences. When the annotator has spent the time finding the first occurrence of the entity, they will have identified many, if not all, of the other occurrences of that entity, and it will be relatively cheap to annotate all the occurrences in the document. A good interface will have predicted and highlighted these occurrences.

If the sample turns out to be negative, e.g. by the proform span (the span in question, as opposed to the antecedent span) being the first span in the document, then allowing the annotator to label cataphoric spans would also contribute towards the goal of increasing annotator efficiency.

The setup in Li et al. (2020) allows a candidate coreferent pair to be disregarded in three ways, where only the third way should be a valid reason for disregarding:

1. The span is incorrectly identified, and is not a valid noun phrase.

2. The span is the first mention of that entity (and thus has no antecedent).

3. The span is the only mention of that entity in the document.

The following section will elaborate on the experiments to improve upon these shortcomings.

3 Methodology

The experiments reported in this paper investigate a set of different methods for conducting manual annotation during an active learning scenario.

3.1 Discrete annotation with cataphoric links

Previous approaches to active learning for coreference resolution have focused primarily on antecedent labelling, ignoring potential occurrences following an entity. The OntoNotes dataset is not made with specific cataphoric linkings. This makes it more difficult to test how well the system performs when adding cataphoric data. It is still however possible to retrieve cataphoric mentions of an entity from the dataset.

Even though the sample selection algorithm will only select entities with a candidate *antecedent*, it should be possible for the annotator to choose cataphoric occurrences. Our simulated experiment will test whether allowing the annotator to select cataphoric mentions will have an impact on how many label queries are disregarded.

3.2 Annotating all spans for the queried entity in the document

This is motivated by the experience that it is easier to label multiple spans of the same entity in the same document than it is to annotate just one instance, even if the document contains several occurrences of that entity. Even though more samples are being labelled, and those samples are not necessarily the most informative ones, they will still provide more information per query and per clock-time than strictly pair-wise or discrete annotation.

The improvement would be made by adding multiple ML and CL constraints for each query. Every time a suggested pair is not the final pair of that query a CL constraint is applied, and every label the annotator selects receives a ML constraint. This, combined with transitivity constraints (elaborated in Li et al. (2020)), is hypothesised to increase the amount of information available to the learner.

3.3 Annotation error

Whether the annotator is helped by interface highlighting of predictions or not, a potential challenge with asking an annotator to label all occurrences of an entity in the document is that they are susceptible to losing focus due to boredom or time pressure. In these situations it is plausible that there will be a certain amount of error. Taking inspiration from Sachan et al. (2015), which included user labelling error as a hyperparameter, we include labelling error in our experiments.

3.4 Enabling span editing and annotating all spans

In previous approaches to active learning for coreference resolution, when an annotator is queried with a span which is incorrectly identified as a span, that query is disregarded. There is no difference between a CL constraint because of correctly identified spans not linking, and a CL constraint caused by correctly linked but incorrectly identified spans. These kinds of boundary errors are common in entity recognition, and these frequent errors can have a big impact on downstream performance. In the discrete annotation, Li et al. (2020) improved this problem by making the user click all the words in the antecedent span, building the span word by word. However, they did not allow the user to correct the proform span. This limitation also applies to their simulated experiments.

We therefore allow the user to correct the proform span. The method for manually correcting the proform span is letting the annotator choose which words belong to the span. In the simulated experiment we scan the indeces of all spans in that document for the closest span that belongs to a coreference cluster in the dataset. We then find an antecedent to the new proform, and make a new ML constraint, leaving a CL constraint to the initial candidate pair. If the nearest span is not coreferent with any other span in the document, the incorrectly identified span is unlikely to be a boundary error, and the query is therefore disregarded as not coreferring.

4 Evaluation

We compare the baseline discrete labelling system versus enhanced labelling using the standard English CoNLL-2012 coreference resolution dataset (Pradhan et al., 2012). Following both Li et al. (2020) and Sachan et al. (2015), user labelling is simulated from the gold standard labels in the CoNLL dataset.

4.1 Evaluation metric

In the field of coreference resolution there are multiple ways of scoring a system, each with their own benefits and drawbacks. A somewhat standardised option, and the one chosen to evaluate the experiments reported in this paper, is to combine the recall and precision from MUC (Vilain et al., 1995), B^3 (Bagga and Baldwin, 1998) and CEAFe (Luo, 2005) as an average F1 score. We compute this score with the official CONLL-2012 evaluation scripts.

We also compare the amount of successful queries in each AL session as a metric of how successful the annotation approach is at providing positive training examples. A successful query is a query which returns a coreferent pair, regardless of whether the original proform or antecedent candidate were coreferent or not. This way, there will be at least one ML constraint from that query. An unsuccessful query does not return a coreferent pair, and the only thing that can be learnt from that query is that the original proform and antecedent candidates are not coreferent, resulting in only one CL constraint.

4.2 Neural network architecture

For the sake of comparison we use the same coreference model as in (Li et al., 2020). They use the AllenNLP implementation of Lee et al. (2017), which keeps all the hyperparameters, except that it excludes speaker features, variational dropout and limits the maximum number of considered antecedents to 100. In Lee et al. (2017), they use GloVe embeddings (Pennington et al., 2014) as word embeddings. They use a bidirectional LSTM (Hochreiter and Schmidhuber, 1997), where the hidden states have 200 dimensions, to represent the aggregated word spans. The model internal scoring for determining whether a span is a mention, and whether two mentions are coreferring, is using feed-forward neural networks consisting of two hidden layers with 150 dimensions and rectified linear units (Nair and Hinton, 2010). The optimiser used is ADAM (Kingma and Ba, 2014).

4.3 Experiments

We ran simulated AL experiments with the OntoNotes 2012 Coreference Resolution dataset using the following setup. Each experiment is based on Li et al. (2020), using their entropy selector as sample selection algorithm, selecting 20 queries from each document. The OntoNotes is split into 2802 training documents, 343 validation documents and 348 testing documents. The validation set is used to compute F1 score while training, whereas the test set is used only for final F1 score computation after training has finished.

A 700-document subset of the training data is set aside, and the initial model is trained on this subset. The model trains until convergence with a patience of 2 epochs, up to 20 epochs, before adding more data. Then 280 documents are labelled in an AL session. After these 280 documents are labelled, they are added to the 700 documents, and training continues on the now 980 documents in the set aside training subset.

This continues until all the 2802 documents in the training set have been labelled. Finally, a new model trained on all the 2802 training documents with all the model and training parameters reset. This last step is to make the final model comparable to other models trained without AL, and use the same hyperparameter as Lee et al. (2017). There are 20 span-pair queries per document in the AL session, meaning 5600 queries per AL session, and a total of 39200 queries over the 8 AL sessions.

For labelling with error, 10% of the labels retrieved in the annotation session are set to a random span in the document. We implement this by introducing a 10% chance of having a random span chosen instead of a coreferring span. This is to prevent the erroneous labels systematically having the same index each AL session.

We include one baseline experiment from Li et al. (2020). The experiment is using discrete annotation with the same parameters as our experiments, but we report the F1 score for the baseline with the best performing experiment from Li et al. (2020), which uses a query-by-committee system with three models. This is done to compare the results of our experiments to the currently best performing coreference resolution system using AL.

In the baseline experiment and Experiments 1 and 3, the annotator is only allowed to select one occurrence of the proform entity. In Experiment 2 the annotator labels all the anteceding occurrences of the proform, whereas in 4 and 5 the annotator labels all the occurrences of that entity.

We also perform a timed annotation exercise with the same setup as in Li et al. (2020). We recruited 10 annotators with experience in text processing, who annotated for 30 minutes each. Li et al. (2020) used annotators with NLP experience, whereas our annotators did not that but are skilled in working with speech transcripts. This might impact the absolute annotation time, but the relative annotation time within our group of annotators should still be informative. The annotators in Li et al. (2020) were asked a pair-wise question first, and in the case of non-coreference they were asked to annotate the *first* instance of the entity. In contrast, we asked our annotators to label *all* instances of the entity in the case. When an annotator provided only one extra instance of the entity, that was noted as a "follow-up question", whereas when they labelled more than one extra instance of the entity it was noted as a "multi-response". We used the same annotation interface as in Li et al. (2020), but altered it to allow cataphoric labelling as well as multiple labels per query.

4.4   Results

Table 1 shows the results from our timed annotation exercise. In our experiment the annotators spent longer on the initial question (20.66 s), but were faster on supplying answers for the follow-up question (12.61 s). When annotating more than one extra occurrence, the time taken for each of those occurrences was lower than answering the initial question.

The average normalised annotation time per occurrence was 16.57 seconds. In contrast, the annotators' median normalised annotation time was only 10.26 seconds per occurrence. This indicates that the distribution of annotation times is higher at the lower end, and that there were a few queries with very

		Avg. Time per query
Li et al. (2020)	Initial question	15.96s
	Follow-up question	15.57s
	ONLY Follow-up question	28.01s
Our experiments	Initial question	20.66s
	Follow-up question	12.61s
	Normalised multi-response	16.57s

Table 1: Results for the timed annotation exercise. We first list the results from the corresponding timed exercise reported in Li et al. (2020). The fourth and fifth results for our equivalent experiments, with the exception that the annotators were allowed to select any instance of the entity in the follow-up, not just the first. The final time in the table is the average time taken for the annotators to label every instance of the entity, normalised by the number of labels in each query.

Validation F1 score for each epoch in training

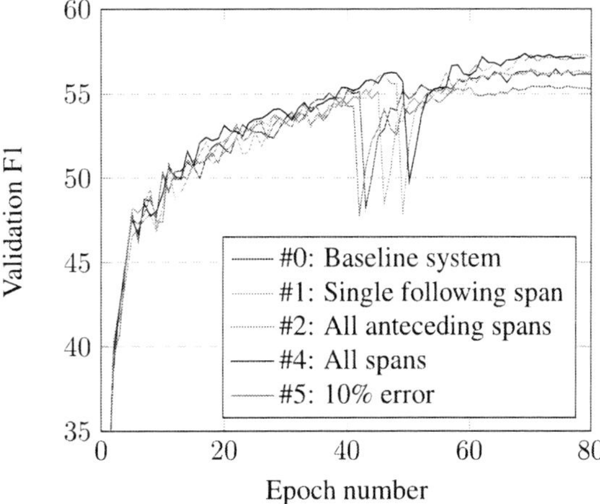

Figure 2: The F1 score while training for each experiment. This score is computed using the validation dataset. As expected, the scores are similar at the earlier stages, when the model is trained on the same number of labels. For the later epochs the models trained on more labels, Experiment 2 and 4, perform marginally better than the other models. The dip in F1 score around epoch 50 represent the retraining of the model from scratch after all the documents have been labelled.

long times which might have skewed the average. The fastest annotations for the multi-response queries were made in 2.07 when normalised for the number of labels annotated in that query. The slowest annotations took 124.95 seconds.

Figure 2 plots the F1 score over the training epochs, using the validation data. The improvements in F1 over the epochs are very similar for each of the training methods in the early stages, but in the later stages the active learning approaches which allow multiple labelling come out on top.

In the baseline experiment 49% of the queries return a coreferent label pair, which means over half of the queries did not result in a ML constraint. In Experiment 1 that number is increased to 54%, as can be seen in Table 2. This is a reduction of disregarded queries by 11%. In Experiment 2 and 4 the simulated annotator is instructed to label all the occurrences of the entity in the given document, which results in several label pairs per query. For Experiment 2 there are 0.93 label pairs per query, whereas for Experiment 4 there are 1.41 label pairs per query.

There was no difference between the labels retrieved for Experiment 3, where the annotator was allowed to edit proform spans and the results for the baseline experiment. A total of 6 spans were edited

#	Experiment	Successful labels per query	CONLL F1 score
0	Discrete annotation (Li et al., 2020)	0.51	57.08
1	Allowing following spans	0.54	**58.01**
2	Annotating all anteceding spans	0.93	57.18
3	Allowing proform edit	0.51	56.09
4	Combining 1 and 2	**1.41**	57.37
5	Combining 1 and 2 with 10% error	0.52	55.48

Table 2: Experiments for the AL models, with the F1 score representing the performance on the final models on the test set. The "Successful label per query" column explains how many queries returned with positive coreferent pairs. The F1 score for the baseline (Experiment 0) is achieved using a sample selector with the query-by-committee approach. When Experiment 2 and 4 are close to and exceeding 1 that is because they are returning more than one label pair per query.

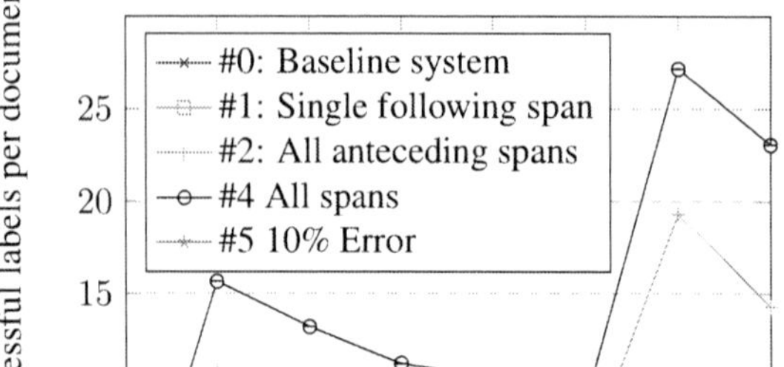

Figure 3: The number of successful queries for each AL session. The sessions have been normalised for document length, as some of the sessions have significant longer document lengths. Experiment 3 is not included, as it was overlapping with the baseline system. The approaches in Experiment 2 and 4 are more effective at providing successful label pairs than the other experiments, particularly with longer documents.

under the simulated experiment.

In Figure 3 the label pair counts are separated into the active learning sessions, and normalised by average document length for that session. This measure can be seen as an average number of successful label-pairs per document. In Experiment 1 there are marginally more labels successfully identified than in the baseline system. For both Experiment 2 and 4 the AL sessions provide many more label pairs per document, up to an average 27.16 label pairs for Experiment 4 in AL session 6. The efficacy of the combined model is reduced when 10% labelling error is added in each AL session, but Experiment 5 still provided more labels than the baseline system.

5   Analysis and Discussion

The timed annotation exercise show that the cost of annotating all the labels of an entity in a text is low when the annotator has already read the text to make a judgement on the initial coreference pair. The results also show that there might be a cut tail distribution of annotation times. The majority of the multi-response annotations were faster than the initial and the single-response follow-up question responses.

On average it took our annotators longer time for the initial question in our implementation of the same timed annotation exercise as in Li et al. (2020), but shorter time for the follow-up question. People working in NLP are likely to be more experienced with seeing text containing bracketed annotation. It is possible that our set of annotators were slower at responding for the initial question because of the lack of experience in NLP.

One reason the average time for answering the follow-up question was lower in our setup might be that the annotators were allowed to label any instance of the occurrence, not just the first. Particularly for longer texts it might be faster to label an occurrence closer to the proform entity than the first occurrence.

From Figure 3 we can see that the labelling approach in Experiment 1 returns more labels per query than the baseline approach, through the AL sessions. The same is true for Experiment 4 and 2 respectively. This indicates that cataphoric occurrences contain unused information, which should be used for training. The sudden jump in successful queries in AL sessions 6 and 7 for Experiment 2 and 4 can partly be ascribed to an increase in document length in those sessions, even though the graph is normalised to document length. This might mean that models trained on datasets with longer documents are able to benefit more from the improved label retrieval rate.

Even with 10% of the labels chosen at random the combined approach retrieved more successful label pairs than the baseline system, but the final F1 score was somewhat lower. This lower score F1 was expected, as the erroneous labelling would add confusion to the model. Care should therefore be taken when designing a labelling system to ensure that errors are minimised.

The small improvement in the validation F1 score shown in Figure 2 indicates that the added labels under the current system do not translate into having an impact on how fast high accuracy is achieved. Despite this, the final F1 score on the separate test data is marginally higher for Experiment 4 than the baseline experiment.

This lack of impact could have several causes. As the machine learning algorithm is the same as in the baseline system, it might not be best suited to make use of the extra available information. In addition, the OntoNotes dataset does not inherently support cataphoric linking of entities, so a dataset which does contain inherent cataphoric links might also contribute towards making use of the extracted data more efficiently.

The negative results for Experiment 3 can have multiple causes. One of these is that the algorithm for selecting replacement proform spans was purposefully conservative in choosing the closest span. This was to retain ecological validity in the annotation simulation, as an annotator would look close to the span to determine whether the error was a boundary error.

6 Conclusion and Future Research

The contribution of the research in this article is the improved techniques for extracting more information from user labelling. We have seen that allowing annotators to leverage cataphoric information, especially in combination with annotating several occurrences per query, can contribute to optimising the time spent by annotators hand labelling a dataset. Even though the machine learning models did not perform markedly better earlier in the training process, the amount of disregarded queries dropped by a noticeable amount just by adding cataphoric labels.

We have also seen that the amount of successful label pairs per query is over 1 for the approaches allowing multiple responses. This means that it is possible to extract much more information than with previous approaches. Our timed annotation exercise indicate that labelling several occurrences of an entity in the same query is faster than answering multiple queries with only one set of labels. It would be interesting to investigate whether choosing labels closer or further from the proform label would have an impact on the learning.

These findings are interesting for the real world application of coreference resolution systems, particularly for long form documents, such as in the legal sector, where there is a lot more information to leverage than in short form documents. A future project would look into making changes to the machine learning model for more effective use of the new data.

Future research would also look into testing which interface design would best aid the human annotator in the labelling process, especially for long form documents.

References

Chinatsu Aone and Scott William Bennett. 1995. Evaluating automated and manual acquisition of anaphora resolution strategies. In *Proceedings of the 33rd annual meeting on Association for Computational Linguistics*, pages 122–129. Association for Computational Linguistics.

Amit Bagga and Breck Baldwin. 1998. Algorithms for scoring coreference chains. In *The first international conference on language resources and evaluation workshop on linguistics coreference*, volume 1, pages 563–566. Granada.

D. Boyle. 2017. T2: Trainspotting. United Kingdom: TriStar Pictures, Inc., Sony Pictures Releasing.

Kevin Clark and Christopher D Manning. 2015. Entity-centric coreference resolution with model stacking. In *Proceedings of the 53rd Annual Meeting of the Association for Computational Linguistics and the 7th International Joint Conference on Natural Language Processing (Volume 1: Long Papers)*, pages 1405–1415.

Kevin Clark and Christopher D Manning. 2016a. Deep reinforcement learning for mention-ranking coreference models. *arXiv preprint arXiv:1609.08667*.

Kevin Clark and Christopher D Manning. 2016b. Improving coreference resolution by learning entity-level distributed representations. *arXiv preprint arXiv:1606.01323*.

Dennis Connolly, John D Burger, and David S Day. 1997. A machine learning approach to anaphoric reference. In *New methods in language processing*, pages 133–144.

Jacob Devlin, Ming-Wei Chang, Kenton Lee, and Kristina Toutanova. 2018. Bert: Pre-training of deep bidirectional transformers for language understanding. *arXiv preprint arXiv:1810.04805*.

Greg Durrett and Dan Klein. 2013. Easy victories and uphill battles in coreference resolution. In *Proceedings of the 2013 Conference on Empirical Methods in Natural Language Processing*, pages 1971–1982.

Caroline Gasperin. 2009. Active learning for anaphora resolution. In *Proceedings of the NAACL HLT 2009 Workshop on Active Learning for Natural Language Processing*, pages 1–8.

Aria Haghighi and Dan Klein. 2010. Coreference resolution in a modular, entity-centered model. In *Human Language Technologies: The 2010 Annual Conference of the North American Chapter of the Association for Computational Linguistics*, pages 385–393. Association for Computational Linguistics.

Sepp Hochreiter and Jürgen Schmidhuber. 1997. Long short-term memory. *Neural computation*, 9(8):1735–1780.

Ryu Iida, Kentaro Inui, Hiroya Takamura, and Yuji Matsumoto. 2003. Incorporating contextual cues in trainable models for coreference resolution. In *Proceedings of the 2003 EACL Workshop on The Computational Treatment of Anaphora*.

Mandar Joshi, Omer Levy, Daniel S Weld, and Luke Zettlemoyer. 2019. Bert for coreference resolution: Baselines and analysis. *arXiv preprint arXiv:1908.09091*.

Mandar Joshi, Danqi Chen, Yinhan Liu, Daniel S Weld, Luke Zettlemoyer, and Omer Levy. 2020. Spanbert: Improving pre-training by representing and predicting spans. *Transactions of the Association for Computational Linguistics*, 8:64–77.

Diederik P Kingma and Jimmy Ba. 2014. Adam: A method for stochastic optimization. *arXiv preprint arXiv:1412.6980*.

Florian Laws, Florian Heimerl, and Hinrich Schütze. 2012. Active learning for coreference resolution. In *Proceedings of the 2012 Conference of the North American Chapter of the Association for Computational Linguistics: Human Language Technologies*, pages 508–512, Montréal, Canada, June. Association for Computational Linguistics.

Kenton Lee, Luheng He, Mike Lewis, and Luke Zettlemoyer. 2017. End-to-end neural coreference resolution. *arXiv preprint arXiv:1707.07045*.

David D Lewis and William A Gale. 1994. A sequential algorithm for training text classifiers. In *SIGIR'94*, pages 3–12. Springer.

Belinda Li, Gabriel Stanovsky, and Luke Zettlemoyer. 2020. Active learning for coreference resolution using discrete annotation. *arXiv preprint arXiv:2004.13671*.

Xiaoqiang Luo. 2005. On coreference resolution performance metrics. In *Proceedings of the conference on human language technology and empirical methods in natural language processing*, pages 25–32. Association for Computational Linguistics.

Joseph F McCarthy and Wendy G Lehnert. 1995. Using decision trees for coreference resolution. *arXiv preprint cmp-lg/9505043*.

Tomas Mikolov, Ilya Sutskever, Kai Chen, Greg S Corrado, and Jeff Dean. 2013. Distributed representations of words and phrases and their compositionality. In *Advances in neural information processing systems*, pages 3111–3119.

Vinod Nair and Geoffrey E Hinton. 2010. Rectified linear units improve restricted boltzmann machines. In *ICML*.

Vincent Ng. 2010. Supervised noun phrase coreference research: The first fifteen years. In *Proceedings of the 48th annual meeting of the association for computational linguistics*, pages 1396–1411. Association for Computational Linguistics.

NIST. 2004. Automatic content extraction (ace).

Fredrik Olsson. 2009. A literature survey of active machine learning in the context of natural language processing.

Jeffrey Pennington, Richard Socher, and Christopher D Manning. 2014. Glove: Global vectors for word representation. In *Proceedings of the 2014 conference on empirical methods in natural language processing (EMNLP)*, pages 1532–1543.

Sameer Pradhan, Alessandro Moschitti, Nianwen Xue, Olga Uryupina, and Yuchen Zhang. 2012. Conll-2012 shared task: Modeling multilingual unrestricted coreference in ontonotes. In *Joint Conference on EMNLP and CoNLL-Shared Task*, pages 1–40. Association for Computational Linguistics.

Mrinmaya Sachan, Eduard Hovy, and Eric P Xing. 2015. An active learning approach to coreference resolution. In *Twenty-Fourth International Joint Conference on Artificial Intelligence*.

Andrew I Schein and Lyle H Ungar. 2007. Active learning for logistic regression: an evaluation. *Machine Learning*, 68(3):235–265.

Burr Settles. 2009. Active learning literature survey. Technical report, University of Wisconsin-Madison Department of Computer Sciences.

Yanyao Shen, Hyokun Yun, Zachary C Lipton, Yakov Kronrod, and Animashree Anandkumar. 2017. Deep active learning for named entity recognition. *arXiv preprint arXiv:1707.05928*.

Marc Vilain, John Burger, John Aberdeen, Dennis Connolly, and Lynette Hirschman. 1995. A model-theoretic coreference scoring scheme. In *Proceedings of the 6th conference on Message understanding*, pages 45–52. Association for Computational Linguistics.

Kellie Webster, Marta Recasens, Vera Axelrod, and Jason Baldridge. 2018. Mind the gap: A balanced corpus of gendered ambiguous pronouns. *Transactions of the Association for Computational Linguistics*, 6:605–617.

Sam Wiseman, Alexander Matthew Rush, Stuart Merrill Shieber, and Jason Weston. 2015. Learning anaphoricity and antecedent ranking features for coreference resolution. In *Proceedings of the 53rd Annual Meeting of the Association for Computational Linguistics and the 7th International Joint Conference on Natural Language Processing (Volume 1: Long Papers)*. Association for Computational Linguistics.

Xiaofeng Yang, Guodong Zhou, Jian Su, and Chew Lim Tan. 2003. Coreference resolution using competition learning approach. In *Proceedings of the 41st Annual Meeting on Association for Computational Linguistics-Volume 1*, pages 176–183. Association for Computational Linguistics.

Xiaofeng Yang, Jian Su, and Chew Lim Tan. 2008. A twin-candidate model for learning-based anaphora resolution. *Computational Linguistics*, 34(3):327–356.

Shanheng Zhao and Hwee Tou Ng. 2014. Domain adaptation with active learning for coreference resolution. In *Proceedings of the 5th International Workshop on Health Text Mining and Information Analysis (Louhi)*, pages 21–29, Gothenburg, Sweden, April. Association for Computational Linguistics.

Reference in Team Communication for Robot-Assisted Disaster Response: An Initial Analysis

Natalia Skachkova and Ivana Kruijff-Korbayová

DFKI / Saarland Informatics Campus / 66123 Saarbrücken Germany

`natalia.skachkova@dfki.de; ivana.kruijff@dfki.de`

Abstract

We analyze reference phenomena in a corpus of robot-assisted disaster response team communication. The annotation scheme we designed for this purpose distinguishes different types of entities, roles, reference units and relations. We focus particularly on mission-relevant objects, locations and actors and also annotate a rich set of reference links, including co-reference and various other kinds of relations. We explain the categories used in our annotation, present their distribution in the corpus and discuss challenging cases.

1 Introduction

We present the findings of an initial analysis of contextual reference phenomena in team communication in robot-assisted disaster response. Disaster response teams operate in high risk situations and must make critical decisions quickly, despite partial and uncertain information. For better safety and operational capability, first responders increasingly deploy mobile robots for remote reconnaissance of an incident site. The work in this paper contributes to our ongoing effort to develop methods for interpreting the verbal communication in a response team, in order to extract *run-time mission knowledge* from it. Mission knowledge encompasses the mission goals, which tasks have been assigned to whom, the state of their execution, the relevant points of interest (POIs) and the possibly changing information about them, etc. We work on using mission knowledge extracted from the verbal team communication and integrated with information from other sources, such as the sensors carried by the robots, to provide situation awareness and teamwork assistance both during and after a mission, as described in (Willms et al., 2019).

As part of extracting mission knowledge from the verbal team communication, it is important to identify *mission-relevant objects, locations, actors, tasks, events etc.* that are being referred to and the links between them. This is the goal of reference resolution. In order to get a better understanding of how this task can be performed, we analysed the corpus of robot-assisted disaster response team communication from the TRADR project (TRADR project website, 2020), (Kruijff-Korbayová et al., 2015). The corpus contains the communication in teams of first responders who are using ground and airborne robots to explore an area, searching for victims and hazards, to carry out measurements and gather samples in the aftermath of an industrial incident, such as a fire or explosion. In the first phase of reference phenomena analysis, the results of which we present in this paper, we focused on the references to and links between mission-relevant objects, locations and actors. We aimed to gain insight regarding the kinds of reference cases in the data, their distribution and the challenges for reference resolution. We annotated the data in order to systematically capture the various cases and be able to access them later for deeper analysis. Our aim was not to create an ultimate annotated resource and/or a novel annotation scheme. We designed the annotation scheme specifically for our analysis, and it was evolving as the annotation progressed. The present paper reports our findings and indicates what our reference resolution system would need to deal with. In Section 2 we overview existing approaches to co-reference and anaphora annotation in text and dialogue. Section 3 gives more details about our data. Section 4 describes the cases of reference to

Proceedings of the 3rd Workshop on Computational Models of Reference, Anaphora and Coreference (CRAC 2020), pages 122–132,
Barcelona, Spain (online), December 12, 2020.

and links between mission-relevant objects, locations and actors that we identified and how we captured them in our annotation scheme, accompanied by typical examples as well as illustrations of some tricky cases and challenges. In Section 5 we summarize and indicate our future steps.

2 Approaches to co-reference and anaphora annotation

The study of co-reference and anaphoric relations has long tradition in linguistics, and there exist numerous approaches to annotation. They are rather difficult to systematise, due to proliferating terminologies and combinations of heterogeneous phenomena, such as different types of references, referents and relations. Since a proper discussion of the similarities and differences would exceed the space we have available here, we present the relevant previous work in a close to chronological order.

The first annotation scheme for anaphoric relations appeared in 1992 (Fligelstone, 1992). In the late 1990s this field of research got a push, when the 6th and 7th Message Understanding Conferences (MUC-6, MUC-7) took place. MUC-7 Coreference Task Definitions (Hirschman and Chinchor, 1998) defined *co-reference* as a symmetric identity relation between two noun phrases (NPs) if both of them refer to the same entity. Among the researchers who worked on co-reference annotation schemes around this time are McEnery et al. (1997), Ge (1998), Rocha (1999). There also appeared some works investigating not only relations between entities introduced by NPs, but also event co-reference and temporal relations between events, e.g. by Bagga and Baldwin (1999), or Setzer and Gaizauskas (2000).

At the same time, interest in the annotation of a wider range of semantic relations emerged. Among these relations is *anaphoric reference*. While co-reference is an equivalence relation, anaphoric reference is not - the interpretation of an anaphoric expression always depends on its antecedent. Deemter and Kibble (2000) discussed the differences between anaphora and co-reference in detail. They stressed that they can coincide, but are not interchangeable, and pointed out that co-reference is not to be mixed with bound anaphora, where an anaphor relates to a generic antecedent, which does not actually refer to any specific entity. They also showed the difference between co-reference and an intensional relation between an entity and a predicative expression that refers to a whole set of entities.

One of the more fine-grained approaches to co-reference annotation was presented by Hasler et al. (2006). Aiming at creating corpora for event processing, they investigated NP and event co-reference and created a co-reference annotation scheme. They introduced relations between NPs (identity, synonymy, generalisation, specialisation and other) and co-reference types (NP, copula, apposition, bracketed text, speech pronoun and other).

Among more recent papers on co-reference annotation are the works by Cohen et al. (2017) about identity and appositive relations in biomedical journal articles, Dakle et al. (2020) on co-reference in emails, Wright-Bettner et al. (2019) on cross-document co-reference.

While all the above mentioned works mostly deal with text data, Poesio et al. (1999) developed the MATE 'meta-scheme' for anaphora annotation in dialogue. This generic scheme consists of a core scheme for annotating identity relations (co-reference) between the entities introduced by NPs, and three extensions for annotating references to the visual situation, bridging and anaphoric relations involving an extended range of anaphoric expressions and antecedents. The bridging extension was later realized in the GNOME annotation project (Poesio, 2004).

Poesio et al. (1999) also formulated the difficulties that any designer of an annotation scheme for anaphora faces, namely, that almost every word or phrase in a coherent text can potentially be linked to something that was introduced earlier (cf. also the concept of cohesion (Halliday and Hasan, 1976)).

Speaking of anaphora, sometimes researches try to concentrate only on the identity relation between entities, e.g. (Poesio, 2004) or Aktaş et al. (2018). But often anaphora is understood in a broader sense. Nissim et al. (2004) and Elango (2005) discussed in various types of anaphors and antecedents. Zinsmeister and Dipper (2010) researched the annotation of abstract (discourse-deictic) anaphora. Anaphoric relations between different types of events were also studied by Caselli and Prodanof (2010). Pocsio et al. (2008), annotating the ARRAU corpus, introduced an anaphoric relation between single anaphoric expression and plural antecedents, as well as references to events, actions and plans.

Kruijff-Korbayová and Kruijff (2004) developed a discourse-level annotation scheme that covered a broad range of discourse reference properties, e.g. semantic sort, delimitation, quantification, familiarity status, and anaphoric links (co-reference and bridging).

There also emerged some classifications of anaphora types and other relations. So, Tetreault et al. (2004) annotated the Monroe corpus, consisting of task-oriented dialogues from an emergency rescue domain. They focused on co-referential pronouns and NPs (identity relation), but also presented a classification of relations for non-co-referential pronouns with the following relation types: indexicals, action, demonstrative, functional, set, hard and dummy. Botley (2006) distinguished three types of abstract anaphora: label anaphora (encapsulates stretches of text), which has several sub-types, situation anaphora (for linking events, processes, states, facts, propositions) and text deixis. Another classification by Eckart de Castilho et al. (2016) included the following anaphora types: individual anaphors, reference to abstract objects, vague anaphors, inferrable-evoked pronouns and unmarked anaphors.

All these classifications were developed with a certain corpus and task in mind, and none can be considered universal, standard and pervasive. Although none of the existing classifications was entirely suitable to us, given our domain and the goal of our analysis, they were fundamentally helpful in devising our own annotation scheme.

So, following Hasler et al. (2006), we try to differentiate between an explicit identity, when expressions are linked via a copula, and an implicit one. Defining the bridging relation, we relied on works of Poesio (2004) and Kruijff-Korbayová and Kruijff (2004). Our intensional relation can be traced back to both bound anaphora and intensional predicates presented by Deemter and Kibble (2000), and the notion of vague anaphor is similar to that defined by Eckart de Castilho et al. (2016).

We started the annotation effort with the aim to keep the annotation scheme quite simple, distinguishing between main types of mission-relevant entities, locations and actors, and focusing on the reference relation types. As we proceeded with the annotation, we found it necessary to extend the scheme with certain more fine-grained distinctions to capture sometimes quite special cases.

3   Data: The TRADR Team Communication Corpus

The TRADR corpus consists of dialogues that represent human-human team communication in robot-assisted disaster response. The dialogues were recorded during exercises on different industrial sites performed as part of the TRADR project (TRADR project website, 2020), (Kruijff-Korbayová et al., 2015). The exercises simulated situations after a industrial accident, such as fire, explosion, etc. and involved teams of firefighters using ground and airborne robots for reconnaissance.

There are 15 files with dialogues in the corpus, each corresponding to a mission or sometimes a part of a mission. Nine files contain dialogues in German, and six - in English. The German dialogues were recorded in 2015 and 2016, the English data is from 2017. The firefighters who took part in the 2017 experiment were Dutch, and so non-native English speakers. In total the joint corpus contains about 2,9k dialogue turns (see Table 1).

Recording	Mission	Duration	Turns
TJex2015			**363**
	Day 1	48:21 min	186
	Day 2	33:21 min	177
TEval 2015			**1,279**
	Day 1	58:23 min	359
	Day 2	65:04 min	356
	Day 3	57:15 min	272
	Day 4	53:22 min	292
TEval 2016			**422**
	Day 1	n.a.	312
	Day 2	n.a.	110
TEval 2017			**811**
	Day 1	64:02 min	239
	Day 2	149:20 min	400
	Day 3	56:36 min	172

Table 1:   TRADR corpus composition (based on (Anikina and Kruijff-Korbayová, 2019))

The TRADR experiments involve teams of first responders exploring complex dynamic environments using robots, namely unmanned ground vehicles (UGVs) and unmanned aerial vehicles (UAVs). The robots are used for reconnaissance, mainly to look for points of interest (POIs), including victims and hazard sources, such as smoke, fire, or contamination; and check if the site is safe enough for human first responders to enter. The robots are equipped with gas detectors, a standard camera and an infrared one. Pictures taken by the robot cameras can be shared among the team members. Some UGVs have a mechanical arm for picking up, turning, pushing or moving objects.

The team consists of operators (UGV-1, UGV-2, UAV) who control the robots, a team leader (TL) and in some missions also a mission commander (MC). A MC is in charge of the whole mission and gives tasks to teams. The TL distributes the tasks between the operators, coordinates their actions and reports to the MC (if present). The operators use robots to perform the tasks assigned to them and report to the TL about the results or possible difficulties.

The team members use a shared situation awareness interface, consisting of a digital map on which POIs are marked and robots' positions are displayed; a repository of shared photos made with the robot camera; and in 2017 also a task list which the TL can manually edit.

The team communication in the TRADR scenarios has the following characteristics:

- Participants follow the radio communication protocol (albeit somewhat loosely), i.e. they use special phrases to start/finish a conversation, check the connection quality, accept/reject requests, etc.
- Information flows through a rather complex communication pipeline with several participants. This sometimes leads to repeating information or requests.
- TL switches between the operators, so the flow of information is usually split into several interlaced threads. This sometimes leads to confusion and misunderstandings.
- The participants sometimes refer to objects on the display, i.e., the shared digital map, photos or task list.
- The fact that the participants perceive the environment via a medium (here the robot's camera(s)) is reflected in language usage. Often, when the TL assigns tasks and gives commands, they speak to an operator, but mean a robot. Similarly, an operator may refer to an icon on the digital map as a real object or location, and vice versa. We call this *double reality representation*.
- Like any spontaneous speech TRADR dialogues are characterized by repetitions, elliptical constructions, fillers/hesitation markers, such as 'erm', 'uh', etc. and other disfluencies, incomplete and/or ungrammatical utterances.

4   Annotation and Analysis of Reference in the TRADR Corpus

The analysis we present aims to gain initial insight in the kinds and distribution of references to entities and relations between them in the TRADR corpus, as a preparatory step before developing reference resolution modules as part of the team communication interpretation in our system (Willms et al., 2019).

In this section we explain the categories that we distinguished in the analysis, show their distribution in the TRADR corpus and discuss the challenges we encountered during annotation.

We used the WebAnno tool (Eckart de Castilho et al., 2016) to perform the annotation. Originally, only one annotator, the first author, performed the annotation, under the guidance of the second author. All spurious cases were discussed by both authors and the annotation was updated based on the decision. We adjusted and extended our annotation scheme in the process. We did not involve multiple independent annotators, because our aim was mainly to get an overview of the reference resolution issues. To test the reliability of the resulting annotation scheme, another person annotated a small subset of the corpus, consisting of one dialogue, which contained 57 utterances. We measured inter-annotator agreement using Cohen's kappa following (Carletta, 1996). We obtained a kappa score of 0.704 for the *Entities* layer, 1.0 for *Comments*, 0.895 for *Roles*, 0.573 for *Reference Units* and 0.845 for *Reference Links*. This shows good agreement, except for reference units.

4.1   Annotation Scheme

Our annotation scheme has four separate layers: *Entities, Roles, Reference units* and *Comments*. We use separate layers, so that each layer can have its own set of markable expressions and a separate corresponding tag set. We keep the tag sets flat for practical reasons.

At the *Entities* layer we annotate mission-relevant objects (POIs), locations, mission participants (actors) and other mentioned entities. At the *Roles* layer we annotate the role of each mention of a mission participant, such as MC, TL, OP-UGV1, OP-UAV, etc. The purpose of the *Reference Units* layer is to annotate reference links as well as the syntactic category of the expressions that constitute the source and target of the link. Finally, at the *Comments* layer we annotate several special cases: expletive pronouns, deictic pronouns referring to displayed objects, incorrect transcriptions, uncertain and vague cases. The annotation of entities, roles and reference units and links is discussed in more detail below.

A given expression may be marked simultaneously at different layers. For example, the expression 'UGV one' may be marked at the *Entities* layer as an actor, at the *Roles* layer as OP-UGV1 and at the *Reference Unit* layer as an NP.

Table 2 shows the full list of tags for each layer and their distribution in the TRADR corpus. Of the 7067 entities in total 51.2% are actors, 17.48% are various kinds of objects, 11.07% locations, 0.92% displayed POIs and 19.34% do not fit into one of these classes and are labeled as other. As for roles, 31.35% refer to the TL and 1.2% to the MC, 53.61% to the robot operators, 5.15% to the robots and 1.41% are other roles. We marked a total of 4385 reference units, of which 80.21% are nominal expressions and 19.79% other markables.

Table 3 shows the distribution of reference links. We annotated in total 2502 relation instances. The largest group is basic anaphora, which makes up almost 55% of all relation instances. Bridging constitutes 12.35%, implicit identity and base identity are also among the common relations with 9.6% and 7.5%, respectively. Other relations occur much less often.

4.2 Entities

We marked expressions referring to mission-relevant entities and assigned them a tag characterizing their semantic type. As we were particularly interested in mission-relevant objects (POIs), locations and actors, we distinguished these explicitly, and the rest received the tag "other". We considered NPs and NP-like expressions as primary markables. For locations we included also other types of expressions, esp. prepositional phrases and adverbials.

From the viewpoint of reference resolution we identified the need to make the following distinctions: (a) *object/location* that the participants know exists (object) or where it is (location), (b) *potential object/location*: the participants are not sure it exists (object) or it is a hypothetical place, (c) *undefined object/location*: the participants know it exists but not what it is (object) or it is an unknown place (location). Example 4.1 illustrates the three cases in (a), (b) and (c) respectively.[1]

Layer	Tag set and distribution
Entities Total: 7067	actor (3618 / 51.2%), object (1082 / 15.31%), potential object (128 / 1.81%), undefined object 25 / 0.35%), location (741 / 10.49%), potential location (9 / 0.13%), undefined location (32 / 0.45%), POI (65 / 0.92%), other (1367 / 19.34%)
Roles Total: 3764	MC (45 / 1.2%), TL (1180 / 31.35%), TEAM (136 / 3.61%), OP-UGV1 (986 / 26.2%), OP-UGV2 (649 / 17.24%), OP-UAV (312 / 8.29%), OP-PL (71 / 1.89%), UGV1 (59 / 1.57%), UGV2 (65 / 1.73%), UAV (38 / 1.01%), OP+ROBOT (138 / 3.67%), ROBOT-SG (13 / 0.35%), ROBOTS-PL (19 / 0.5%), OTHER-SG (45 / 1.2%), OTHER-PL (8 / 0.21%)
Reference units Total:4385	np (2904 / 66.23%), pro (581 / 13.25%), num (20 / 0.46%), name (12 / 0.27%), adv (582 / 13.27%), vp (40 / 0.91%), pp (18 / 0.41%), clause (156 / 3.56%), discourse (72 / 1.64%)
Comments Total: 303	EXPLETIVE (121 / 39.93%), INCORRECT (68 / 22.44%), DEICTIC (36 / 11.88%), UNCERTAIN (53 / 17.49%), VAGUE (25 / 8.25%)

Table 2: Reference annotation layers, tag sets and their distribution

Reference links Total: 2502	basic anaphora (1375 / 54.96%), bridging (309 / 12.35%), discourse anaphora (37 / 1.48%), propositional anaphora (103 / 4.12%), identity (183 / 7.31%), potential identity (32 / 1.28%), implicit identity (240 / 9.59%), implicit potential identity (44 / 1.76%), asking for identity (11 / 0.44%), intensional reference (82 / 3.28%), negative reference (38 / 1.52%), continuation (43 / 1.72%), metonymy (5 / 0.2%)

Table 3: Reference link types and their distribution

Example 4.1 *Object/location: (a) real, (b) potential, (c) undefined*
(a) UAV: Ich habe jetzt bei [der zweiten Person] auch eventuell Rauch gefunden. (I also found possible smoke near [the second person].)
(b) TL: Yes, only the outside, looking for [smoke] or [victims]. Over.
(c) TL: Can you see a... [what is a... that smoke from]? Over.

---

[1]Square brackets enclose the markable(s) in focus in each example. We do not indicate all markables for the sake of legibility. For German examples we provide an English translation that we make as near-literal as possible.

The analysis of inter-annotated agreement showed that it is especially difficult to distinguish between displayed POIs and objects, and to decide whether we have a mission-relevant POI (*object* or *location*) or an irrelevant one (*other*). Furthermore, we detected the following aspects that need further consideration in the future. First, in most cases locations are not clearly delimited, e.g., *'the north-west corner of the plant'*, which is a challenge for example for rendering them in the digital map. Second, we currently do not distinguish between absolute locations, e.g., *'the north-west corner of the plant'* and locations relative to the current position of the robot. Third, the same or similar expression may be interpreted as a reference to an object in one context, and location in another. For example, the two staircases in Example 4.2(a) are objects, but a staircase can be a location in another case. Fourth, the expressions referring to locations (and objects) can be nested, cf. Example 4.2(b). The nested structure can be quite complex.

Example 4.2 *Entities – challenges: (a) object vs. location, (b) nesting*
(a) UGV-1: Ja, ich hab gerade ein Foto geschossen, hier sind [zwei Treppen] auf der linken Seite, allerdings kein Angriffstrupp. (Yes, I have just taken a photo, here are [two staircases] on the left but there's no attack squad.)
(b) UGV-1: eine Person gesichtet, ist [[auf der Ebene, auf der auch die Leckage ist], [hinter dem ersten Hochofen]]. (One person sighted, is [[at the same floor as the leakage] [behind the first furnace]].)

A special type of entity is a *displayed POI*. This is an icon on the digital map that represents a physical POI, like in Example 4.3(a). We use the displayed POI tag when it is clear that an expression refers to an icon on the map. In many cases it is difficult or even impossible for the annotator to distinguish between a physical POI and its displayed POI, they are used interchangeably. Example 4.3(b) illustrates this.

Example 4.3 *(a) displayed POI, (b) physical and displayed POI mix-up*
(a) TL: Can you make [a POI from the victim the photo you sent]? Over.
(b) TL: Yeah. Tango goes to [fire thirty nine] and Romeo goes to [victim thirty eight].

4.3 Roles

Role resolution is needed as a basis for tracking who is assigned which task. We mark every expression that refers to a mission participant (or a group thereof), and label it with a tag reflecting their role. Besides full NPs, including names and personal pronouns, which are also annotated as actors at the *Entity* layer, the markables at the *Roles* layer include reflexive and possessive pronouns, in order to capture really all references to mission participants. The primary roles are MC, TL, the robot operators and the robots themselves. The examples above and below provide various illustrations. In addition we had to introduce a tag for the entire team (TEAM) and tags for subgroups (OP+ROBOT, ROBOTS-PL, OTHER-PL).

Role annotation has the following challenges. First, the resolution of roles for pronouns and personal names is context dependent, and sometimes the annotator cannot figure it out. Second, an operator and their robot often act and are perceived as a single unit, which makes it difficult to distinguish between them in the annotation. Third, reference is sometimes made to some (sub)group, of the participants, and it is not clear who is meant.

4.4 Reference Units and Relations

Reference units are those expressions whose referents are, or have the potential to be, linked to the referents of other expressions by a reference relation. We annotate the syntactic type of the markable expression. Because we originally focused on entities, nominal expressions are the primary markables: we distinguish between noun phrases (*np*), pronouns (*pro*) and numerals (*num*). As we proceeded with the annotation we added other markable types: adverbial (*adv*), verb phrase (*vp*), prepositional phrase (*pp*), *clause* and *discourse*. The examples discussed further below provide various illustrations.

The inter-annotator agreement is the lowest for this layer. Disagreement concerned mostly the following pairs of labels: *adv* vs. *pp*, *np* vs. *clause*, *discourse* vs. *clause*.

Reference units are connected via *Reference links*. Our annotation scheme includes the traditional link types that we apply according to their usual definitions: *basic anaphora* as in (Deemter and Kibble, 2000), *bridging* (associative relations), *discourse anaphora* (reference to a multi-sentence descriptive passage in the dialogue) and *propositional anaphora* (reference to a statement, proposition or fact not longer than a clause). In addition, we introduce several new link types in order to capture the kinds of relationships we observe in our data. The latter we describe below.

The *identity* link captures the cases where it is more or less explicitly asserted that two expressions have identical referents or describe the same phenomenon. Identity is typically expressed by a copula construction, but other forms are also found, like in Example 4.4(a). When the identity relation needs to be inferred, we label it *implicit identity* (see Example 4.4(b) and (c)). Sometimes, the speakers may not even know that they refer to the same entity. This may happen throughout a dialogue, and it is important that reference resolution recognizes it, to keep track of mission-relevant objects, locations and tasks. The difficulty here is that the related reference units may be far apart.

Sometimes it is difficult to differentiate between *identity* and *implicit identity*, for example, when someone is explaining something giving additional details or paraphrasing, as in Example 4.4(d).

Example 4.4 *identity vs. implicit identity link*
(a) Op1: Eeh. Team leader for operator one. I sent you a picture with [the BIO hazards]. [Codes eight and three].
(b) TL: Ok. I have [a task] for you. Emm. I create an area and then you have to [explore it].
(c) Op2: I will give [my status] for about thirty seconds. Over. ... Op2: [I am at the position of the north-west corner of the plant.]
(d) TL: Das gleiche Bild, was du jetzt gemacht hast, [da in die Mitte] reinzoomen, [da wo die Rauchentwicklung ist]. (The same picture you've taken now but zooming [in the middle] [there where the smoke development is].)

For cases where it is not clear (to the dialogue participants or the annotator) whether identity holds between some reference units, we introduce the link types *potential identity* and *implicit potential identity*.

Example 4.5 *(a) potential vs. (b) implicit potential identity link*
(a) UAV: Es könnten [Personen] sein [das was hell leuchtet]. (It could be [people], [that what is brightly glowing].)
(b) UGV1: I see a victim. It's looks like he's sitting on [a chair]. Is that the same victim you see? UGV2: Negative. It's an... erm... maybe. M- my victim is also sitting on [an chair]. ... UGV2: UGV one, I think, I'm seeing your victim. Is also sitting on a blue chair.   *—probably the same chairs*

These relations pose a challenge for reference resolution, because the hypothetical identity may turn out to be untrue later in the dialogue (not because of an annotator's mistake, but because of belief revision due to additional information available to the participants).

The link *asking for identity* is applied in cases when a participant poses a question concerning the identity of two or more entities. In this case the speaker may suggest a possible candidate for identity, or the speaker does not have any candidates in mind and wants to have an answer (see Example 4.6).

Example 4.6 *Asking for identity link*
UAV: Also - die Person müsste hinter [dem großen Hochofen] auf dem freien Weg sein. TL: Ist das [welcher Hochofen] ist es, der rechte oder der linke von uns aus gesehen? (So, the person must be behind [the big furnace] on the free path. [Which furnace] is it, the right one or the left one seen from our direction?)   *welcher Hochofen → dem großen Hochofen*

Example 4.5(b) above demonstrates a combination of basic anaphora, asking for identity, implicit identity and potential implicit identity regarding the reference to the victim(s).

Because we differentiate between actual and hypothetical (or potential) entities, we also need a separate reference link type for the latter, in order to be consistent. The *intensional reference* link, illustrated in Example 4.7, serves this purpose. We use this link type also for references to generic objects.

Example 4.7 *Intensional reference link*
TL: Kannst du mir mal [ein Foto von deiner Position] machen? UGV-2: Ja ich mach dir mal [ein Snapshot]. (Can you make a photo from your position for me? - Yes, I'll make you a snapshot.)
—a photo does not exist yet

To correctly keep track of things during a mission, we also need information about entities referred to in the scope of a negation operator. We introduce the link *negative reference* illustrated in Example 4.8.

Example 4.8 *Negative reference link*
TL: Habt ihr neuen Status zum [Standort der Person oder der Chemikalien]? Ich krieg [keinen Standort].
(Do you have a new status of [the location of the person or the chemicals]? I don't get [any location].)

Challenges   Our annotation scheme includes various data-, domain- and task-specific types of reference units and relations. Such an extensive approach gives rise to additional challenges.

First of all, since we only use one type of *bridging* link, the annotated cases encompass a range of different association types. This includes the typical ones, such as set membership, part-whole, entity-attribute, as well as some rather special ones, for instance, contextual association as in Example 4.9(a) between a physical mission entity (POI) and a corresponding displayed POI, or (b) between a picture and what is depicted, as well as (c) between an adverbial pronoun (in German) and an entity. We knowingly overloaded the bridging link for the sake of the initial analysis, and intend to split it in the future.

Example 4.9 *Bridging relation: specific associations*
(a) Op1: Emm. [The fire] is on the north site. North, north-east site. Took on the corner. TL: Can eeh you put [the point of interest]?   the point of interest → the fire
(b) UGV-2: Ich hab dir gerade [ein Bild] geschickt. [Da] steht ein Stuhl auf dem Stuhl liegt ein Paket und vor dem Stuhl steht ein Paket. (I've just sent you [a picture]. [There] is a chair, on the chair lies a package, and in front of the chair lies another package.)   – da (there) → ein Bild (a picture)
(c) UGV-1: [Grüne Fass] mit Flasche [drauf]. ([Green barrel] with a bottle [on it]. ˙
– drauf (on it) → grüne Fass (green barrel)

German adverbial pronouns sometimes refer to propositions or larger pieces of dialogue. We annotate these cases as *propositional* or *discourse anaphora*. An exception is the case when an entity referred to by an adverbial pronoun is introduced after it within the same sentence, as in Example 4.10. For now we use the identity link here, but it actually does not fully capture this kind of relation.

Example 4.10 *Adverbial pronouns: identity relation*
TL: Bitte [darauf] achten, [eine Bezeichnung auf dem Kanister zu erkennen]. (Please take care to recognize a label on the canister.)

Moreover, there are some other associative relations that we currently do not annotate. Here we have cases when an entity in plural form has several singular antecedents (Example 4.11(a)), cases with negative noun phrases as antecedents (Example 4.11(b)), and cases where a noun phrase to be resolved contains words 'more', 'another' and so on (Example 4.11(c)).

Example 4.11 *Unlabeled associative relations*
(a) UAV: [Ein Lagebild von oben] komplette Lage und [ein Lagebild zwischen den beiden Türen], verstanden. ... UAV: Ja, [beide Bilder] in Infrarot ebenfalls. ([A picture of the whole situation from above] and [a picture of the situation between the two doors], roger. ... Yes, [both pictures] also in infrared.)
(b) UGV2: UGV two. [No alert]. Over. TL: All right. I've got [a couple of them] from location you are now. Over.
(c) TL: Only I have [a picture from mmm that is him]. I don't, I don't have [more information].

Next, there are cases of *implicit identity* that we do not currently annotate, such as when we have two different antecedents and a singular entity that refers to them, like in Example 4.12.

Example 4.12 *Implicit identity: several antecedents for a singular entity*
TL: Operator one for team leader. I create an area. Can you [explore that area], please? ... TL: It's operator two for team leader. I create an area. Can you [explore that area], please? TL: Operator one and operator two. Here is team leader. Can you accept [your task]? Over.
– your task → explore that area (operator one), your task → explore that area (operator two)

Communication problems, such as in Example 4.13, also evoke annotation difficulties. Currently we do not annotate the cases, when the participants mishear, misspeak or misjudge a situation or what is on the screen, although such cases are also relevant for keeping track of entities or events accurately.

Example 4.13 *Communication problems*

Op2: Yeah. [What's area] do you mean? TL: [Area on the west site]. Over. Op2: [The area on the left site]. Ok. TL: [The area on the west site]. Over. Op2: [On the west site].

One more issue that requires further consideration is how the *double representation of reality* is annotated. Generally, we follow the convention that we treat physical objects and the corresponding symbols on the screen as the same entities, because they are used interchangeably by the mission participants. However, this is not always possible, as it can happen that the difference between a physical object and its symbolic representation is brought under discussion, like in Example 4.14. In such cases we differentiate them, but this sometimes leads to complications, for example with co-reference chains.

Example 4.14 *Real object vs. its symbolic representation*

UGV2: I'm searching for [$_{object}$ the victim] in area, where it's... where- where the picture I can see in the plot. Over. TL: You can see [$_{poi}$ a victim] in the plot. [$_{object}$ The real victim] will be more to the right side of the- [$_{poi}$ it]. Over.

Finally, our annotation of *interrogative pronouns* and noun phrases that include them is currently not quite consistent. In Example 4.15(a), we connect 'welchem Bild' with 'einem Wärmebild' and 'einem richtigen Foto' via two potential identity links, as these phrases are the only possible candidates. But we do not link 'what' and 'the whole area' in Example 4.15(b).

Example 4.15 *Interrogative pronouns*

(a) TL: Auf [welchem Bild] jetzt auf [einem Wärmebild] oder auf [einem richtigen Foto]? (On [which picture], on [a heat image] or on [a usual photo]?)

(b) TL: [What] did you explore? What- UGV-1: I did explore [the whole area].

5 Conclusions and Outlook

We presented a preliminary analysis of reference phenomena in a corpus of team communication for robot-assisted disaster response, done in preparation for developing reference resolution modules for a system that interprets such team communication to extract run-time mission knowledge and use it for various forms of teamwork assistance. Our annotation scheme has separate layers for mission-relevant entities, roles of actors, reference units with links between them, as well as comments for special cases.

Among the mission-relevant entities we focused on objects, locations and actors. Although these constitute the majority of objects referred to, there is a large number of other entities that remain to be classified in more detail. For the sake of reference resolution we found it important to distinguish between objects and locations that are known to exist, and those that are potential/hypothetical or undefined. This is however very difficult to do during annotation. Moreover, information about mission entities evolves during the dialogue, and this creates challenges for co-referential links. Another interesting challenge is the double reality representation, which means that mission objects in the physical reality and those displayed in a digital map are mostly referred to interchangeably, but sometimes need to be distinguished. In this regard we plan to review the literature on visual co-reference resolution as a next step.

Our analysis shows that a content representation using slots and fillers, as is commonly done in dialogue systems, clearly does not suffice for this domain, a proper discourse representation is required.

As for referential links, basic anaphora together with identity relationships dominate. Bridging is next, and then there are various different cases which are not that frequent but quite tricky for reference resolution. Analyzing different kinds of bridging in more detail and properly describing the other kinds of links remains a topic for our future work. The annotated corpus is currently being used for testing existing co-reference resolution models, including the AllenNLP model (Lee et al., 2017), NeuralCoref by HuggingFace (Wolf et al., 2020) and the CoreNLP framework (Manning et al., 2014). The results of these experiments will help determine our future steps for reference resolution.

Acknowledgements

This work was done as part of the project "A-DRZ: Setting up the German Rescue Robotics Center", funded by the German Ministry of Education and Research (BMBF), grant No. I3N14856.[2] We would like to thank our colleagues from the A-DRZ project for discussions, Tatiana Anakina for additional reference annotation and the reviewers of the CRAC 2020 Workshop on Computational Models of Reference, Anaphora and Coreference for valuable comments.

References

Berfin Aktaş, Tatjana Scheffler, and Manfred Stede. 2018. Anaphora resolution for Twitter conversations: An exploratory study. In *Proceedings of the First Workshop on Computational Models of Reference, Anaphora and Coreference*, pages 1–10.

Tatiana Anikina and Ivana Kruijff-Korbayová. 2019. Dialogue act classification in team communication for robot assisted disaster response. In *Proceedings of SIGDIAL 2019*.

Amit Bagga and Breck Baldwin. 1999. Cross-document event coreference: Annotations, experiments, and observations. In *Coreference and Its Applications*.

Simon Philip Botley. 2006. Indirect anaphora: Testing the limits of corpus-based linguistics. *International Journal of Corpus Linguistics*, 11(1):73–112.

Jean Carletta. 1996. Assessing agreement on classification tasks: The kappa statistic. *Comput. Linguist.*, 22(2):249–254, June.

Tommaso Caselli and Irina Prodanof. 2010. Annotating event anaphora: A case study. In *LREC*.

K. Bretonnel Cohen, Arrick Lanfranchi, Miji Joo-young Choi, Michael Bada, William A. Baumgartner, Natalya Panteleyeva, Karin Verspoor, Martha Palmer, and Lawrence E Hunter. 2017. Coreference annotation and resolution in the Colorado Richly Annotated Full Text (CRAFT) corpus of biomedical journal articles. *BMC bioinformatics*, 18(1):1–14.

Parag Pravin Dakle, Takshak Desai, and Dan Moldovan. 2020. A study on entity resolution for email conversations. In *Proceedings of The 12th Language Resources and Evaluation Conference*, pages 65–73.

Kees van Deemter and Rodger Kibble. 2000. On coreferring: Coreference in MUC and related annotation schemes. *Computational linguistics*, 26(4):629–637.

Richard Eckart de Castilho, Éva Mújdricza-Maydt, Seid Muhie Yimam, Silvana Hartmann, Iryna Gurevych, Anette Frank, and Chris Biemann. 2016. A web-based tool for the integrated annotation of semantic and syntactic structures. In *Proceedings of the Workshop on Language Technology Resources and Tools for Digital Humanities (LT4DH)*, pages 76–84, Osaka, Japan, December. The COLING 2016 Organizing Committee.

Pradheep Elango. 2005. Coreference resolution: A survey. *University of Wisconsin, Madison, WI*.

Steve Fligelstone. 1992. Developing a scheme for annotating text to show anaphoric relations. *New Directions in English Language Corpora: Methodology, Results, Software Developments*, pages 153–170.

Niyu Ge. 1998. Annotating the Penn treebank with coreference information. *Technical report*.

Michael A.K. Halliday and R. Hasan. 1976. *Cohesion in English*. Longman, London, U.K.

Laura Hasler, Constantin Orasan, and Karin Naumann. 2006. NPs for events: Experiments in coreference annotation. In *LREC*, pages 1167–1172. Citeseer.

Lynette Hirschman and Nancy Chinchor. 1998. Appendix F: MUC-7 coreference task definition (version 3.0). In *Seventh Message Understanding Conference (MUC-7): Proceedings of a Conference Held in Fairfax, Virginia, April 29 - May 1, 1998*.

Ivana Kruijff-Korbayová and Geert-Jan M Kruijff. 2004. Discourse-level annotation for investigating information structure. In *Proceedings of the Workshop on Discourse Annotation*, pages 41–48.

---

[2]rettungsrobotik.de

Ivana Kruijff-Korbayová, Francis Colas, Mario Gianni, Fiora Pirri, Joachim de Greeff, Koen Hindriks, Mark Neerincx, Petter Ögren, Tomáš Svoboda, and Rainer Worst. 2015. TRADR project: Long-term human-robot teaming for robot assisted disaster response. *KI - Künstliche Intelligenz*, 29(2):193–201, Jun.

Kenton Lee, Luheng He, M. Lewis, and Luke Zettlemoyer. 2017. End-to-end neural coreference resolution. In *EMNLP*.

Christopher D. Manning, Mihai Surdeanu, John Bauer, Jenny Finkel, Steven J. Bethard, and David McClosky. 2014. The Stanford CoreNLP natural language processing toolkit. In *Association for Computational Linguistics (ACL) System Demonstrations*, pages 55–60.

Tony McEnery, Izumi Tanaka, and Simon Botley. 1997. Corpus annotation and reference resolution. In *Operational Factors in Practical, Robust Anaphora Resolution for Unrestricted Texts*.

Malvina Nissim, Shipra Dingare, Jean Carletta, and Mark Steedman. 2004. An annotation scheme for information status in dialogue. In *LREC*. Citeseer.

Massimo Poesio, Florence Bruneseaux, and Laurent Romary. 1999. The MATE meta-scheme for coreference in dialogues in multiple languages. In *Towards Standards and Tools for Discourse Tagging*.

Massimo Poesio, Ron Artstein, et al. 2008. Anaphoric annotation in the ARRAU corpus. In *LREC*.

Massimo Poesio. 2004. The MATE/GNOME proposals for anaphoric annotation, revisited. In *Proceedings of the 5th SIGdial Workshop on Discourse and Dialogue at HLT-NAACL 2004*, pages 154–162.

TRADR project website. 2020. Long-term human-robot teaming for robot-assisted disaster response (TRADR). http://www.tradr-project.eu/. Accessed: 2020-04-30.

Marco Rocha. 1999. Coreference resolution in dialogues in English and Portuguese. In *Coreference and Its Applications*.

Andrea Setzer and Robert J Gaizauskas. 2000. Annotating events and temporal information in newswire texts. In *LREC*, volume 2000, pages 1287–1294. Citeseer.

Joel Tetreault, Mary Swift, Preethum Prithviraj, Myroslava O Dzikovska, and James Allen. 2004. Discourse annotation in the Monroe corpus. In *Proceedings of the Workshop on Discourse Annotation*, pages 103–109.

Christian Willms, Constantin Houy, Jana-Rebecca Rehse, Peter Fettke, and Ivana Kruijff-Korbayová. 2019. Team communication processing and process analytics for supporting robot-assisted emergency response. In *International Conference on Safety, Security, and Rescue Robotics (SSRR)*.

Thomas Wolf, Lysandre Debut, Victor Sanh, Julien Chaumond, Clement Delangue, Anthony Moi, Pierric Cistac, Tim Rault, Rémi Louf, Morgan Funtowicz, Joe Davison, Sam Shleifer, Patrick von Platen, Clara Ma, Yacine Jernite, Julien Plu, Canwen Xu, Teven Le Scao, Sylvain Gugger, Mariama Drame, Quentin Lhoest, and Alexander M. Rush. 2020. Huggingface's transformers: State-of-the-art natural language processing.

Kristin Wright-Bettner, Martha Palmer, Guergana Savova, Piet de Groen, and Timothy Miller. 2019. Cross-document coreference: An approach to capturing coreference without context. In *Proceedings of the Tenth International Workshop on Health Text Mining and Information Analysis (LOUHI 2019)*, pages 1–10.

Heike Zinsmeister and Stefanie Dipper. 2010. Towards a standard for annotating abstract anaphora. In *LREC*, pages 54–59.

Resolving Pronouns in Twitter Streams: Context can Help!

Anietie Andy
University of Pennsylvania
andyanietie@gmail.com

Chris Callison-Burch
University of Pennsylvania
ccb@cis.upenn.edu

Derry Tanti Wijaya
Boston University
wijaya@bu.edu

Abstract

Many people live-tweet televised events like Presidential debates and popular TV-shows and discuss people or characters in the event. Naturally, many tweets make pronominal reference to these people/characters. We propose an algorithm for resolving personal pronouns that make reference to people involved in an event, in tweet streams collected during the event.

1 Introduction

Pronoun resolution is an important task in natural language processing (Denis and Baldridge, 2007; Clark and Manning, 2015; Cheri et al., 2016; Yin et al., 2018). However, not a lot of work has been done to address pronoun resolution in Twitter streams related to events. During a televised event such as a Presidential debate or TV-shows, individuals publish tweets about people in the context in which they are being portrayed in the event (Andy et al., 2017; Andy et al., 2019). Some of these tweets make reference to people using third-person singular pronouns like *he*, *him*, *his*, *she*, and *her*. For example, here are some tweets about an episode of the TV-show, Game of Thrones season 7 (GoTS7) that were published during the same minute while the episode was airing: (i) *"she took his face"*, (ii) *"walder frey?! probably just before arya killed him"*, and (iii) *"wait where is arya did she change to his face"*. With short text such as these event-related tweets, although some tweets might mention the referents in the same tweets as the pronouns (e.g., in (ii) where *"him"* makes reference to the character *"Walder Frey"* in the same tweet), some other tweets may not contain the referents in the same tweets (e.g., in (i) and (iii), the pronouns {*"she"*, *"his"*} and *"his"* respectively refer to the characters, {*"Arya"*, *"Walder Frey"*} and *"Walder Frey"* that are not mentioned in (i) and (iii) respectively).

Resolving a pronominal mention in an event-related tweet is a challenging task because a tweet with pronominal mentions either: (i) does not mention any person, (ii) makes reference to a person not mentioned in the tweet, and (iii) mentions more than one person (who may or may not have the same gender as the pronoun).

In this paper, taking advantage of the context in which a pronoun is mentioned in the tweet, the tweet's temporal information, and the context in which other people are mentioned in tweets about the same event published at the same time period, we develop an algorithm to automatically resolve these third-person singular pronouns.

We evaluate our algorithm on tweets collected around two events: (1) a United States (US) Democratic party Presidential debate and (2) an episode of a popular TV-show, GoTS7. We show that our algorithm outperforms baselines. We will make these datasets available to the research community.

2 Related Work

A lot of work on resolving pronouns in text has been done. In Denis and Baldridge (2007), a ranking approach for resolving pronouns in text was proposed. In Clark and Manning (2015), an entity-based coreference model which incrementally learns to resolve coreference was proposed. Yin et al. (2018) proposed a self-attention method to model zero pronouns. In Cheri et al. (2016), the eye movements of

Proceedings of the 3rd Workshop on Computational Models of Reference, Anaphora and Coreference (CRAC 2020), pages 133–138,
Barcelona, Spain (online), December 12, 2020.

participants annotating documents were tracked to gain insights to some of the processes people use in coreference resolution. Lee et al. (2017) proposed an end-to-end coreference resolution model that is based on a neural model; the proposed model takes into consideration all the spans in a given text and given a span, it determines if there is a previous span which is an antecedent. Abzaliev (2019) proposed a coreference resolution model which uses fine-tuned BERT embeddings. In Kocijan et al. (2019), a large coreference resolution dataset was constructed. In Rudinger et al. (2018), gender bias in coreference resolution was studied and it was shown that gender bias exists in some coreference resolution systems. In Zhao et al. (2018), a coreference resolution dataset focused on gender bias was constructed and similar to Zhao et al. (2018) it was shown that some coreference resolution systems are gender biased; a model was proposed to remove these biases while maintaining the performance on coreference datasets.

Not a lot of prior work has been done to resolve pronouns in Twitter data. The closest related work to our work is Aktaş et al. (2018), which studies pronominal anaphora on conversations in Twitter and constructs a corpus to determine relevant factors for resolving anaphora in Twitter conversation data.

Our algorithm is different from Aktaş et al. (2018) because it focuses on resolving pronouns in tweets that make reference to people and characters portrayed in an event.

3 Dataset and Labeling

Our dataset consist of tweets collected during the airing of an hour-long episode of the popular HBO show, GoTS7 and tweets collected during night 1 of the first 2020 US Democratic party Presidential debate (the first debate was held on 2 nights).

3.1 GoTS7 dataset

Using a Twitter streaming API, we collected 4,223 time-stamped tweets that contained *"#got"* - a popular hashtag for the show, while episode 3 of GoTS7 was airing. From these we identified tweets that mentioned a third-person singular pronoun and we collected the timestamp in which each of these tweets was published. In this episode of GoTS7, 35 characters were portrayed, 24 of which were male and 11 female. From our dataset, we observed that in this episode an average of 93 posts were published per minute.

Labeling: The day after each episode of GoTS7 aired, the New York Times (NYTimes) published a summary of the episode. We collected the NYTimes summary of this episode. We showed this summary to 3 annotators who had watched the episode. Then given a tweet with a third-person singular pronoun mention and the timestamp this tweet was published, we asked the annotators to identify the character that was being referred to in the tweet. We selected a character for each pronoun mention if at least 2 of the annotators identified the same character as the one the pronoun was referring to. Using kappa calculation, we calculated the agreement between the annotators and got 0.86. Our labeled dataset contains 154 tweets with resolved pronominal references to characters. 59% (i.e., 91) of the labeled tweets contained both a third-person singular pronoun and the character that was being referenced by the pronoun, and 41% (i.e., 63) mentioned a third-person singular pronoun and did not contain the character that was being referenced by the pronoun.

3.2 US Presidential debate dataset

Similar to section 3.1, we collected 46,142 time-stamped tweets that contained the word *"debate"* while the Presidential debate was airing and identified tweets containing a third-person singular pronoun and their corresponding timestamps. There were 10 candidates who participated in the debate, 7 of which were male and 3 female. From our dataset, we observed that on the average, 431 posts were published per minute in our Presidential debates.

Labeling: While the debate was airing, NYTimes had a live-blog with some political reporters discussing and analyzing the debate in real-time[1]. We collected these live-blog discussions and analysis and showed

---

[1] https://www.nytimes.com/interactive/2019/06/26/us/politics/democratic-debate-live-chat.

them to 3 annotators who had watched the debate. Given a tweet with a mention of a third-person singular pronoun and the timestamp in which the tweet was published, the annotators were asked to identify the Presidential candidate that was being referenced by the pronoun. A candidate was selected if at least 2 of the annotators identified the same candidate as the one being referenced in the tweet. Using kappa calculation, we calculated the agreement between the annotators and got 0.83. Our labeled dataset is made up of 141 tweets with resolved pronominal references to Presidential candidates. 84% (i.e., 118) of the labeled tweets contained both a third-person singular pronoun and the candidate that was being referenced by the pronoun and 16% (i.e., 23) of the labeled tweets mentioned a third-person singular pronoun and did not contain the candidate that was being referenced by the pronoun.

The annotators mostly agreed, however, some of the tweets in which the annotators did not agree on made reference to characters using third-person singular pronouns without mentioning any characters in the tweet, as shown by the following examples from GoTS7: (1) *"lol he can't stop himself #gots7"*, (2) *"noo shes my favorite #gots7"*, and (3) *"now it's time to get her rocks off #gots7"*.

4 Our Algorithm

Our algorithm has 3 steps:

4.1 Step 1: Candidate/Character Identification:

Prior to the Presidential debate, NYTimes published the names of the Presidential candidates who would be debating[2]. We selected the candidate names from the NYTimes article. For GoTS7, we identified characters by selecting all the character names listed in the Wikipedia page of GoTS7.

Some event-related tweets mention people by their names or aliases (Andy et al., 2017), hence for each candidate/character in each of these events, we construct an alias list which consists their first name (which is unique in both the Presidential debates and GoTS7), their last name if it is unique in the event, and the nickname listed in the first paragraph of the character (person entity) Wikipedia page. We also selected the gender of each candidate and character from the candidates and shows Wikipedia page, respectively.

4.2 Step 2: Identifying the context in tweets

To determine the context of pronoun mentions and candidate/character mentions, we use the pre-trained BERT (Devlin et al., 2018) language representation model. We input each tweet containing the pronoun or candidate/character mentions to the pre-trained BERT-Base model and extract the 768-dimensional contextual embeddings of the pronoun or candidate/character tokens, which we take as their contextual representations in the tweet, generated from the final hidden layer of the pre-trained model. For multi-token candidates/characters, we use the average of their token embeddings.

4.3 Step 3: Pronoun resolution

A tweet with a pronominal mention either contains possible persons being referred to by the pronoun (section 4.3.2) or it does not (i.e., either because it does not contain any person mention or it does not contain person mentions with the same gender as the pronoun) (section 4.3.1). Our algorithm handles both cases.

4.3.1 Case 1: Tweets with pronouns but no possible person referent

Given a tweet t with a third-person singular pronoun mention and the timestamp it was published, our algorithm identifies all the candidates/characters that were mentioned more than k times in tweets published in the same minute as tweet t and groups the tweets that mention the same candidate/character together. To identify the optimal value for k, we collected tweets published around 2 other episodes of GoTS7 and tweets published around another US Presidential debate and randomly selected tweets published in a 20 minute time period in each of these events; we varied the number of candidate/character mentions (between 1 to 5) per minute and observed that on the average, candidates/characters mentioned

---

html
[2]https://www.nytimes.com/2019/06/26/us/politics/democratic-debate-lineup.html

more than 3 times in tweets published in a minute, were referred to by a pronoun in the same minute, hence we choose $k=3$. For each group of tweets, where tweets in each group make reference to the same candidate/character, our algorithm calculates the cosine similarity between the BERT embedding of the third-person singular pronoun mention and the BERT embedding of the candidate or character mentions in each tweet in each group. The average cosine similarity between the pronoun mention and the candidate/character mentions in each group is calculated. Since we know the gender of each of the candidates/characters (section 4.1), our algorithm identifies the candidate/character being referred to by the pronoun in the tweet by selecting the candidate/character with the largest average cosine similarity to the pronoun embedding, above or equal to a threshold (0.3), and its gender matches the pronoun's. We chose 0.3 as the threshold by using selected tweets published in two other GoTS7 episodes and another US Presidential debate to compare candidate/character embeddings to pronoun embeddings published in the same minute and observed that a threshold of 0.3 gave optimal results for matching pronouns to their referents.

Algorithms	Precision	Recall	F1
Our Model	**0.79**	**0.65**	**0.71**
Last person mention	0.47	0.40	0.43
Spike per minute	0.68	0.48	0.56

Table 1: Results of applying our algorithm and baselines to tweets with pronoun mentions but no possible referent mention in our Presidential debate dataset

Algorithms	Precision	Recall	F1
Our Model	**0.73**	**0.65**	**0.68**
Last person mention	0.61	0.23	0.33
Spike per minute	0.69	0.62	0.65

Table 2: Results of applying our algorithm and baselines to tweets with pronoun mentions but no possible referent mention in our GoTS7 dataset

4.3.2 Case 2: Tweets with pronoun mentions and possible person referents

Given a tweet t with a third-person singular pronoun mention and person mentions, and the timestamp this tweet was published, our algorithm identifies all the candidates/characters that were mentioned more than $k=3$ times in tweets published in the same minute as tweet t and groups the tweets that mention the same candidate/character together.

In some cases, the pronoun in the tweet t could be making reference to the candidate/character mentioned in t. Therefore, we also select the candidate/character mentioned in the tweet as a candidate/character mention; here, we do not give any additional weight or preference to the mentioned candidate/character because it is possible that the pronoun might be making reference to a different character as shown in the following examples : (1) *"Cersei is about to kill her"* and (2) *"Cersei is taunting her"*, where in both cases, *"her"* refers to a different character, *"Ellaria"*.

Similar to Section 4.3.1, for each group of tweets, where tweets in each group make reference to the same candidate/character, our algorithm calculates the cosine similarity between the BERT embedding of the third-person singular pronoun and the BERT embeddings of each of the candidate/character mentions. The candidate/character with the highest average cosine similarity to the pronoun embedding, above or equal to a threshold (0.3), and its gender matches the pronoun in the given tweet, is selected as the candidate/character that resolves the pronoun.

5 Experiments

5.1 Case 1: Tweets with pronouns but no possible person referent:

Here we compared our algorithm to the following baselines:

Algorithms	Precision	Recall	F1
Our Model	**0.95**	**0.82**	**0.88**
Stanford Coref	0.90	0.63	0.74
Spike per minute	0.91	0.49	0.64
Neural model	0.75	0.55	0.63

Table 3: Results of applying our algorithm and baselines to tweets with pronoun mentions and mention of possible person referents in our Presidential debate dataset

Algorithms	Precision	Recall	F1
Our Model	**0.91**	**0.82**	**0.86**
Stanford Coref	0.73	0.30	0.43
Spike per minute	0.78	0.60	0.68
Neural model	0.83	0.71	0.77

Table 4: Results of applying our algorithm and baselines to tweets with pronoun mentions and mention of possible person referents in our GoTS7 dataset

Most frequent candidate/character mention per minute (Spike per minute): Given a tweet t with a pronoun mention, the tweets published in the same minute as t are identified. The candidate/character with the most mentions in these tweets, and is the same gender as the referenced third-person singular pronoun is identified as the candidate/character the pronoun is referring to.

Last person mentioned in tweet by author: For each given tweet t with a third-person singular pronoun, we select the last candidate/character that was mentioned in a tweet by the author of t.

Tables 1 and 2 show the results from our algorithm compared to these baselines on the Presidential debate and GoTS7 datasets, respectively.

5.2 Case 2: Tweets with pronoun mentions and possible person referents:

In this section, we compare our algorithm to the baseline, *Spike per minute*, described in Section 5.1. We also compare our algorithm to the Stanford coreference toolkit (Manning et al., 2014) and a neural coreference resolution model (neural model) (Lee et al., 2017); this model, when given a span of text, determines if any of the previous spans of text is an antecedent. Tables 3 and 4 show the results.

6 Error Analysis and Future Work

In this work, we focused on gathering context in the form of tweets published in the same minute as the tweet with the pronominal mention. One of the challenges we observed is that in some cases a pronominal mention might make reference to a character or person not mentioned in the same minute, hence in the future, we plan to explore how far back in time we should expand this context prior. With regards to tweets with pronouns but no possible person referent, one future avenue to explore is to prepend these tweets with previous tweets published by the same authors and apply state-of-the-art coreference model on these expanded tweet "paragraphs". However, as we observe in our experiments, the last tweet prior may not contain the referent (as evident from the low recall of the "Last person mention" baseline). Therefore, we plan to explore how far back in tweet (or time) we should prepend these tweets.

7 Conclusion

In this work, we develop an algorithm that resolves third-person singular pronouns in Twitter data related to two events: a Presidential debate and GoTS7. We show that our algorithm can help resolve third-person singular pronouns in these event-related tweets, even in cases where there are no possible person referent mentioned in a tweet. We also show that our method outperforms baselines.

References

Artem Abzaliev. 2019. On gap coreference resolution shared task: insights from the 3rd place solution. In *Proceedings of the First Workshop on Gender Bias in Natural Language Processing*, pages 107–112.

Berfin Aktaş, Tatjana Scheffler, and Manfred Stede. 2018. Anaphora resolution for twitter conversations: An exploratory study. In *Proceedings of the First Workshop on Computational Models of Reference, Anaphora and Coreference*, pages 1–10.

Anietie Andy, Mark Dredze, Mugizi Rwebangira, and Chris Callison-Burch. 2017. Constructing an alias list for named entities during an event. In *Proceedings of the 3rd Workshop on Noisy User-generated Text*, pages 40–44.

Anietie Andy, Derry Tanti Wijaya, and Chris Callison-Burch. 2019. Winter is here: Summarizing twitter streams related to pre-scheduled events. In *Proceedings of the Second Workshop on Storytelling*, pages 112–116.

Joe Cheri, Abhijit Mishra, and Pushpak Bhattacharyya. 2016. Leveraging annotators' gaze behaviour for coreference resolution. In *Proceedings of the 7th Workshop on Cognitive Aspects of Computational Language Learning*, pages 22–26.

Kevin Clark and Christopher D Manning. 2015. Entity-centric coreference resolution with model stacking. In *Proceedings of the 53rd Annual Meeting of the Association for Computational Linguistics and the 7th International Joint Conference on Natural Language Processing (Volume 1: Long Papers)*, volume 1, pages 1405–1415.

Pascal Denis and Jason Baldridge. 2007. A ranking approach to pronoun resolution. In *IJCAI*, volume 158821593.

Jacob Devlin, Ming-Wei Chang, Kenton Lee, and Kristina Toutanova. 2018. Bert: Pre-training of deep bidirectional transformers for language understanding. *arXiv preprint arXiv:1810.04805*.

Vid Kocijan, Oana-Maria Camburu, Ana-Maria Cretu, Yordan Yordanov, Phil Blunsom, and Thomas Lukasiewicz. 2019. Wikicrem: A large unsupervised corpus for coreference resolution. *arXiv preprint arXiv:1908.08025*.

Kenton Lee, Luheng He, Mike Lewis, and Luke Zettlemoyer. 2017. End-to-end neural coreference resolution. *arXiv preprint arXiv:1707.07045*.

Christopher D Manning, Mihai Surdeanu, John Bauer, Jenny Rose Finkel, Steven Bethard, and David McClosky. 2014. The stanford corenlp natural language processing toolkit. In *Proceedings of 52nd annual meeting of the association for computational linguistics: system demonstrations*, pages 55–60.

Rachel Rudinger, Jason Naradowsky, Brian Leonard, and Benjamin Van Durme. 2018. Gender bias in coreference resolution. *arXiv preprint arXiv:1804.09301*.

Qingyu Yin, Yu Zhang, Weinan Zhang, Ting Liu, and William Yang Wang. 2018. Zero pronoun resolution with attention-based neural network. In *Proceedings of the 27th International Conference on Computational Linguistics*, pages 13–23.

Jieyu Zhao, Tianlu Wang, Mark Yatskar, Vicente Ordonez, and Kai-Wei Chang. 2018. Gender bias in coreference resolution: Evaluation and debiasing methods. *arXiv preprint arXiv:1804.06876*.

Coreference Strategies in English-German Translation

Ekaterina Lapshinova-Koltunski
University of Hildesheim/
Saarland University
`e.lapshinova`
`@mx.uni-saarland.de`

Marie-Pauline Krielke
Saarland University
`mariepauline.krielke`
`@uni-saarland.de`

Christian Hardmeier
Edinburgh University/
Uppsala University
`christian.hardmeier`
`@lingfil.uu.se`

Abstract

We present a study focusing on variation of coreferential devices in English original TED talks and news texts and their German translations. Using exploratory techniques we contemplate a diverse set of coreference devices as features which we assume indicate language-specific and register-based variation as well as potential translation strategies. Our findings reflect differences on both dimensions with stronger variation along the lines of register than between languages. By exposing interactions between text type and cross-linguistic variation, they can also inform multilingual NLP applications, especially machine translation.

1 Introduction

Coreference devices and their usage vary both across and within languages depending on several factors such as register and style among others. Moreover, translation process evokes a number of translation phenomena, such as explicitation or interference (Blum-Kulka, 1986; Toury, 1995) that also have an impact on the choice of linguistic expressions used. We assume that variation in coreference devices depends on the following factors: (a) language-specific constraints, (b) functional variation across language registers as well as (spoken or written) mode and (c) effects of the translation process.

Translating between languages involves transformation of the source coreference patterns into the target ones. Analysing such patterns can give insights into translation strategies for referring expressions in texts. Variation along the above stated lines (a, b, c) causes a number of problems in multilingual coreference resolution or coreference annotation projection (Postolache et al., 2006; Ogrodniczuk, 2013; Grishina and Stede, 2015; Novák, 2018). Although several studies describe such problems (Grishina and Stede, 2015; Lapshinova-Koltunski and Hardmeier, 2017; Lapshinova-Koltunski et al., 2019b), there is still a lack of understanding as to which linguistic phenomena and concretely, which structures cause these problems. In this paper, we attempt to detect such phenomena for English-German translations in a data set containing two different text registers: TED talks, which represent spoken language, and news, a type of written discourse. Previous studies show that the choice of referring expressions depends on the mode of text production in both languages under analysis (Kunz et al., 2016; Kunz et al., 2017).

The phenomena we analyse are not restricted to expressions referring to simple, nominal antecedents, but also comprise expressions referring to events. We also include cases of comparative reference, substitution and ellipsis, which according to Kunz and Steiner (2012) trigger a type reference relation (and not the relation of identity), or "sloppy identity".

Our main goal is to shed light on cross-lingual differences in coreference expressions. Another goal is to explore possible translation strategies for the language pair under analysis and the given text types. For this, we perform an empirical, corpus-based analysis using a number of coreference features as indicators of cross-lingual variation. The features are extracted from an existing corpus annotated with coreference chains. They include morpho-syntactic and functional properties of referring expressions, as well as chain properties. Using correspondence analysis and hierarchical cluster analysis we detect specific features of coreference distinctive for the two dimensions (language contrast and register variation) under

Proceedings of the 3rd Workshop on Computational Models of Reference, Anaphora and Coreference (CRAC 2020), pages 139–153,
Barcelona, Spain (online), December 12, 2020.

analysis. Our results show that both language and register (or mode) give rise to differences in our data and the coreference features vary depending on the dimensions.

Knowledge on the differences in the realisation of the coreference phenomena depending on the language or register is valuable to cross-lingual coreference resolution, as it was already acknowledged in the community, e.g. the CoNLL-2012 shared task on coreference resolution included multiple languages, registers and modes within OntoNotes (Recasens and Pradhan, 2016). Knowledge of the analysed variation is even more important for contrastive linguistics and (machine) translation.

2   Related Work

Several studies in the area of translation have addressed the importance of coreference (Baker, 2011; Becher, 2011; Königs, 2011). However, these works are example-based and provide neither a comprehensive account, nor empirical evidence for their claims. There are a few corpus-based studies of coreference translation (Zinsmeister et al., 2012; Novák and Nedoluzhko, 2015; Lapshinova-Koltunski et al., 2019b), addressing mostly the challenge of translating pronouns. The awareness of this challenge has also increased in the MT community (Voita et al., 2019; Lapshinova-Koltunski et al., 2019a; Guillou et al., 2018; Bawden et al., 2018; Miculicich Werlen and Popescu-Belis, 2017; Guillou, 2016; Hardmeier and Federico, 2010), and its relevance for multilingual coreference resolution is beyond doubt (Green et al., 2011; Novák and Žabokrtský, 2014; Grishina and Stede, 2017). Still, coreference translation is affected by many factors and remains poorly understood.

Kunz et al. (2017) analyse coreference and other means of explicit discourse phenomena in English and German comparable texts. They find that English and German differ in the linguistic means available in their language systems to convey coreference. English provides less syntactic flexibility and is restricted in the distribution of referents. German has more options and tends to use more grammatical means of coreference than English (Kunz et al., 2017), which indicates that English and German differ in how coreference chains are built up in terms of form and type of referring expressions within the chains. Kunz et al. (2017) base their analyses on the assumptions within contrastive pragmatics (House, 1997) suggesting that meanings are expressed more explicitly by linguistic signals in German than in English. However, Kunz et al. (2017) claim that translation strategies cannot rely on knowledge about contrastive lexico-grammar alone – awareness of preferred patterns that distinguish the languages and registers are essential for translators. The authors state that translating coreference chains from English into German implies using a higher number of coreferring expressions, and at the same time, chains of two elements may drop out because of remetaphorisation (i.e. change in word class). The authors use comparable corpora of original texts in both languages for their analyses, which does not provide them with the insights of what is actually happening in translation in the given language pair. Their findings include recommendations for translation strategies, but not the observation of the translation behaviour.

Lapshinova-Koltunski and Martínez Martínez (2017) focus on cohesive devices in English and German original (spoken and written) texts and report a higher degree of cohesiveness in German than in English, while overall spoken texts show more cohesive devices than written texts. Lapshinova-Koltunski et al. (2019b) analyse incongruences in the annotation of nominal coreference in English-German translations. The majority of the discovered incongruences are caused by explicitation – German translations contain more explicit linguistic devices triggering coreference. They point out that these cases of explicitation do not necessarily arise from the translation process, but can also be caused by idiosyncrasies of the two languages in terms of coreference properties. However, while looking into parallel chains, the authors do not provide analyses of the differences in the type of referring expressions in the source and the target texts. Moreover, their analysis is restricted to nominal coreference only.

Based on the previous literature, we can assume that the German translations contain more referring expressions and more chains than the English source texts. Conversely, shorter chains should be more common in the English originals than in the German translations. In terms of the structure and function of coreference chain members, there should be more explicit linguistic devices expressing coreference in the translations. In particular, translations would prefer demonstrative forms instead of personal reference, and entity reference instead of events (with entity reference being more concrete). In addition to such differences between originals and translations, we also expect variation in terms of register or mode, which may occasionally be even more prominent than that between languages (Kunz et al., 2016).

3 Analysed Features

In our analyses, we use a number of coreference features that are related to the form, functional and structural properties of chain members, as well as chain properties. First of all, we are driven by the structures available in the annotated corpus at hand. The morpho-syntactic and functional subtypes of anaphors and cataphors (which we collectively refer to as referring expressions) are motivated by the analyses by Becher (2011), who grades various types of referring expressions according to their degree of explicitness. This is important for our analyses, as our data contains translations, and explicitation – a higher explicitness of linguistic means in translated texts – is a well-known effect of the translation process. The levels of explicitness of referring expressions are related to Ariel (1990)'s concept of Accessibility. Morpho-syntactic types of referring expressions are related not only to accessibility, but also to the givenness or salience of a referent in the recipient's mind (Prince, 1981; Grosz et al., 1995; Gundel et al., 2003).

In studies involving register or genre variation, the distribution of morpho-syntactic types of mentions, such as the prevalence of pronouns vs. nouns, also plays an important role (Fox, 1987; Biber et al., 1999; Amoia et al., 2012; Kunz et al., 2016). Morpho-syntactic subtypes of referring expressions, substitution and ellipsis, as well as the scope of antecedents were analysed by Kunz et al. (2017) and Lapshinova-Koltunski and Martínez Martínez (2017) to reveal differences between registers and between the languages English and German. The scope of coreference is reflected in the differentiation between reference to entities vs. events, and in the form of the antecedent (nominal, verbal, clausal). As referring expressions can have more than one antecedent, the distinction between split and simple antecedent is also important. The resolution of anaphors with multiple antecedents differs in its processing from the resolution of single anaphors (Eschenbach et al., 1989).

The accessibility of a referent is also related to certain chain properties (Eckert and Strube, 2000): a high degree of accessibility is related to low distance between anaphors in long coreference chains and a low overall number of different coreference chains. The distance between anaphors and their antecedents is an important metric in many coreference resolution systems. Distance can be measured in different ways. The distance measure used in this work is the number of intervening sentence boundaries. This metric was also used by Nguy et al. (2011) for coreference resolution in Czech and by Amoia et al. (2012) for the analysis of variation in spoken and written texts.

In this study we include the following categories to analyse variation in the English-German coreference chains (a more detailed description is contained in Table 2 in the Appendix):

1. **morpho-syntactic types of all mentions** (including antecedents and referring expressions): pronoun (pp.m), noun phrases (np.m), verbal phrases (vp.m), clause (clause.m);

2. **types of reference**: pronouns functioning as anaphors (pp.anap), as cataphors (pp.cat), expressing substitution (pp.subs), comparative reference (pp.cmp), extratextual (extrtxt.ref) and pleonastic pronouns (pp.pleon);
   nominal phrases used as apposition (np.app), as comparative reference (np.cmp), as referring expression (np.ref),

3. **morpho-syntactic types of anaphoric expressions**:

   - pronouns: personal (pers.pp), possessive (poss.pp), demonstrative (dem.pp), reflexive (refl.pp), relative (rel.pp);
   - noun phrases sorted by their modifiers: possessive (poss.np), demonstrative (dem.np), def-article (def.np), indefinite (indef.np), bare noun phrases (bare.np);
   - comparative reference: particular and general (np.cmp.part, pp.cmp.part, np.cmp.gen and pp.cmp.gen);
   - substitution: nominal (np.subs) and verbal (vp.subs);

- ellipsis: nominal (np.ell) and verbal (vp.ell);

4. **types of referring expressions** measured by types of antecedents they refer to: referring expressions to entities (entity.ant.ref), referring expressions to events (event.ant.ref) and referring expressions to generics (gen.ant.ref); simple antecedent (simple.ant.ref), split reference (split.ant.ref), no explicit antecedent (noexpl.ant.ref);

5. **types of antecedents** by their form: pronoun (pp.ant), nominal phrase (np.ant), verbal phrase (vp.ant), clauses (clause.ant);

6. **chain properties**:
   - number of chains: total number (nr.chain)
   - chain length: mean chain length (mn.chain.lngth), median chain length (mdn.chain.lngth), standard deviation of chain length (stddv.chain.lngth), longest chain (lngst.chain), number of shortest, i.e. two-member chains (m2.chain), three-member chain (m3.chain), four-member chain (m4.chain) and five and more member chain (m5.chain)
   - distance between chain members measured in sentences (chain.dist).

4   Data and Methods

4.1   Data

For our analyses, we use ParCorFull (Lapshinova-Koltunski et al., 2018), a parallel corpus of English-German translations that is manually annotated for full coreference chains[1]. Coreference chains in this corpus consist of (mostly) chain-initial antecedents and anaphoric expressions that include pronouns, nouns, nominal phrases. Verbal phrases and clauses are also included as antecedents of event anaphors. The authors annotated elliptical constructions and cases of substitution, see details described by Lapshinova-Koltunski and Hardmeier (2017) and Lapshinova-Koltunski et al. (2018). The corpus contains transcribed TED talks and news texts in English (EN) and their corresponding German translations (DE). The summary statistics for the corpus data are given in Table 1.

subcorpus	texts	tokens	sentences	mentions	chains
EN-TED	20	70,736	3,379	5,970	2,121
DE-TED	20	66,783	3,555	5,911	2,206
EN-news	19	10,798	543	684	213
DE-news	19	10,602	543	576	269
EN-TOTAL	39	81,534	3,922	6,654	2,334
DE-TOTAL	39	77,385	4,098	6,487	2,475

Table 1: Corpus statistics

The corpus contains 39 parallel texts varying in their size from 368 tokens (the shortest news text) to 6,128 tokens (the longest TED talk). Although the number of texts in the news and in the TED part are similar, the size of the news portion in terms of tokens is much smaller. The news texts and part of the TED talks are aligned on the sentence level.

4.2   Methods

We extract frequency distributions of the features defined in Section 3 above from the corpus, save them in a contingency table with subcorpora or texts in rows and features in columns. Then, we use two explorative multivariate techniques to analyse the data: Correspondence Analysis (CA) and Hierarchical Cluster Analysis (HCA). Both analyses are performed in R environment (R Core Team, 2017, R version 3.6.1): we use the package `ca` to perform correspondence analysis and `pvclust` and `pvrect` to perform hierarchical cluster analysis.

---

[1]The corpus is available from the LINDAT repository at `http://hdl.handle.net/11372/LRT-2614`.

Correspondence analysis (Greenacre, 2007) is an extension of principal component analysis and fits good to explore relations between variables in a data set, as it summarises and visualises data in a two-dimensional plot. CA allows to study both sets of variables – those constituting the rows and those in columns of the contingency table[2]. We use CA to see which variables, in our case subcorpora, have similarities and how these subcorpora correlate with the coreference features contributing to the similarities. Weighted Euclidean distances, termed the χ^2 distances are measured on the basis of the feature distributions across the subcorpora. The data in the contingency table is scaled so that rows (subcorpora) and columns (features) are treated in an identical manner and so, the row and column projections in the new space may both be plotted on the same graph. The larger the differences between the subcorpora, the further apart they are on the map. Likewise, dissimilar categories of coreference features are further apart. Proximity between subcorpora and coreference features in the merged map is an approximation of the correlation between them. CA transforms the correlations between subcorpora and features in our table into a set of uncorrelated variables – principal axes or dimensions. These dimensions are computed in such a way that any subset of k dimensions accounts for as much variation as possible in one dimension, the first two principal axes account for as much variation as possible in two dimensions, and so on. Like this, we can identify new meaningful underlying variables, which should ideally correlate with such variables as language or register, indicating the reasons for the similarities or differences between the subcorpora. The position of the dots (subcorpora) and triangles (coreference features) indicates the relative importance of a feature for a subcorpus (see Figure 1). Moreover, the angle formed by the lines connecting the subcorpus or feature labels to the origin must be taken into account. Small angles indicate association, 90 degrees angle means no relation and angles up to 180 degrees mean negative association. The length of the lines also indicates association between subcorpora and features: the longer the line, the stronger is the association.

We use HCA (Everitt et al., 2011; Hothorn and Everitt, 2014), an unsupervised technique derived from exploratory data mining, that allows us to identify groups in the data which were not previously known. We do not prescribe what the groupings could be, since we want the algorithm to work on its own to discover all kinds of unknown patterns in the data. Specifically, we aim to see how our coreference features naturally group without applying prior knowledge of what the output groups should be. The core idea of HCA is that objects, in our case coreference features, are more related to nearby objects than to objects farther away. Coreference features are connected to form clusters based on their Euclidean distance measured here on the basis of the feature distributions (as also in the case of CA). The results are represented graphically in a dendrogram, a branching diagram that shows the relationships of similarity among a group of entities. The arrangement of the branches tells us which features are most similar to each other. We apply a technique based on bootstrap resampling, with the help of which we are able to produce *p-value*-based clusters, i.e. the ones that are highly supported by the data will have large *p-values*. For the sake of visibility our output dendrogram demonstrates AU (Approximately Unbiased) *p-value* only, which is computed by multi-scale bootstrap resampling and is a better approximation to unbiased *p-value* – indicated with red colour in Figure 2 below. The red numbers indicate the support for the split into clusters using an unbiased estimate. We draw rectangles around significant clusters (with the threshold value for p-values of 0.95). The resulting significant clusters demonstrate groups of features that are observed in our data.

5 Results

We first perform a correspondence analysis with all the features described in Section 3 above to get a general overview of how features are distributed along the lines of text types or languages. The resulting two-dimensional graph is shown in Figure 1. A detailed output of all the three CA analyses with the information on feature weights, contribution to eigenvalues, their distance to the centroid, etc. is given in Tables 3, 4, 5 in Appendix. The most obvious information we can obtain from this is that variance is most strongly pronounced between the two registers, while language contrast only marginally seems to play a role. The registers vary along dimension 1 (x-axis) explaining a very high portion (84.6%) of

---

[2]In PCA, either the rows or the columns would be considered.

the variation, while languages vary along dimension 2 (y-axis) explaining only 14% of variance. The outcome is not surprising, since on the one hand, feature distribution is strongly connected to register types, on the other hand, language contrast is expected to be weaker in translations due to shining through effects (i.e original text structures are kept in the target texts).

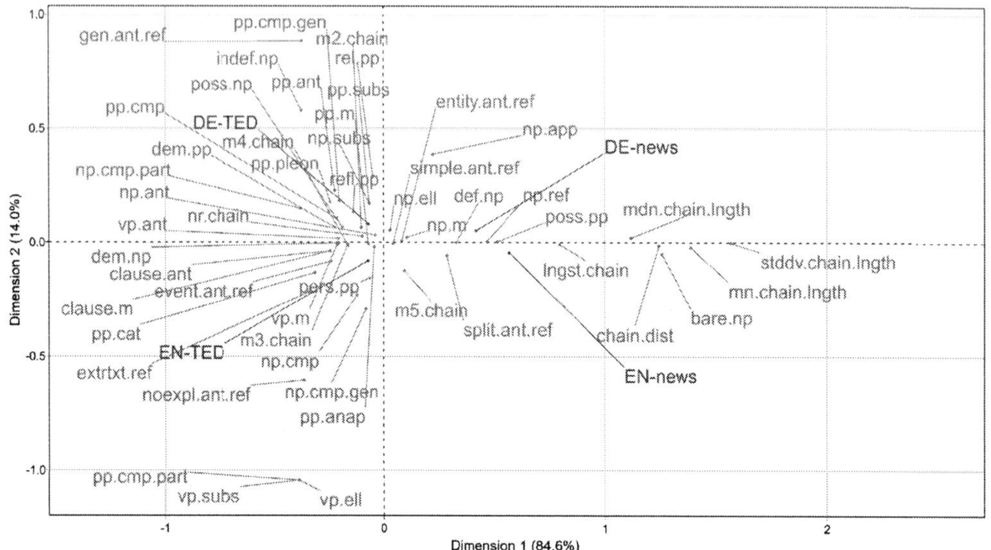

Figure 1: CA for all subcorpora with all features

In the next step, we perform clustering of features – an unsupervised analysis to explore groups of features that arise in our data. We hope that the resulting feature groups will help us to find specific features responsible for the observed register or language contrasts.

The cluster analysis (Figure 2) shows that there are two clear cut groups of features. A closer look at the distributions of the features reveals that the smaller group of features consists of the nine more general and also most common features in all subcorpora, while the other group is much more diverse including more fine-grained features, which are also less common.

Next, we perform a correspondence analysis on the two groups of features that resulted from HCA, starting with the smaller group (Figure 3). We find that the biggest part of the variation is explained by dimension 1 (x-axis, 71.3%) indicating a strong variance between the registers. The language contrast, i.e. the difference between originals and translations is seen in the second dimension (y-axis). Although its contribution is small (explaining 28.5% variation in the data), it is twice as big as the contribution to dimension 2 in Figure 1 above, showing that this first feature group reveals more differences between originals and translations than the whole group of features. The features that especially contribute to language contrast are two-member chains and personal pronouns.

Looking at the first dimension, EN news is the most distinct subcorpus, least associated with the selected features with only very weak associations with simple and entity antecedents. In the DE news texts we see a moderate association with NPs as referring expressions. This is most likely due to the high number of nominal references to a human antecedent (i.e. *Simone Biles, die Turnerin, die 19-jährige amerikanische Turnerin, die Amerikanerin, Biles, dieses Mädchen, der 19-Jährigen.*). Short, two-member chains are most strongly associated with the translated TED talks (DE-TED), as well as NPs as antecedents. These two features suggest that in the DE-TED translations, two member chains with an NP antecedent are relatively common. It is possible that some of these short chains are instances where in English there is no chain at all, for instance due to a reduced relative clause as in example (1), or other implicit references in the source text made explicit in the target text.

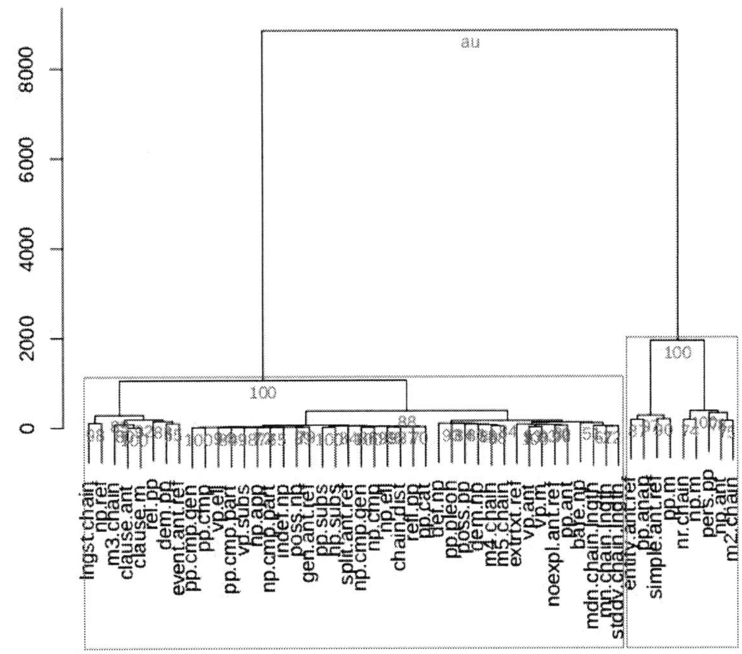

Figure 2: Clustering of all features under analysis

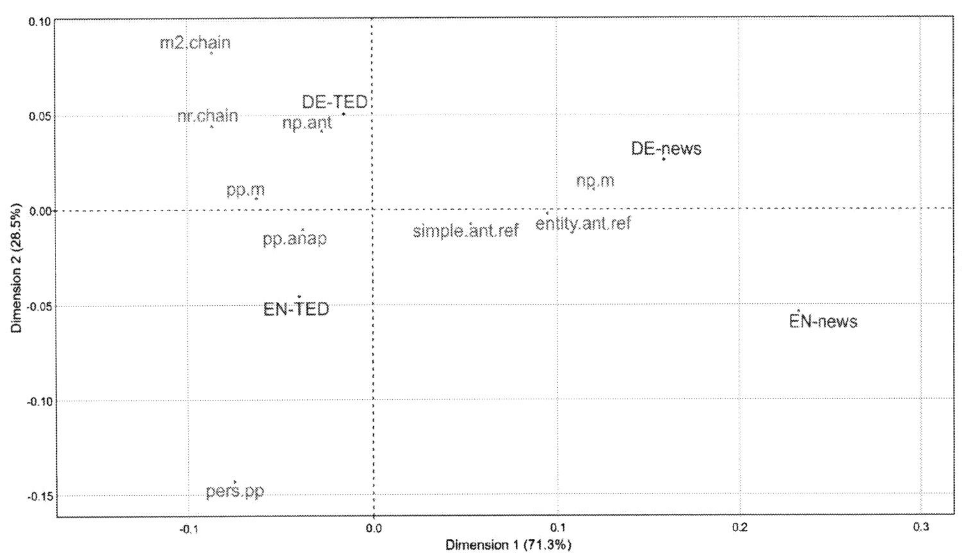

Figure 3: CA for all subcorpora with the first group of features resulting from HCA

(1)   a.   *Everybody talks about happiness these days. I had somebody count the number of books with "happiness" in the title published in the last five years [...].*

       b.   *Jeder spricht heutzutage über das Glück. Ich habe einige Leute die Anzahl [der Bücher] zählen lassen, [die] mit "Happiness" im Titel in den letzten fünf Jahren veröffentlicht wurden [...].*

Two-member chains might therefore not indicate a general tendency towards shorter chains in the German translations but rather be an indicator of explicitations of cases where the original keeps the reference implicit. The EN-TED talks show a strong association with personal pronouns, indicating frequent pronominal reference. Pronominal reference hints at a relatively low level of formality (Lapshinova-Koltunski and Martínez Martínez, 2017). The frequent use of personal pronouns in TED talks points to recurring reference to persons as the topic of the talks, see example (2) for illustration.

(2)   *Now, I should mention that [Nathaniel] refuses treatment because when [he] was treated it was with shock therapy and Thorazine and handcuffs, and that scar has stayed with [him] for [his] entire life. But, as a result now, [he] is prone to these schizophrenic episodes. The worst of which can manifest themselves as [him] exploding, and then disappearing for days, wandering the streets of Skid Row, exposed to its horrors, with the torment of [his] own mind unleashed upon [him].*

The second group of features shows an even stronger variation along dimension 1 (*x*-axes), explaining 86.2% of the variation between the two registers (see Figure 4).

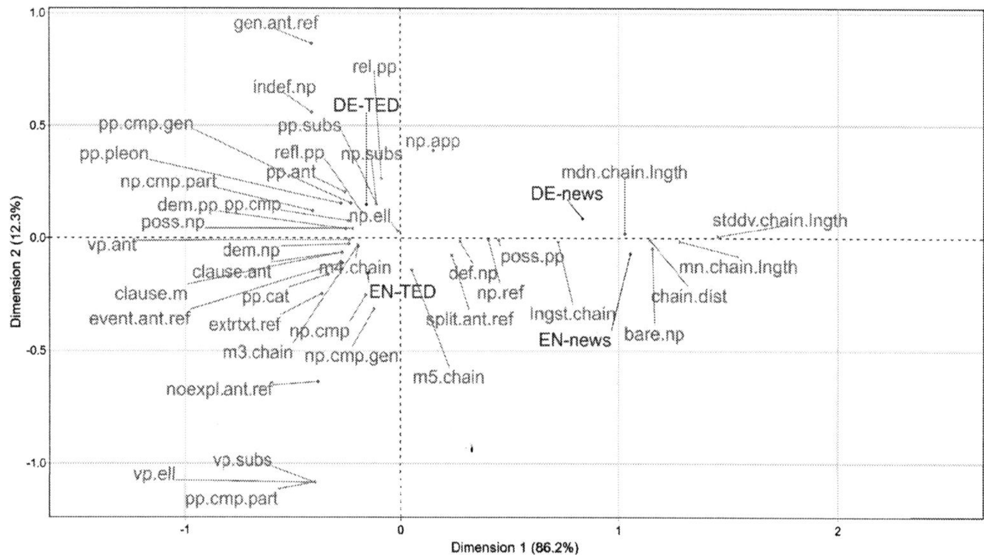

Figure 4: CA for all subcorpora with the second group of features resulting from HCA

Here, the language contrast, i.e. the difference between originals and translations is much less prominent. This indicates that the groups we detected by clustering vary in their explaining power for language contrast. While the first group explained 28% of variation between the languages, the second group explains only half of that (12.3%). The second group rather seems to represent distinctiveness between the registers. News texts are highly distinct from TED talks on this graph. Responsible features for their distinctiveness are *mdn.chain.lngth* and *stddv.chain.lngth* indicating a strong variation in chain length. Also the feature *lngst.chain* is associated with news in both languages, reflecting the fact that news texts often deal with one topic that is focused throughout the whole text. Appositions are associated with DE-news as well as DE-TED Talks. Appositions can represent explicitations, as in example (3), further defining a referent.

(3)   a.   *Boundless Informant is a program that the NSA hid from Congress.*
        b.   *["Boundless Informant"] ["Informant ohne Grenzen"] ist ein Programm, das die NSA vor dem Kongress verborgen hielt.*

The EN-news texts are most strongly associated with bare NPs and features related to chain length and distance. Bare NPs in English are, besides plural indefinites, mostly names. Their strong association reflects the fact that the EN-news texts tend to reiterate the names while German texts tend to reformulate and substitute proper names. In news texts the distance between mentions in a chain seems to be very long, which is especially not problematic for cohesiveness if the referent is reiterated.

The EN-TED talks show the strongest association with verbal ellipsis (see Example (4)) and substitution. These are cohesive devices which represent implicit and "sloppy" ways of creating coreference and are therefore susceptible to explicitation by a translator.

(4)   a.   *Nobody wants to change [how they live] just because [it] 's good for the world, or because we are [supposed to].*

        b.   *Niemand möchte [sein Leben ändern], weil [es] gut für die Umwelt ist oder weil wir [es] sollten.*

The same holds true for comparative reference (*np.cm.part, pp.cmp.gen*) as well associated with EN-TED talks. For extratextual reference we find a moderate association with EN-TED talks. Plausibly so, since TED talks are video talks where speakers often point at visualization material (presentations, pictures, videos or even other people present on the stage). Extratextual reference is often not retained in the target texts, since deictic reference is especially hard to match in subtitles, see example (5). The same mechanism seems to be at work with the feature "no explicit antecedent", even more strongly associated with the EN-TED talks. In cases, where a cue to a possible extratextual referent cannot be found in the text material, the annotator has the option of labelling a referring expression "no explicit". The German translators frequently avoid reference to undefined antecedents leaving them out altogether as illustrated in example (6).

(5)   a.   *[These] are ancient dice, made out of sheep's knuckles. Right?*

        b.   *[Es] gibt diese antiken Würfel, aus Schafsknöcheln. Wissen Sie?*

(6)   a.   *There was a case study done in 1960 's Britain, when [they] were moving from grammar schools to comprehensive schools.*

        b.   *In den 60er Jahren wurde in Großbritannien eine Fallstudie durchgeführt. Damals wurden Gymnasien in Gesamtschulen umgewandelt.*

The DE-TED talk translations are most strongly associated with generic and indefinite NPs. On the German translation side these distinctive features may be results of explicitation attempts, inserting a generic noun where in the English source texts there is no explicit antecedent. Also relative clauses distinctive for DE-TED texts are typical cases of explicitation. While English offers the option of a reduced variant (in object relative clauses), as well as participle (*-ing* and *-ed* clauses), in German, these options do not exist. Since TED talks often deal with more complex, scientific topics where a sound understanding by the listener/reader is essential, the feature is found more strongly related to the TED talks than to the news texts. Regarding this second group of features, the TED talks differ more from each other than the news texts. One plausible explanation might be the fact that the originally spoken texts through translation are turned into more written-like texts, which is reflected by the distinctive features respectively in the two languages.

6 Conclusion

In the present paper, we explored a number of coreference features in English-German translations that contain texts belonging to two registers. The results show that there is more variation in terms of registers or modes (spoken vs. written) than of languages, which means that English originals and their German translations differ to a lesser extent than news texts and TED talks. This confirms findings of other studies, e.g. Kunz et al. (2016) who show that variation along the dimension of mode is more prominent than that along the dimension of language. The authors show this using a set of comparable texts, whereas our data contains originals and their translations, i.e. the same texts in two languages.

By using cluster analysis we found two clusters of the features at hand, showing that the more general features represent language contrast better, while a more fine-grained classification of feature categories reflects the register or mode variation. This finding indicates that more general features reveal the differences between originals and translations, whereas a more fine-grained classification of feature categories reflects the register or mode variation. However, we were not able to discover features that would strongly indicate concrete differences between the original and the translated texts, which was one of our original goals.

In our future work, we plan to integrate further techniques, such as feature selection technique, e.g. information gain, as used by Lapshinova-Koltunski and Martínez Martínez (2017) to see which features are more informative to predict the two languages in the analysed data. Furthermore, it would be interesting to extend our analyses to the other translation direction and see if we observe the same translationese phenomena for the German-English translations. Another extension of the work would be adding translations of the same texts into further languages.

Acknowledgements

Christian Hardmeier was supported by the Swedish Research Council under grant 2017-930. The ParCorFull annotation work was funded by the European Association for Machine Translation. We would also like to thank our reviewers for their useful comments and suggestions.

References

Marilisa Amoia, Kerstin Kunz, and Ekaterina Lapshinova-Koltunski. 2012. Coreference in Spoken vs. Written texts: a Corpus-based Analysis. In *Proceedings of the Eighth International Conference on Language Resources and Evaluation (LREC'12)*, pages 158–164, Istanbul, Turkey, May. European Language Resources Association (ELRA).

Mira Ariel. 1990. *Accessing Noun-phrase Antecedents*. Routledge, London.

Mona Baker. 2011. *In Other Words: A Coursebook on Translation*. Taylor & Francis.

Rachel Bawden, Rico Sennrich, Alexandra Birch, and Barry Haddow. 2018. Evaluating Discourse Phenomena in Neural Machine Translation. In *Proceedings of the 2018 Conference of the North American Chapter of the Association for Computational Linguistics: Human Language Technologies, Volume 1 (Long Papers)*, pages 1304–1313, New Orleans, Louisiana, June. Association for Computational Linguistics.

Viktor Becher. 2011. *Explicitation and Implicitation in Translation. A Corpus-based Study of English-German and German-English Translations of Business Texts*. Ph.D. thesis, Universität Hamburg.

Douglas Biber, Edward Finegan, Stig Johansson, Susan Conrad, and Geoffrey Leech. 1999. *Longman Grammar of Spoken and Written English*. Longman, Harlow, 1 edition.

Shoshana Blum-Kulka. 1986. Shifts of Cohesion and Coherence in Translation. In Juliane House and Shoshana Blum-Kulka, editors, *Interlingual and intercultural communication*, pages 17–35. Gunter Narr, Tübingen.

Miriam Eckert and Michael Strube. 2000. Dialogue acts, synchronizing units, and anaphora resolution. *Journal of Semantics*, 17(1):51–89.

Carola Eschenbach, Christopher Habel, Michael Herweg, and Klaus Rehkämper. 1989. Remarks on Plural Anaphora. In *Proceedings of the fourth conference on European chapter of the Association for Computational Linguistics*, pages 161–167. Association for Computational Linguistics.

Brian S. Everitt, Sabine Landau, Morven Leese, and Daniel Stahl. 2011. *Cluster Analysis*. Wiley Series in Probability and Statistics. Wiley.

Barbara A. Fox. 1987. *Discourse Structure and Anaphora: Written and Conversational English*. Cambridge University Press, Cambridge.

Spence Green, Nicholas Andrews, Matthew R Gormley, Mark Dredze, and Christopher D Manning. 2011. Cross-lingual Coreference Resolution: A New Task for Multilingual Comparable Corpora. Technical Report 6, HLT-COE, Johns Hopkins University.

Michael J. Greenacre. 2007. *Correspondence Analysis in Practice*. Chapman & Hall/CRC, Boca Raton.

Yulia Grishina and Manfred Stede. 2015. Knowledge-lean Projection of Coreference Chains across Languages. In *Proceedings of the 8th Workshop on Building and Using Comparable Corpora*, page 14, Beijing, China.

Yulia Grishina and Manfred Stede. 2017. Multi-source Annotation Projection of Coreference Chains: Assessing Strategies and Testing Opportunities. In *Proceedings of the 2nd Workshop on Coreference Resolution Beyond OntoNotes (CORBON 2017)*, pages 41–50. Association for Computational Linguistics.

Barbara J. Grosz, Aravind K. Joshi, and Scott Weinstein. 1995. Centering: A Framework for Modeling the Local Coherence of Discourse. *Computational Linguistics*, 21.

Liane Guillou, Christian Hardmeier, Ekaterina Lapshinova-Koltunski, and Sharid Loáiciga. 2018. A Pronoun Test Suite Evaluation of the English–German MT Systems at WMT 2018. In *Proceedings of the Third Conference on Machine Translation: Shared Task Papers*, pages 570–577, Belgium, Brussels, October. Association for Computational Linguistics.

Liane Guillou. 2016. *Incorporating Pronoun Function into Statistical Machine Translation*. Ph.D. thesis, School of Informatics. University of Edinburgh.

Jeanette Gundel, Michael Hegarty, and Kaja Borthen. 2003. Cognitive Status, Information Structure, and Pronominal Reference to Clausally Introduced Entities. *Journal of Logic, Language and Information*, 12(3):281 – 299.

Christian Hardmeier and Marcello Federico. 2010. Modelling Pronominal Anaphora in Statistical Machine Translation. In *Proceedings of the IWSLT (International Workshop on Spoken Language Translation)*, pages 283–289, Paris, France.

Torsten Hothorn and Brian S. Everitt. 2014. *A Handbook of Statistical Analyses Using R*. Chapman & Hall/CRC Press, 3rd edition.

Juliane House. 1997. *Translation Quality Assessment: A Model Revisited*. Tübinger Beiträge zur Linguistik. G. Narr.

Karin Königs. 2011. *Übersetzen Englisch - Deutsch. Lernen mit System*. Oldenbourg Verlag, Oldenbourg, 3 edition. vollstäädig überarbeitete Auflage.

Kerstin Kunz and Erich Steiner. 2012. Towards a Comparison of Cohesive Reference in English and German: System and Text. In M. Taboada, S. Doval Suárez, and E. González Álvarez, editors, *Contrastive Discourse Analysis. Functional and Corpus Perspectives*. Equinox, London.

Kerstin Kunz, Ekaterina Lapshinova-Koltunski, and José Manuel Martínez Martínez. 2016. Beyond Identity Coreference: Contrasting Indicators of Textual Coherence in English and German. In *Proceedings of the Workshop on Coreference Resolution Beyond OntoNotes (CORBON 2016)*, pages 23–31, San Diego, California, June. Association for Computational Linguistics.

Kerstin Kunz, Stefania Degaetano-Ortlieb, Ekaterina Lapshinova Koltunski, Katrin Menzel, and Erich Steiner. 2017. Gecco – an Empirically-based Comparison of English-German Cohesion. In Gert De Sutter, Marie-Aude Lefer, and Isabelle Delaere, editors, *Empirical Translation Studies: New Methodological and Theoretical Traditions*, volume 300 of *TILSM series*, pages 265–312. Mouton de Gruyter. TILSM series.

Ekaterina Lapshinova-Koltunski and Christian Hardmeier, 2017. *Coreference Corpus Annotation Guidelines*, December.

Ekaterina Lapshinova-Koltunski and José Manuel Martínez Martínez. 2017. Statistical Insights into Cohesion: Contrasting English and German across Modes. In Markéta Janebová, Ekaterina Lapshinova-Koltunski, and Michaela Martinková, editors, *Contrasting English and Other Languages*, pages 130–163. Cambridge Scholars Publishing, Newcastle upon Tyne.

Ekaterina Lapshinova-Koltunski, Christian Hardmeier, and Pauline Krielke. 2018. ParCorFull: a Parallel Corpus Annotated with Full Coreference. In Nicoletta Calzolari (Conference chair), Khalid Choukri, Christopher Cieri, Thierry Declerck, Sara Goggi, Koiti Hasida, Hitoshi Isahara, Bente Maegaard, Joseph Mariani, Hélène Mazo, Asuncion Moreno, Jan Odijk, Stelios Piperidis, and Takenobu Tokunaga, editors, *Proceedings of 11th Language Resources and Evaluation Conference*, pages 423–428, Miyazaki, Japan, may. European Language Resources Association (ELRA).

Ekaterina Lapshinova-Koltunski, Cristina España-Bonet, and Josef van Genabith. 2019a. Analysing Coreference in Transformer Outputs. In *Proceedings of the Fourth Workshop on Discourse in Machine Translation (DiscoMT 2019)*, pages 1–12, Hong Kong, China, November. Association for Computational Linguistics.

Ekaterina Lapshinova-Koltunski, Sharid Loáiciga, Christian Hardmeier, and Pauline Krielke. 2019b. Cross-lingual Incongruences in the Annotation of Coreference. In *Proceedings of the Second Workshop on Computational Models of Reference, Anaphora and Coreference*, pages 26–34, Minneapolis, USA, June. Association for Computational Linguistics.

Lesly Miculicich Werlen and Andrei Popescu-Belis. 2017. Validation of an Automatic Metric for the Accuracy of Pronoun Translation (APT). In *Proceedings of the Third Workshop on Discourse in Machine Translation*, pages 17–25, Copenhagen, Denmark, September. Association for Computational Linguistics.

Giang Linh Nguy, Michal Novák, and Anna Nedoluzhko. 2011. Coreference Resolution in the Prague Dependency Treebank. Technical report, UFAL, Prague. Technical report.

Michael Novák and Anna Nedoluzhko. 2015. Correspondences between Czech and English Coreferential Expressions. *Discours*, 16.

Michal Novák and Zdeněk Žabokrtský. 2014. Cross-lingual Coreference Resolution of Pronouns. In *Proceedings of COLING 2014, the 25th International Conference on Computational Linguistics: Technical Papers*, pages 14–24, Dublin, Ireland.

Michal Novák. 2018. A fine-grained large-scale analysis of coreference projection. In *Proceedings of the First Workshop on Computational Models of Reference, Anaphora and Coreference*, pages 77–86, New Orleans, Louisiana, June. Association for Computational Linguistics.

Maciej Ogrodniczuk. 2013. Translation- and Projection-based Unsupervised Coreference Resolution for Polish. *Language Processing and Intelligent Information Systems, IIS 2013*, 7912.

Oana Postolache, Dan Cristea, and Constantin Orasan. 2006. Tranferring Coreference Chains through Word Alignment. In *Proceedings of the 5th International Conference on Language Resources and Evaluation*.

Ellen F. Prince. 1981. Towards a Taxonomy of Given-new Information. In P. Cole, editor, *Radical Pragmatics*, pages 223–255. Academic Press, New York.

R Core Team, 2017. *R: A Language and Environment for Statistical Computing*. Vienna, Austria.

Marta Recasens and Sameer Pradhan. 2016. Evaluation Campaigns. In *Anaphora Resolution – Algorithms, Resources, and Applications*, pages 165–208.

Gideon Toury. 1995. *Descriptive Translation Studies - and Beyond*. John Benjamins Publishing Company, Benjamins edition.

Elena Voita, Rico Sennrich, and Ivan Titov. 2019. When a Good Translation is Wrong in Context: Context-Aware Machine Translation Improves on Deixis, Ellipsis, and Lexical Cohesion. In *Proceedings of the 57th Annual Meeting of the Association for Computational Linguistics*, pages 1198–1212, Florence, Italy, July. Association for Computational Linguistics.

Heike Zinsmeister, Stefanie Dipper, and Melanie Seiss. 2012. Abstract Pronominal Anaphors and Label Nouns in German and English: Selected Case Studies and Quantitative Investigations. *Translation: Computation, Corpora, Cognition*, 2(1).

A Appendix

feature	description	example
	Count features	
np.cmp.gen	general comparison NP	*a different person*
np.cmp.part	particular comparison NP	*a taller person*
pp.cmp.gen	general comparison pronoun	*other one*
pp.cmp.part	particular comparison pronoun	*bigger one*
np.ell	NP ellipsis	*I count the [neighboring balls].., the answer's always twelve [].*
vp.ell	verb ellipsis	*They knew about this. I did not [].*
def.np	NP with def. article	*the person*
dem.np	demonstrative NP	*this person*
indef.np	indefinite NP	*any person*
bare.np	NP without modifier	*person*
poss.np	possesive NP	*my sister*
dem.pp	demonstrative pronoun	*these*
pers.pp	personal pronoun	*he, she it, etc.*
poss.pp	possessive pronoun	*hers, his, its, etc.*
refl.pp	reflexive pronoun	*herself, himself*
rel.pp	relative pronoun	the person *who*
pp.subs	any pronoun expressing substitution	
vp.subs	verb substitution	*Has the plane landed? – Yes, it has [done].*
np.subs	nominal substitution	*He wants a green apple, but she wants the red [one].*
noexpl.ant.ref	reference to a non identifiable antecedent	*see example (6)*
simple.ant.ref	reference to one single referent	*He eats [peas]. They are green.*
split.ant.ref	two or more antecedents	*[Tim] likes [Tom]. They are happy.*
clause.ant	clausal antecedent	*[Tim hates Tom]. This is sad.*
np.ant	antecedent is an NP	*Tim likes [cats]. They are soft.*
pp.ant	pronominal antecedent	*Tim likes [them]. They are soft.*
vp.ant	verbal antecedent	*Tim [writes]. It is his hobby.*
entity.ant.ref	reference to an entity	*Tim likes [Tom].He is blond.*
event.ant.ref	reference to an event	*Tim loves Tom.[This] is nice.*
gen.ant.ref	reference to generic antecedent	*Pigs are clever.[They] can read.*
np.app	nominal apposition	*A friend, [Marco], got married.*
np.cmp	all cases of comparative nominal phrases	
np.ref	any reference to an NP	
pp.anap	any anaphoric pronoun	
pp.cat	cataphoric pronoun	*[She] is strong. Her name is Uma.*
pp.comp	any pronoun expressing comparative reference	
extrtxt.ref	reference to an extratextual referent	*see example (5)*
pp.pleon	pleonastic *it*	*[It]'s raining.*
clause.m	all clausal mentions	
np.m	all nominal mentions	
pp.m	all pronominal mentions	
vp.m	all verbal mentions	
nr.chain	total number of coreference chains	
m2.chain	chain with two members	
m3.chain	chain with three members	
m4.chain	chain with four members	
m5.chain	chain with five or more members	
	Other features	
lngst.chain	maximum chain length	
mn.chain.lngth	mean chain length	
mdn.chain.lngth	median chain length	
stddv.chain.lngth	standard deviation of chain length	
chain.dist	mean distance in sentences between mentions in same chain	

Table 2: Overview of all features under analysis with definitions and examples

feature	Mass	ChiDist	Inertia	Dim. 1	Dim. 2
np.cmp.gen	0.000663	0.316624	0.000066	-0.436676	-3.789908
np.cmp.part	0.000108	0.414074	0.000018	-1.985124	1.930274
pp.cmp.gen	0.000231	0.297027	0.000020	-1.072092	2.377709
pp.cmp.part	0.000015	1.127224	0.000020	-2.032161	-13.533658
np.ell	0.000678	0.064981	0.000003	0.162947	0.686875
vp.ell	0.000062	1.127224	0.000078	-2.032161	-13.533658
def.np	0.005950	0.329001	0.000644	1.734675	0.000025
dem.np	0.007630	0.211763	0.000342	-1.089966	-0.031847
indef.np	0.000139	0.713970	0.000071	-1.968138	7.514472
bare.np	0.008709	1.256376	0.013746	6.624325	-0.650892
poss.np	0.000493	0.207501	0.000021	-1.002061	0.877135
dem.pp	0.020130	0.236394	0.001125	-1.186002	0.887559
pers.pp	0.059773	0.169113	0.001709	-0.337756	-2.030630
poss.pp	0.009294	0.518437	0.002498	2.733614	0.039440
refl.pp	0.000832	0.255761	0.000054	-0.738817	1.742443
rel.pp	0.020084	0.301273	0.001823	-0.262351	3.750173
pp.subs	0.001233	0.226172	0.000063	-0.353595	2.217421
vp.subs	0.000031	1.127224	0.000039	-2.032161	-13.533658
noexpl.ant.ref	0.002435	0.707096	0.001218	-1.901654	-7.843646
simple.ant.ref	0.133726	0.044202	0.000261	0.231679	-0.062243
split.ant.ref	0.001988	0.307337	0.000188	1.505294	-0.740406
clause.ant	0.009988	0.245664	0.000603	-1.281402	-0.487098
np.ant	0.057446	0.052750	0.000160	-0.214535	0.421710
pp.ant	0.002682	0.326889	0.000287	-1.177903	2.949368
vp.ant	0.003961	0.208049	0.000171	-1.093846	0.229017
entity.ant.ref	0.117434	0.084428	0.000837	0.444521	0.077095
event.ant.ref	0.015567	0.254615	0.001009	-1.270361	-1.075932
gen.ant.ref	0.000200	0.990971	0.000197	-1.956178	11.446540
nr.chain	0.070686	0.103485	0.000757	-0.526150	0.353133
lngst.chain	0.003160	0.807960	0.002063	4.192428	-0.117235
mn.chain.lngth	0.000215	1.389670	0.000415	7.334646	-0.275031
mdn.chain.lngth	0.000123	1.122915	0.000155	5.899956	0.270630
stddv.chain.lngth	0.000248	1.568046	0.000610	8.271408	-0.013635
m2.chain	0.045546	0.124456	0.000705	-0.548020	0.845941
m3.chain	0.012762	0.166895	0.000355	-0.869407	-0.101058
m4.chain	0.005379	0.165987	0.000148	-0.867163	-0.172977
m5.chain	0.006982	0.157495	0.000173	0.509968	-1.595385
chain.dist	0.000074	1.242745	0.000115	6.558996	-0.176087
np.app	0.000262	0.739706	0.000143	1.180567	5.032233
np.cmp	0.000771	0.276492	0.000059	-0.653459	-2.989083
np.ref	0.023351	0.472276	0.005208	2.487352	0.042190
pp.anap	0.110683	0.049181	0.000268	-0.232044	-0.262816
pp.cat	0.001187	0.342668	0.000139	-1.641004	-1.711176
pp.cmp	0.000247	0.267869	0.000018	-1.132096	1.383249
extrtxt.ref	0.003591	0.402488	0.000582	-1.787352	-2.817923
np.subs	0.001233	0.226172	0.000063	-0.353595	2.217421
pp.pleon	0.007737	0.315157	0.000769	-1.284026	2.307029
clause.m	0.009988	0.245664	0.000603	-1.281402	-0.487098
np.m	0.082631	0.109066	0.000983	0.562322	0.291150
pp.m	0.127607	0.071472	0.000652	-0.375570	-0.088586
vp.m	0.004054	0.211373	0.000181	-1.115253	-0.084960

Table 3: Output of CA with all features: masses or weights of features (Mass), chi-squared distances of feature points to the centroid, i.e. their average (ChiDist), feature contribution to principal inertias or eigenvalues (Inertia) and standard coordinates in Dimension 1 (Dim1) and Dimension 2 (Dim2))

feature	Mass	ChiDist	Inertia	Dim. 1	Dim. 2
pers.pp	0.074203	0.161340	0.001932	-0.999866	-3.018902
simple.ant.ref	0.166010	0.053775	0.000480	0.710814	-0.158291
np.ant	0.071314	0.049546	0.000175	-0.360819	0.875915
entity.ant.ref	0.145785	0.094975	0.001315	1.267290	-0.047300
nr.chain	0.087750	0.097184	0.000829	-1.155579	0.929273
m2.chain	0.056542	0.120464	0.000821	-1.157407	1.756098
pp.anap	0.137404	0.039039	0.000209	-0.498657	-0.217014
np.m	0.102579	0.120281	0.001484	1.599027	0.226883
pp.m	0.158413	0.062801	0.000625	-0.830071	0.128954

Table 4: Output of CA with the 1st group of features: masses or weights of features (Mass), chi-squared distances of feature points to the centroid, i.e. their average (ChiDist), feature contribution to principal inertias or eigenvalues (Inertia) and standard coordinates in Dimension 1 (Dim1) and Dimension 2 (Dim2))

feature	Mass	ChiDist	Inertia	Dim. 1	Dim. 2
np.cmp.gen	0.003481	0.345312	0.000415	-0.314363	-2.160139
np.cmp.part	0.000567	0.427257	0.000103	-1.048137	0.847752
pp.cmp.gen	0.001214	0.304792	0.000113	-0.600798	1.069651
pp.cmp.part	0.000081	1.167677	0.000110	-1.027334	-7.448581
np.ell	0.003562	0.036934	0.000005	-0.031473	0.227877
vp.ell	0.000324	1.167677	0.000441	-1.027334	-7.448581
def.np	0.031245	0.274728	0.002358	0.711096	-0.104608
dem.np	0.040068	0.242720	0.002361	-0.621538	-0.182838
indef.np	0.000729	0.709433	0.000367	-1.055649	3.843650
bare.np	0.045735	1.156825	0.061204	3.003787	-0.313568
poss.np	0.002590	0.230630	0.000138	-0.581516	0.304382
dem.pp	0.105716	0.260101	0.007152	-0.665836	0.300682
poss.pp	0.048811	0.455132	0.010111	1.181082	-0.059239
refl.pp	0.004371	0.259922	0.000295	-0.469710	0.795526
rel.pp	0.105473	0.290837	0.008922	-0.226358	1.831489
pp.subs	0.006476	0.220449	0.000315	-0.286092	1.051881
vp.subs	0.000162	1.167677	0.000221	-1.027334	-7.448581
noexpl.ant.ref	0.012790	0.745846	0.007115	-0.983296	-4.389810
split.ant.ref	0.010442	0.267015	0.000744	0.611908	-0.521618
clause.ant	0.052453	0.279416	0.004095	-0.706994	-0.438857
pp.ant	0.014085	0.333571	0.001567	-0.668673	1.408843
vp.ant	0.020803	0.238604	0.001184	-0.619869	-0.051979
event.ant.ref	0.081756	0.291118	0.006929	-0.701308	-0.752017
gen.ant.ref	0.001052	0.983372	0.001018	-1.060938	5.953188
lngst.chain	0.016594	0.736247	0.008995	1.877954	0.129035
mn.chain.lngth	0.001128	1.284371	0.001861	3.338840	-0.098603
mdn.chain.lngth	0.000648	1.033924	0.000692	2.675730	0.130440
stddv.chain.lngth	0.001303	1.456807	0.002766	3.785737	0.049886
m3.chain	0.067024	0.201356	0.002717	-0.515901	-0.218129
m4.chain	0.028250	0.201405	0.001146	-0.514197	-0.257608
m5.chain	0.036669	0.151949	0.000847	0.134401	-0.979939
chain.dist	0.000391	1.144067	0.000512	2.973885	-0.065053
np.app	0.001376	0.692390	0.000660	0.389001	2.682152
np.cmp	0.004047	0.308970	0.000386	-0.417091	-1.739034
np.ref	0.122634	0.408645	0.020479	1.060135	-0.052987
pp.cat	0.006233	0.377442	0.000888	-0.868716	-1.112941
pp.cmp	0.001295	0.283857	0.000104	-0.627456	0.537262
extrtxt.ref	0.018860	0.438271	0.003623	-0.942805	-1.692524
np.subs	0.006476	0.220449	0.000315	-0.286092	1.051881
pp.pleon	0.040635	0.325911	0.004316	-0.719559	1.067513
clause.m	0.052453	0.279416	0.004095	-0.706994	-0.438857

Table 5: Output of CA with the 2nd group of features: masses or weights of features (Mass), chi-squared distances of feature points to the centroid, i.e. their average (ChiDist), feature contribution to principal inertias or eigenvalues (Inertia) and standard coordinates in Dimension 1 (Dim1) and Dimension 2 (Dim2))

Sequence-to-Sequence Networks
Learn the Meaning of Reflexive Anaphora

Robert Frank[*]
Yale University
bob.frank@yale.edu

Jackson Petty[*]
Yale University
jackson.petty@yale.edu

Abstract

Reflexive anaphora present a challenge for semantic interpretation: their meaning varies depending on context in a way that appears to require abstract variables. Past work has raised doubts about the ability of recurrent networks to meet this challenge. In this paper, we explore this question in the context of a fragment of English that incorporates the relevant sort of contextual variability. We consider sequence-to-sequence architectures with recurrent units and show that such networks are capable of learning semantic interpretations for reflexive anaphora which generalize to novel antecedents. We explore the effect of attention mechanisms and different recurrent unit types on the type of training data that is needed for success as measured in two ways: how much lexical support is needed to induce an abstract reflexive meaning (i.e., how many distinct reflexive antecedents must occur during training) and what contexts must a noun phrase occur in to support generalization of reflexive interpretation to this noun phrase?

1 Introduction

Recurrent neural network architectures have demonstrated remarkable success in natural language processing, achieving state of the art performance across an impressive range of tasks ranging from machine translation to semantic parsing to question answering (Sutskever et al., 2014; Cho et al., 2014; Bahdanau et al., 2016). These tasks demand the use of a wide variety of computational processes and information sources (from grammatical to lexical to world knowledge), and are evaluated in coarse-grained quantitative ways. As a result, it is not an easy matter to identify the specific strengths and weaknesses in a network's solution of a task.

In this paper, we take a different tack, exploring the degree to which neural networks successfully master one very specific aspect of linguistic knowledge: the interpretation of sentences containing reflexive anaphora. We address this problem in the context of the task of semantic parsing, which we instantiate as mapping a sequence of words into a predicate calculus logical form representation of the sentence's meaning.

(1) a. Mary runs $\rightarrow$ RUN(MARY)

    b. John sees Bob $\rightarrow$ SEE(JOHN, BOB)

Even for simple sentences like those in (1), which represent the smallest representations of object reflexives in English, the network must learn lexical semantic correspondences (e.g., the input symbol *Mary* is mapped to the output MARY and *runs* is mapped to RUN) and a mode of composition (e.g., for an intransitive sentence, the meaning of the subject is surrounded by parentheses and appended to the meaning of the verb). Of course, not all of natural language adheres to such simple formulas. Reflexives, words like *herself* and *himself*, do not have an interpretation that can be assigned independently of the meaning of the surrounding context.

Proceedings of the 3rd Workshop on Computational Models of Reference, Anaphora and Coreference (CRAC 2020), pages 154–164,
Barcelona, Spain (online), December 12, 2020.

(2) a. Mary sees herself $\rightarrow$ SEE(MARY, MARY)

    b. Alice sees herself $\rightarrow$ SEE(ALICE, ALICE)

In these sentences, the interpretation of the reflexive is not a constant that can be combined with the meaning of the surrounding elements. Rather, a reflexive object must be interpreted as identical to the meaning of verb's subject. Of course, a network could learn a context-sensitive interpretation of a reflexive, so that for any sentence with *Mary* as its subject, the reflexive is interpreted as MARY, and with *Alice* as its subject it is interpreted as ALICE. However, such piecemeal learning of reflexive meaning will not support generalization to sentences involving a subject that has not been encountered as the antecedent of a reflexive during training, even if the interpretation of the subject has occurred elsewhere. What is needed instead is an interpretation of the reflexive that is characterized not as a specific (sequence of) output token(s), but rather as an abstract instruction to duplicate the interpretation of the subject. Such an abstraction requires more than the "jigsaw puzzle" approach to meaning that simpler sentences afford.

Marcus (1998) argues that this kind of abstraction, which he takes to require the use of algebraic variables to assert identity, is beyond the capacity of recurrent neural networks. Marcus's demonstration involves a simple recurrent network (SRN, Elman 1990) language model that is trained to predict the next word over a corpus of sentences of the following form:

(3) a. A rose is a rose.

    b. A mountain is a mountain.

All sentences in this training set have identical subject and object nouns. Marcus shows, however, that the resulting trained network does not correctly predict the subject noun when tested with a novel preamble 'A *book is a ...*'. Though intriguing, this demonstration is not entirely convincing: since the noun occurring in the novel preamble, *book* in our example, did not occur in the training data, there is no way that the network could possibly have known which (one-hot represented) output should correspond to the reflexive for a sentence containing the novel (one-hot represented) subject noun, even if the network did successfully encode an identity relation between subject and object.

Frank et al. (2013) explore a related task in the context of SRN interpretation of reflexives. In their experiments, SRNs were trained to map input words to corresponding semantic symbols that are output on the same time step in which a word is presented. For most words in the vocabulary, this is a simple task: the desired output is a constant function of the input (*Mary* corresponds to MARY, *sees* to SEE, etc.). For reflexives however, the target output depends on the subject that occurs earlier in the sentence. Frank et al. tested the network's ability to interpret a reflexive in sentences containing a subject that had not occurred as a reflexive's antecedent during training. However, unlike Marcus' task, this subject and its corresponding semantic symbol did occur in other (non-reflexive) contexts in the training data, and therefore was in the realm of possible inputs and outputs for the network. Nonetheless, none of the SRNs that they trained succeeded at this task for even a single test example.

Since those experiments were conducted, substantial advances have been made on recurrent neural network architectures, some of which have been crucial in the success of practical NLP systems.

- **Recurrent units**: More sophisticated recurrent units like LSTMs (Graves and Schmidhuber, 2005) and GRUs (Cho et al., 2014) have been shown to better encode preceding context than SRNs.

- **Sequence-to-Sequence architectures**: The performance of network models that transduce one string to another, used in machine translation and semantic parsing, has been greatly improved by the use of independent encoder and decoder networks (Sutskever et al., 2014).

- **Attention mechanism**: The ability of a network to produce contextually appropriate outputs even in the context of novel vocabulary items has been facilitated by content-sensitive attention mechanisms (Bahdanau et al., 2016; Luong et al., 2015).

These innovations open up the possibility that modern network architectures may well be able to solve the variable identity problem necessary for mapping reflexive sentences to their logical form. In the experiments we describe below, we explore whether this is the case.

2 Experimental Setup

Our experiments take the form of a semantic parsing task, where sequences of words are mapped into logical form representations of meaning. Following Dong and Lapata (2016), we do this by means of a sequence-to-sequence architecture (Sutskever et al., 2014) in which the input sentence is fully processed by an encoder network before it is decoded into a sequence of symbols in the target domain (cf. Botvinick and Plaut 2006, Frank and Mathis 2007 for antecedents). This approach removes the need to synchronize the production of output symbols with the input words, as in Frank et al. (2013), allowing greater flexibility in the nature of semantic representations.

The sequence-to-sequence architecture is agnostic as to the types of recurrent units for the encoding and decoding phases of the computation, and whether the decoder makes use of an attention mechanism. Here, we explore the effects of using different types of recurrent units and including attention or not. Specifically, we examine the performance and training characteristics of sequence-to-sequence models based on SRNs, GRUs, and LSTMs with and without multiplicative attention (Luong et al., 2015).

In all experiments, we perform 5 runs with different random seeds for each combination of recurrent unit type (one layer of SRN, LSTM or GRU units for both the encoder and decoder) and attention (with or without multiplicative attention). All models used hidden and embedding of size of 256. Training was done using Stochastic Gradient Descent with learning rate of 0.01. Models were trained for a maximum of 100 epochs with early stopping when validation loss fails to decrease by 0.005 over three successive epochs.

We conduct all of our experiments with synthetic datasets from a small fragment of English sentences generated using a simple context-free grammar. This fragment includes simple sentences with transitive and intransitive verbs. Subjects are always proper names and objects are either proper names or a reflexive whose gender matches that of the subject. Our vocabulary includes 8 intransitive verbs, 7 transitive verbs, 15 female names, and 11 male names. The grammar thus generates 5,122 distinct sentences. All sentences are generated with equal probability, subject to the restrictions imposed by each experiment. We use a unification extension to CFG to associate each sentence with a predicate calculus interpretation. The symbols corresponding to the predicates and the entities in our logical language are identical with the verbs and names used by our grammar, yielding representations like those shown in (1) and (2). The output sequences corresponding to the target semantic interpretations include parentheses and commas as separate symbols. Quite clearly, this dataset does not reproduce the richness of English sentence structure or the distribution of reflexive anaphora, and we leave the exploration of syntactically richer domains for future work. However, even this simple fragment instantiate the kind of contextual variable interpretation found in all cases of reflexive interpretation and therefore it allows us to probe the ability of networks to induce a representation of such meanings.

As discussed in the previous section, we are interested in whether sequence-to-sequence models can successfully *generalize* their knowledge of the interpretation of sentences containing reflexives to ones having novel antecedents. To do this, we employ a *poverty of the stimulus* paradigm that tests for systematic generalization beyond a finite (and ambiguous) set of training data (Chomsky, 1980). In our experiments, we remove certain classes of examples from the training data set and test the effect on the network's success in interpreting reflexive-containing sentences. Each of our experiments thus defines a set of sentences that are withheld during training. The non-withheld sentences are randomly split 80%–10%–10% between training, validation, and testing sets. Accuracy for each set is computed on a sentence-level basis, i.e., an accurate output requires that all symbols generated by the model be identical to the target. Our experiments focus on two sorts of manipulations of the training data: (1) varying the number of lexical items that do and do not occur as the antecedents of reflexives in the training set, and (2) varying the syntactic positions in which the non-antecedent names occur. As we will see, both of these manipulations substantially impact the success of reflexive generalization in ways that vary across network types.

3 Experiment 1: Can Alice know herself?

In the first experiment, we directly test whether or not networks can generalize knowledge of how to interpret *herself* to a new antecedent. We withhold all examples whose input sequence includes the reflexive *herself* bound by the single antecedent *Alice*, of the form shown in (4).

(4) Alice *verbs* herself → *verb*(ALICE, ALICE)

Sentences of any other form are included in the training-validation-test splits, including those where *Alice* appears without binding a reflexive.

3.1 Results

All network architectures were successful in this task, generalizing the interpretation of *herself* to the novel antecedent *Alice*. Even the simplest networks, namely SRN models without attention, achieve 100% accuracy on the generalization set (sentences of the form shown in (4)). This is in sharp contrast the negative results obtained by Frank et al. (2013), suggesting an advantage for training with a language with more names as well as for instantiating the semantic parsing task in a sequence-to-sequence architecture as opposed to a language model.

4 Experiment 2: Doesn't Alice know Alice?

While the networks in Experiment 1 are not trained on sentences of the form shown in (4), they are trained on sentences that have the same target semantic form, namely sentences in which *Alice* occur as both subject and object of a transitive verb.

(5) Alice *verbs* Alice → *verb*(ALICE, ALICE)

In Experiment 2 we consider whether the presence of such semantically reflexive forms in the training data is helpful to networks in generalizing to syntactically reflexive sentences. We do this by further excluding sentences of the form in (5) from the training data.

4.1 Results

All architectures except SRNs without attention generalize perfectly to the held out items. Inattentive SRNs also generalize quite well, though only at a mean accuracy of 86%. While success at Experiment 1 demonstrates the networks' abilities to generalize to novel input contexts, success at Experiment 2 highlights how models can likewise generalize to produce entirely new outputs.

5 Experiment 3: Who's Alice and who's Claire?

So far, we have considered generalization of reflexive interpretation to a single new name. One possible explanation of the networks' success is that they are simply defaulting to the (held-out) ALICE interpretation when confronted with a new antecedent, as an elsewhere interpretation (but see Gandhi and Lake 2019 for reasons for skepticism). Alternatively, even if the network has acquired a generalized interpretation for reflexives, it may be possible that this happens only when the training data includes overwhelming lexical support (in Experiments 1 and 2, 25 out of the 26 names in our domain appeared in the training data as the antecedent of a reflexive). To explore the contexts under which networks can truly generalize to a range of new antecedents, we construct training datasets in which we progressively withhold more and more names in sentences of the forms shown in (6), i.e., those that were removed in Experiment 2.[1]

---

[1] Since *himself* and *herself* are different lexical items, it is unclear if the network will learn their interpretations together, and whether sentences containing *himself* will provide support for the interpretation of sentences containing *herself*. We therefore withhold only sentences of this form with names of a single gender. We have also experimented with witholding masculine reflexive antecedents from the training data, but the main effect remains the number of female antecedents that is withheld.

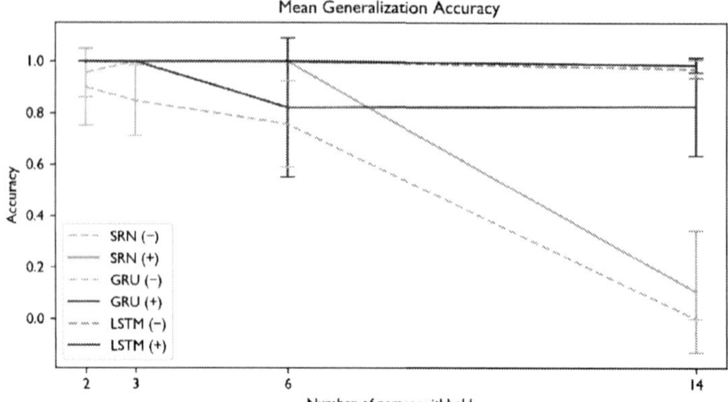

Figure 1: Mean generalization accuracy by number of names withheld in Experiment 3. The $(+)$ or $(-)$ next to the type of recurrent unit indicates the presence or absence of attention. Error bars display the standard deviation of accuracies.

(6) a. *P verbs* herself $\rightarrow verb(P,P)$

    b. *P verbs P* $\rightarrow verb(P,P)$

Our domain contains 15 distinct feminine antecedents; we perform several iterations of this experiment, withholding progressively more feminine names from appearing in the contexts in (6), until only a single feminine name is included in the training data as the antecedent of a reflexive.

5.1   Results

As shown in Figure 1, reducing the set of names that serve as antecedents to reflexives in the training data resulted in lower accuracy on the generalization set. SRNs, especially without attention, show significantly degraded performance when high numbers of names are withheld from reflexive contexts during training. With attention, SRN performance degrades only when reflexives are trained with a single feminine antecedent (i.e., 14 names are held out). In contrast, LSTMs both with and without attention maintain near-perfect accuracy on the generalization set even when the training data allows only a single antecedent for the feminine reflexive *herself*. The performance of GRUs varies with the presence of an attention mechanism: without attention, GRUs achieve near perfect generalization accuracy even for the most demanding case (training with a single feminine antecedent), while the performance of GRUs with attention has mean accuracy near 80%.

We also explored how recurrent unit type and attention affect *how* models learn to generalize. One way to gauge this is by examining how quickly networks go from learning reflexive interpretation for a single name to learning it for every name. Table 1 shows the mean number of epochs it takes from when a network attains 95% accuracy on a single antecedent contexts[2] to when it has attained more than 95% accuracy on *all* held out antecedent contexts.[3]

This 'time to learn' highlights the disparate impact of attention depending on the type of recurrent unit; SRNs with attention and LSTMs with attention acquire the generalization much faster than their attentionless counterparts, while attention increases the length of time it takes for GRUs to learn for all but the condition in which 14 antecedents were withheld. Figure 2 illustrates another important aspect of reflexive generalization: it proceeds in a piecemeal fashion, where networks first learn to interpret reflexives for the trained names and then generalize to the held out antecedents one by one. In Figure 2 we show an SRN without attention, but the same pattern is representative of the other networks tested.

---

[2]An 'antecedent context' is the set of all reflexive sentences with a particular antecedent.

[3]Note that this doesn't mean that models retained more than 95% accuracy on all contexts — some models learned a context, only to forget it later in training; this measurement does not reflect any such unlearning by models.

Architecture	# contexts withheld			
	2	3	6	14
SRN ($-$)	7.5	5.0	—	—
SRN ($+$)	0.6	0.6	0.6	—
GRU ($-$)	1.8	2.2	3.4	9.4
GRU ($+$)	2.2	3.6	5.3	1.5
LSTM ($-$)	1.2	2.2	4.4	12.2
LSTM ($+$)	0.6	0.8	1.4	3.4

Table 1: Average number of epochs between having learned one context and having learned all contexts, calculated as the mean difference among runs which succeeded in eventually learning all contexts once. A '—' in a row indicates that no models were able to achieve this degree of generalization.

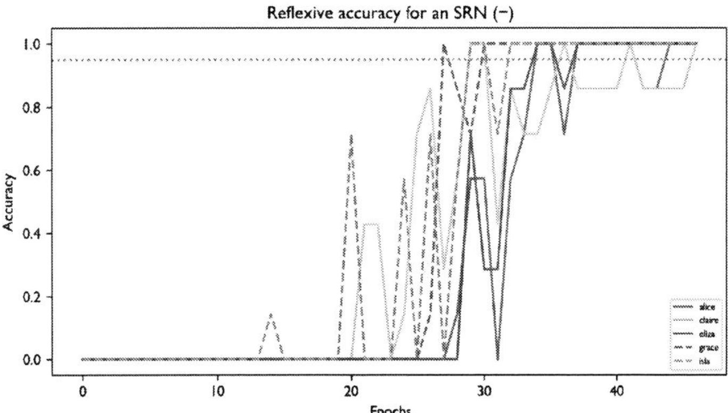

Figure 2: Reflexive accuracy with different antecedents during training of an SRN without attention. *Alice*, *Claire* and *Eliza* were withheld during training while *Grace* and *Isla* present in the training data.

6 Experiment 4: What if Alice doesn't know anyone?

The experiments we have described thus far removed from the training data input sentences and logical forms that were exactly identical to those associated with reflexive sentences. The next pair of experiments increases the difficulty of the generalization task still further, by withholding from the Experiment 2 training data all sentences containing the withheld reflexive antecedent, *Alice*, in a wider range of grammatical contexts, and testing the effect that this has on the network's ability to interpret *Alice*-reflexive sentences.

Experiment 4a starts by withholding sentences where *Alice* appears as the subject of a transitive verb (including those with reflexive objects, which we already removed in earlier experiments). This manipulation tests the degree to which the presence of *Alice* as a subject more generally is crucial to the network's generalization of reflexive sentences to a novel name. We also run a variation of this experiment (Experiment 4b) in which sentences containing *Alice* as the subject of intransitives are also removed, i.e., sentences of the following form:

(7) Alice *verbs* $\rightarrow$ *verb*(ALICE)

If subjecthood is represented in a uniform manner across transitive and intransitive sentences, the absence of such sentences from the training data might further impair the network's ability to generalize to reflexive sentences.

Experiment 4a	SRN (−)	SRN (+)	GRU (−)	GRU (+)	LSTM (−)	LSTM (+)
Alice-reflexive	0.00	0.80	0.03	0.26	0.00	**1.00**
Alice-subject (trans)	0.02	**0.83**	0.04	0.29	0.03	0.28

Experiment 4b	SRN (−)	SRN (+)	GRU (−)	GRU (+)	LSTM (−)	LSTM (+)
Alice-reflexive	0.00	0.63	0.00	0.80	0.00	**0.83**
Alice-subject (trans)	0.00	0.25	0.01	**0.78**	0.03	0.23
Alice-subject (intrans)	0.00	0.80	0.58	0.95	0.98	**1.00**

Table 2: Mean accuracy on generalization sets for Experiments 4a and 4b.

6.1 Results

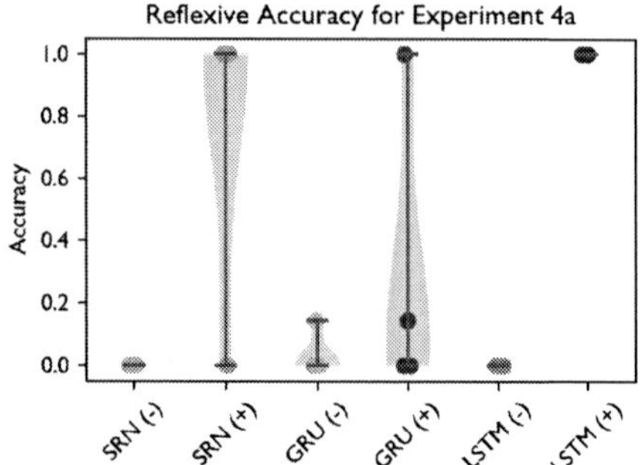
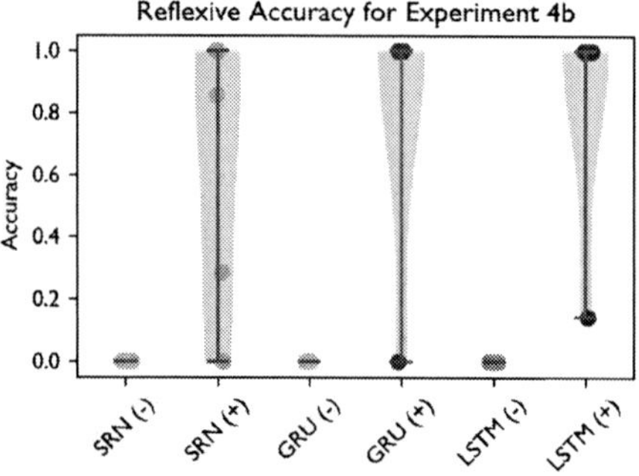

Figure 3: Mean accuracy on *Alice*-reflexive sentences in Experiments 4a (left) and 4b (right).

Experiment 4a   The left plot in Figure 3 shows the reflexive generalization accuracy for the runs of the different architectures in the first variant of this experiment. Models without attention uniformly perform poorly across all recurrent unit types. With attention, performance is more variable: LSTMs perform at ceiling and SRNs do well for most random seeds, while GRUs perform poorly for most initializations with a single seed performing at ceiling. The top portion of Table 2 contrasts the means of these results with the generalization performance on transitives with *Alice* subjects. Here again LSTMs without attention performed poorly while those with attention did much worse on *Alice*-transitives than on *Alice*-reflexive sentences.

This result at once highlights the role that attention plays in learning this type of systematic generalization; attention appears to be necessary for recurrent architectures to generalize in this context. The pattern of results also demonstrates a substantial effect of model architecture: attentive SRNs substantially outperform the more complex LSTM and GRU architectures on generalization to *Alice*-transitives, though this was not the case for reflexive sentences, where LSTMs showed a substantial advantage.

Experiment 4b   The right plot in Figure 3 shows the impact of withholding *Alice*-intransitive sentences from training. As before, models without attention fail on interpreting *Alice*-reflexive sentences. LSTMs and SRNs with attention perform nearly as well as in Experiment 4a, with some seeds performing at ceiling and a somewhat larger number than before failing to doing so. In contrast, the performance of attentive GRUs is improved in this context. The bottom of Table 2 shows the mean generalization accuracy for transitive and intransitive sentences with *Alice* subjects. In some cases the transitive subject performance is as in Experiment 4a or worse, but in one case, namely attentive GRUs, it improves in this more difficult context, paralleling what we saw for reflexive generalization.

The reversal of GRU (+) and SRN (+) accuracies better lines up with what we might expect given the complexity of the network architectures, with the more complex GRUs now outperforming the simpler SRNs. These results also reinforce the connection observed in those from Experiment 4b on the effects of

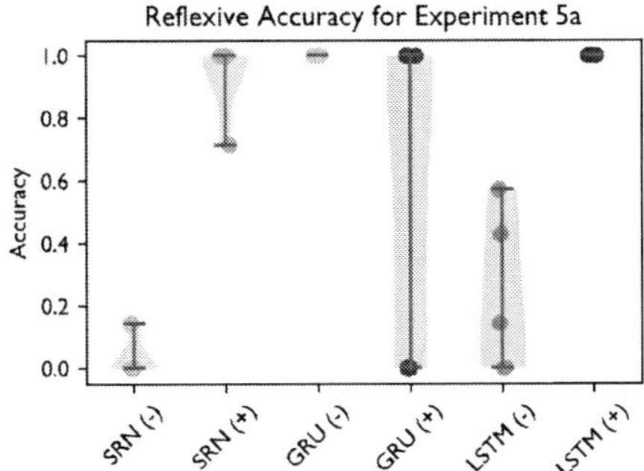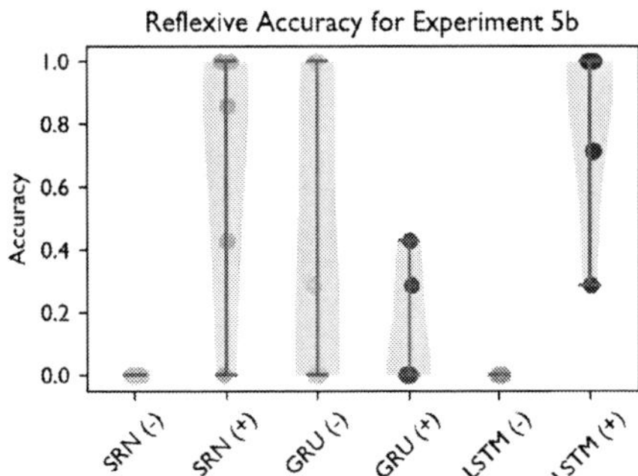

Figure 4: Mean accuracy on *Alice*-reflexive sentences in Experiments 5a (left) and 5b (right).

attention in generalization.

While withholding more information during training as we move from Experiment 4a to 4b might be expected to impair generalization for attentive GRUs, as it did for all other architectures, we in fact see an increase in performance on *Alice*-reflexive sentences. One possible explanation of this surprising result is that the attentive GRU networks in experiment 4a have learned from the training data a context-sensitive regularity concerning the distribution of the withheld name *Alice*, namely that it occurs only as the subject of intransitive verbs. In Experiment 4b, however, the absence of evidence concerning the types of predicates with which *Alice* may occur allows the network to fall back to a context-free generalization about *Alice*, namely that it has the same distribution as the other names in the domain. Note that this explanation is possible only if the network treats intransitive and transitive subjects in a similar way.

7 Experiment 5: What if nobody knows Alice?

In the final experiment, we restrict the grammatical context in which *Alice* appears by removing from the training data of Experiment 2 all instances of transitive sentences with *Alice* in object position (but it is retained in subject position, apart from reflexive sentences). In a second variant (Experiment 5b), we further restrict the training data to exclude all intransitive sentences with *Alice* subjects. Although English, as a language with nominative-accusative alignment, treats subjects of intransitives in a grammatically parallel fashion to subjects of transitives, other languages (with ergative-absolutive alignment) treat intransitive subjects like transitive objects. Though the word order of our synthetic language suggests nominative-accusative alignment, intransitive subjects have in common with transitive objects being the final argument in the logical form, which might lead to them being treated in similar fashion.

7.1 Results

Experiment 5a The left plot in Figure 4 shows reflexive generalization accuracy when the missing antecedent *Alice* is withheld from transitive objects. In contrast to the results in Experiment 4, the effect of attention is more varied here. While SRNs and LSTMs without attention perform poorly, GRUs without attention perform well (for some seeds). As the top panel in Table 3 shows, no models without attention performed well on sentences with *Alice* in object position. For the models with attention, SRNs and LSTMs perforrmed uniformly well while the performance of GRUs was more mixed. On *Alice*-object sentences attentive SRNs again showed excellent performance, whereas the GRUs and LSTMs fared less well. At the same time, while GRUs with attention outperformed GRUs without attention on *Alice*-object sentences (25% to 4%), they greatly underperformed them on the reflexive sentences (60% to 98%).

Experiment 5b The right plots in Figure 4 shows the effects of further withholding *Alice*-intransitive sentences for *Alice*-reflexive sentences. This manipulation has devastating effects on the performance of all models without attention. For models with attention, there is also a negative impact on reflexive generalization, but not as severe. As shown in the bottom portion of Table 3, this manipulation has little impact on the network's performance on *Alice*-object sentences, with SRNs with attention continuing to

Experiment 5a	SRN ($-$)	SRN ($+$)	GRU ($-$)	GRU ($+$)	LSTM ($-$)	LSTM ($+$)
Alice-reflexive	0.03	0.94	0.98	0.60	0.23	**1.00**
Alice-object	0.00	**0.97**	0.04	0.25	0.04	0.37

Experiment 5b	SRN ($-$)	SRN ($+$)	GRU ($-$)	GRU ($+$)	LSTM ($-$)	LSTM ($+$)
Alice-reflexive	0.00	0.65	0.45	0.14	0.00	**0.80**
Alice-object	0.00	**0.94**	0.03	0.09	0.03	0.17
Alice-subject (intrans)	0.00	0.13	0.00	0.00	0.00	**0.40**

Table 3: Mean accuracy on generalization sets for Experiments 5a and 5b.

perform strongly and the other models performing less well. GRUs continue to interact with attention in unusual ways. While they perform poorly on *Alice*-object and *Alice*-intransitive sentences with and without attention, inattentive GRUs continue to outperform attentive ones on reflexive sentences.

Overall, as in Experiment 4, LSTMs with attention show the highest accuracy on the *Alice*-reflexive sentences by a wide margin, while SRNs with attention attain the best performance on *Alice*-object sentences. Unlike in Experiment 4, withholding the *Alice*-intransitive sentences from training does not yield any benefit for GRUs with attention in performance on the reflexive set, in fact the opposite is true. This may be interpreted once again as evidence that GRUs are treating transitive and intransitive subjects as belonging to the same category. In Experiment 5a, *Alice* occurs in both positions, leading the network to treat it as a subject like any other, and therefore potentially capable of serving as a subject of a reflexive. *Alice*'s absence from object position does not impact the formation of this generalization. In Experiment 5b, on the other hand, where *Alice* occurs only as a transitive subject, it leads the attentive GRU to treat it as name with a distinctive distribution, which impairs generalization to reflexive sentences.

8 Conclusions

Because of their abstract meaning, reflexive anaphora present a distinctive challenge for semantic parsing that had been thought to be beyond the capabilities of recurrent networks. The experiments described here demonstrate that this was incorrect. Sequence-to-sequence networks with a range of recurrent unit types are in fact capable of learning an interpretation of reflexive pronouns that generalizes to novel antecedents. Our results also show that such generalization is nonetheless contingent on the appearance of the held-out antecedent in a variety of syntactic positions as well as the diversity of antecedents providing support for the reflexive generalization. Additionally successful generalization depends on the network architecture in ways that we do not fully understand. It is at present unknown whether the demands that any of these architecture impose on the learning environment for successful learning of reflexives are consistent with what children experience, but this could be explored with both corpus and experimental work. Future work will also be necessary to elucidate the nature of the networks' representations of reflexive interpretation and to understand how they support lexical generalization (or not).

The question we have explored here is related to, but distinct from, the issue of systematicity (Fodor and Pylyshyn, 1988; Hadley, 1994), according to which pieces of representations learned in distinct contexts can freely recombine. This issue has been addressed using sequence-to-sequence architectures in recent work with the synthetic SCAN robot command interpretation dataset (Lake and Baroni, 2018) and on language modeling (Kim and Linzen, 2020), in both cases with limited success. One aspect of the SCAN domain that is particularly relevant to reflexive interpretation is commands involving adverbial modifiers such as *twice*. Commands like *jump twice* must be interpreted by duplicating the meaning of the verb, i.e., as JUMP JUMP, which is similar to what we require for the interpretation of the reflexive object, though in a way that does not require sensitivity to syntactic structure that we have not explored here. Recently, Lake (2019), Li et al. (2019) and Gordon et al. (2020) have proposed novel architectures that increase systematic behavior, and we look forward to exploring the degree to which these impact performance on reflexive interpretation.

Our current work has focused exclusively on recurrent networks, ranging from SRNs to GRUs and

LSTMs. Recent work by Vaswani et al. (2017) shows that Transformer networks attain superior performance on a variety of sequence-to-sequence tasks while dispensing with recurrent units altogether. Examining both the performance and training characteristics of Transformers will allow us to compare the effects of attention and recurrence on the anaphora interpretation task. This is especially interesting given the impact that attention had on performance in our experiments.

Finally, while our current experiments are revealing about the capacity of recurrent networks to learn generalizations about context-sensitive interpretation, there are nonetheless limited in a number of respects because of simplifications in the English fragment we use to create our synthetic data. Reflexives famously impose a structural requirement on their antecedents (c-command). In the following example, the reflexive's antecedent must be STUDENT and cannot be TEACHER.

(8) The student near the teacher sees herself → SEE(STUDENT, STUDENT)

We do not know whether the architectures that have succeed on our experiments would do similarly well if the relevant generalization required reference to (implicit) structure. Past work has explored the sensitivity of recurrent networks to hierarchical structure, with mixed results (Linzen et al., 2016; McCoy et al., 2020). In ongoing work, we are exploring this question by studying more complex synthetic domains both with the kind of recurrent sequence-to-sequence network used here as well networks that explicitly encode or decode sentences in a hierarchical manner. A second simplification concerns the distribution of reflexives themselves. English reflexives can appear in a broader range of syntactic environments apart from transitive objects (Storoshenko, 2008). It would be of considerable interest to explore the reflexive interpretation in a naturalistic setting that incorporate this broader set of distributions.

Acknowledgments

For helpful comments and discussion of this work, we are grateful to Shayna Sragovicz, Noah Amsel, Tal Linzen and the members of the Computational Linguistics at Yale (CLAY) and the JHU Computation and Psycholinguistics labs. This work has been supported in part by NSF grant BCS-1919321 and a Yale College Summer Experience Award. Code for replicating these experiments can be found on the Computational Linguistics at the CLAY Lab GitHub `transductions` and `logos` repositories.

References

Dzmitry Bahdanau, Kyunghyun Cho, and Yoshua Bengio. 2016. Neural machine translation by jointly learning to align and translate.

Matthew M. Botvinick and David C. Plaut. 2006. Short-term memory for serial order: A recurrent neural network model. *Psychological Review*, 113:201–233.

Kyunghyun Cho, Bart Van Merriënboer, Caglar Gulcehre, Dzmitry Bahdanau, Fethi Bougares, Holger Schwenk, and Yoshua Bengio. 2014. Learning phrase representations using RNN encoder-decoder for statistical machine translation. *arXiv preprint arXiv:1406.1078*.

Noam Chomsky. 1980. *Rules and Representations*. Columbia University Press.

Li Dong and Mirella Lapata. 2016. Language to logical form with neural attention. In *Proceedings of the 54th Annual Meeting of the Association for Computational Linguistics (Volume 1: Long Papers)*, pages 33–43, Berlin, Germany. Association for Computational Linguistics.

Jeffrey L Elman. 1990. Finding structure in time. *Cognitive science*, 14(2):179–211.

Jerry A. Fodor and Zenon W. Pylyshyn. 1988. Connectionism and cognitive architecture: A critical analysis. *Cognition*, 28:3–71.

Robert Frank and Donald Mathis. 2007. Transformational networks. In *Proceedings of the 3rd Workshop on Psychocomputational Models of Human Language Acquisition*.

Robert Frank, Donald Mathis, and William Badecker. 2013. The acquisition of anaphora by simple recurrent networks. *Language Acquisition*, 20:181–227.

Kanishk Gandhi and Brenden M. Lake. 2019. Mutual exclusivity as a challenge for deep neural networks.

Jonathan Gordon, David Lopez-Paz, Marco Baroni, and Diane Bouchacourt. 2020. Permutation equivariant models for compositional generalization in language. In *International Conference on Learning Representations*.

Alex Graves and Jürgen Schmidhuber. 2005. Framewise phoneme classification with bidirectional LSTM and other neural network architectures. *Neural networks*, 18(5-6):602–610.

Robert F. Hadley. 1994. Systematicity in connectionist language learning. *Mind and Language*, 9:247–272.

Najoung Kim and Tal Linzen. 2020. COGS: A compositional generalization challenge based on semantic interpretation. In *The 2020 Conference on Empirical Methods in Natural Language Processing*.

Brenden M. Lake. 2019. Compositional generalization through meta sequence-to-sequence learning. In *Advances in Neural Information Processing Systems 32*, pages 9791–9801.

Brenden M. Lake and Marco Baroni. 2018. Generalization without systematicity: On the compositional skills of sequence-to-sequence recurrent networks. In *Proceedings of the 35th International Conference on Machine Learning, volume 80 of Proceedings of Machine Learning Research*, pages 2873–2882, Stockholm, Sweden.

Yuanpeng Li, Liang Zhao, Jianyu Wang, and Joel Hestness. 2019. Compositional generalization for primitive substitutions. In *Proceedings of the 2019 Conference on Empirical Methods in Natural Language Processing and the 9th International Joint Conference on Natural Language Processing (EMNLP/IJCNLP)*, pages 4293—4302, Hong Kong, China.

Tal Linzen, Emmanuel Dupoux, and Yoav Goldberg. 2016. Assessing the ability of LSTMs to learn syntax-sensitive dependencies. *Transactions of the Association for Computational Linguistics*, 4(1).

Thang Luong, Hieu Pham, and Christopher D. Manning. 2015. Effective approaches to attention-based neural machine translation. In *Proceedings of the 2015 Conference on Empirical Methods in Natural Language Processing*, pages 1412–1421, Lisbon, Portugal. Association for Computational Linguistics.

Gary F. Marcus. 1998. Can connectionism save constructionism? *Cognition*, 66:153–182.

R. Thomas McCoy, Robert Frank, and Tal Linzen. 2020. Does syntax need to grow on trees? Sources of hierarchical inductive bias in sequence-to-sequence networks. *Transactions of the Association for Computational Linguistics*, 8:125–140.

Dennis Ryan Storoshenko. 2008. The distribution of reflexive pronouns in English: A corpus analysis. In *Proceedings of the 24th Northwest Linguistics Conference*, pages 67–74.

Ilya Sutskever, Oriol Vinyals, and Quoc V Le. 2014. Sequence to sequence learning with neural networks. In *Advances in neural information processing systems*, pages 3104–3112.

Ashish Vaswani, Noam Shazeer, Niki Parmar, Jakob Uszkoreit, Llion Jones, Aidan N. Gomez, Lukasz Kaiser, and Illia Polosukhin. 2017. Attention is all you need. *CoRR*, abs/1706.03762.

A Dataset for Anaphora Analysis in French Emails

Hani Guenoune [♣][◊], Kevin Cousot [♣], Mathieu Lafourcade [◊]
Melissa Mekaoui [♣], Cédric Lopez [♣]
[♣] Emvista, Rond-Point Benjamin Franklin, 34000 Montpellier, France
[◊] LIRMM, 161 Rue Ada, 34095 Montpellier, France

Abstract

In 2019, about 293 billion emails were sent worldwide every day. They are a valuable source of information and knowledge for professionals. Since the 90's, many studies have been done on emails and have highlighted the need for resources regarding numerous NLP tasks. Due to the lack of available resources for French, very few studies on emails have been conducted. Anaphora resolution in emails is an unexplored area, annotated resources are needed, at least to answer a first question: Does email communication have specifics that must be addressed to tackle the anaphora resolution task? In order to answer this question 1) we build a French emails corpus composed of 100 anonymized professional threads and make it available freely for scientific exploitation. 2) we provide annotations of anaphoric links in the email collection.

1 Introduction

Emails significantly increase the extent of communications in companies. In 2019, about 293 billion emails were sent worldwide every day. They are of great interest for professionals as they represent a valuable source of information and knowledge. Natural Language Processing (NLP) techniques are commonly used for email analysis, to generate a history of the knowledge they convey (Matta et al., 2014), to retrieve redundant problem solving elements (Francois et al., 2016), or to identify tasks in order to help the user manage its time (Khosravi and Wilks, 1999).

Many studies have been conducted on emails since the late 1990s, especially for the analysis of the English language, thanks to the publicly available Enron corpus (250 000 emails sent or received by 87,000 employees of Enron) (Klimt and Yang, 2004).

Our review of French corpora reveals that only one collection of emails is available, which is a subset of the EASY Evaluation Package (provided as part of the Evaluation Campaign for Parsers of French, containing 2,250 anonymised personal emails (Paroubek et al., 2006)). Given this lack of email corpora for the French language, recent works on French emails needed to create their own corpora (Kalitvianski, 2018), However, similarly to the EASY Corpus, the corpora resulting from these works are not freely available to the research community, therefore comparing systems is still unfeasible, as recently highlighted by (Mekaoui et al., 2020).

Anaphora and coreference resolution are core components of the NLP field. These tasks aim to detect and resolve repeated mentions of the same entities in a given document. Many NLP tasks rely on the ability to resolve entities efficiently and could be prominently improved by using robust automatic strategies of anaphora and coreference resolution. In order to design suitable strategies dealing with a natural language phenomenon, one would require to analyse a sufficient number of occurrences of the said phenomenon.

Several studies on annotating French texts with anaphoric links have been conducted (Landragin, 2019; Landragin, 2018; Muzerelle et al., 2014; Tutin et al., 2000), resulting in a few available corpora. The texts covered in these corpora are of various genres and natures, nonetheless, emails are part of none of these datasets.

Proceedings of the 3rd Workshop on Computational Models of Reference, Anaphora and Coreference (CRAC 2020), pages 165–175,
Barcelona, Spain (online), December 12, 2020.

In order to capture the characteristics of referring expressions in this particular kind of discourse (*cf.* Section 3.1), we undertook the process of manually marking the occurrences of each type of anaphora that we considered relevant to the needs of typical NLP issues (*cf.* Section 3.5) in a collection of anonymized professional French emails.

Our work leads to the following contributions: Making available the first free French email corpus for scientific exploitation; Providing annotations for the anaphora discourse phenomenon in French emails; Giving a first quantitative overview of anaphora and coreference in emails.

In this paper, we describe the dataset and its anonymization process (*cf.* section 2), then, we focus on anaphora and coreference annotation (*cf.* section 3). Finally, we describe the annotated corpus and our future works (*cf.* section 5).

2 Dataset

As for (Krieg-Holz et al., 2016), our dataset is made of French professional emails which were requested from individual email authors on the basis of a volunteer act. In our case, authors are employees of a company that wished to remain anonymous. The corpus consists of 100 threads made of 314 emails (7163 words), out of mailing lists, exchanged between June and September 2017.

2.1 Data collection

Technically, the threads were collected through two email inboxes. This implies that the recipients of the threads are always the two same individuals, but emails are from 53 authors. Given the user-centered applications that we considered for this data collection, we made the decision to exclude emails received from automated mailing lists. A thread contains between 1 and 18 emails. Each email consists of the message, the signature if any, and the metadata ("from","to","subject", and "date"). The presence of attachments is indicated. A first cleaning step ensured that no text segments were duplicated in the thread (for instance, through the use of the email forwarding function).

We decided not to structure the threads and share them in their original state, so that the user could have complete freedom over the use of the dataset (no bias according to the structure and no format is imposed). For instance, splitting by sentences or by token is a prepossessing step that embeds several crucial choices we wanted to avoid.

2.2 Anonymization

In order to anonymize the dataset, we used a state-of-the-art named entity recognizer (Lopez et al., 2019) to locate names of people, places, names of organizations, phone numbers, websites, email addresses and so on. Then, all detected mentions have been replaced by dummy data (for instance, "Peter" could have been replaced by "Kevin", and "Marseille" could have been replaced by "Paris"). An important point is that the consistence of the corpus is preserved: all identical mentions have been replaced by a given mention. This assures that the anonymizations of coreferent polylexical entites such as "Marc Sullivan" and "Marc John Sullivan" remain consistent with the original form of the entities. Moreover, the case has been respected ("Peter" and "peter" could have been respectively replaced by "Kevin" and "kevin"). This allows the corpus to be used for the evaluations of other NLP tasks, such as named entity recognition, for instance. Finally, a manual iteration certifies that no mentions have been left out and that the corpus is fully anonymized. All in all, 9,277 mentions were replaced.

3 Anaphora annotation

Corpora with annotated anaphoric links are essential in NLP and in linguistics. Large sets of annotations give the opportunity to study the anaphora phenomenon. Allowing to craft rule-based systems (manually or automatically generated rules) and machine learning models. Annotated corpora also allow the evaluation of those systems.

The first goal of this study is to address the scarcity of French resources for anaphora study, especially ones containing emails texts (Guenoune et al., 2019). We aim to do so by making available the first free French email corpus with anaphoric links annotations. This work results in a relatively small dataset primarily designed for analysis and evaluation purposes, and represents, in our opinion, a useful starting point (Landragin, 2018). This will allow us to undertake experiments and comparisons to highlight the singularity of automatic anaphora resolution in the email genre (cf. Section 3.1). And thus, serve as a foundation for designing a rule-based resolution system that takes into account the writing conventions observed in this kind of texts.

Two large French corpora are annotated with coreference and anaphoric links. ANCOR (Muzerelle et al., 2014) contains a collection of spoken French transcriptions taken from sociolinguistic interviews. DEMOCRAT's corpus is the most recent resource, annotated with coreferential information (Landragin, 2019). Interestingly, the authors took into account coreference chains in the annotation process. In DEMOCRAT, the selection of texts was done in a way that helps capture the variations of the coreference phenomenon across text genres and eras. Nonetheless, emails are not considered in these corpora.

In Section 4, a set of methodological choices is compared to those of larger-scale projects ; *ANCOR* (Muzerelle et al., 2014), *ARRAU* (Poesio and Artstein, 2008) and *OntoNotes* corpora (Pradhan et al., 2007).

In the following section, we discuss the specificity of annotating anaphoric links in the context of emails (*cf.* section 3.1), then describe our annotation protocol and the typology used (*cf.* section 3.3)).

3.1 Emails singularities

Email writings show some singularities that make the tasks of anaphora annotation and resolution difficult. The two main challenges encountered when dealing with emails are:

- The structural level : Due to the segmented form of the communication (message/thread), emails redefine the binding scope of an anaphoric mention (Reinhart, 1983). An expression can refer to antecedents mentioned within the same message or not. Antecedents may be located in different emails in the thread, or even in different threads. This particular aspect impels us, from an annotation point of view, to design a scheme that handles these extended scopes, and deals with internal and external antecedents. It also affects the resolution task, which becomes analogous to a Cross-Document (CD) problem (Barhom et al., 2019) in which every email thread represents a document. As opposed to Within-Document (WD) anaphora resolution that has been extensively studied during the last decades, the CD task, that aims to locate coreferent entities across multiple documents, remains, as far as we are aware, totally unexplored for French.
  In addition to that, the writings in emails obey to a certain number of stylistic and functional rules making their content singular. One example is the mentions of entities in the metadata of each mail (Sender, recipients, signatures..) that can be antecedents to anaphoric expressions used in the email body.

- The morphological aspects : Similarly to every other kind of user-generated texts, the morphological level affects both the tasks of manual annotation of anaphora and its automatic resolution. For example, gender and number traits being some of the most decisive features in anaphora resolution, rely on meticulous spelling and require a high level of morphological accuracy. However, considering the "non standard" nature of emails writings (Tarrade et al., 2017), morphological errors can produce ambiguous phrasings.

3.2 Annotation protocol

The task was performed by a group of 3 MSc/PhD annotators with Linguistics background, and of different French language proficiency levels. Including one expert annotator whose annotations were considered as gold standard in the agreement study.

The process consisted of six stages (including three iterative steps):

1. **Initialization of the guideline:** The first strategy emerged from discussions about the general purposes and requirements of the resulting corpus.
   The initial draft was defined in such a way that allowed evolution and adaptations to the cases eventually encountered by the annotators.

2. **Selecting a small set of threads:** The goal was to select a portion of the collection that contains the types that are most likely to lead to annotation disparities.

3. **Annotating the selected threads with the current guidelines:** The human annotators were given guidelines regarding the types of mentions and anaphoric expressions to mark. Every annotator trained on a separate portion of the collection.

4. **Agreement study:** In order to assess the operability of the resulting typology, agreement studies have been undertook on the threads selected in step 2. Unlike for other NLP tasks (typically classification ones), annotators are expected to mark words from the text as antecedents, this makes it difficult to establish *a priori* the set of all possible annotations for a given anaphor. Provided that the Kappa measure relies on the set of possible class labels, implementing it to capture agreements on anaphora annotation is challenging. Several methods were used to address this particular aspect (Artstein and Poesio, 2008).

   In our experiments, we chose to isolate the identification and delimitation of antecedents from the classification task. The formal experiments concerned the task of classification of annotated anaphoric mentions into the set of types defined. It was designed to determine in what proportion the annotators agree that an anaphoric markable belongs to a given type, then analyse the reasons for eventual disagreements. Two agreement scores were calculated to assess the consistency of both the typology and the guidelines : A first pairwise (annotator$_i$, gold) agreement score (Cohen's Kappa), and an overall agreement experiment, namely Fleiss' Kappa (Fleiss, J et al., 1981).

5. **Discussion and evolution of the guidelines:** Regular discussions led to several developments in the original typology and annotation protocol (cf. Special operators. Section 3.4). The exchanges mainly dealt with the most commonly encountered difficulties and ambiguous cases. Depending on the pairwise and overall agreement scores, we decide to go back to step 3 or continue to step 6 when a strong agreement is achieved.

6. **Applying the final guidelines to the entire dataset:** We decided to apply the final guidelines to the entire dataset once the Cohen' and Fleiss' Kappa scores (that establish K = *0.6* as good agreement) reached at least *0.70* for the classification task (anaphora types annotation). We chose to keep the typology and the guidelines stable for several sessions, then we decided to proceed with the annotation of the entire collection of threads.

Disagreement

Typically, the cases that resulted in disagreements between annotators concerned the indirect and bridging anaphora phenomena, especially the ones that show through the use of first and second person pronouns in reference to the sender and receiver of the email (this particular case is discussed in Section 5). Multiple disagreements have also been observed in evolving referents annotation (Charolles, 2001) and the inclusive and exclusive use of singular third person pronoun *"On"* (Delaborde and Landragin, 2019). Although not formally assessed, we also note consequent dissension regarding the delimitation of phrasal and abstract antecedents (Amsili et al., 2005).

3.3 Annotation scheme

The major focus in the study was directed towards conceiving a scheme that allows the annotation task to be performed within a reasonable time-frame while maintaining a satisfactory coverage in dealing with the different intricacies of the anaphora phenomenon and consistency with formal specifications.

The anaphoric relation impose a constraint of dependence in interpretation between two distinct mentions, where the first (the antecedent) would be essential to the comprehension of the second (the anaphoric mention) (Mitkov et al., 2012). Therefore, unlike the symmetrical identity (coreference), the relation between an anaphoric mention and its antecedent must be an oriented one. This is represented in the annotation through the choice of a *link-based* strategy. Moreover, as argued in (Poesio et al., 2016), despite the fact that adopting this strategy embeds the necessity to decide which of the antecedents must be marked, it gives the advantage of making the annotation of uncertainty easier.

The strategy used for the annotation task is inspired, in its main aspects, from the guidelines introduced by the MATE Markup Scheme (Poesio, 2005) which seems to us as a straightforward approach to linking lexical units within a text. Slight adjustments have been made in order to maintain a satisfactory level of genericity and to keep the task simple for human annotators. Following the recommendations of the MATE Scheme, we use two distinct elements (<PHRASE> and <ANA>) to mark discourse entities and anaphoric relations. We used the standard XML format for the final form of the dataset. However, for readability and speed purposes, the annotation was originally performed using a custom tagging language.

This section presents the method used for the identification of different types of mentions, then the representation of the anaphoric relations, with supporting examples in french, followed by their translation.

Entities identification

The annotated markables have been restrained to those involved in anaphoric or coreference relations, for the annotation task to remain manageable and feasible in a reasonable period of time.

The first step is therefore to locate the lexical units that should be linked. The <PHRASE> element is used to mark the mentions of discourse entities. It has the numeric attribute id that uniquely identifies the mention within the thread. We define the <PHRASE> element as the segment that may refer to a concrete or abstract entity of the world, including facts, events or situations. The antecedent syntactical representation could thus be a noun, a verbal phrase or a hole sentence (Amsili et al., 2005). We chose to mark the maximal projection of the head noun. Any modifier, determiner or apposition involved in the description of the entity referred to by the mention, is included in the <PHRASE> element, like in the example below.

```
<PHRASE id="1">le nouveau directeur de recherche</PHRASE>

           "The new research supervisor"
```

In addition to nouns' maximal projections, we also mark anaphoric demonstrative and personal pronouns as well as possessive determiners (*cf.* Section 3.5).

Linking referring mentions

Anaphoric relations between mentions are encoded using the <ANA> element and are linked to the corresponding <PHRASE> elements using the attributes loc, thread, src and ant and assigned an anophora type through the attribute type, like in the following text, supposedly located in the thread 1.

```
<PHRASE id="1">le nouveau directeur de recherche</PHRASE> s'occupera des
recrutements, <PHRASE id="2">il</PHRASE> fera passer des entretiens dès la
première semaine.
<ANA id="1" loc="I" thread="1" src="2" ant="1" type="PIS"/>

"The new research supervisor will be responsible of recruitment, he will
conduct job interviews beginning the first week"
```

The loc attribute takes the values I, E, or Et (respectively for Internal, External and External thread) and indicates whether the antecedent appears in the same message as the anaphoric mention, in a different message of the same thread or in a completely different thread.

The thread attribute identifies the thread that contains the antecedent, it allows to retrieve antecedents located in external threads.

Relations are represented by linking the values of the src and ant attributes of the element <ANA> to the id of the <PHRASE> elements corresponding to the anaphoric mention and its antecedent (resp.).

3.4 Special cases

In order to be able to deal with special forms of anaphoric relations between mentions, a number of special operators have been introduced.

Split antecedents

A split antecedent is an antecedent formed by two separate noun phrases (Chomsky, 1981). A frequent occurrence of this type of anaphoric relation involving a combined antecedent shows through the use of plural pronouns (typically third person `ils` and `elles` - "They"). Since noun phrases involved in a split antecedent can be mentioned in different segments of the text, we chose to identify each one separately with a `<PHRASE>` element. The combined antecedent is marked in the `<ANA>` element using the character "-".

```
Marc et Eric sont partis, ils étaient pressés. / "Marc and Eric are gone, they were
in a rush."
```

```
<PHRASE id="1">Marc</PHRASE> et <PHRASE id="2">Eric</PHRASE>
sont partis,<PHRASE id="3">ils</PHRASE> étaient pressés.
<ANA id="1" loc="I" thread="1" src="3" ant="1-2" type="PIC"/>
```

Dual antecedents

Possessive pronouns [`mien, tien, notre...`] "[`mine, yours, ours...`]" require the identification of two different discourse segments to be fully interpreted. The possessive pronoun relates to a first noun phrase designating the entity that possesses (the owner in the example below). The second dependence is a determining one and binds the pronoun with the phrase that indicates the semantic type of what is possessed, which is omitted from the direct context of the pronoun.

We mark each relation of this phenomenon in the `ant` attribute of the `ANA` element, using a separating symbol.

```
Salut <PHRASE id="1">Rodolphe</PHRASE>,
<PHRASE id="2">le bureau</PHRASE> de Josette est plus grand que le
<PHRASE id="3">tien.</PHRASE>
<ANA id="1" loc="I" thread="1" src="3" ant="1^2" type="PPS"/>

"Hi Rodolphe, Josette's office is bigger than yours."
```

Chains

Multiple mentions of a given entity are encoded in the element of the anaphoric relation that points to one of the mentions. We try, whenever possible, to mark all previous lexical occurrences of the entity referenced within the `ant` attribute of the `ANA` element as follows :

```
<PHRASE id="1">Pierre Dupont</PHRASE>...<PHRASE id="2">Mr Dupont</PHRASE>...
<PHRASE id="3">Pierre</PHRASE> ...<PHRASE id="4">Il</PHRASE>.
<ANA id="1" loc="I" thread="1" src="4" ant="1&2&3" type="PIS"/>

          "Pierre Dupont...Mr Dupont...Pierre...He.."
```

The strategy of marking only left (previous) coreferents leads to the presence of partial sequences, it means that only the most recent anaphor is linked to a complete coreference chain. This choice has been made in order to avoid the continual correction of preceding annotations manually which would represent an enormous amount of work. In every new apparition, the annotators reuse the previous partial chain and enrich it with the newly mentioned coreferent. This makes the building of chains a sequential procedure that is complete only when the last anaphor of the text has been marked.

Uncertainty

For some special cases, we found it necessary to implement a strategy that deals with fuzzy antecedents. As it happens that the annotator cannot choose unambiguously the correct antecedent between a set of possible mentions. Different methods aim to tackle this issue (Landragin, 2007), we chose to use an annotation with *alternatives*, where the annotator provides a list of all possible mentions separated with "|".

This strategy allows us to deal with the case of evolving referents (Charolles, 2001) and the "non strict" use of singular third person pronoun `"on"` (Delaborde and Landragin, 2019).

3.5 Anaphoric expressions types

In this section, we begin by listing the syntactic types (parts-of-speech) of the anaphoric expressions we chose to mark. Then, we discuss the semantic types of the relationships between anaphoric mentions and antecedents. Anaphoric expressions retained for annotations are the following.

Pronouns and possessive determiners

Personal, demonstrative (celui, celle... "the one") and possessive (*cf.* Dual antecedents, in 3.4) pronouns are selected.

```
"As agreed, they will offer you a new full-time contract with a trial period of
one month. The old one will be canceled. Charles is in the same case. He will receive
his next week.
Point to check during the month of September, your ability to react responsively
to our production needs."
```

Nouns

Nominal anaphora is marked by selecting noun variations that refer to the same entity, in the typical cases, marked nouns are often labels of the semantic class of the named-entity antecedent.

```
"I have received a complaint from FlashDR, apparently the client is not
satisfied at all."
```

Adjectival pointers

A typical case of elliptical phrasing is the use of the attributes of a mention instead of its nominal representation in order to avoid repetition. In the annotation, we target adjectives such as [le premier, le dernier..."the first, the last"] which are used without the noun they are supposed to describe. The determiner is included in the marking element.

```
"Here are the two phones in question. For the first I wish an estimate,
at the same time can you send me a estimate for the second ?"
```

Non-anaphoric forms

This type is provided to annotators, in order to mark phrasings seemingly anaphoric, but should not be considered by a resolution procedure (specifically pronouns in their impersonal use such as the pleonastic *it*, or referential mentions in idiomatic phrases).

3.6 Semantic relations types

The types of anaphoric links we chose to consider are based on the nature of the semantic relation between the two linked mentions.

Identity

The first class of types contains those where the anaphoric mention and the antecedent have a referential identity, the anaphoric unit points to the whole entity referenced by the antecedent. Coreferent mentions are part of this class.

Association

Often referred to by bridging anaphora, this class contains all non coreference relations between the anaphoric mention and their respective antecedents. Theses semantic relations can be of various natures. It could be a meronymic/holonymic relation where one is part of the entity designated by the second, they could also be linked with a contextual association of ideas. We chose not to distinguish between different semantic relations of bridging anaphora. However, in order not to limit the whole category to the *part-of* relation, we chose to rank every non identity relation within the generic association type.

```
"FreeMine has two Bluboo in warranty exclusion in their possession, they would like
to know what they should do?"
```

Synthetic

This type of relation takes place between a phrasal antecedent and the anaphoric mention (mostly demonstrative and personal pronouns or nouns). The pronoun operates a summary of an idea that has been previously described (Lefeuvre, 2012). Anaphora relations involving abstract entities such as ideas, events, fact or situations (Amsili et al., 2005) fall into this category.

```
"Message 1: Our orders are not being validated since yesterday. If it suits you,
we take stock of the problem tomorrow in a meeting.
Message 2: It's ok for me!
Message 3: That's fine with me!"
```

Indefinite pronouns
```
    "If some engineers no longer use our tools, we wonder what they are for!"
```

4 Comparison with other annotated corpora

In this section, we highlight the disparities in methodological choices and conceptual decisions between our annotation protocol and other well-known corpora in the field of anaphora and coreference studies. A synthesis is reported in Table 1 which focus on a series of common issues that are considered important choices to be made in order to design an annotation scheme for anaphora (Poesio et al., 2016).

Corpus	MD	Annotated NPs	Predicative NPs	Conjunct.	Pleo.	D-deixis.
ARRAU	*MaxP+MinA*	*All*	non-referring	*Split*	yes	yes
OntoNotes	*MaxP*	*All*	no	*Coord*	no	no
ANCOR	*MaxP*	*Ana*	no	*Coord*	yes	yes
Ours	*MaxP*	*Ana*	no	*Split*	yes	yes

Table 1: Comparison with ARRAU/OntoNotes

Markables' delimitation (MD).   Defining the span of text to be annotated is a consequent question as it raises several issues in the implementation of an evaluation protocol.
In most of the cases, annotation projects chose to mark the maximal projection of the antecedent (noted *MaxP* in table 1). Others, such as the MUC Corpora, add a MIN attribute containing the head of the NP to each markable annotation.
The ARRAU Corpus uses maximal projection and includes the MIN attribute as well (noted *MinA*).

Annotated NPs.   In Table 1, we note the distinction between corpora that annotate all NPs and those that choose to mark only NPs involved in anaphoric relations (we use *All* and *Ana* respectively).
For the sake of simplicity and speed of the process, we chose not to mark all NPs.

Predicative NPs.   Previous works on annotation diverge on whether predication is to be considered as reference and should or not be linked to the corresponding NP. While several works choose not to not mark them. In ARRAU, predicative NPs are marked but labelled as non-referring.

Conjunction. (Conjunct.)   One common issue is to decide whether to mark coordinated NPs (*Coord*) as in "Mark and Eric" as NPs. This allows the segment to be linked to a plural third person pronoun ("They"). The alternative solution, implemented in this work, is to take into consideration split antecedents (noted *Split* in Table 1), allowing the annotator to link the plural pronoun with two distinct NPs introduced in different segments.

Pleonastic pronouns annotation (Pleo).   Whether to consider pleonastic pronouns as markables is another important choice to be made in the annotation process. In our corpus, pleonastic pronouns are annotated as being non referring.

Discourse-deixis annotation (D-deixis).   Is a reference to antecedents introduced by phrasal segments, such as references to ideas, events, and abstract objects.

5 Discussion and future work

The analysis of the annotated corpus leads to several axes of study. Referential identity annotation between named entities is complex and raises the question of cross-document coreference. Intuitively, it seems that entities of some semantic types are easier to bind across email threads than others. For instance, it is effortless for a human to decide that two occurrences of the word "Coca-Cola", refer to the same entity, even if each word is mentioned in a separate email thread. On the contrary, it is more challenging to decide whether two mentions of ""Bernard"" appearing in different threads are coreferent or not. A contextual analysis is needed to link such entities.

Another issue deriving from the conversational nature of emails is the question of the identity of the speakers in the metadata, referred to by first person pronouns. The results of our annotation process showed that in a professional setting, plural first and second person pronouns often lead to ambiguous interpretations. For example, an occurrence of the pronoun "we" can refer to the group formed by the sender and the recipients of the email, or to the organisation, mentioned in the signature of the email, to which the speaker belongs.

Using this email corpus we plan to tackle anaphora resolution. The evaluation of the different state-of-the-art machine learning models and symbolic systems will allow us to identify the most significant locks and issues of anaphora resolution in emails.

By taking into account the behaviour of anaphora in such a specific setting, we can focus our efforts towards the challenging cases and the most frequently encountered types of anaphora.

Rel.	*Identity*				*Association*			*Synth.*			*Ellip.*	*Indef.*	*Pleo.*
POS	*PR*	*N*	*Adj*	*Sum*	*PR*	*N*	*Sum*	*PR*	*N*	*Sum*	*Det*	*PR*	*PR*
Count	1008	246	23	**1367**	173	36	**252**	94	20	**114**	**10**	**13**	**103**

Table 2: Typology distribution.

The corpus contains 1856 annotations which gather six relation types (*cf.* Table 2 where possessive determiners have been merged with pronouns under the column *PR* and *N* and *Adj* stand for adjective pointers and nouns respectively). Identity is the most represented relation type (1367 occurrences), followed by association (252) and synthetic (114) relations. As expected, pronominal anaphora is frequent in emails. These links are in most cases internal to the email, as the attached metadata usually defines the antecedent (particularly in the case of first and second person pronouns). In addition to their number, our corpus also contains a high density of pronominal anaphors (74,8%) compared to other corpora ; for instance, the ANCOR corpus contains 41,1% of pronominal anaphors. As a result, only 16,2% of referring nominal mentions are observed, against 45% in ANCOR. Let us note that, interestingly, 90 external relations (identity) have been annotated between two different emails of the same thread, and 23 relations between mentions of separate threads.

6 Conclusion

The detection and resolution of anaphoricity on French emails is an unexplored area that is essential to NLP systems applied to electronic communication. In this paper, we highlight the necessity of building annotated emails corpora. We introduce a small dataset of French emails annotated with anaphoric relations which will be freely distributed. The purpose of the dataset is to make possible the analysis of anaphora's behaviour in an email setting and to serve as a foundation for resolution systems taking into account the writing conventions in this kind of texts. An overview of the distribution of anaphora types in emails gives pointers regarding the challenging aspects of the forthcoming resolution task. We begin by listing the singularities of annotating anaphoric links in emails, then we present the annotation scheme used to deal with special cases and external antecedents. The paper is concluded by comparing important aspects of anaphora annotations to other larger-scale corpora.

References

Barhom, S., Shwartz, V., Eirew, A., Bugert, M., Reimers, N., Dagan, I. (2019). Revisiting Joint Modeling of Cross-document Entity and Event Coreference Resolution. IN ACL.

Artstein, R., Poesio, M. (2008). Inter-Coder Agreement for Computational Linguistics. IN Computational Linguistics, 34, 555-596.

Amsili, P., Denis, P., Roussarie, L., and Umr, C. P. (2005). Anaphores abstraites en français : représentation formelle. IN Traitement Automatique des Langues. ATALA.

Charolles, M. (2001). *"Référents évolutifs et évolution de la référence"*. In Les référents évolutifs entre linguistique et philosophie.

Delaborde, M. and Landragin, F. (2019). De la coréférence exacte à la coréférence complexe : une typologie et sa mise en œuvre en corpus. 10èmes Jounées internationales de Linguistique de Corpus, Université Grenoble Alpes, Grenoble, France.

Francois, R., Nada, M., and Hassan, A. (2016). Ktr: an approach that supports knowledge extraction from design interactions. *IFAC-PapersOnLine*, 49(12):473–478.

Guenoune, H., Cédric, L., Tisserant, G., Lafourcade, M., and Mekaoui, M. (2019). Vers une résolution des relations anaphoriques dans la communication électronique médiée. 11.

Kalitvianski, R. (2018). *Traitements formels et sémantiques des échanges et des documents textuels liés à des activités collaboratives*. Ph.D. thesis, Université Grenoble Alpes.

Khosravi, H. and Wilks, Y. (1999). Routing email automatically by purpose not topic. *Natural Language Engineering*, 5(3):237–250.

Klimt, B. and Yang, Y. (2004). Introducing the enron corpus. In *CEAS*.

Krieg-Holz, U., Schuschnig, C., Matthies, F., Redling, B., and Hahn, U. (2016). Code alltag: A german-language email corpus. In *Proceedings of the Tenth International Conference on Language Resources and Evaluation (LREC'16)*, pages 2543–2550.

Landragin, F. (2007). L'anaphore à antécédent flou : une caractérisation et ses conséquences sur l'annotation des relations anaphoriques. In Journée d'étude de l'Association pour le Traitement Automatique des LAngues (ATALA) sur la résolution des anaphores. Paris, France.

Landragin, F. (2018). Étude de la référence et de la coréférence : rôle des petits corpus et observations à partir du corpus mc4. In Bases, Corpus, Langage - UMR 7320.

Landragin, F. (2020). Rapport final du projet ANR Democrat, "Description et modélisation des chaînes de référence : outils pour l'annotation de corpus et le traitement automatique. ANR (Agence Nationale de la Recherche - France).

Lefeuvre, F. (2012). Les anaphores résomptives en c', cela, ça et ceci dans Juste la fin du Monde et Derniers remords avant l'oubli de Jean-Luc Lagarce, June. Analyse des anaphores résomptives dans des pièces de théâtre de J.-L. Lagarce.

Lopez, C., Mekaoui, M., Aubry, K., Bort, J., and Garnier, P. (2019). Reconnaissance d'entités nommées itérative sur une structure en dépendances syntaxiques avec l'ontologie nerd. In *Extraction et Gestion des Connaissances: Actes de la conférence EGC'2019*, volume 79, pages 81–92. BoD-Books on Demand.

Matta, N., Atifi, H., and Rauscher, F. (2014). Knowledge extraction from professional emails. In *IFIP International Workshop on Artificial Intelligence for Knowledge Management*, pages 43–57. Springer.

Everitt, B. and Fleiss, J. (1981). Statistical Methods for Rates and Proportions.

Massimo Poesio. (2004). The MATE/GNOME scheme for anaphoric annotation.

Chomsky, N. (1981). Lectures on government and binding.

Mekaoui, M., Tisserant, G., Dodard, M., and Lopez, C. (2020). Extraction de tâches dans les emails : une approche fondée sur les rôles sémantiques. In *Proceedings of the Extraction and Gestion des Connaissances (EGC'20)*, page to appear.

Mitkov, R., Evans, R., Orasan, C., Dornescu, I., and Rios, M. (2012). Coreference resolution: To what extent does it help nlp applications? In *TSD*.

Muzerelle, J., Lefeuvre, A., Schang, E., Antoine, J.-Y., Pelletier, A., Maurel, D., Eshkol-Taravella, I., and Villaneau, J. (2014). Ancor_centre, a large free spoken french coreference corpus: description of the resource and reliability measures. In *LREC*.

Poesio, M. and Artstein, R. (2008). Anaphoric annotation in the arrau corpus. In *LREC*.

Poesio, M., Stuckardt, R., and Versley, Y. (2016). *Anaphora Resolution: Algorithms, Resources, and Applications*. ISBN 978-3-662-47908-7.

Pradhan, S. S., Hovy, E. H., Marcus, M., Palmer, M., Ramshaw, L. A., and Weischedel, R. M. (2007). Ontonotes: a unified relational semantic representation. *Int. J. Semantic Computing*, 1:405–419.

Reinhart, T. (1983). Coreference and bound anaphora: A restatement of the anaphora questions. *Linguistics and Philosophy*, 6:47–88.

Tarrade, L., Lopez, C., Panckhurst, R., and Antoniadis, G. (2017). Typologies pour l'annotation de textes non standard en français. TALN 2017, June. Poster.

Tutin, A., Trouilleux, F., Clouzot, C., Gaussier, E., Zaenen, A., Rayot, S., and Antoniadis, G. (2000). Annotating a large corpus with anaphoric links. Third International Conference on Discourse Anaphora and Anaphor Resolution (DAARC2000), 2000, United Kingdom. pp.2

Paroubek,P., Robba, I., Vilnat, A., Ayache, C. (2006). Data, Annotations and Measures in EASY the Evaluation Campaign for Parsers of French. Proceedings of the Fifth International Conference on Language Resources and Evaluation (LREC'06)", 2006, Genoa, Italy.

Association for Computational Linguistics
209 N. Eighth Street
Stroudsburg, Pennsylvania 18360

ISBN 978-1-7138-2824-2